MUSIC IN AMERICAN LIFE

Ellington

Duke Ellington, 1925 (Frank Driggs Collection)

Ellington

THE EARLY YEARS

Mark Tucker

UNIVERSITY OF ILLINOIS PRESS

Urbana and Chicago

Illini Books edition, 1995
©1991 by the Board of Trustees of the University of Illinois
Manufactured in the United States of America
2   3   4   5   C   P   5   4   3   2   1

Permissions for music and lyrics cited
in the text follow the index.

This book is printed on acid-free paper.

Library of Congress Cataloging-in-Publication Data

Tucker, Mark, 1954–
    Ellington : the early years / Mark Tucker.
        p.   cm. — (Music in American life)
    List of compositions and discography: p.
    Includes bibliographical references and index.
    ISBN 0-252-01425-1 (cloth : alk. paper). — ISBN 0-252-06509-3
(pbk. : alk. paper)
    1. Ellington, Duke, 1899–1974. 2. Jazz musicians—United States—
Biography. I. Title. II. Series.
ML410.E44T8   1990
781.65'092—dc20
    [B]   90-36360
                                                                          CIP
                                                                          MN

To my parents

Contents

Preface   xi

Acknowledgments   xv

Key to Symbols Used in Transcriptions   xix

Part One
WASHINGTON • 1899–1923

1	Ellington's Washington	3
2	Young Edward	16
3	Soda Fountain Rag	28
4	The Duke's Serenaders	47
5	Washington Bandleader	63

Part Two
NEW YORK • 1923–1927

6	New in New York	79
7	Washingtonians on the Great White Way	96
8	The Songwriter: From "Jim Dandy" to "Yam Brown"	119
9	The First Recordings	140
10	On Tour in New England	183
11	The Rise of Duke Ellington	194
12	A Composer and His Band	211

Appendix:
Compositions and Recordings of Duke Ellington,
1914–November 1927   259

Notes   273

Note on Sources   309

Interviews   315

Bibliography   317

General Index   325

Index of Compositions, Recordings, and
Arrangements of Duke Ellington   341

Preface

Edward Kennedy "Duke" Ellington first gained widespread fame while appearing with his orchestra at the Cotton Club in Harlem from late 1927 until 1931. During that period his music reached many Americans over the CBS radio network, which transmitted regular broadcasts from the New York night spot, and on recordings issued by Victor, Brunswick, OKeh, and other companies. By the early thirties Ellington was becoming known as a composer for such pieces as "Mood Indigo" (1930), "Creole Rhapsody" (1931), "Sophisticated Lady" (1933), and "Solitude" (1934). At the same time his orchestra had begun to win national popularity contests and readers' polls sponsored by magazines and newspapers. As a writer for the *Pittsburgh Courier* exclaimed in 1931, "He is declared to be the 'King of Jazz' in America today. Long live the Duke and may he reign upon the throne for many moons."[1]

The salvo became prophecy as Ellington went on to enjoy a lengthy and majestic career. Over the next forty years, until his death in 1974, he was recognized as one of America's leading musicians. Constant touring and frequent recording helped him attract a large international audience for his music. Some bandleaders, such as Count Basie, may have traveled as strenuously; others probably sold more recordings. Yet none came close to writing so much music —over 1,500 compositions, it is estimated—and few drew such critical acclaim. A long list of Ellington's "Honors and Awards" appears at the end of his memoirs, *Music Is My Mistress* (1973), and includes the Presidential Medal of Freedom (1969), honorary degrees from fifteen colleges and universities, keys to more than a dozen cities, from Niigata, Japan, to Birmingham, Alabama, and Amsterdam, Holland, and an International Humanist Award (1972) for "global public service."

The general outlines of Ellington's post-Cotton Club career are relatively well known. He was, after all, a charismatic public figure whose activities were closely followed by the media and a famous musician whose work was richly documented by recordings. Nevertheless, Ellington always managed to remain something of a mystery. While his music often seemed to be jazz (or steeped in the jazz tradition), Ellington spurned the label, resisting efforts by critics to categorize him or his work. He appeared before audiences as a popular entertainer yet spoke and acted like visiting royalty. He led a big band that played for high-school proms and country-club dances yet was equally at home giving concerts in Carnegie Hall or London's Palladium. Working in a musical field perceived by many to be trivial and ephemeral, he brought high ideals and a determination to celebrate and memorialize the African-American experience: "The music of my race is something which is going to live," he wrote in 1931, "something which posterity will honor in a higher sense than merely that of the music of the ballroom today."[2]

To understand the origins of Ellington's character and the roots of his art, it is necessary to explore his life before the Cotton Club —before he had become famous as a composer, bandleader, and recording artist. This early and tantalizingly obscure chapter in the Ellington chronicle, from 1899 to 1927, forms the basis of the present study, which falls into two main parts. The first focuses on Ellington's youth in Washington, D.C., where he was born and raised and where he would spend nearly the first third of his life. Washington's black community played an important role in shaping Ellington's character, and his family imbued him with values that sustained him both as man and artist. Moreover, black musicians in Washington affected Ellington's development in significant ways: training him as a pianist, bandleader, and businessman; influencing his musical tastes and attitudes toward performing; helping to forge his identity as an African-American artist.

The second part begins with Ellington's move to New York in 1923 and follows his efforts to establish himself there as a pianist, bandleader, songwriter, and composer. During much of this time Ellington's band was based in Times Square at the Kentucky Club (or the Hollywood, as it was first called), where he gained experience accompanying singers and dancers, and evolved distinctive approaches to orchestration and composition which would characterize his later work. Players such as trumpeter Bubber Miley, trombonist Joe Nanton, drummer Sonny Greer, and saxophonists Otto Hardwick and Harry Carney laid a foundation for the Ellington orchestra of the future. This period culminated with the twenty-eight-year-old bandleader's debut at the Cotton Club, on December 4, 1927. It is there, on the brink of a new phase in Ellington's creative and professional life, that this study ends.

Ellington's years before the Cotton Club have received scant attention, partly because information about this period has been less accessible, also because Ellington's later achievements have eclipsed his early efforts. With a few exceptions, critics and historians have tended to pass over the pre-1928 recordings, considering them inferior to those that followed and peripheral to Ellington's major output. Yet a closer look at the circumstances surrounding record dates yields information about repertory and personnel which may account for the varying standards of performance. Instead of reading Ellington's history from the aural evidence, then, I have viewed recordings as only one of many sources that contribute to the story. Others include published sheet music and stock arrangements, accounts in contemporary newspapers, periodicals, and trade publications, testimony from friends, family, and fellow musicians, and Ellington's own statements offered over the years in writings and interviews. Together these sources suggest that beneath the deceptively placid surface of the early years, forces were at work that helped set Ellington in motion, propelling him toward the Cotton Club stage in 1927 and preparing him for one of the most remarkable careers in twentieth-century musical life.

Acknowledgments

I am grateful to the many people who assisted me in this study. Some are no longer with us: Professor Mercer Cook, son of Ellington's mentor, Will Marion Cook, who provided information about Ellington in Washington and who read and commented on several early chapters; Ellington trombonists Lawrence Brown and Juan Tizol; singer and organist Revella Hughes; and Ellington's first cousin Bernice Wiggins, who shared her memories of a distant time and place, letting me experience directly the warmth of the Ellington family.

At Howard University's Moorland–Spingarn Research Center, James P. Johnson and Deborrah Richardson guided me expertly to different corners of the collection. During 1983 and 1984, when I was a Fellow at the Smithsonian's National Museum of American History, Cynthia Hoover and her colleagues in the Division of Musical Instruments created ideal working conditions. The same was true in 1988 when John Hasse, curator in the Division, and John Fleckner, director of the Archives Center, invited me to be among the first to explore the Smithsonian's newly acquired Duke Ellington Collection.

At Yale University I was assisted with Ellington oral-history materials by Harriet Milnes, Jan Fournier, and the director of Oral History, American Music, Vivian Perlis. I am also indebted, like so many others, to Dan Morgenstern, director of the Institute of Jazz Studies, Rutgers University-Newark, New Jersey. Early on he patiently answered questions and pointed out fruitful avenues of research to follow. One led to Phil Schaap, whose knowledge and expertise came to the rescue more than once.

Among those who let me use their personal collections were Vince Giordano, who made available orchestral stocks and sheet music I was unable to locate elsewhere, and Thornton Hagert. John Leifert, George Blacker, and the late Carl Kendziora supplied me with tape copies of rare recordings. Throughout my research I have benefited from the conscientious work of Stanley Dance; he and his wife, Helen Oakley Dance, have done much to facilitate future Ellington scholarship.

In many ways, this study would not have been possible without the generosity of three individuals who shared with me their extensive knowledge of, and love for, the music of Duke Ellington: Brooks Kerr, Jerry Valburn, and Jack Towers. To learn from these devoted students of Ellingtonia has been deeply rewarding.

I would also like to thank the following people who contributed in various ways: Maurice Banks; Tommy Benford; Ed Berger; Garvin Bushell; Ruth Ellington Boatwright; Marilyn Tyler Brown; W. Montague Cobb; A. P. Davis; Bessie Dudley; Roy Ellis; Sammy Fain; Lawrence Gushee; June Hackney and Alice Spraggins; Adelaide Hall; Andrew Homzy; Jehu and Alice Hunter; Oscar Lucas; Juanita Middleton; Michael Montgomery; Toots Mondello; Jon Newsom; Mitchell Parish; Delia Perry; Essie Sorrel; John Steiner; Mrs. Maximillian A. Tufts; De Priest Wheeler; Erik Wiedemann. A special thanks to Steven Lasker for information on recordings that will eventually appear in his definitive discography of Ellington, 1923–42.

Two grants were important in the beginning and later stages of work: a research assistance grant from the Sinfonia Foundation in 1983, and a research fellowship for recent recipients of the Ph.D. from the American Council of Learned Societies in 1987.

Martin Williams read an early draft of the manuscript and made valuable suggestions. At the University of Michigan Judith Becker, Piotr Michalowski, and James Dapogny offered sound criticism. Richard Crawford initially steered me toward a study of Ellington's early years, asked the unanswered questions, and inspired me to do better.

Finally I thank my parents, Beverley and Louis Leonard Tucker, and my grandmother Dorothy B. Jones, who have given me constant love and support; my brother Lance, who stepped in at a crucial time with some computer wizardry; and Carol Oja, my closest reader, who was always there when it mattered most.

Key to Symbols Used in Transcriptions

♩	scoop up to pitch
⌐⌐	slide between pitches
⌐~⌐	bent note
(♪)	ghosted note, implied or lightly sounded
~~	terminal vibrato
↑ ♯	actual pitch sounds slightly higher than notated
↓ ♭	actual pitch sounds slightly lower than notated
𝄃	growl
×	blurred pitch
×	accidental cluster
• or ••	note sounded is a mistake; probable correct note appears below example next to asterisks

Note: All musical examples of recorded performances have been transcribed by the author. It is conventional in jazz transcriptions for ♫ to represent ♩ ♪ or more rarely ♫ . For the most part this interpretation is assumed in my transcriptions, although often the notation does not reflect the performers' rhythmic subtleties. Departure from this practice is indicated by the marking "even"; when the triplet feeling is quite strong, the marking ♫ = ♩ ♪ appears above or in the example.

Part One

WASHINGTON · 1899–1923

1

Ellington's Washington

Once upon a time a beautiful young lady and a very handsome young man fell in love and got married. They were a wonderful compatible couple, and God blessed their marriage with a fine baby boy. . . . They loved their little boy very much. . . . They raised him in the palm of the hand and gave him everything they thought he wanted. Finally, when he was about seven or eight, they let his feet touch the ground.

Duke Ellington, *Music Is My Mistress*, x

In the storybook prologue to his memoirs, *Music Is My Mistress*, Duke Ellington almost seems to be speaking the words aloud. The delivery is smooth and self-assured; the tone has that characteristic blend of graciousness, irony, and pure put-on which made it difficult to know his true point of view. This is the voice Ellington used to charm kings and queens, to win over audiences, and to keep prying interviewers at arm's length. It is the voice of someone who had been in the spotlight for many years: a master of illusion adept at presenting a vivid image to the public while carefully protecting his private life.

Ellington began developing that image in Washington, D.C., long before he became a celebrity, even before he became a musician and entertainer. As a child there, he was exposed to his father's fanciful language and teasing wit. In school he was taught that "proper speech and good manners were our first obligations."[1] As a teenager he learned to dress well and with taste, thus earning the nickname "Duke." Growing up black in a segregated city—where skin color determined one's basic rights and social status—he discovered how appearances counted for a great deal. But the way he spoke, dressed, and carried himself was not just an act calculated to win acceptance. For Ellington also inherited from Washington's black community a fierce pride and innate sense of privilege. These qualities would later help him succeed in a highly competitive profession. More important, they inspired him to become a composer who could express in music the feelings and aspirations of his race.

The city of Ellington's youth shaped his character in complex and profound ways. Later, when looking back on his childhood, Ellington depicted Washington as a wonderful, nurturing environment. In *Music Is My Mistress* a warm nostalgia suffuses his reminiscences like haze over the Potomac River on a hot summer day. But Washington was a place of stark contrasts. In the early 1900s it had one of the largest and most distinguished black communities in America; yet this community was cut off from the majority white population by near-total segregation and divided within by strong class distinctions. In Washington, black high-school students who might gain entrance to some of the nation's best colleges could not get served in downtown restaurants. The city's white press seldom acknowledged black achievements but often printed accounts of black crime, real or alleged. And while intellectuals like writer Alain Locke and historian Carter G. Woodson lectured up at Howard University, other blacks eked out a living in the dingy alleys of Capitol Hill.

Ellington was born into a black urban community that had experienced slow but steady growth during the nineteenth century. In the early 1800s educational and economic opportunities for both freed blacks and slaves in Washington had been severely limited. The 1822 city directory showed most freed black women employed as domestic servants, while freed men worked in such professions as "bricklayers, carpenters, oystermen, carters, livery-stable hands, hackmen, blacksmiths, shoemakers, waiters, barbers and hairdressers, tailors, cooks, and common laborers."[2] Some better-educated blacks were drawn to Washington in hope of finding government jobs, but few realized this ambition during the antebellum period.

The Civil War and its aftermath brought freedom for Washington's blacks and positive steps toward full citizenship. A law requiring that the city provide black public schools was passed in 1864. Three years later Howard University received its charter as "the first university south of the Mason-Dixon Line to be expressly dedicated to biracial education."[3] That same year black males won the right to vote in local elections. Such social progress, and the lure of government jobs, attracted many blacks to the capital. The young Booker T. Washington noted in 1878–79 that "the city was crowded with coloured people," many of them "drawn to Washington because they felt that they could live a life of ease there."[4] By the turn of the century, Washington had the largest black community in the nation—87,000 (31 percent of the city's total population), ahead of New Orleans, Philadelphia, and New York. But beyond its sheer number of blacks, Washington was notable for "the extraordinary cultivation and intellectual distinction of the upper-class colored community" which made it, in the words of the city's chief historian, Constance McLaughlin Green, "the undisputed center of Negro civilization."[5]

The city planned by Pierre L'Enfant in 1791 was divided into four quadrants and laced with a grid of perpendicular streets and diagonal avenues radiating from the Capitol. In the early 1900s many of Washington's middle- and upper-class blacks settled in the Northwest section, especially the area bounded by "15th Street on the west, Florida Avenue on the north, 1st Street on the east and M Street on the south."[6] Ellington's family always lived in Northwest Washington, although some of his relatives were scattered in other parts: Aunt Laura in Northeast, Aunt Ella in Southwest, and Aunt Emma in Georgetown.[7] U Street became the black community's center of commerce. Among its establishments were the Dunbar Hotel, the Industrial Savings Bank, the print shops of John Goins and the Murray brothers, and the Lincoln Theater. U Street also had halls for dancing, like Murray's Palace Casino (above the brothers' print shop) and the True Reformers' Hall, where Ellington would play one of his first jobs. Another important thoroughfare, running north-south, was Seventh Street. In the mid-1920s, the young poet Langston Hughes loved this "long, old, dirty street, where the ordinary Negroes hang out."[8]

The economic and educational advantages enjoyed by some of

Washington's blacks helped to form an elite segment of the population. Langston Hughes complained that members of this group "drew rigid class and color lines within the race against Negroes who worked with their hands, or who were dark in complexion and had no degrees from colleges." [9] Drummer Sonny Greer, a resident of Washington around 1920 and a long-time associate of Ellington, put it more bluntly: "I could play the dances but I couldn't mingle with all the highfalutin doctors and lawyers and all the fancy chicks from the university. They looked at me like I was nothin'— and I'm the sharpest guy in the damn hall!" [10] Even Ellington, who usually avoided sensitive topics, had to admit that such attitudes characterized his hometown: "I don't know how many castes of Negroes there were in the city at that time, but I do know that if you decided to mix carelessly with another you would be told that one just did not do that sort of thing. It might be wonderful for somebody, but not for me and my cousins." [11]

Ellington's experience growing up in a segregated and stratified community may have been one factor behind his later aversion to categories and labels, whether applied to himself or his music. He tried to avoid the word "jazz," preferring the terms "Negro" or "American" music. He claimed there were only two types of music, "good" and "bad." He wrote pieces like *Black, Brown, and Beige* (1943) and *My People* (1963) that celebrated the common heritage of all African-Americans. And he embraced a phrase coined by his colleague Billy Strayhorn—"beyond category"—as a liberating principle.

But if young blacks faced social snobbery from within their community and rank prejudice from without, they still could feel "lucky," as did historian Rayford W. Logan (b. 1897), "in having been born and educated in Washington, D.C." [12] During Ellington's youth, Washington's blacks could take pride in their independent churches, schools, theaters, and civic organizations. At Dunbar, the first public high school for blacks in America, a student had the chance to work with Jessie Fauset, a Phi Beta Kappa graduate of Cornell and a novelist and poet who later joined the staff of W. E. B. Du Bois's magazine, *Crisis*. In 1923 Dunbar's music faculty included Alston Burleigh (son of composer-singer Harry T. Burleigh); Mary L. Europe (James Reese Europe's sister, who wrote the school's alma mater); and Henry Lee Grant, composer, pianist, teacher, and a founder of the National Association of Negro Musicians. Performers such as Roland Hayes and Marian Anderson gave concerts at Dunbar and the school had its own orchestra, founded by Henry Grant in the 1920s.[13]

The other black high school in Washington in the early 1900s was the Samuel H. Armstrong Technical High School, which Ellington would attend. Armstrong opened as a vocational school in 1902, offering an alternative to the college-preparatory program at Dunbar (then called the M Street High School). Ellington's son Mercer has characterized Armstrong as "rough": "If you went there you were practically regarded as incorrigible."[14] But Oscar Lucas, another Washingtonian and a Dunbar graduate, has said that the differences between the two schools have been exaggerated.[15]

Sources of pride for Dunbar, Armstrong, and the community at large, the high-school cadet corps and their competitive drills gave training and discipline to black males and helped develop leadership qualities. A number of prominent Dunbar graduates participated in the cadet corps, among them the composer and bandleader James Reese Europe, historian Rayford W. Logan, poet Sterling Brown, scholar and diplomat Mercer Cook (son of Will Marion Cook), army lieutenant-colonel West Hamilton, federal judge William H. Hastie, and blood-plasma researcher Dr. Charles H. Drew.[16] The cadet corps' smart dress, bright colors, and precise maneuvers made the competitive drill a festive occasion. Writing in 1927, Howard University sociologist William H. Jones devoted a chapter to the Armstrong-Dunbar competition, which "lends as much color and ostentatiousness to the activities of the Negro population of Washington as any other annual affair."[17] At a time when blacks were allowed to watch—but not play—most professional sports, the drill provided a large-scale competitive event in which blacks were organizers and participants as well as spectators.

While competitive drills fostered pride in community, historical pageants, often put on by church and school groups, stimulated pride in race. The most extravagant pageant during Ellington's youth was *The Star of Ethiopia,* presented in October 1915 at the American League Ball Park. In 1913 W. E. B. Du Bois had produced it in New York for the National Emancipation Exposition. The program for the Washington production gave the following description: "The Story of the Pageant covers 10,000 years and more of the history of the Negro race and its work and suffering and triumphs in the world. The Pageant combines historic accuracy and symbolic truth. All the costumes of the thousand actors, the temples, the weapons, etc., have been copied from accurate models." [18]

The historic drama had five scenes—"Gift of Iron," "Dream of Egypt," "Glory of Ethiopia," "Valley of Humiliation," "Vision Everlasting"—and featured "music by colored composers, lights and symbolic dancing." Elzie Hoffman's band took part, as did 1,000 actors and a chorus of 200. J. Rosamond Johnson was music director. A spectator would have heard his brother James Weldon Johnson's song, "Walk Together, Children," also Verdi's "Celeste Aida." It is not known whether the sixteen-year-old Ellington attended the pageant; he did work at the ball park as a youngster, and rehearsals for the pageant were held at his high school. But *The Star of Ethiopia* seems to have been a major community event. Nearly seventy years later, the noted physician and longtime Washington resident Dr. W. Montague Cobb (Dunbar 1921) would speak of it as "very impressive." [19]

Washington's black citizens carried on a richly varied musical life. The community was noted for its choral ensembles, concert artists, musical theater, bands, and teachers. In his memoirs Ellington focused mainly on one aspect of the scene: the popular music played by pianists and small ensembles. But while this was the field that drew his interest, he was surrounded by other kinds of musicians who helped shape his outlook. Concert music thrived alongside the more popular fare.

One of the earliest black musical organizations in America was Washington's Colored American Opera Company, founded in 1872 and directed by John Esputa of the Marine Band. In 1873 the company's performance of Julius Eichberg's *The Doctor of Alcantara* featured singer and teacher Henry Fleet Grant, whose son Henry Lee Grant would give Ellington composition lessons in the late 1910s. [20]

Professor J. Henry Lewis of Howard University directed the Amphion Glee Club, which often performed for state occasions and for the Mu-So-Lit Club, a black cultural and literary organization. Lewis conducted a performance of *Emmanuel*, the "first all-colored oratorio," and trained a seventy-member chorus for "A Mammoth Cake Walk and Jubilee Entertainment" given in Convention Hall.[21] In 1919 Lewis became director of the Federated Choral Society of Washington; the group's accompanist was Louis N. Brown, a popular pianist and bandleader praised by Ellington in *Music Is My Mistress*.

One of Ellington's first employers, Russell Wooding, was a horn player and bandleader who directed the Wooding Jubilee Quintette, a small vocal ensemble. The group performed spirituals and jubilees at concerts and receptions.[22] In February 1921 Wooding wrote an operetta—*Halcyon Days in Dixie*—which was, according to *The Negro Musician,* an "attempt at music drama based on themes of Negro life and music." Wooding's Quintette starred in the operetta, assisted by violinist Joseph Douglass (grandson of Frederick Douglass) and by two "interpretative dancers." Although the reviewer (probably Henry L. Grant) called Wooding's composition "scarcely impressive as a work possessing marked racial characteristics," he did find it a "laudable effort viewed . . . in the light of a venture in Negro Opera." [23]

Washington's black community boasted other musical organizations, among them the Dvořák Musical Association, the Treble Clef Club, the Washington Permanent Chorus, the Burleigh Choral Society, and the Georgetown Music Association. Perhaps the most ambitious group was the Samuel Coleridge-Taylor Choral Society. Formed in 1901, anticipating an American visit by the African-English composer, the society aimed "to develop a wider interest in the masterpieces of the great composers and especially diffuse among the masses a higher musical culture and appreciation of works that tend to refine and elevate." [24] The society gave the American premiere of Coleridge-Taylor's *Hiawatha* and in 1908 put on *The Atonement,* his "Musical Representation of Christ's Passion." Its musical director and founder was John Turner Layton, for many years head of music in Washington's black public schools. (Layton's son, John Turner Layton, Jr., went on to a successful career as a popular pianist and songwriter; among his best-known songs were "After You've Gone" and "Way Down Yonder in New Orleans." Ellington remembered Layton, Jr., as a fine pianist.)[25] The main accompanist for the Coleridge-Taylor Choral Society was Dunbar music teacher Mary Europe. Ellington apparently knew her; in later years he would ask his friend Maurice Banks to "look her up" in Washington and make sure she was getting along.[26]

Howard University had an active music program during Ellington's childhood. Its music department was founded in 1870, and in 1905 a University School of Music was established. The university sponsored a glee club, also a ladies' chorus and a Teachers College choral society; the last of these groups eventually became the Howard University Choir, well known for its performances under director Dean Warner Lawson.[27] In addition to J. Henry Lewis, one of the early conductors of the Howard University Glee Club was Roy W. Tibbs, who also directed the choir at the Nineteenth Street Baptist Church, which the Ellington family attended. Tibbs was a pianist who had studied at Oberlin and in Paris. Among his pupils was Claude Hopkins (1903–84), one of Ellington's keyboard rivals in the early 1920s and later a popular bandleader.

Two important institutions that would touch Ellington's musical development sprang up virtually next door to each other in Northwest Washington: the Washington Conservatory of Music and School of Expression, and the Howard Theater.

The Washington Conservatory was established in 1903 by Oberlin-trained pianist Harriet Marshall Gibbs. At first located in the True Reformers' Hall (12th and U streets, N.W.), the conservatory found new quarters in 1904 at 902 T Street, N.W.[28] By 1910 eleven students were graduated in its first commencement. One was Henry L. Grant, who received a diploma in the Artist's Course for piano and theory. Other conservatory students were to have connections with Ellington. Singer Ernest Amos, a scholarship student in 1910, later became Ellington's music teacher at Armstrong and also taught at Dunbar. And three students who performed in Washington Conservatory recitals—Gertrude Wells, Claude Hopkins, and Louis Brown—were among Washington's finest ragtime and popular pianists by 1920.[29]

In addition to putting on concerts and providing blacks with music instruction, the conservatory served as a springboard for several important ensembles. The Washington Concert Orchestra, founded in 1913, included such players as Sylvester Thomas and Russell Wooding, who went on to lead their own popular orchestras. Henry L. Grant conducted the L'Allegro Glee Club and played in the Samuel Coleridge-Taylor Trio with cellist Leonard Jeter and violinist Felix Weir. The Euterpeans—a male quartet that had both Grant and Ernest Amos as members—presented recitals at the Howard Theater in 1915 and 1916. Grant and Amos were also involved in the Afro-American Folk-Song Singers, a vocal ensemble founded in 1913. That year, Will Marion Cook directed the group in a program of works that suggested the group's nationalistic aims. The evening began with choral arrangements of Negro folk songs. It continued with Abbie Mitchell singing folk-inspired pieces by Tchaikovsky and Dvořák, Henry Grant playing Mendelssohn's Rondo capriccioso, and the chorus performing excerpts from Coleridge-Taylor's *Hiawatha*. And it ended with four "Characteristic Afro-American compositions" by Will Marion Cook: "Swing Along," "Lovers Lane," "Rain Song," and "Exhortation."[30] The Folk-Song Singers gave accomplished black musicians the opportunity to perform music reflecting their heritage next to mainstream classical works. Such a program challenged musical categories; perhaps it even helped break them down.

A few blocks west of the Washington Conservatory, at 620 T Street, N.W., the Howard—Washington's first theater intended for the black population—opened on August 22, 1910. With a balcony and eight proscenium boxes, it could seat 1,500 people.[31] Besides hosting vaudeville and black revues, the Howard sponsored local variety shows and special musical events. By 1911 the Washington Conservatory had begun using the Howard for its recitals, guest-artist concerts, and commencement exercises. That same year Andrew Thomas was named manager of the theater. Thomas went on to become a successful businessman and a much-admired figure in the black community. In 1917 a lead article in the *Bee* credited him with making the Howard "the greatest colored-managed theatre in the nation."[32]

Whether or not the *Bee* was correct in its proud claim, the Howard did serve as an important outlet for local talent and brought to Washington some of the country's top black singers, instrumentalists, actors, and comedians. Many of the performers and musical ensembles were based in New York. While Ellington was growing up, the Howard presented James Reese Europe's Clef Club Orchestra, Will Marion Cook and his Southern Syncopated Orchestra, and

Ford Dabney's Syncopated Orchestra. Ellington saw pianist Luckey Roberts at the Howard, also Noble Sissle and Eubie Blake in a traveling production of *Shuffle Along*.[33] He also might have seen Will Vodery conduct one of the "Smart Set" orchestras and heard singers like Mamie Smith, Sissieretta Jones ("the Black Patti"), Gertrude Saunders, and Aida Ward. He could have attended shows like *Strut Yo' Stuff* and *Broadway Rastus* and observed troupes like Collins's Alabama Minstrels and Herbert's Minstrels.[34]

The Howard Theater was a place for recreation and entertainment. Yet its high standards of performance and presentation made it a symbol of black accomplishment. Audiences went to see not only outstanding black vaudevillians, blues singers, and jazz bands but also concert artists. Besides hosting the Washington Conservatory's recitals and commencement programs, the Howard sponsored Sunday afternoon concerts and other events featuring art music. In 1911 the theater put on a musical production called *The Evolution of the Negro in Picture, Song, and Story.* Once again, Henry Grant was involved, directing the L'Allegro Glee Club accompanied by Mary Europe. The program included texts by William Dean Howells and Paul Laurence Dunbar, and music by von Suppé, Chaminade, and Brahms. Most interesting was the structure of the presentation:

> Overture
> Night of Slavery—Sorrow Songs
> Dawn of Freedom
> Day of Opportunity

Like the pageant *The Star of Ethiopia,* this event brought together music and stories to celebrate the history of black Americans. Such endeavors may have left their mark on Ellington. Years later he would compose works that treated similar themes using similar forms. His *Symphony in Black,* written for a Paramount music short in 1934, had an overture, a section titled "The Laborers," and a "Hymn of Sorrow." And in the extended composition *Black, Brown, and Beige* of 1943, Ellington attempted to give a "tone parallel to the history of the American Negro." The piece moved from past to present and again featured work songs and a "spiritual theme," "Come Sunday."[35] The man who devoted so much of his career to championing the achievements of his race through music and words grew up amidst people whose art could express the same ideals.

While institutions like the Washington Conservatory, the Howard Theater, Howard University, and Dunbar High School gave a forum for the development of Washington's black musical talent, newspapers and periodicals kept the community informed of progress. The city's main black newspaper, the Washington *Bee* (begun in 1887), regularly reviewed concerts and featured articles on well-known performers and teachers. The paper also ran a column by Wellington A. Adams called "The Musical World." Although Adams usually covered the concert-music scene he sometimes ventured opinions on popular music trends. He was one of the city's most energetic musical entrepreneurs: he gave voice recitals, wrote music and poetry, opened and managed the W. A. Adams Music House on U Street, and in 1916 founded his own school, the Columbia Conservatory. In 1918 or 1919 Adams began a periodical, *The Music Master,* which covered black musical events in town and around the country. Other local periodicals devoted to concert music and pedagogy were the *Negro Music Journal* (which became the official organ of the Washington Conservatory in 1903) and *The Negro Musician,* edited by Henry Grant.[36]

Blacks in Washington could receive musical training from teachers like Wellington A. Adams, in schools like the Washington Conservatory, also in bands. The Elks sponsored a brass band that played for parades, picnics, and concerts. World War I stimulated band activity. In March 1919 the *Bee* ran notices for an "overseas" band that J. H. Willis was forming as he attempted to enlist black musicians returning from France. The next month A. Jacob Thomas, bandmaster of the 368th Infantry, wanted to open a conservatory to train band musicians.[37] In 1921 the *Bee* noted that white high schools were just organizing a regimental band, two years or so after black high schools had taken the step.[38]

One of Washington's most prominent black bandleaders in the early 1900s was Elzie Hoffman. Hoffman's band played for many different functions: parades, Howard University commencements, cadet competitive drills, outdoor parties, even at a downtown white theater, supplying music for the race-track and buck-dance scenes in a film. By 1920 the *Bee* was listing Hoffman as one of the "Big Five" who entertained "official Washington night after night throughout the year." [39] Although Hoffman's repertory may have differed from that of ensembles Ellington played in, sometimes links were formed by musicians like Bill Jones who crossed between various groups and styles. Remembering his early efforts in piano contests, Ellington called Jones one of the "great drummers" who had tried to confound him with sudden shifts of meter. [40] Jones played both in Hoffman's band and in one led by James E. Miller.

Miller, later a teacher at Armstrong, organized a band of twenty-four musicians at the Garnet Community Center in 1918. By 1921 Miller's "Community Band" was praised as "the only one of color playing for the city during the concert season." [41] Miller was an organizational man; he not only taught in the public schools and channeled his efforts through the community centers but belonged to the Crescendo Club, a musicians' protective group, and helped form an American Federation of Musicians local for black musicians in 1922. [42] Among the products of Miller's bands were Sandy Williams, later trombonist with Fletcher Henderson, also the bandleader's sons Bill, Felix, and "Devil" Miller, all members of Duke Ellington's first band.

While Elzie Hoffman and James Miller were probably little known outside Washington, other musicians from Ellington's home town made impressive reputations elsewhere. In 1904 Washington-reared James Reese Europe (1881–1919) went to New York, where he became a popular society musician, organized the Clef Club —a fraternal and protective organization for black musicians— and eventually directed a brass band overseas during World War I. Two prominent members of New York's Clef Club also came from Washington: Will Marion Cook (1869–1944), a violinist, conductor, and successful composer for the stage; and Ford Dabney (1883–1958) who, like Europe, was a popular society bandleader and led a "syncopated orchestra." All three commanded respect for their accomplishments and musicianship. They composed music, conducted large instrumental ensembles that fused popular and "classical" repertories from both America and Europe, and brought their own groups to Washington in the 1910s and 1920s, during Ellington's formative years. [43]

In the early 1900s Washington's black community was a place of promise. Its institutions were strong and its leading figures—in music, as in other professions—were men and women of learning, ambition, and discipline. Ellington may have spent his earliest years in a city deeply divided by race and class. But this same city inspired its black citizens to aim high and, in so doing, to move beyond category.

2

Young Edward

1899–1914

Ellington's rosy view of Washington in *Music Is My Mistress* resulted in large part from close family ties and long-standing loyalties. Whatever tensions or troubles may have marked his childhood, they found no place in his memoirs.[1] The subject of family, in particular, brought forth sweet sentiments and superlatives from Ellington, as in the autobiographical tribute "My Mother, My Father" (from *My People*, 1963):

> My mother—the greatest—and the prettiest
> My father—just handsome—but the wittiest
> My granddaddy natural born proud
> Grandma so gentle—so fine
> The men before them worked hard and sang loud
> About the beautiful women in this family of mine . . .
> From sun to sun
> Their hearts beat as one
> My mother—my father—and love[2]

Such a description might seem cloying to some, not to say unbelievable. Yet a similar pride and loyalty characterize the memories of those relatives most familiar with Ellington's early years: his sister Ruth Ellington Boatwright (b. 1915), his first cousin Bernice Wiggins (1904–88), and his son Mercer Ellington (b. 1919). The more one listens to their voices, the more Ellington's singular traits unfold as part of a larger family pattern.

Duke Ellington's father, James Edward Ellington (called J.E. by some, Uncle Ed by others), was born in Lincolnton, North Carolina, on April 15, 1879, and moved with his parents to Washington, D.C., in the early 1890s or shortly before.[3] The Ellingtons may have come to Washington in search of better jobs and living conditions, joining many blacks from southeastern towns and rural areas who relocated to northern cities in the years between the Civil War and World War I. Although it could offer little employment in industry, Washington did have positions for blacks in government (nearly 2,400 of 23,144 federal workers were black in 1891) and in business, where they served the needs of whites, especially in catering and domestic service.[4]

Little is known about the Ellington family's early days in Washington. In *Music Is My Mistress* Duke did not mention his paternal grandparents, only his cousin and companion William ("Sonny"), the son of John Ellington, one of J.E.'s brothers. Even the size of J.E.'s family is open to question: Barry Ulanov, Ellington's first biographer, put the number at fourteen, and Duke pushed the total to twenty.[5] Some clues about the employment and various residences of the Ellington males, however, are provided by city directories. J.E.'s brothers John and William Ellington were laborers in the 1890s. When J.E. was seventeen, in 1896, he worked as a waiter. From this point until 1920 his life changed steadily. He had fourteen different addresses in twenty-four years and a series of progressively better occupations: coachman (1898, 1901), driver (1899, 1900, 1903), butler (1903–4, 1906–7, 1909–17), caretaker (1918–19), and Navy Yard employee (1920).[6]

Despite apparent flux, J.E. enjoyed a stable relationship with one employer throughout most of this period. As early as 1894 (according to Ulanov) or 1898 (city directory), he began working for Middleton F. Cuthbert, a prominent Washington doctor who lived at 1462 Rhode Island Avenue, N.W. At first J.E. seems to have been Cuthbert's coachman or driver. In time he became the butler who "made the decisions around the house" and oversaw the activities of the cook and maid.[7] J.E. seems to have had a good personal relationship with Cuthbert; Ulanov described him as the doctor's "confidant and very close friend."[8] Because of his association with Cuthbert, J.E. was able to pick up work as a caterer for other wealthy families in Washington society, including occasional stints at the White House. These jobs brought in extra income and gave J.E. a network of connections that later helped Duke find "society" band work outside the black community.

J.E.'s connection with Cuthbert helped in other ways, too. When Duke was eighteen years old and needed treatment for a hernia, Cuthbert recommended the specialist and supervised the operation.[9] And Ruth Ellington Boatwright has said that Cuthbert was her childhood doctor. She added that her father—who told her he did not go beyond grade school—educated himself by reading his way around Cuthbert's library, "from the floor to the ceiling, all four walls."[10] J.E. also may have acquired his polished speech and formal manners from working in a wealthy white household. Mercer Ellington described dinner at J.E.'s house as having an elegant style bequeathed from Cuthbert to J.E. and on to Duke: "The way the table was set was just like those at which my grandfather had butlered. This, you might say, is where the dukedom began— his experience of being around at a time when [J.E.] was working for very splendid people."[11]

J.E. quit his job as a butler sometime during World War I. For a few years he made his income from catering and renting out rooms in a house on K Street, "in the fashionable area where all the suffragettes were."[12] By 1920 J.E. was working as a blueprint maker in Washington's huge Navy Yard, situated on the north bank of the Potomac River, in the southeastern section of the city. J.E. retired from this position around 1930.[13]

J.E. was gregarious and witty. His sense of style and sophisticated air impressed his son. So did his way with language, especially when addressing women. Duke wrote that he always hoped to be able to speak like his father: "He knew exactly what to say to a lady—high-toned or honey-homey."[14] Beyond his charming outward manner, though, J.E. seems to have had a powerful inner drive. He showed enterprise and industry in his work as a caterer, butler, and landlord. Later, when he was working as a blueprinter at the Navy Yard and arthritis made his job painful, he wanted to continue rather than quit and move to New York.

If Duke Ellington admired and strove to emulate his father, he loved his mother with a passionate intensity bordering on worship. In *Music Is My Mistress* Ellington began the "Washington" section by stating how difficult it was to describe her, since "no one else but my sister Ruth had a mother as great and as beautiful as mine." But in fact he had no difficulty celebrating the woman who doted on him when he was sick, escorted him to and from grade school, and later took him on summer vacations to the New Jersey shore. Bernice Wiggins once said of Ellington's mother-love: "I never saw anything like it—so devoted. You know, he was the same way about his whole family."[15] Ellington would continue to cherish his mother's memory long after her death in 1935. At a White House reception in 1969 he announced: "There is no place I would rather be tonight, except in my mother's arms."[16] The sentiment is strong for one who had lost his mother over thirty years earlier; the savoir faire of the line might have made his father smile.

Daisy Kennedy Ellington was born in Washington, D.C., on January 4, 1879. According to Bernice Wiggins, Daisy's paternal grandfather was a white senator from King and Queen County, Virginia, and her grandmother an Indian. Daisy's father, James William Kennedy, married Alice Williams, of mixed Indian and Negro descent. Photographs in *Music Is My Mistress* show both of Daisy's parents. James William Kennedy looks proud in his police officer's uniform, for good reason: in 1910, when there were nearly 95,000 blacks in Washington, only forty were policemen.[17] Daisy had four brothers (John, James William, and two who died at an early age) and four sisters (Marie, Maud, Gertrude, and Florence).[18] Mercer Ellington has described the Kennedys as being more artistically inclined than the Ellingtons. Duke did not confirm this, but he remembered being a young boy in the midst of a "wonderfully warm family . . . spoiled rotten by all the women."[19]

Ellington characterized his mother as a spiritual person "mainly interested in knowing and understanding God." He credited her with teaching him that all races were equal, regardless of skin color. Daisy spoke quietly but with authority. Once she told her son: "Edward, you are blessed. You don't have anything to worry about. Edward, you are blessed!" Reflecting on this years later, Ellington still conveyed a childlike belief in her encouraging words, knowing that "anything she told me was true."[20] In his biography of Ellington, Barry Ulanov emphasized Daisy's formality, calling her "a woman of rigorous moral principle, stiff-lipped and, in direct contradiction of her beautiful face and figure, prim of mien and manner."[21] While J.E. gave polish to his son's outward bearing,

Daisy helped him cultivate inner qualities of discipline and spirituality. Her faith in him would be inspiring for many years to come.

Daisy Kennedy and James Edward Ellington were married on
January 3, 1898.[22] They lost a first child in infancy. But on April
29, 1899, a son was born: Edward Kennedy Ellington. A midwife
delivered the baby at 2129 Ward Place, N.W., where J.E.'s parents
lived.[23] Soon after their son's birth, the Ellingtons moved in with
J.E.'s family on Ward Place.[24]

By his own account, Ellington's boyhood was happy and trouble-
free. Unlike Howard University historian Rayford W. Logan, who
grew up in Washington with the "horror and fear of lynching,"
Ellington gave no hint that he faced racial problems.[25] He remembered savoring delicious family meals; walking all over town to
visit relatives and to sample cakes and ice cream; chasing rabbits
and squirrels in Rock Creek Park. The Ellington of *Music Is My
Mistress* seems a typical American boy who reads detective stories,
likes to draw, and dreams about becoming an athlete.

Young Edward showed no great enthusiasm for music even
though he was surrounded by it at home. Like many American families of the time, the Ellingtons owned a piano. J.E. played by ear
such popular songs as "Smiles" and "It's a Long Way to Tipperary";
he also performed operatic arias "in a florid way" and could strum
a guitar.[26] Daisy had received some musical training and could read
music. She preferred "pretty things" like C. S. Morrison's "Meditation" (1896) and pieces by Carrie Jacobs Bond.[27] Ulanov described
how a four-year-old Edward wept at his mother's rendition of "The
Rosary" by Ethelbert Nevin. Daisy also liked to play hymns and
even ragtime, but she disapproved of the blues.[28]

Other members of the Kennedy clan shared Daisy's musical inter-
ests. Her sister Florence played piano and may have given informal
instruction to her nephew Edward. Another sister, Gertrude, had
a daughter Florence who was a good ragtime pianist. Both Ruth
and Mercer have recalled the keyboard skill of Elizabeth, another
Kennedy cousin.

Informal singing also took place in the Ellington home. During "whist meetings" J.E. used to lead a group of friends in songs
like "Sweet Adeline." Apparently J.E. made up the arrangements,
hummed the individual parts, and conducted from the piano.[29]

Young Edward, ca. 1903–1904 (Courtesy of the Archives Center, NMAH, Smithsonian Institution)

Many years later, Ellington composed *The Girls Suite,* a work incorporating "Sweet Adeline," "Peg O' My Heart," "Juanita," and "Sylvia"—four songs which, as Stanley Dance noted, "his father and friends [had] rendered in barbershop fashion."[30]

Outside the home, another source of musical exposure for young Edward was the church. Actually he attended two: his mother's, the Nineteenth Street Baptist Church, and his father's, John Wesley AME Zion. At first he sat with his parents in the regular service; when a little older he attended Sunday school, which gave him "a wonderful feeling of security."[31] In both places he heard hymns and spirituals that his mother probably played at home.

During Ellington's youth the Nineteenth Street Baptist Church used *The Baptist Hymnal* (1883), which was revised in 1926 and published as *The New Baptist Hymnal.* Bernice Wiggins, a longtime church member, recalled some of her own favorite hymns as "Abide with Me," "Blest Be the Tie," and "Onward Christian Soldiers." All are in *The New Baptist Hymnal,* which also contains "From Greenland's Icy Mountains," "Rock of Ages," and "Nearer, My God, to Thee." Such pieces were known and loved not just by black Baptists in Washington but by many American Protestants. In 1907 a special program at the Nineteenth Street Church featured "Hymns of Bye-Gone Days, Soul Satisfying Songs, as sung years ago." These included "Some Things I Remember," "When I Was Young," "Good Old Times," and "Blest Be the Tie."[32] Later Nineteenth Street choirs were directed by Professor Roy W. Tibbs (from 1915 to 1925) and Benjamin Washington (from 1925 to 1939), both accomplished musicians who taught in the music department at Howard University.

The John Wesley AME Zion Church, now at 1615 14th Street, N.W., was located on 18th Street between L and M streets when Ellington went there. Ruth has said that her family attended this church because of its proximity to their house. She remembered the music as "very formal," with hymns like "Onward Christian Soldiers" performed as well as arrangements of spirituals by Harry T. Burleigh.[33] Mrs. Essie Sorrel, a member of John Wesley AME Zion since the early 1900s, recalled the Ellington family attending the church but did not believe that Edward was an active member.[34] Still, as Ruth has said of her brother, "Edward was moved by everything he heard." The emotional values of this sacred music would surface later in such works as "Hymn of Sorrow" from *Symphony in Black,* "Come Sunday" from *Black, Brown and Beige,* and the sacred concerts.

Ellington's first brush with formal music instruction came when he was about seven years old. At the time he was attending Garnet Elementary School—records show him there from 1905 to 1908. In *Music Is My Mistress* he related how his mother decided it was time for piano lessons after he hurt himself playing baseball. His teacher was Marietta (Mrs. M. Harvey) Clinkscales, whose name has been spelled variously as Klinkscale, Klinkscales, Klingscale, even Chinkscales. Mrs. Clinkscales introduced the boy to the basics of keyboard technique, hand position, and theory. It is not known how far he advanced or whether he learned any complete pieces. Ellington apparently missed more lessons than he took. He did, however, take part in one of Mrs. Clinkscales's pupil recitals held at a local church.[35] As the one student who had not mastered his piece, he was required to play the bass part while his teacher played the treble. But Ellington remembered the experience as more instructive than embarrassing: "The umpy-dump bottom was, of course, the foundation and understanding of that part of piano-playing I later learned to like."[36] Elsewhere in *Music Is My Mistress* Ellington claimed his early lessons helped in his first attempt at composition and introduced him to notation. But in the 1940s he told Barry Ulanov that his lessons "all slipped away from me" for six or seven years, and in a 1965 interview he denied their importance altogether, saying they "had nothing to do with the thing that followed when I became fourteen."[37] Whatever Ellington may have thought about his lessons later, at the time they did not fuel his musical ambitions or reveal any special talent.

Perhaps young Edward found the formal worlds of parlor, church, and piano lessons too restrictive. For early on, the boy enjoyed cutting loose and putting on a show. When very young he used to entertain his cousins by playing the Jew's harp, dancing the buck-and-wing, and telling jokes. While still in grade school he tagged along with a magician friend of his father, learning tricks and performing locally. He also had a gift for dramatic pronouncements about his talents: he told his mother that he would become "one of the greatest musicians in the world" and made his female cousins bow down to him to show respect and loyalty.[38] His parents did not discourage these theatrical tendencies. Indeed, he probably acquired a flair for exaggeration from J.E., who called Daisy his "queen," Ruth his "princess," and whose idea of a flattering remark was: "The millions of beautiful snowflakes are a celebration in honor of your beauty."[39]

Young Edward also experienced the theater first-hand. By age twelve he was sneaking into burlesque shows at the Gayety Theater on 9th Street. The Gayety was owned and managed by whites but blacks were allowed to sit in the balcony. There, having "a tendency toward instruction as well as entertainment," Ellington studied the dramatic presentations and began learning the craft of show business.[40]

In later years Ellington described his childhood as a time of security, prosperity, even indulgence. His parents "were very strict," he once confessed, "about seeing that I got everything I wanted."[41] J.E. kept the house "loaded with the best food obtainable," Daisy protected her little "jewel," and his relatives were "all great . . . the greatest cooks in the world."[42] But his family gave him more than a sense of being well fed and much loved: they instilled in him a pride about who he was and what he could achieve. J.E. and Daisy told both Edward and Ruth that they could be the best and "do anything anyone else can do."[43] They encouraged young Edward when he took an interest in art, and they continued their support when he later turned to music. The Ellingtons believed in stressing the positive aspects of life and not discussing the negative. As Ruth has said, she and her brother grew up in a house "full of love, where people did not talk about hostile incidents. . . . I guess that was their way of protecting us."[44] This atmosphere of love and positive reinforcement might have made some people unable to withstand the harsher winds blowing outside the cottage walls. But in Edward it helped strengthen character and build up a solid core of confidence.

Expectations of high achievement may have been common among middle- and upper-class blacks in Washington. Oscar Lucas (b. 1906) felt great pressure from his family to become either a doctor or teacher; fellow members of his 1922 Dunbar High School class, he has said, faced the same two options since other professional occupations were open only to whites.[45] Another Dunbar graduate, pianist and composer Billy Taylor (b. 1921), has spoken of the positive benefits of career expectations: "I had much reinforcement in terms of who I was, what I was about, and the tremendous contributions that black people have made to science, music, art, government. Black accomplishment was very visible in Washington what with the judges, lawyers, and other over-achievers—so I had no problems. I was led to believe that any field that I wanted to go into, I had the possibility of success."[46] When Ellington later recalled the source of inspiration for his early composing, he cited a similar attitude: "The driving power was a matter of wanting to be —and to be heard—on the same level as the best."[47]

Another factor that shaped young Edward's character was his family's secure economic status. Not in the highest rank of black families, but far better off than the unskilled workers or alley dwellers, the Ellingtons occupied a relatively comfortable position in the middle of the economic spectrum for Washington's blacks. When he worked for Cuthbert, J.E. must have made a decent income, which he supplemented with outside catering jobs. Daisy worked, too, as a laundress, a domestic, and one year as a painter's assistant in the Bureau of Painting.[48] J.E. earned enough money to rent the house at 1621 K Street in 1918 and to buy his own home two years later at 1212 T Street, N.W., near Le Droit Park, one of the better black neighborhoods.[49] But perhaps more important than the amount of J.E.'s actual income was the attitude of privilege he conveyed to his family. Duke wrote that his father "lived like a man who had money, and he raised his family as though he were a millionaire."[50] In this environment of love, material comforts, and imagined royal splendor, a middle-class black child could grow up a duke.

Ellington used to say that he received two educations—one in school, the other in the pool hall.[51] During the eighth grade at Garrison Junior High School (1913–14), he had an English teacher, Miss R. A. Boston (also the principal), who emphasized the importance of proper speech and deportment as well as pride in self: "I think she spent as much time in preaching race pride as she did in teaching English, which, ironically and very strangely, improved your English—she would explain that everywhere you go, if you were sitting in a theater next to a white lady . . . or you were on stage representing your race . . . your responsibility is to command respect for the race."[52] Miss Boston's teachings may have reflected a wider movement spreading through Washington's black schools that year. At the annual meeting of the Colored School Settlement in December of 1913, the assistant superintendant of black schools stressed the "importance of teaching children about the great men of our race" so they might "escape being overwhelmed by white prestige and avoid impairment of colored initiative."[53] A student like Ellington benefited from this philosophy.

Ellington also learned race pride could be carried too far, as when the "proud Negroes" of Washington opposed school desegregration because they did not want their educational standards lowered.[54] And he saw how this pride could become prejudice in a black community where caste distinctions were made on the basis of skin color. Perhaps to escape this stratification, Ellington sought out places like Frank Holliday's poolroom at Seventh and T streets, a place that showed "how all levels could and should mix."[55] There he found college graduates, professional gamblers, Pullman porters, law and medical students (probably from nearby Howard University), and musicians. In school Ellington studied Negro history and learned to be proud of his people; in the poolroom he was taught "the art of hustle" by card sharks, check-forgers, and pickpockets. But even these small-time criminals, with their worldly airs and slick style, were worthy of emulation: "At heart, they were all great artists."[56]

In the summers after school was out, young Edward sometimes accompanied his mother on vacations to Atlantic City or Asbury Park, New Jersey—two resorts along the Atlantic seaboard that were popular with urban residents, including Washington's blacks. From June to August Atlantic City became a major center of musical activity, drawing musicians from New York, Newark, Philadelphia, Baltimore, and Washington. James Hubert "Eubie" Blake spent most of his summers there between 1905 and 1917, and James P. Johnson and Willie "the Lion" Smith were also on the scene before World War I. In his memoirs Smith wrote that there was a great demand in Atlantic City hotels and clubs for solo pianists and small group combinations in 1915 and 1916.[57] Ellington did not mention hearing music in these cabarets—perhaps his youth prevented him from entering night spots.

One summer, probably in 1913 or 1914, Ellington traveled with his mother to Asbury Park, up the coast from Atlantic City. Despite being underage he found work as a dishwasher at the Plaza

Hotel. He told his supervisor, a man named "Bowser," that he had been listening to pianists in Washington. Later Bowser suggested that Ellington go hear Harvey Brooks, a pianist in Philadelphia. At summer's end Ellington followed the advice. He was impressed by Brooks's "swinging" and his "tremendous left hand." And Brooks seems to have been kind to his young admirer: "Harvey was not selfish. When I told him about my resolve, he encouraged me, and taught me many of the shortcuts . . . to successful playing." [58] Ellington's comment suggests he already may have been experimenting with popular piano styles. Back in Washington he began to apply himself in earnest.

3

Soda Fountain Rag

1914–1917

Ellington's interest in music grew stronger after 1914. His instruction from Mrs. Clinkscales had been only rudimentary, but over the next two-and-a-half years, while attending Armstrong High School, he worked hard to become a better pianist. By 1917 he was playing with professionals and had already begun to earn a living from music. If Harvey Brooks sparked Ellington's drive to improve, other pianists in his hometown provided further inspiration, encouragement, and instruction. "Washington," Ellington said later, "was a very good climate for me to come up in musically." [1] The flourishing musical scene in the city's black community, together with Ellington's zest to entertain and family-given desire to excel, helped him grow.

On the surface, Ellington's musical development during these years appears casual, even haphazard. As a black high-school student serious about music, he could have pursued formal training at the Washington Conservatory (as did his near-contemporary, Claude Hopkins), at Wellington Adams's Columbia Conservatory, or with private teachers. But such instruction could not help him learn what he wanted to play: ragtime, popular songs, and dance music. The best way to master these idioms was to listen carefully to other musicians, practice what he remembered, then entertain at parties and dances for on-the-job experience. Ellington's later accounts of his musical progress mention all three activities but emphasize the social advantages of playing for others more than the rewards of solitary practice. For Ellington, as for James P. Johnson and Willie "the Lion" Smith, the high status of the piano "tickler"—not just a desire for musical accomplishment—made the profession seem glamorous and inviting.[2] He admired the flamboyant style and sharp dress of the Washington pianists: "Those ragtime pianists sounded *so* good to me! And they looked so good! Particularly when they flashed their left hands."[3]

Yet long hours of practice lay behind the image of natural talent and spontaneity that the pianists projected. Occasionally Ellington acknowledged this: "I could see that the ragtime pianists employed more affected fingering than the concert pianists and that attracted me very much. I hit that fingering very hard and somehow it seemed to come natural to me."[4] More often, though, he joined these other musicians in assuming an easy air of accomplishment—as when he called his first composition the result of "fiddling around on the piano, using what was left over from my piano lessons."[5] A neighbor gave another version of this "fiddling around," recalling how (around 1916) Ellington used to practice at night : he would strike a chord "and plunk and plunk and plunk it out . . . two or three hours of plunking the same chord or a few notes running away from it got to be pretty wearisome."[6] Such persistence helped Ellington gain technical mastery and may have influenced later habits of composing.

Between 1914 and 1917 Ellington mainly listened to and emulated black pianists in Washington. Someone with more training might have picked up elements of popular piano style from sheet music, either in song accompaniments or ragtime pieces. But Ellington was not yet a proficient reader of music and probably relied little on notation.[7] Ellington did acknowledge learning from piano rolls recorded by James P. Johnson. Yet the earliest he could have heard them was May or June 1917, when they were first issued; by then Ellington had already left high school and acquired basic keyboard techniques. If Ellington was exposed to the few recordings of solo ragtime by such white pianists as Mike Bernard, Harry Thomas, and Roy Spangler, he did not say so. Perhaps local black pianists made a greater impression—or perhaps Ellington wanted to give credit to his otherwise unsung hometown musical heroes.

An aspiring popular pianist who spurned formal instruction and made little use of written and recorded sources had to develop keen ears and a retentive memory. Pianist James P. Johnson claimed to be able to "catch" a piece after hearing it played once or twice.[8] In the 1920s he told Will Marion Cook and Cook's son Mercer that he had learned this skill by accompanying contestants in talent shows, "not knowing in advance what song they had chosen."[9] Willie "the Lion" Smith remembered that he and his contemporaries "learned a melody by ear and then tried to beautify it with our own ideas."[10] Ellington stressed a similar approach in his early years: "I used to spend nights listening to Doc Perry, Louis Brown, Louis Thomas— they were the schooled musicians, they'd been to the conservatory. And I listened to the unschooled, to Lester Dishman, Sticky Mack. There was a fusion of the two right where I was standing, leaning over the piano with both my ears twenty feet high."[11]

The idea of Ellington's ears creating a fusion of "schooled" and "unschooled" styles is intriguing. Yet the ingredients of this fusion are not known. None of the Washington pianists mentioned by Ellington is known to have made recordings. Except for Ellington, no other musician seems to have left descriptions of these players. And Ellington's characterizations tend to be vague: Lester Dishman had "the *great* left hand"; Clarence Bowser was the "top ear man," and his music "majestic"; Blind Johnny played "a lot of piano."[12] As a result, one can only speculate about the style and repertory of the Washington ragtime pianists from whom Ellington learned.

Washington, like Baltimore and other East Coast cities, had a tradition of ragtime piano that extended back to the late nineteenth century. Louis N. Brown, whom Ellington heard as a teenager, said that he learned ragtime around 1901 from Bud Minor, who had been born in the 1850s.[13] Philadelphia pianist Walter Gould (b. 1875) had heard of Old Man Sam Moore, who had been "ragging the quadrilles and schottisches before I was born." And Eubie Blake cited a number of early ragtime pianists active in his native Baltimore. Among the better known "unschooled" players were Sammy Ewell and William Turk. According to Blake, Turk had "a left hand like God. He didn't even know what key he was playing in, but he played them all." Another player, "One-Leg" Willie Joseph, supposedly had studied at the Boston Conservatory before working opposite Blake at Baltimore's Goldfield Hotel around 1907 and

1908. Blake admired Joseph: "Nobody could copy him. He knew everything, the heaviest classics and any kind of rags."[14]

But while the names of older ragtime pianists in Washington and other East Coast cities have been preserved, their music for the most part is lost. Ragtime compositions by midwesterners like Scott Joplin and Joseph Lamb date back to the turn of the century. The earliest published rags composed by black players on the East Coast, however, include "Pork and Beans" and "The Junk Man Rag" (both 1913) by Charles Luckeyth "Luckey" Roberts, and "The Chevy Chase" and "Fizz Water" (both 1914) by Eubie Blake. These pieces only approximate a style that was probably more complicated in performance. Blake has told how music publishers urged composers to avoid technical difficulties that would inhibit sales;[15] Roberts's "The Junk Man Rag" is even marked "Simplified" under the title. Although accounts vary about the degree of improvisation in ragtime, many East Coast pianists seem not to have relied much on notation. Rather, they improvised on set melodies or pieces, adding their own embellishments. Blake said that most of the music played by the ragtime pianists was not written down; instead, pieces were "built on tricks that nobody else but you could do."[16] In the early 1900s James P. Johnson first heard Scott Joplin rendered by New Jersey "ticklers" who "just play sections of [rags] that they heard someplace."[17] In such a tradition, much important "composing" occurred during performance.

Efforts to describe an East Coast style have been hampered by a lack of biographical and musical evidence. In *They All Played Ragtime,* for example, Blesh and Janis state that by the 1880s the "Eastern" style had moved from rural areas of Virginia and the Carolinas into cities like Baltimore, Washington, Philadelphia, and New York.[18] Such a claim is hard to substantiate without more information about the backgrounds of individual pianists. Similarly, when these two authors distinguish East Coast style from the Midwestern type of Scott Joplin, James Scott, Joseph Lamb, and others, they may be describing one person (e.g., James P. Johnson) or even one piece (his "Carolina Shout") rather than an entire school, as in the following excerpt: "Slow-drag ragtime was already considered out of date by a new generation that emphasized the brilliant, fast techniques of the shouts, which utilize the ragtime bass, but in which the traditional trio is generally omitted. The shout piles one intricate theme on top of another and interrupts the 'stride' with complex broken bass rhythms. Its effectiveness depends on a constant building up of tension and excitement to the sudden, staccato ending."[19] Johnson himself, who first heard ragtime in Jersey City in the early 1900s, maintained that "East Coast playing was based on cotillion dance tunes, stomps, drags, and set dances . . . all country tunes."[20] But while Johnson's origins (a Virginia-born mother) and tune titles ("Carolina Shout" and "Carolina Balmoral") suggest an East Coast line of descent, clarinetist Garvin Bushell has traced the pianist's roots elsewhere: "He played things that were very close to what pianists in Ohio and the West were doing."[21] Terry Waldo has extended the range of influence even further, writing that Luckey Roberts and Eubie Blake absorbed not only Midwestern ragtime but "anything they could get their hands on," including European sources (operetta, opera, "classical" instrumental compositions) as well as American.[22]

Recordings, like the written and verbal testimony, also bear witness to the variety in East Coast ragtime. Together with Luckey Roberts (whose two sides recorded by Columbia in 1916 were never released), James P. Johnson and Eubie Blake are the best-known black Eastern ragtime pianists to record before 1920. Their piano rolls from 1917 and 1918 indicate that each man could perform pieces in different styles.[23] The phrasing and rhythmic feeling of Johnson's "Caprice Rag" (1917) is closer to that of 1920s Harlem stride, while his "Stop It" (also 1917) has an older, march-like character. Blake's "Charleston Rag" (1917) features a walking bass in broken octaves, flashy arpeggiated breaks, chromatic seventh chords, and certain rhythmic tricks that turn up in none of Johnson's 1917 rolls:[24]

Example 1. Eubie Blake, "Charleston Rag" (1917 piano roll), C strain, mm. 15–16.

By contrast, Blake's versions of "Somebody's Done Me Wrong" and "Goodnight Sweet Angeline" are moderately embellished treatments of popular songs.

These few observations illustrate the difficulty in defining a general regional style for pianists whose influences were diverse, whose repertories were varied, and whose individual trademarks and "tricks" made them sound different from one another. In the absence of more written and recorded evidence, generalizations about East Coast ragtime must remain tentative and suggestive.

Just as the individual styles of Washington ragtime pianists are lost in memory, their repertory is also unknown. Ellington, for example, never mentioned pieces played by pianists in Washington. Like their northern counterparts, they probably performed a variety of works. James P. Johnson's account of his repertory in New York around 1912 gives a sense of the mixture there: "I played 'That Barbershop Chord' . . . 'Lazy Moon' . . . Berlin's 'Alexander's Ragtime Band.' Some rags, too, my own and others . . . Joplin's 'Maple Leaf Rag' (everybody knew that by then) . . . his 'Sunflower Slow Drag' . . . 'Maori' by Will Thiers [Tyers] . . . 'The Peculiar Rag' and 'The Dream' by Jack the Bear. Then there were 'instrumentals'; piano arrangements of medleys of Herbert and Friml, popular novelties and music-hall hits—many by Negro composers."[25] Eubie Blake's repertory in Baltimore was similar. At the Goldfield Hotel around 1907 to 1910 patrons requested popular songs such as "Heart of My Heart," "I've Got Rings on My Fingers," "Cheyenne," and "Casey Jones."[26] Blake also played his own pieces ("The Baltimore Todolo," "Kitchen Tom," "Poor Katie Redd") and improvised on operatic themes. The technique of "ragging" classical compositions may have been practiced in Washington, especially by pianists who had received conservatory training.

By 1914 Ellington was listening more intently to ragtime players in Washington. Around the same time, inspired by their example and in need of a repertory of his own, he composed his first piece, "Soda Fountain Rag," also known as "Poodle Dog Rag."[27] Precise dating of "Soda Fountain Rag" is impossible: Ellington did not notate the piece or record it in the studio.[28] But over the years he performed the rag (or parts of it) in concerts and discussed it in interviews. In

Music Is My Mistress he claimed to have composed it "just before" he entered high school. This would date it around 1914, close to the time he heard Harvey Brooks and began to take more interest in the piano. The title comes from the Poodle Dog Café, a soda fountain where Ellington worked while attending school. No record of such a place survives from the mid-1910s.[29] In 1920, however, a restaurant by that name opened on Seventh Street and Florida Avenue, N.W., and it featured jazz musicians.[30] Claude Hopkins played there and so might have Ellington. Either Ellington came up with "Soda Fountain Rag" earlier and re-named it when he performed at the Poodle Dog, or else he pushed back the date of its composition by a few years.

Just as the precise origin of "Soda Fountain Rag" is elusive, so is a sense of the entire composition. Instead of a "set" piece like James P. Johnson's "Carolina Shout," "Soda Fountain Rag" consists of a few musical ideas that serve as a basis for improvised elaboration. Indeed, when Ellington first performed "Soda Fountain Rag" he knew few other pieces, so he would change the rag's tempo and rhythms to come up with a "one-step, two-step, waltz, tango and fox trot."[31] This adaptable quality remained part of the piece's performing tradition.

The history of "Soda Fountain Rag" unfolds most clearly retrospectively. On a "Bell Telephone Hour" program broadcast on October 13, 1967, Ellington played a few strains of a rag before abruptly breaking off. He identified the music as the beginning of "Soda Fountain Rag," claiming he could not continue because "It's too hard. I can't finger it any more."[32] The first strain of this 1967 "Soda Fountain Rag" turned up earlier in a May 8, 1937, radio broadcast of "The Saturday Night Swing Club." Here Ellington called the piece "Swing Session" ("swing" being a more appealing label in 1937 than "rag"). "Swing Session" led off a medley of Ellington's own compositions.[33]

The A strain of both the 1967 "Soda Fountain Rag" and the 1937 "Swing Session" first appeared in the middle of "Oklahoma Stomp," recorded by an Ellington band (under the name the Six Jolly Jesters) on October 29, 1929. Two takes of "Oklahoma Stomp" survive, and in each Ellington played virtually the same solo. Moreover, before that solo he used the eight-bar introduction from "Swing

Session" to usher in a trumpet solo (in D minor). The trumpet's sixteen-bar chorus is based on virtually the same chord progression as Ellington's piano solo:

Example 2. "Oklahoma Stomp" (October 29, 1929), chord progressions.
a. Trumpet solo, mm. 1–8.

$$\text{i} \qquad \text{V7} \qquad \text{i} \qquad \text{V7} \qquad \text{i} \qquad {}^{\flat}\text{VI}^{\flat}7 \quad \text{V7} \qquad \text{\%}$$

b. Piano solo, mm. 1–8.

$$\text{i} \qquad \text{V7} \qquad \text{i} \qquad \text{V7} \qquad \text{i} \qquad \text{V7} \qquad \text{\%} \qquad \text{\%}$$

The chord progression during the trumpet solo (repeated to fill out sixteen bars), the eight-bar piano introduction, and Ellington's sixteen-bar solo chorus make up the oldest recorded evidence for the piece Ellington later called "Soda Fountain Rag."[34]

It is hard to know what "Soda Fountain Rag" sounded like in 1914–15, when Ellington ostensibly composed the piece. By 1929, when part of it was first recorded, Ellington had spent half a dozen years in New York, where he was exposed to more pianists (James P. Johnson, Willie "the Lion" Smith, Richard "Abba Labba" McLean, Thomas "Fats" Waller, and others) and more styles than he had ever heard in Washington. Still, some parts of "Soda Fountain Rag" resemble pieces that Ellington could have known around 1914—or at least share traits with a style of piano ragtime popular before 1920. The introduction, for example, is similar to one used by Eubie Blake in "The Chevy Chase" (1914):

Example 3 a. Eubie Blake, "The Chevy Chase," published version, introduction, mm. 1–4.

3 b. Ellington, "Swing Session" (May 8, 1937), introduction, mm. 1–4.

Willie "the Lion" Smith remembered "The Chevy Chase" as a popular piece among pianists in the period from 1913 to 1917.[35] Ellington may not have known Blake's piece, but he might have heard such an introductory idea played by Blake or other pianists in Atlantic City in 1914.

The A strain of Ellington's "Soda Fountain Rag" (in the 1929, 1937, and 1967 incarnations), with its minor mode, driving rhythm, simple harmony, and short, repeated motives in the treble, bears comparison with James P. Johnson's "Steeplechase Rag" (1917) and Luckey Roberts's "The Junk Man Rag" (1913):

Example 4. "Swing Session," third A strain, mm. 9–12.[36]

In the 1937 and 1967 versions, Ellington played different second
strains. "Swing Session" has a dissonant, mock-classical call-and-
response after the A strain:

Example 5. "Swing Session," B strain, mm. 1–4.

Later, after the introduction and the A strain return, a new section
in F major begins (Example 6); in the second half of the first two
eight-bar phrases, a right-hand melody appears that would emerge

Example 6. "Swing Session," C strain, mm. 1–8.

* Should be:

** Should be:

six weeks later as the theme of "Sponge Cake and Spinach," re-corded by Ellington with Barney Bigard and his Jazzopators (June 16, 1937). A repeated figure played by Fats Waller in his "Viper's Drag" (Example 7) may have inspired Ellington's phrase.

Example 7. Fats Waller, "Viper's Drag" (November 16, 1934), middle section, second chorus, mm. 1–2.

In the 1967 version Ellington omitted the call-and-response section from the B strain of "Swing Session"; instead, after the A strain he played a chorus pointing in the direction of 1920s Harlem stride, with ringing right-hand thirds that evoke James P. Johnson and a rising scale figure that seems to come from Fats Waller's 1929 "Handful of Keys":

Example 8. "Soda Fountain Rag" (1967), B strain, mm. 1–6.

* Should be:

**Should be:

The elements of variation and adaptability that mark Ellington's performances of "Soda Fountain Rag" over a span of some forty years reflect the piece's original function as "filler" for his early repertory. In 1929 he used it as part of a band arrangement, "Oklahoma Stomp." In 1937 it became a solo vehicle for a radio broadcast. At a Paris concert in 1965 it served as a brilliant introduction to "Rockin' in Rhythm." And in 1972, when his former drummer Sonny Greer walked onstage at Carnegie Hall, Ellington played it to evoke a bygone era of good feelings and shared experiences. Ellington's treatment of "Soda Fountain Rag" illustrates one of his basic compositional methods: taking older, pre-existing musical ideas and placing them in new contexts.

Another early piano piece (or fragment of one) was never publicly acknowledged by Ellington. In 1971 he told Brooks Kerr that the brief piano solo in "Beige"—the third movement of his 1943 work, *Black, Brown, and Beige*—was "Bitches' Ball," dating from 1914.[37] In the 1943 Carnegie Hall performance Ellington played an eight-bar chord progression, first as a slow, Spanish-tinged near-blues, then as a nimble flight for the right hand:

Example 9. "Beige" (January 23, 1943), piano solo, mm. 1–16.

* Should be:

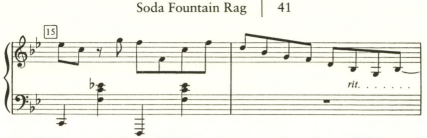

The first part of the solo seems harmonically advanced for 1914 (especially the F# and A against the G minor chord in m. 3). Also, the single-note right-hand lines (mm. 5–8) have more chromatic embellishment than is common in pre-1920 ragtime (compare with the diatonic lines in the last strain of James P. Johnson's "Caprice Rag" from 1917). But the fancy right-hand figuration of the second part recalls Ellington's comment about the "affected" fingering of the ragtime players he was emulating. And the technique of varying the tempo and rhythm—"ragging" the piece—suggests what Ellington might have done in the early days with "Soda Fountain Rag." "Bitches' Ball," like "Soda Fountain Rag," is a blueprint for improvisation and individual "tricks," not a finished composition.

Pianists like Eubie Blake, Willie "the Lion" Smith, and James P. Johnson worked in cabarets, sporting houses, and hotels. As a fledgling ragtime player still in high school, Ellington was either too young or too inexperienced for such employment. Instead he played in school, entertained at parties and dances sponsored by his peers, and joined other musicians at informal sessions. Cato Adams, a 1907 graduate of Armstrong High School, later assistant principal, has said that Ellington used to cut classes and play piano in the gymnasium. This earned him the wrath of teachers whose students slipped out of clases to dance while Ellington played.[38] Another longtime Washingtonian, Mrs. Essie Sorrel, remembered Ellington going around with a group of boys to various houses, "plunking" the piano and singing the latest songs.[39] Piano-playing made Ellington popular among his classmates. And his stylish dress and aristocratic airs inspired a friend to start calling him "Duke."[40]

Soon after entering Armstrong High, Ellington entertained at a party for fellow students and played what he claimed was his second composition, "What You Gonna Do When the Bed Breaks Down?" He characterized this bawdy tune as a "pretty good 'hug-and-rubbin' crawl."[41] Yet in later years he rarely played it in public. Once, however, during a September 1964 interview in Toronto conducted by "Byng" Whitteker, Ellington demonstrated the piece, accompanied by bass and drums, and discussed its relation to dancing.[42] In this performance, his introduction featured a rolling bass line, "crushed" notes in the right hand, and a harmonic sequence based on secondary dominants:

Example 10. "What You Gonna Do When the Bed Breaks Down?" mm. 1–4.

In the main section of the piece, while playing this cadential pattern over and over again, Ellington commented, "Real parlor social music . . . with 10,000 repeats on this part . . . the kids are still rockin'."

Example 11. "What You Gonna Do When the Bed Breaks Down?" mm. 17–18..

Then he instructed his bassist and drummer to play on the after-beat

("In Washington they used to dance on the after-beat"), changing the pattern to:

Example 12. "What You Gonna Do When the Bed Breaks Down?" mm. 24–26.

On this occasion, Ellington took a loose and fairly unstructured approach to the song. He sang none of the lyrics, and Whitteker interrupted him a few minutes into the piece.

In 1972 Brooks Kerr heard Ellington perform "What You Gonna Do When the Bed Breaks Down?" on electric piano at a seventy-third birthday celebration. Kerr remembers the piece with the same secondary-dominant sequence that Ellington played in Toronto. He also recalls the lyrics sung by Ellington. Below is a lead-sheet version of the song based on a performance by Kerr on October 5, 1984.

Example 13. "What You Gonna Do When the Bed Breaks Down?" mm. 1–8.

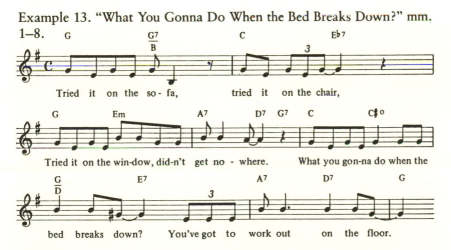

The text suggests why the song may have become, as Ellington said in Toronto, "very popular locally." And Mercer Cook vouched for the piece's popularity among students at Dunbar High School in 1918 and 1919.[43]

In *Music Is My Mistress* Ellington mentioned skipping school and attending a "hop" at a house where other pianists had gathered: Roscoe Lee, Earl Hyman, "Shrimp" Brauner, Claude Hopkins, and Gertie Wells. At such spontaneous get-togethers pianists played for each other and exchanged keyboard tips. Ellington described the atmosphere as more cooperative than competitive: "Everyone seemed to get something out of the other's playing—the ear cats loved what the schooled guys did, and the schooled guys, with fascination, would try what the ear cats were doing. It was a wonderful, healthy climate for everybody."[44] Ellington flourished in this environment. As a "constant listener and hanger-on," he found most every Washington pianist "wide open and approachable."

One of the pianists Ellington approached during his high-school years was Oliver "Doc" Perry. According to Ellington, Perry was a "reader," one of the "conservatory boys." He was also one of the most popular black bandleaders in Washington when Ellington was growing up; the Washington *Bee* and the *Chicago Defender* (J. Le C. Chestnut's "Under the Capitol Dome" column) gave many notices of his performances from 1917 to the early 1920s. Perry replaced Wellington Adams as music editor of the *Bee* in 1921, covering developments in both the classical and popular fields.

Although he admired and associated with the "unschooled" ragtime players, Perry was a different breed of musician. Oscar Lucas has described Perry's playing as "smooth"; Mrs. Delia Perry has called it "soft . . . Doc had the 'touch.' "[45] Ellington pointed out how Perry could "switch from his own precise, clean style to that of any other piano player he heard."[46] This versatility, together with his refined personal qualities, put Perry in demand as a performer at fancy functions. A description of a formal reception for the Magnets Club, held on February 2, 1917, at the Knights of Pythias Temple (12th and U streets, N.W.), gives an idea of the elegant surroundings in which Perry worked. The main hall was "draped in evergreens and decorated at intervals with colored lights and fine art paintings." Doc Perry's Society Band "played the latest dance music and a local artist sang popular songs through a megaphone while beautifully gowned young women tangoed with their well-groomed partners."[47]

Perry took an interest in the young Ellington, perhaps after meeting him at a playing session. In time Ellington began visiting Perry at his home on U Street, where the older man generously shared his knowledge. Later Ellington would recall these sessions with gratitude: "[Doc Perry] was absolutely the most perfect combination of assets I could have encountered at that time. He first taught me what I called a system of reading the lead and recognizing the chords, so that I could have a choice in the development of my ornamentation. He was my piano parent and nothing was too good for me to try."[48] Elsewhere Ellington credited Perry with teaching him to "read notes, not just spell 'em out."[49]

Ellington filled in for Perry at Wednesday afternoon dances when the latter had to play for dinner at the Ebbitt House, a fashionable downtown hotel. Soon Ellington began to take on other "relief" work in clubs and cafés patronized by blacks. In a 1966 interview he described how this came about: "After I mastered ["Soda Fountain Rag"] I was a soda jerk. They used to have a piano player there and he'd get tired and sleepy and fall off his piano stool. . . . I'd go in as a relief man. Then I would substitute on various other occasions and then people began to . . . look at me as a piano player of some sort."[50] Doc Perry's guidance helped Ellington develop not just musical skills but a professional attitude toward performing; Perry used to say that he "trained Duke for public work."[51] The public performer Ellington later became shared qualities with Perry, who "talked with a sort of semi-continental finesse," was "extremely dignified, clean, neat," and was "respected by musicians, show people, and the laymen as well."[52]

About this time Ellington also came in contact with Louis N. Brown (ca. 1889–1974), another schooled musician. Like Perry, Brown led bands that played for dances, dance classes, parties, and receptions. He was active in other aspects of musical life in Washington's black community, playing piano and organ at the Lincoln Theater on U Street, appearing as soloist on concert programs, and directing church choirs.[53] Mercer Cook remembered Brown as a tall, charismatic bandleader who was popular among Dunbar High School students in 1920; Brown even performed for the Dunbar fiftieth class reunion in 1970.[54] Ellington remarked on Brown's "unbelievable technique," citing his ability to play speedy chromatic thirds and his wide-reaching left hand, which could stretch "elevenths in any key."[55]

Ellington and other "ear cats" admired the technique and aplomb of pianists like Brown and Perry. Perhaps less original than the Lester Dishmans, Clarence Bowsers, and Sticky Macks, these disciplined musicians were more versatile and, as a result, more popular. They could play the "classics," read the latest popular songs and show tunes from sheet music, and improvise on almost anything. Their varied skills allowed them to perform in casual sessions and fancy society balls. From these men Ellington learned how being both a gracious entertainer and a well-rounded musician could lead to success.

During his years at Armstrong High School, Ellington may have concentrated more on extracurricular activities than on studying. His grades were average in English, history, and math and poor in the sciences. The only grade for a music course that appears on his transcript is a "D" ("deficient"). Ellington maintained his earlier interest in art, however, as his generally good marks in freehand and mechanical drawing suggest.[56] He entered a poster contest sponsored by the NAACP and won first prize. In his senior year he was offered a scholarship to Brooklyn's Pratt Institute but turned it down because "by playing piano, and by booking bands for dances, I was making a lot of money."[57] Up until this point music had seemed more "a gift or a bonus." Now Ellington began to think of making it a career.

When he left high school in February of 1917, Ellington decided to keep pursuing music while taking side jobs in commercial art to supplement his income.[58] His musical skills were newly developed, his professional experience still limited. But he was by no means a beginner. From practicing on his own and sharpening his ear he had acquired sufficient technique and repertory to allow him to participate in the musical life of Washington's black community. From playing informally around town and substituting for working pianists he had come to be known as a "pretty good piano player."[59] Studying with Doc Perry had boosted his confidence as a performer. Though lacking conventional formal training, Ellington had absorbed, as he said, the important "emotional" and "technical" values of music-making.[60] These values, reinforced by a driving ambition to push beyond what he already knew, prepared Ellington to become a professional.

4

The Duke's Serenaders

1917–1919

In April 1917, a few months after Ellington left high school, America declared war against Germany. Some blacks, like Harlem's Reverend Adam Clayton Powell, Sr., bridled at the idea of their young men going off to defend an unjust society: "As a race we ought to let our government know that if it wants us to fight foreign powers we must be given some assurance first of better treatment at home."[1] Black Washingtonians tended to be less outspoken. A few community leaders saw the war as an opportunity to improve economic conditions and to break down color lines.[2] At Howard University the Central Committee of Negro College Men was set up in May to organize young blacks willing to serve. Gradually blacks around the country fell into rank, and by July 700,000 had registered for the draft.

Ellington passed his eighteenth birthday April 29, 1917, but since men in their early twenties were the only ones required to register, he was still too young to do so.[3] For a black teenager seeking employment, wartime Washington was not such a bad place to be. The nation's capital became a "busy, martial city."[4] Departing servicemen left behind jobs to be filled. Wages rose. And black musicians had plenty of opportunities to play. In June the Stenographers Club held a dance featuring [Joe] Rochester's Baltimore Orchestra and Doc Perry's Peerless Harmony Band. In July Louis Brown's orchestra played for the intermission of the Doves' dancing class. And in August, Brown's "Society Orchestra" provided music for a picnic at Greenwillow Park.[5]

Ellington's employment immediately after high school was varied. His talent for drawing and painting brought work making signs and posters; in time he went into partnership with Ewell Conaway (or Conway), whose brother Sterling would play banjo and guitar with him around 1918 and 1919. The 1917 city directory gives Ellington's occupation as "steward." Perhaps he joined his father (still listed as "butler") in working for Dr. Cuthbert. Also, sometime during 1917 or 1918, Ellington found work as a messenger, first at the Navy Department, then for the State Department. He later claimed to have held this job until the end of the war.

In addition to his day jobs Ellington kept busy at night with music. Until then he had performed chiefly as a solo pianist or in small, informal groups. But by 1917 he was getting experience with larger and more disciplined ensembles. A few encounters revealed that, despite his grooming by Doc Perry, he was not quite ready for such assignments. One of his first professional jobs, Ellington later said, was with a dance band led by the pianist Louis Thomas.[6]

Louis Thomas was one of the most popular black musicians in Washington from 1915 to 1920. He came from a notable family. His brother Sylvester led the Columbian Orchestra, which often performed for picnics and parades. Andrew Thomas, another brother, was the enterprising manager of the Howard Theater. Like Doc Perry and Louis Brown, Louis Thomas was a "reader" whose bands could play the latest songs and dance tunes. He did well enough to send out various groups under his name, at times using white musicians who worked for Meyer Davis. Claude Hopkins remembered Thomas as getting "all the society work around Washington" at the time.[7]

Thomas's organizational skills contributed to his success. He owned a building at 9th and R streets, N.W., which by 1916 had become headquarters for his Capital City Clef Club (probably modeled on New York's Clef Club, founded by James Reese Europe in 1910).[8] Thomas's Clef Club served as a booking agency and meetingplace for Washington's black musicians. Later Thomas opened a cabaret, restaurant, and dance hall in the building. Thomas's orchestras played frequently at the New Ebbitt Café in Washington and filled engagements in places as distant as Pinehurst, North Carolina, and Michigan. In February 1917 the *Bee* reported that Thomas's Capital City Clef Club was "making great progress," having become "very popular with the white as well as colored patrons."[9]

Sometime in September of 1917 Ellington may have made his first appearance with one of Thomas's groups. The job could have been at Mrs. Flora C. Dyer's dance class, 1517 R Street, N.W., "where all the nice young society kids used to go" and where Thomas performed regularly.[10] For this occasion Ellington was told to learn "The Siren's Song," a popular piece from the Jerome Kern–P. G. Wodehouse musical *Leave It To Jane,* which had opened August 28 in New York. Ellington recalled that he labored over the part all afternoon. (The sheet music version is rather easy—although Ellington's part may have been more challenging.) That night he knew "The Siren's Song" but did not fare as well with the band's other "legitimate" numbers, and he really started to worry when Thomas's musicians began talking about "correct chords."[11] Still, Thomas was not too hard on the young substitute pianist; Ellington remembered working for Thomas, either as a single or in different bands, for "a couple of years."[12]

Russell Wooding provided Ellington with further opportunity to play in an ensemble. Wooding was another well-organized bandleader who worked society jobs. By 1915 he was booking three bands out of his Northeast office under the name "Wooding's Smart Set Orchestras."[13] It may have been one of these that Ellington played with around 1917. The orchestra was large—a later account would put the total at thirty-four: five pianos, ten saxophones, twelve fiddles, six banjorines, and drums.[14] Ellington took one of the piano parts but was fired by Wooding for straying from the written page and adding his own embellishments. This probably resulted more from Ellington's poor reading skills than from abandoning the notes in favor of improvisation.[15]

Through contact with musicians like Louis Thomas, Russell Wooding, Louis Brown, and Doc Perry, Ellington absorbed a bandleader's basic training: finding jobs, negotiating fees, paying musicians, choosing music to play, even dressing for work. (Ellington later recalled the scolding he got from Doc Perry for wearing a shepherd's plaid suit to a formal dance at the British Embassy.[16]) Soon, as a recognized pianist about town, Ellington was asked to field small bands of his own. But a leader of pick-up groups did not necessarily have to write out arrangements or compose original material. Ellington probably contacted musicians, met them on the job, then relied on their collective musical knowledge and improvising skills to get through an evening's work. One of the first jobs Ellington played with his own hand-picked group was at the True Reformers' Hall at 12th and U streets, N.W., in the heart of Washington's black community.

The True Reformers' Hall, previously owned by a black civic group, the Grand United Order of True Reformers, had been bought by the Knights of Pythias in January 1917 and renamed the Pythian Hall (or the Pythian Temple).[17] Ellington and others, however, always referred to it as True Reformers' Hall. A large four-story structure advertised as "the best-equipped public hall owned by colored people in the country," it served as headquarters for various civic organizations and rented out rooms to individuals and groups for special functions. In 1913 the Magnolia Dancing Class met Wednesday and Saturday nights in the hall, with music supplied by Carroll's Columbia Orchestra and the Yale Orchestra, admission fifteen cents.[18] In 1916 a social group called "The Happy Four L. M. Club" sponsored an "entertainment" in Room 5 of the hall, advertising "Good Music" for a charge of ten cents.[19] More formal events also took place at True Reformers', like the "Masque L'Allegro Frolik" on February 23, 1917, where "serpentine waltzes, confetti showers, characteristiques, etc. were danced to the strains of divine music under the direction of the unexcelled Louis M. [sic] Brown." It was an elegant affair: a solo dancer interpreted "Poor Butterfly" and the Orphean Quartette sang Ethelbert Nevin's "The Rosary."[20]

Ellington's first job at the True Reformers' Hall probably took place on a less auspicious occasion. Events like the "Masque L'Allegro Frolik" were staged in the main auditorium and used an orchestra of ten to twelve players. Ellington most likely assembled a small three- or four-piece group and played in Room 5 or 10, which accommodated forty to fifty people.[21] These are the two rooms mentioned by Ellington in *Music Is My Mistress,* and these are where Roy Ellis also recalled hearing Ellington. While attending Dunbar High School from 1914 to 1918, Ellis belonged to a social club called "The Rockaways," a half-dozen or so friends who promoted parties and dances (or "hops"). According to Ellis, Ellington played for smaller functions at True Reformers' Hall, bringing along a drummer or sometimes a banjo player. If a large group were needed, the Rockaways would hire Doc Perry. [22]

The groups Ellington played with at True Reformers' Hall most likely had changing personnel. In 1917 Ellington was not well-enough established to offer musicians regular work, so he drew from a pool of friends as jobs came up. Regular sidemen included the three Miller brothers—Bill on guitar, Felix on saxophone, "Devil" or "Brother" on drums—guitarist William Escoffery, and drummer Lloyd Stewart. A bit later, when he "was old enough to go out and play," Otto Hardwick joined on bass fiddle, then on C-melody saxophone. [23] And Arthur Whetsol sometimes played trumpet or cornet.

These young men, in varying combinations, made up "The Duke's Serenaders," the earliest name Ellington chose for his group and one he would continue to use in the 1920s after leaving Washington. In Hardwick, Whetsol, and the Miller brothers, Ellington had found musicians who could read music as well as improvise. The Millers were sons of James Miller, the Armstrong High music teacher and leader of community center bands. Trombonist Sandy Williams (b. 1906), a member of Fletcher Henderson's and Chick Webb's orchestras in the 1930s, studied with the elder Miller and occasionally did "parade work" with his band. He also played with Miller's sons at the Howard Theater in the early 1920s: "The sons' band played jazz and they had quite a repertoire. It wasn't just barrelhouse. They used to have stocks sent them from different publishers in New York, and you had to be able to read music to play with them." [24] Williams considered the Miller brothers "first-class musicians."

Otto Hardwick (1904–70) was a native Washingtonian who attended Dunbar High School and as a teenager played bass with Carroll's Columbia Orchestra. [25] In a 1964 interview he said he met Ellington when both were high-school students. This seems unlikely given their age difference: when Ellington left Armstrong in February 1917, Hardwick was only twelve. Still, Hardwick's family lived at 1345 T Street, about a block away from 1212 T Street, where J.E., Daisy, and Ruth moved in 1919 or 1920. By this time Ellington was married and living on Sherman Avenue, but he probably paid frequent visits to his family on T Street, where he could have met Hardwick. Hardwick remembered that he was just starting out in "the band business" when Ellington gave him one of his first opportunities to play, and later Ellington took credit for encouraging Hardwick to learn the C-melody saxophone.[26] He also recalled being surprised by the young man's ability: "He read very well and played even better, so he was no longer looked on as too young to be called for a job." Soon Hardwick became Ellington's friend and "first chair saxophone around Washington."[27]

Arthur Whetsol (1905–40) was another neighborhood friend. His mother, Mrs. Schiefe, ran a boardinghouse at 905 R Street, N.W., right next to Louis Thomas's Clef Club building.[28] His stepfather, "Elder" Schiefe, was a Seventh-Day Adventist minister. Whetsol and Hardwick were schoolmates at Garnet Elementary School.[29] Whetsol may have attended Armstrong but apparently played in the Dunbar High School orchestra (together with Hardwick) under the direction of Henry Grant.

In Ellington's bands of the 1920s and 1930s, Arthur Whetsol was known for his "propriety, clean appearance, and reliability," also for his good grammar.[30] Whetsol's style may have reflected that of his minister stepfather but also seemed characteristic of the neighborhood in which Ellington and his musician friends grew up. Barry Ulanov has noted a certain outlook shared by Washington jazz musicians that set them apart from others: "Duke had it . . . so had Otto Hardwick, the Miller brothers, Bill Escoffery, Claude Hopkins, Arthur Whetsol, Elmer Snowden, Rex Stewart, all the musicians who were born or bred in the capital. . . . There was a Washington pattern: it involved a certain bearing, a respect for education, for the broad principles of the art of music; a desire for order, for design in their professional lives."[31] Doc Perry and Louis Brown could be added to Ulanov's list. Such qualities may have helped these black musicians find acceptance with white audiences. At the same time, the reading ability of Hardwick, Whetsol, and the Millers filled out the repertory requirements of dance jobs and parties where Ellington might not have made it so easily on his own.

Ellington played apart from the Serenaders, too. Rex Stewart (1907–67), a later Ellingtonian who lived in Washington from 1914 to about 1922, recalled "Eddie" Ellington with a small group at the Odd Fellows Hall in Georgetown. The band was led by a saxophonist named "Tobin." In addition to Ellington it featured Hardwick on bass fiddle and a drummer named "Stickamackum." Stewart's account of a Saturday night dance (probably in the early 1920s) describes working conditions rather different from those encountered by the society bands of Doc Perry and Louis Brown. Excessive drinking during the evening led to a brawl. Ellington and a few others escaped by "hotfooting" it down 29th Street. Drummer "Sticks" simply pulled a switchblade and calmly chewed tobacco as he packed up. Stewart heard the band playing "popular tunes of the day," like Shelton Brooks's "Walkin' the Dog," "It's Right Here for You (If You Don't Get It, 'Tain't No Fault of Mine)," and "He May Be Your Man, But He Comes to See Me Sometimes." Stewart also remembered Duke hanging out at the corner of Seventh and T streets and being crowned "king" of Room 10 at True Reformers' Hall, "where the teenagers held their get-togethers." [32]

By 1918 Ellington's musical activity had begun to accelerate. The city directory listed him as "musician" and his name appeared in the yellow pages of the telephone directory under the heading "Musicians." His personal life changed when he married Edna Thompson, whom he had met when both were attending Armstrong. Ellington had been living at his father's place, 1703 8th Street, N.W.; now the newlyweds moved to 1955 3rd Street, N.W. [33]

Around this time Ellington started playing for functions outside the black community. Bernice Wiggins has said that J.E.'s connections with caterers and butlers helped Duke get a dance job at the Women's Democratic Club, on the corner of 17th and K streets, N.W. The occasion was special enough that Mrs. Wiggins was allowed to go and hear her cousin (normally she could not). She looked in the hall to see people dancing in a "gorgeous lighted room." [34] This job led to others. As Ellington later recalled, in 1917 and 1918 "all the embassies and big shots in Washington were hiring small bands to play for parties. It didn't seem to make much difference *what* band—they just hired *a* band." [35]

Ellington's popularity grew partly because of an increased demand for the new music called "jazz" and partly because of good business sense. Black Washington was just awakening to jazz in 1918. An article that year in the *Bee* explained the term, stating that "everyone is delighted with the new syncopated melodies which are now so popular throughout the country." [36] The production of

Broadway Rastus at the Howard Theater featured a "colored ginger jazz orchestra" playing jazz in a "plantation style." Soon after, S. H. Dudley's *Darktown Frolics* brought Dudley's Jazz Band to the Howard. Wellington A. Adams's music store advertised a new blues by quoting its publisher's claim that the piece was "an instrumental JAZZ number and one of the biggest sensations in New York at the present time." [37] By July 1918 Adams's establishment began selling sheet music and player rolls from New York's Pace and Handy Music Company. Less than a year later Washington was visited by W. C. Handy himself and his Original Jazz Band. [38]

White Washingtonians were discovering jazz, too, although the music received less notice in the *Washington Post* and *Evening Star* than in the *Bee*. In 1918 Victor advertised recordings made by the Original Dixieland Jazz Band and Columbia announced Earl Fuller's "jazzed" version of "The Missouri Waltz." The *Post* theater directory carried ads for the Howard, where whites may have gone to hear visiting jazz bands. Most ads for dancing did not mention jazz, but in the summer of 1918 notices for Chevy Chase Lake (which had "two big pavilions" for dancing) listed both an orchestra and a jazz band.[39] If by 1918 white Washingtonians were starting to dance to jazz, it was still a bit early to read in the papers about the new, slightly naughty music.

Advertising helped spread Ellington's reputation. After listing his name under "Musicians" in the 1918 telephone directory, he placed the following ad in June 1919: [40]

JAZZ BAND   COLORED MUSICIANS

The Duke's Serenaders

E. K. ELLINGTON

Pianist

1955 3rd. St. N.W.   PHONE NORTH 8136

Ellington continued the ads in several more issues. In October 1919 the Duke's Serenaders ("Colored Syncopaters") promised "IRRESISTIBLE JASS" to their "Select Patrons." Instead of being listed merely as "pianist" Ellington now was "manager." This designation remained in the ad of October 1920, but with Doc Perry appearing as "President" of the Serenaders.[41]

Other factors increased Ellington's popularity. People may have

Ellington's advertisement in the October 1919 Washington telephone directory

liked his showy keyboard style and his agreeable manner: "I had," he admitted in his memoirs, "a good personality." [42] Being a crafty salesman didn't hurt, either. When prospective employers called him on the phone he used to speak quickly, as though rushed and very busy. [43]

Otto Hardwick once described this period of Ellington's rising fortunes: "All of a sudden, around 1918, we began to get a lot of 'dicty' jobs. We would all pile into my Pullman automobile, nicknamed 'The Dupadilly,' and Duke would direct us to drive to an embassy or private mansion. Other times we would go out to Manassas, Culpepper, Warrenton or Orange [Virginia], for fancy balls and society receptions. This was Meyer Davis territory and none of us was able to figure out how Duke was muscling in." [44] Ellington's ability to get Virginia society jobs came from his promotional efforts and attractive personal qualities, also from his experience working under Louis Thomas. The towns mentioned by Hardwick may have been "Meyer Davis territory," but Thomas had connections there, too. Once Thomas sent Ellington to a solo piano job at the Ashland Country Club. (Ashland is about fifteen miles north of Richmond, sixty miles south of Washington.) Ellington's fee was $100, $90 of which Thomas claimed as commission. It was then that Ellington decided to go into business for himself. [45]

The Virginia towns in which Ellington played varied in distance from Washington—from relatively close Manassas (thirty-seven miles) to more distant Orange (seventy-eight miles)—but all had ties to the capital. Important social events like the Middleburg Hunt were covered regularly by the *Washington Post*. Washington residents had horse farms or private homes in these areas or were invited there for social functions. A train ran from Washington to Warrenton, Culpepper, and Orange. Today all of these towns are under the jurisdiction of the Washington Local 161-710 of the American Federation of Musicians. In Ellington's time black musicians were not part of the union, but they shared the geographic territory with the city's white union members. (Charlottesville and Richmond also supplied bands on occasion.)

Some of Ellington's Virginia jobs may have been linked to annual events on the social calendar, especially the horse shows and hunts. The fox-hunting season usually lasted from October through March. Several famous sporting events took place near the towns mentioned by Ellington: the Middleburg Hunt, the Piedmont Hunt (Loudoun and Fauquier counties), the Warrenton Hunt, and the Orange Fox and Hounds. During the hunt season, often in mid-winter, a ball would be held. For many years one of the most popular entertainers at hunt balls was Chauncey Brown, whom Ellington recalled using as a drummer.

Horse shows, held from May through September, also featured music. Upperville (near Middleburg) has the oldest horse show in the country; Manassas, Warrenton, Culpepper, and Orange all sponsored these annual events in 1919 and 1920. Although large brass bands often performed at horse shows, once Ellington's group was asked to take part in the outdoor festivities: "I think with only four pieces we went out and played louder than they did."[46] More typically, though, Ellington's bands would entertain at dances held after the shows; in 1971 he remembered having done this in Warrenton, Orange, and Middleburg.[47]

Ellington may have also played dances at county fairs, country clubs, and private homes. In Warrenton the Warren Green Hotel sponsored many entertainments. Dances in Orange were put on by the Orange County Cotillion, and in Culpepper by the Pot and Kettle Club. At the New Hotel Culpepper the favorite groups were Colgan's Orchestra (from Charlottesville) and "Happy" Walker and his Golden Pheasants (from Washington). The favorite refreshment was whiskey, two gallons of which would be placed behind the piano.[48] Ellington remembered the liquid fuel: "Those were the days when I was a champion drinker. . . . I was eighteen, nineteen, or twenty [1917, 1918, 1919], and it was customary then to put a gallon of corn whiskey on the piano when the musicians began to play. There were four of us in the group, and one hour later the jug was empty. At the end of every hour the butler would replace the empty jug with another full gallon of twenty-one-year-old corn."[49] Depending on the place, occasion, and supply of corn, these dances probably ranged from very formal to quite loose. Ellington once had to play guitar for a barn dance in Orange when a piano would not fit into the barn. (For this occasion the organizer had requested that Ellington appear in person and not just send out one of his groups.[50]) But Ellington may have also taken part in events like the Warrenton "germans"—cotillion dances marked by "dignity" and "stateliness."[51]

Ellington probably worked in neighboring Maryland as well as Virginia, although he did not mention the state in either *Music Is My Mistress* or interviews. In a 1962 *Washington Post* article, George Hoefer alluded to Ellington's jobs at "Maryland estates" but gave no details. Mercer Ellington described his father taking at least one job in Baltimore; surely there were more.[52]

Although Ellington's talent, pleasing personality, and good business sense worked in his favor, organization was a key factor in helping black musicians get a foothold in segregated Washington. Lacking an independent union until 1922, blacks had formed several groups to increase job opportunities. The only one Ellington seems to have been connected with was Louis Thomas's Capital City Clef Club. By 1919 Ellington had gone off on his own, and by 1920 he was getting assistance from Doc Perry (who previously had led groups for Thomas).

Meanwhile, in June 1919 Henry Crowder and Russell Wooding founded the Crescendo Club, a group similar to Europe's and Thomas's Clef Clubs. Formed in response to "intolerable working conditions," the Crescendo Club was dedicated to "the purpose of stabilizing prices, promoting good will among its members, exploiting the profession generally and placing the colored performers of Washington on a better basis of musical proficiency." The club featured both "permanent" and "transient" bands. Its patrons "included the very best that society possesses . . . Cabinet officers, Senators, their relatives, friends, sweethearts, and servants." Like the Clef Club, the Crescendo Club had an educational purpose beyond its business goals: "A special feature of our organization is the weekly get-together of the full membership in joint rehearsal, which gives sixty-five odd musicians the opportunity to perfect themselves in the art and science of music, preparatory to a series of concerts, which are planned for the near future."[53] Of the Washington musicians mentioned by Ellington in *Music Is My Mistress*, at least four were Crescendo Club members: pianists Louis Brown and Roscoe Lee and drummers Bill Jones and Bill Beasley.

When not entertaining Virginians or Washington high society, Ellington continued to play in the black community for dances and parties sponsored by social clubs, civic groups, or promoters like Alonzo "Shrimp" Collins and G. Frank Jones. Calling themselves "The Stenographers," Collins and Jones put on dances featuring local musicians. In February 1916 the *Bee* reported that the Stenographers' weekly afternoon meetings (held Wednesdays from four to eight) were very popular.[54] Later Ellington would recall filling in for Doc Perry at these matinee dances, which usually took place at the True Reformers' Hall. Ellington's own groups also played for such occasions. In May 1919 his Serenaders gave a "Jazz Matinee" at the Odd Fellows Hall (probably 1606 M Street, N.W.) from 3:45 to 7:45. The next month they performed in the Center Market Coliseum, a larger hall, for a Masonic Victory Reception celebrating the end of the war. The dance followed a "literary and musical program." An advertisement in the *Bee* invited the public "to whirl the hours away, for pleasure is assured." There would be dancing until 2 A.M. and "refreshments in abundance."[55]

While Ellington's career stepped up in 1918 and 1919, he decided that his musicianship was not improving quickly enough and took steps to prevent overexposure of underdeveloped talent: "I finally built up so much of a reputation," he later wrote, "that I had to study music seriously to protect it."[56] For instruction he turned to Henry Grant, who lived just down the street from his family's house on T Street.[57]

By this time Grant had emerged as one of Washington's most important black musicians. His father, the singer Henry Fleet Grant, may have been the first black high-school music teacher in Washington, working at the old M Street High School before it became Dunbar in 1916. The younger Henry studied music at Livingston College in North Carolina and at New York University. He began teaching music at Dunbar in 1916, retiring from the post in 1952. Ellington may have heard of Grant while attending nearby Armstrong. Grant's musical activities, however, ranged beyond the world of public school music.[58] He composed, directed choirs at various churches (John Wesley AME Zion, 15th Street Presbyterian, St. Luke's Episcopal), led the L'Allegro Glee Club, gave solo piano recitals, and concertized in a trio with violinist Felix Weir and cellist Leonard Jeter. Grant also had ties to the Washington Conservatory. After completing the Artist's Course there in 1910 he joined the faculty and in 1919 became director. Grant was a close friend of the singer and teacher Ernest Amos, also of the composer Will Marion Cook. On different occasions he performed with and conducted Cook's Afro-American Folksong Singers.

MASONIC VICTORY RECEPTION
BY THE NEW MASONIC HALL CORPORATION

CENTER MARKET COLOSSEUM

Ninth Street and Pennsylvania Avenue

FRIDAY EVENING, JUNE 6, 1919, from 8 P. M. until 2 A. M.

Literary and Musical Program, one hour, by the following contributing artists: Mr. Frank B. Williams, composer of "Jessamine"; Mrs. Louise Mills Brown, Dr. C. Sumner Wormley, and others. Come and whirl the hours away, for pleasure is assured.

MUSIC BY DUKE ELLINGTON'S SERENADERS
Edward K. Ellington, Director

The public is especially invited. Your comfort will be our effort. Craftmen and Honored Ladies, remember the cause for which we are laboring.

DANCING UNTIL 2 A. M. REFRESHMENTS IN ABUNDANCE.
COMMITTEE ON ARRANGEMENTS:

Dr. W. H. Jackson, Chairman	Mr. William HA Cowan
Mr. Jesse H. Mitchell	Mr. Allen F. Jackson
Mr. Archibald Runner.	Dr. P. W. Price
Mr. Ernest M. Dickerson	Mr. J. H. Meyers
Mr. Charles P. Ford	Mr. E. W. Bundy
Dr. William A. Warfield	Miss J. L. Cox
Mr. Paul R. Stewart	Mrs. Clara Brooks

CARD OF ADMISSION, - - $1.00

Tickets on sale at Ross Pharmacy. Tenth and R streets northwest; Moss Pharmacy, Nineteenth and L streets northwest; Jackson & Whipps, Seventh and T streets northwest.
"Over the Top In Smiles and Pleasure."
Mark your calendar for this rare treat.

opened a piano and vocal studio at 931 Westminster street, Washington, D. C. Mrs. Johnson is a gradu-

OVERSEA MUSICIANS, NOTICE

Musicians of the A. E. F. are re-

Advertisement for the Duke's Serenaders in the Washington *Bee*, May 31, 1919

In addition to his local activity, Grant helped found the National Association of Negro Musicians in 1919. Gearing up for this event, he shared sponsorship of music festivals at Dunbar in 1918 and 1919 that featured some of the leading black concert musicians of the day: singers Florence Cole Talbert, Harry T. Burleigh, and Cleota Collins; pianists Carl Diton and Nathaniel Dett; composer-organist J. Rosamond Johnson; and violinist Clarence Cameron White. The Afro-American Folksong Singers and Howard University Girls Glee Club also participated. While serving as secretary of the NANM, Grant edited its journal, *The Negro Musician*, in 1920 and 1921.[59]

Ellington claimed that he was invited by Grant to study harmony and that he "jumped at the opportunity," since Grant taught "most of the advanced musicians."[60] According to Grant's daughters, Mrs. Alice Spraggins and Mrs. June Hackney, Ellington visited twice a week to work on harmony exercises with their father. These lessons—of which no record survives—seem to have helped develop Ellington's reading skills: "We moved along real quickly, until I was learning the difference between a G-flat and an F-sharp."[61] Ulanov paraphrased Grant (whom he seems to have interviewed) on Ellington as a student: "Harmonizing a simple melody was always an experiment in color with Duke; it was always important to him to create a sound that 'rang,' as he put it, either because it was mellifluous, exquisitely concordant, or because it was bizarre, challengingly discordant. But for all his experimental writing, Duke was anxious to learn the fundamentals."[62] Ulanov also reported that Hardwick and Whetsol studied with Grant.

Fortunately for Ellington, Grant believed that standards of excellence could apply to popular music, not just to more traditional concert forms. Unlike the critic and local musical entrepreneur Wellington A. Adams, Grant did not look down upon popular idioms. When Ford Dabney's Syncopated Orchestra played at Convention Hall in 1921, Grant was there in the audience.[63] And the same year, Grant announced in *The Negro Musician* his intention to interview "successful Negro composers, and organizers, leaders, and performers" in the field of popular music, listing Dabney together with John Turner Layton, Jr., and Will Vodery.[64] Grant's interest in popular music also surfaced in his review of Noble Sissle and Eubie Blake's *Shuffle Along*, which played the Howard Theater in June

1921. Calling it the best music since the shows of Williams and Walker and Cole and Johnson, Grant wrote of black Washington's enthusiastic reaction to *Shuffle Along,* even taking some personal credit:

> Mr. Blake himself was the object of my pride, for it was I who gave him his first lesson in harmony and at the same time urged him to continued study. I marvelled at his natural technique and got my first lesson—an insight into the soul of an exponent of "Ragtime." I little dreamed, up to that time, that inherent musical taste and appreciation of the "Classics" was associated with the thoughts, dreams and reaction [*sic*] of the Jazz artist. Mr. Blake often kept me for hours playing serious compositions and evidenced keen enjoyment and critical judgment of all I had to offer. [65]

Grant was a new kind of teacher for Ellington. He was a versatile musician who composed, conducted, and concertized, an active promoter of Negro music, and someone who believed that popular music could be taken seriously. To a young ragtime "plunker" turned bandleader, Grant represented different musical values from those needed for a Warrenton hunt ball or a "hop" at True Reformers' Hall. Perhaps some of Grant's idealism and musical broadmindedness rubbed off on Ellington—together with tips on good voice-leading and solutions to harmonic puzzles.

5

Washington Bandleader

1919–1923

At twenty, Ellington faced the responsibility of supporting his wife, Edna, and son, Mercer, who had been born March 11, 1919. During the day he worked in partnership with Ewell Conaway, painting signs, sets, and backdrops for the Howard Theater and posters for dance halls like Murray's Casino and the Lincoln Colonnade. At night he played jobs and sent out bands under his name. He also found a way to capitalize on both his artistic and musical talents: "When customers came for posters to advertise a dance, I would ask them what they were doing about their music. When they wanted to hire a band, I would ask them who's painting their signs."[1] Through sign-painting and the music business Ellington earned enough to buy a new Chandler—between $1,800 and $2,500 in 1919—and a house on 2728 Sherman Avenue, N.W.[2]

Ellington later claimed that he was earning $10,000 a year: "I had made a lot of money in Washington. At that time I was a much better businessman than I am now."[3] Mercer Ellington has traced his father's business acumen to friends like "Black Bowie"—who helped get jobs for Ellington's group, then split "the lion's share of the proceeds" with Duke—and to "the poolroom education . . . the art of hustling in back halls and dark alleys."[4] If $10,000 was in fact Ellington's yearly income, this meant he was netting about $200 a week. The usual fee for the Serenaders was $5 a night, so he would have had to rake off high commissions from his other bands and do well in the painting business to average $25 to $30 daily.[5]

It was possible. But years later, Edna Ellington would remember these as "hard days."[6] When it came to matters of finance, Duke shared J.E.'s tendencies to exaggerate and to act "as though he had money, whether he had it or not."[7]

In 1919 and 1920 the Washington musical scene was enlivened by the arrival of new bands and visiting musicians. The Jardin Orchestra (a standard name for one of Louis Thomas's Capital City Clef Club groups) played after a Paul Robeson concert in September 1919, "augmented by Jim Europe's Orchestra members."[8] (Europe's band had dispersed after their leader's murder that May, some members going with Noble Sissle, others with Ford Dabney.) Bands from Baltimore often worked in Washington. In September the Strollers sponsored "Washington's Greatest Ball" at the Odd Fellows Hall on 1606 M Street. Four groups were on hand for the occasion: Doc Perry's Jardin Band, Miss Gertie Wells' Jazz Band, and from Baltimore Miss Naomie's Jazz Band and Joe Rochester's Syncopators.[9] Pianist Rochester (a "big, loudmouth singer," according to Roy Ellis) was playing in Washington by 1917, having taken over the band of fellow Baltimorean Eubie Blake the year before. Of the various pianists Ellington met in Washington, Rochester was "not so easily accessible."[10] But Ellington did strike up a friendship with one of Rochester's band members, Elmer Snowden.

Snowden (1900–1973) had played guitar and banjo on street corners, in movie theaters, and with singers in his native Baltimore. He was a member of Eubie Blake's band in 1915 and 1916, before Rochester took over, then stayed on when the group started finding jobs in Washington.[11] Snowden also worked in Atlantic City in the summers. It was there, he later claimed, that he was first heard by Louis Thomas, who subsequently booked Snowden out of his Washington office. In Atlantic City Snowden had discovered an outstanding drummer named "Diamond" [Elbert], also known as "Black Diamond." Diamond went back to Washington with Snowden and the two of them joined Doc Perry and Otto Hardwick in working for Thomas at the Howard Theater. As Snowden would recall: "Oh, we used to perk it up! We had it so they often didn't want to see the show."[12] The year was probably 1920, since Snowden mentioned Marie Lucas leading the Howard pit orchestra at the time. That same year, the *Bee* announced "Mr. Elmo [*sic*] Snowden, banjo player, formerly with Louis Thomas, has resigned and is now playing with Miss Gertrude Wells' Jazz Orchestra, that none can compare with." [13] Snowden married Wells in November 1920.

Since Snowden worked with Joe Rochester, Louis Thomas, Doc Perry, and Gertie Wells, he was bound to meet Ellington sooner or later. Indeed, Snowden seems to have made quite a stir when he arrived in town. As Ellington wrote: "When Elmer Snowden came to Washington in Joe Rochester's band, all the banjo and banjorine players were playing everything right, right on the nose, according to the city's disciplinary climate. . . . [Snowden] had a flair for soul, plus ragtime, and a jumping thing that tore us all up. He immediately became the No. 1 Banjorine Player." [14] Soon Snowden began taking small-group jobs with Ellington. Otto Hardwick and Arthur Whetsol may have played with the two, as did drummer William Alexander "Sonny" Greer—also known as "Sensational Sonny," "The Sweet Singing Drummer," and "Little Willie from Long Branch."

Greer (ca. 1895–1982) was another recent arrival to Washington, drawn by the prospect of work and a healthy musical scene. Born in Long Branch, New Jersey, Greer played the Keith vaudeville circuit as a teenager. In 1919 he was appearing with Fats Waller at the Plaza Hotel in Asbury Park when he met the Conaway Boys, who invited him to join them in Washington. Greer accepted the offer and wound up at Louis Thomas's place on 9th and R streets with Sterling Conaway on banjo and guitar and Claude Hopkins on piano. In time he met Otto Hardwick, who introduced him to Ellington. [15] Around 1920 Greer was recruited for the Howard Theater pit band when the regular drummer, Lutice "Cutie" Perkins, failed to show up. [16] After the Howard job ended at 10:00 P.M., Greer would play with Hopkins and Eddie White at clubs like the Dreamland.

By 1920 the Howard Theater had become a focal point of activity for Washington musicians. Some, like Ellington, Doc Perry, Hardwick, and Snowden, played in small groups for early evening supper shows, before the main acts began. These shows had been going on for a few years. According to Mercer Cook, a Dunbar High student in 1916, teenagers would meet in the balcony for the shows, even after the admission was raised during World War I from a dime to eleven cents. [17] Local musical talent was the main

draw, as Jerry Rhea, one of Ellington's Washington friends, recalled: "There used to be as many as five bands competing at the
theater between 5 P.M. and 6:30 P.M. There was an orchestra in
each box and one in the pit. The bands alternated and each unit
gave out their version of the popular tunes of the day. . . . The
idea was to see which band got the most applause and Duke's Serenaders won a good share of the time. The customers got all the
fine music during these supper stanzas for an eleven-cent admission
charge." [18] In 1921 the supper shows started receiving more attention in the *Bee:* "Everybody is speaking of the wonderful music at
supper shows. It sounds better and better." Later the paper reported
a new band at the shows: "Washington's leading jazz combination,
Elmer Howden's [*sic*] Jazz Aces with 'Diamond' at the drums." [19]
The jazz groups also filled a function during the main event, Snowden recalled, playing the "intermission and the exit music." [20]

The Howard pit-orchestra musicians held their own in the face
of such jazz rivals. In part their success resulted from the leadership
of trombonist, pianist, and conductor Marie Lucas. Daughter of the
minstrel performer Sam Lucas, she had long been involved with
the theater. She was a cast member of both Cole and Johnson's
The Red Moon (1909) and Creamer and Rogers's *The Old Man's
Boy* (1913).[21] Later she became musical director for the Quality
Amusement Corporation and worked with black theater orchestras along the eastern seaboard. In 1916 she led a female orchestra
at the Colonial Theater in Baltimore. That year, when she paid a
visit to Washington, a newspaper columnist noted that she was "no
stranger to the city." [22] Lucas may have taken over at the Howard
as early as 1917, when the *Bee* reported a "female orchestra" replacing the Howard's old house band.[23] In any case, by 1920 she
was leading the Howard pit orchestra.

Perhaps it was Lucas's idea to recruit new musicians in Puerto
Rico that year. Whatever the reason, the *Bee* noted the addition
of three Puerto Ricans to the Howard Theater orchestra in May
1920. How many others eventually joined is not known. But among
the new arrivals were tuba-player Ralph Escudero (who may have
helped in the recruiting) and trombonist Juan Tizol. [24]

Tizol (1900–1984) remembered meeting Ellington at the Howard in 1920, but he did not play with him until much later (1929)
in New York. Although Tizol was mainly a "legitimate" player

—more accustomed to reading than improvising—he did perform with a few Washington jazz groups, such as Gertie Wells's band, and later with one of the White brothers and Arthur Whetsol.[25] Both Tizol and Greer may have been in the Howard pit band for *Bamboula,* a "Jazzonian Operetta" (October 1920); *Strut Yo' Stuff* with Gertrude Saunders (December 1920); and Sissle and Blake's *Shuffle Along* (April 1921). In addition to providing music for revues and shows, the orchestra probably performed recent stock arrangements and light classical fare. In 1921 the *Washington Tribune* noted that the orchestra rehearsed three hours a day, playing music "from New York publishing houses."[26] Tizol recalled that the pit band usually played "an overture or a little symphony, or a little something legit."[27]

Near the Howard Theater were many other places that sponsored musical activity. On Thanksgiving 1920, Louis Thomas opened up his Capital City Clef Club headquarters as a cabaret on 9th and R streets. In a 1927 study of recreation in Washington's black community, sociologist William H. Jones referred to Thomas's place as "the oldest cabaret in the city for the entertainment of Negroes." On the first floor was a restaurant called the Oriental Grill (or Oriental Gardens). A basement room (four feet below sea level) held about sixty people and upstairs was a larger room. The cover charge in 1927 was twenty-five cents. Criticizing the low roof and poor ventilation, Jones pronounced the Oriental Gardens a "third-class place."[28] Trombonist Sandy Williams, who worked there in the early 1920s after his Howard Theater job, concurred: it was a "hole-in-the-wall" where musicians worked "mostly for tips."[29] These later comments notwithstanding, Thomas's club was popular soon after its opening. In 1921 the conservative *Bee* announced that "the Oriental Grill is becoming the mecca for our leading citizens," later reporting that Thomas had lined up "a splendid array of entertainers this season."[30] Among those who entertained at the cabaret were Claude Hopkins, the singer "Bricktop" (Ada Smith), Sonny Greer, and Ellington.

Another popular place for music and dancing was Murray's Casino—or the Murray Palace Casino—on U Street between 9th and 10th. The hall could hold 1,800 people (although Jones gave 500 as the average number). Jones claimed that "practically all the leading fraternal and social organizations hold their dances here."[31] In

At Louis Thomas's cabaret, Washington, D.C., ca. 1920. Left to right: Sonny Greer, Ellington, Sterling Conaway (Frank Driggs Collection)

the early 1920s Elmer Snowden led the house band at Murray's, which included Arthur Whetsol on trumpet, Otto Hardwick on C-melody saxophone, Bill Beasley on drums, and Snowden on tenor banjo and saxophone. Other groups appearing at Murray's Casino from 1921 through 1923 were Gertie Wells's "Aces," Percy Glascoe's "Jazzeolas," Carroll Boyd's "Jazzers," and Sylvester Thomas's Columbian Orchestra. At times out-of-towners supplied the entertainment. Lucille Hegamin and her "Syncopated Jazz Band" were there in March 1922, and in May the blues singer Trixie Smith came in for a "concert." [32]

Heading west down U Street from Murray's Casino, one passed the True Reformers' Hall and then came to the Lincoln Theater, between 12th and 13th, which had the Lincoln Colonnade in its basement. William H. Jones placed the Colonnade together with Murray's under the heading of "Class A" dance halls. Although by 1922 the Colonnade had black management, it was owned by Crandall's Theatre Corporation, a white company, until 1927. An ad in the 1921 Dunbar High School yearbook called the place "America's Most Beautiful Dance Gardens," proudly noting: "Entire Plant Equipped with Typhoon Cooling System." Since Louis Brown was the regular organist upstairs at the theater, it was probably not unusual to find him leading a band downstairs in the Colonnade. In 1923 both Brown and Elmer Snowden's "Irresistible Demons" played there for a midnight dance sponsored by the Red Circle Pleasure Club. [33]

Members of the black community used places like Murray's Casino, the Lincoln Colonnade, and the True Reformers' Hall for special affairs, parties, and dance classes. For these occasions bands furnished "society music"—popular songs and show tunes—interspersed with jazz, ragtime, and blues. But there were other more informal spots for music-making. The Dreamland Cabaret, around the corner from the Howard Theater on Seventh Street between S and T, opened in 1921. Its atmosphere was looser than that of the U Street dance halls. "Quentin," a reporter for the *Washington Tribune,* encouraged his readers to patronize the Dreamland and hear Bill Miller and Claude Hopkins, "dispensers of Jazz," assisted by singers Mabel White, Louise Walker, and Blanche Clarke. Quentin continued: "After midnight, apparently all the musicians in town weird [wend?] their way to this place of amusement, also

Sonny Grier [*sic*], Washington's most eccentric singing drummer can be heard. The slogan here is to come early and [stay] late, for as long as the patrons stay, you will be served and entertained. Every Tuesday night is Contest night."[34] Claude Hopkins claimed to have launched his career in jazz at the Dreamland, "a highspot in Washington." He remembered celebrities who sometimes stopped by: "Babe Ruth used to come in all the time, and he'd start out with a fifty-dollar bill in the cut-box. I remember one time he had a double-header, and he didn't leave there till 5:30 in the morning. Stoned! He was something."[35]

The long hours may have been fun for visitors but rough on performers. "Jay Bee" wrote in the 1922 *Washington Tribune* that he visited the Dreamland at a late hour. The place was "teeming with gaiety" but the "entertainers appeared rather haggard." He heard singer Mabel White together with "two other chirpers, who are all there with the blues stuff."[36] Occasionally things got out of hand at the Dreamland. William H. Jones cited the place's "unwholesome entertainment" and "disorderly, drunken conduct," and wrote that in December 1923 the Dreamland was raided, shut down, and its manager thrown in jail.[37]

In 1920 the *Bee* noted the opening of the Poodle Dog, on Georgia Avenue, calling it "Washington's latest creation in Chinese and American restaurants." The Poodle Dog served up hot music with its chop suey: "New York has nothing on its jazz orchestra and cabaret."[38] Was this the same Poodle Dog Café in which Ellington later claimed to have worked as a soda jerk? It is hard to imagine the enterprising twenty-one-year-old bandleader serving up chocolate malts at this Chinese-American eatery. More likely, when performing his "Soda Fountain Rag" at the Poodle Dog Café, he may have referred to it as "Poodle Dog Rag."[39]

Near the Poodle Dog on Georgia Avenue was the Paradise Café. Claude Hopkins played there in 1922 with his "Agate-Cracking Jazzers."[40] Despite advertising "Polite Entertainment" and "Excellent Food," the Paradise was lost, according to Professor Jones, in February 1924: closed due to drunken and disorderly conduct.[41]

Another restaurant mentioned by Ellington, the Industrial Café, was a popular spot where musicians went after work for "a general gab-fest and jam."[42] The Industrial was located at 2006 11th Street, N.W., near the Hiawatha Theater. A 1920 ad made no mention of music there, only refreshments: "Soft Shell Crabs, hot cakes, sandwiches, salads, and drinks."[43]

Black Washingtonians in the early 1920s could also hear jazz in larger places like Convention Hall and the Center Market Coliseum. The cost of putting on events there was considerable. The Coliseum rental was $300 and the music could run as high as $100. Nevertheless, the *Bee* noted in 1920 that "colored people of this city are giving more entertainments at the Coliseum than are the white race. Money cuts a small figure with us . . . when it comes to seeking pleasure."[44] And when the hot, muggy summers drove city residents out to the parks and amusement centers, the music followed (or led) the throngs. In September 1920 Ellington appeared at New Fairmount Park, assisted by Doc Perry.[45] Next summer the Anderson Open Air Gardens boasted "the biggest musical attraction in Washington": " 'Take it slow and easy and enjoy the outdoor breezes' is the motto. This is the weekly line-up: Monday night, Duke Ellington's Jazz Premiums; Tuesday night, Snowden and Beasley's; Wednesday night, 'Doc' Perry's Society Jazzers; Thursday night, Duke Ellington; Friday night, 'Doc' Perry; Saturday night, Crowder's Penn Garden Jazzers."[46] The Suburban Gardens, in the northeast section of the city, was another popular park for black residents. On Memorial Day 1922, Gertie Wells and her Syncopated Orchestra provided the music, probably in the Gardens' large dancing pavilion. A few weeks later "Duke Ellington and his Stars" played there for a beauty contest.[47]

Some of the Washington dances that featured jazz bands in the early 1920s incorporated aspects of theater and make-believe. While dancers still may have been performing fox-trots and two-steps, the atmosphere could be exotic and sensual, perhaps eliciting appropriate musical responses. The promoters J. H. Matthews and George H. Tucker had an oriental dancing class that met at Murray's Casino and sponsored "Sultan's Balls" for which both Elmer Snowden's and Gertie Wells's bands played. One August night in 1921 the Stenographers produced "A Night In the Orient" at Suburban Gardens. Henry Crowder's Penn Garden Jazz Band provided the music and the promoters supplied "oriental electric effects, quaint costumes and scenery."[48] For Labor Day weekend the Stenographers cooked up even more sizzling entertainment at Convention Hall. The theme this time was "The Devil's Garden," and on hand were Doc Perry's "Jazz Demons" and Elmer Snowden's "Whooping Devils." The fun lasted from 9 P.M. to 4 A.M., but midnight brought a surprise: "At the stroke of twelve the feature of the evening, the appearance of Mephisto with ten frolicking nymphs in filmy garments, was staged."[49] Playing for costumed dancers, actors, oriental revelers, and fashion models, jazz musicians added strange effects to dance music in an effort to evoke the exotic. Don Redman's 1924 arrangement of "Shanghai Shuffle" for Fletcher Henderson may have grown out of such circumstances, also "Limehouse Blues" (1924), a theater song that became popular as a jazz instrumental. More exoticism surfaced in the late 1920s in music conceived for New York nightclub revues (as in Ellington's "jungle" pieces and his "Arabian Lover" and "Japanese Dream" of 1929). But one might have heard something similar in Washington in 1923, when Louis Brown was "dispensing the weird desert melodies" for a sheik dance given by the "Beau Brummels."[50]

Ellington's professional experience in Washington in the late 1910s and early 1920s, then, embraced a variety of contexts: wealthy society parties, hunt balls and barn dances in Virginia, cabarets and restaurants, dances and dance classes at True Reformers' and the Odd Fellows halls, fashion shows at parks, and supper shows at the Howard Theater. Such experience was valuable training for the young bandleader, exposing him to different audiences with varied musical tastes. During this period Ellington's compositional activity is a mystery. If he composed at all between 1918 and 1923 the pieces have been either lost or forgotten. For Ellington, this was a period of learning about the business of leading bands and reviewing fundamentals with Henry Grant. But if Ellington's composing talent had yet to emerge, his musicianship was being tested and proven in competitions.

Audiences were drawn to contests featuring both bands and individuals. A playful combativeness prevailed at the Howard Theater supper shows when the pit orchestra would play a "straight" version of a piece and a jazz group would provide a "jazzed up" response. In 1922 "Jay Bee" visited a supper show and walked in on a "bitter jazz contest . . . between the Snowden-Diamond jazz pirates and Doc Perry's musical thugs."[51] Ellington took part in one of these contests in April at the "Midnite Show." The results were less than magnificent. Only three of the ten scheduled bands showed up, and the winner was a group led by pianist Walter Slade. Apparently Slade sounded good and Otto Hardwick was having an off night: "Duke had a fair line-up that included Otto Hardwick, the saxophone hound, but with the very liberal assistance of an instrument that sounded mighty like unto a wagon wheel that had not been on speaking terms with A.X.L.E. grease for months, Duke was completely outjazzed."[52] On another occasion, Ellington reported facing similar problems with Blind Johnny's band but managed (together with Sterling Conaway and Sonny Greer) to prevail over Elmer Snowden's eight-piece group. In these encounters psychology counted as much as musical skill. Ellington would "tell fellows in the other band they were going to get cut that night," and he and Greer worked out "a lot of tricks between drums and piano" to insure their victory.[53] Greer was already a flashy drummer when he came to Washington in 1919, and his loud personality and street-wise style probably were assets in these musical personality contests.

Other drummers besides Greer were notable figures in black Washington's musical life. In 1922 the *Washington Tribune* praised Diamond, Snowden's Atlantic City partner, who was "reported to be the world's greatest and most sensational trap-artist."[54] A photograph of Diamond showed him with a snare, a bass drum, cymbals, and chimes that hung suspended from a rack. Greer's set in the Louis Thomas cabaret photo is simpler—just a bass, snare, and cymbal—but he probably had more equipment (i.e., temple blocks, chimes) when he played in the Howard Theater pit. While one of Greer's novelties was his singing, drummers like Bill Jones and Bill Beasley used rhythmic tricks and shifting meters in competitive situations. Ellington remembers how they "would go into three-four and five-four . . . and try to throw me."[55]

Ellington got away from tricky drummers by entering piano contests. One such event was sponsored by the Charles Datcher Lodge No. 15 on September 21, 1921. Doc Perry led the house band, and solo contestants included Ellington, Claude Hopkins, and "Luckyeth Roberts of New York City."[56] The winner of the contest was not reported, but a few months later Ellington came out on top in another: "Duke Ellington was awarded the loving cup offered by manager Greenlease of the Liberty Garden in the piano contest held there last Thursday."[57] Winners of contests could enhance their local reputation and make some cash on the side. Luckey Roberts took part in one Washington event where the prize was $50.

One time Ellington had the chance to play for the celebrated New York pianist James P. Johnson. The occasion was a big event at Convention Hall called "The 20th Century Jazz Revue," held November 25, 1921. The promoters were the same ones active in putting on smaller-scale dances and functions in the black community: J. H. Matthews and George H. Tucker (the Orientals) and Alonzo Collins and G. Frank Jones (the Stenographers). A review of the event in the *Chicago Defender*'s Washington column captured the colorful flavor of jazz at the time:

> Among the artists appearing were Gertie Wells and her Jassimba Sextet, "Doc" Perry's Jazz Bandits, Branson's Hypnotic Arcade Hounds, Snowden's Eccentric Serenaders, Caroline Thornton's Harmony Aces, Duke Ellington's Wild Cats, Mose Duncan's International Jazz Hounds, from Baltimore, Md.; "Diamond," Atlantic City's sensational drummer; Beaseley, "the ace of all drummers." In addition the following celebrated stars appeared: Lucille Hegamin, Famous Art Record Phonograph Star; Mrs. Florence Parham, formerly of Nora Bayes Company, and J. P. Johnson, piano wizard of New York City. A capacity audience crowded Convention Hall.[58]

Johnson may have visited Washington before, but most likely this was the night when the twenty-two-year-old Ellington played "Carolina Shout" for its thirty-one-year-old composer. In 1962 Ellington remembered seeing Johnson at Convention Hall and being urged by "his local following" to go up and "cut" James P. with his own piece.[59] Apparently Johnson was impressed and afterwards accompanied his young admirer on "a tour of the South-West district" until ten o'clock the next morning.[60]

In Washington Ellington was exposed to other luminaries besides pianists James P. Johnson, Luckey Roberts, and Eubie Blake. When Mamie Smith visited in 1922 she brought along tenor saxophonist Coleman Hawkins. The *Washington Tribune* described Hawkins (erroneously) as "a former local boy," now a "saxophone king" who "made the old horn do everything but talk."[61] This may have been the occasion when Smith was on tour with Fletcher Henderson. Ellington recalled how Henderson and Hawkins came to hear him

—"just a scuffling, little piano player"—at Jack's on Seventh Street. But when fighting and shooting broke out, all three musicians ended up not on, but under, the bandstand.[62]

Another great reed player Ellington heard in Washington was Sidney Bechet. Ellington remembered seeing him at the Howard Theater in 1921. Mercer Cook speculated that it may have been as early as 1919, when Bechet was on tour with Will Marion Cook's New York Syncopated Orchestra.[63] However, John Chilton, Bechet's biographer, has put the date as January 22–28, 1923, when Bechet appeared at the Howard in the show *How Come.*

Other famous orchestras passed through town. New York's Clef Club Orchestra made annual visits until 1919. W. C. Handy and Ford Dabney brought their groups, as did Leroy Smith, who played the Belasco Theater. Smith's large, disciplined orchestra impressed Ellington, who was accustomed to playing in smaller, looser ensembles: "It was well dressed and well rehearsed, and all the musicians doubled on different instruments." The band's versatility, according to Ellington, "caused an explosion in my desire to explore the further reaches of music's possibilities."[64]

Playing around Washington may have been fun and relatively profitable, but Ellington was not satisfied. If as a teenager he was excited by poolroom accounts of distant places like Cleveland and Chicago, now as a young man he was attracted by the luster of New York and its musical life. The city and its celebrities "filled our imagination." Harlem beckoned from afar: the place "did indeed have the world's most glamorous atmosphere."[65] In one of the photographs taken at Louis Thomas's cabaret, Ellington looks pensive, even bored. He seems too big for his clothes and cramped by the walls with their homey, pastoral murals.[66]

In 1923 he decided it was time to break away.

Part Two

NEW YORK · 1923–1927

6

New in New York

New York in 1923 offered more than glamor and celebrity to a young black bandleader from Washington. Then, as now, it boasted a rich concentration of musical talent and represented the proving ground for achievement. Musicians flocked to New York in search of good jobs, high wages, and opportunities to sell and distribute their music through publishing houses and record companies.

Some of Ellington's friends in Washington had already begun to explore recording possibilities in New York. After speaking with bandleader Elmer Snowden in April 1922, a writer for the *Washington Tribune* reported, "This guy and his destroyers of musical instruments have almost jazzed their way into the studio of the Columbia Phonograph Company."[1] Nothing came of Snowden's venture immediately. However, in November he went to New York with trumpeter Arthur Whetsol and pianist Claude Hopkins to accompany blues singer Sara Martin on a date for Columbia. The two sides—"I Loved You Once But You Stayed Away" and "'Tain't Nobody's Biz-ness If I Do"—were never released. But the three must have returned to Washington with cash from the session and hopes of getting more recording work.

The resident New York expert in Ellington's circle was drummer Sonny Greer. For several years Greer had been entertaining his friends in Washington with tales about the city and its colorful inhabitants: "I was an authority, because my two aunts lived [in New

York] and I had spent a good part of my schooldays in the city. I painted a glowing picture, a fabulous picture. We sat around drinking corn and telling lies, and I won the lying contest."[2] Greer may have been the one who lured Ellington to New York for a brief visit in 1921, when the two played at Busoni's Balconnade opposite the Original Dixieland Jazz Band.[3]

Beyond the stories swapped by black musicians in Washington, a more direct link to New York came from the traveling shows that played theaters like the Howard, Lincoln, and Gayety. In August 1922 one of those shows brought the successful New York-based songwriter and publisher Clarence Williams to the Lincoln Theater. There he met Ellington and heard the young bandleader play piano. When Ellington wondered if he could make it in New York, Williams encouraged him: "I think you could—in fact, I know you could."[4] Not long after, another musician visited Washington who would give Ellington a chance to try out Williams's advice.

Clarinetist Wilbur Sweatman (1882–1961) was a veteran vaudeville performer who had begun his career with W. C. Handy and the Musical Spillers in the early 1900s. In 1913, when he opened at Hammerstein's Victoria Theater in New York, he was billed as "The Musical Marvel of the Twentieth Century," presumably because of his ability to play three clarinets at once.[5] By the early 1920s he was a fairly prolific recording artist for Columbia, making over twenty sides between March 1918 and September 1919. He often toured on the Keith and Orpheum circuits with a singer and jazz band.

Sometime in the summer of 1922, Sweatman's itinerary took him to Washington, where he may have appeared at the Howard Theater.[6] There he met Sonny Greer and perhaps also Ellington. Back in New York in February 1923, Sweatman needed a drummer and wired for Greer. Greer agreed to go if Sweatman would hire Otto Hardwick and Ellington. Greer got his way. By the end of February the *New York Clipper* carried an ad for Sweatman and his new personnel (although not listing any specific performing dates). A photograph of the group also showed John Anderson on trombone. According to Hardwick, Ellington was reluctant to leave his band business in Washington, but the offer to play at Harlem's Lafayette Theater proved too tempting.[7]

PHONOGRAPH ARTIST
WILBUR SWEATMAN
ORIGINATOR AND MUCH IMITATED RAGTIME
AND JAZZ CLARIONETIST

Assisted by Flo Dade, and his Acme of Syncopators
Duke Ellington, Piano   Maceo Jefferson, Banjo   Otto Hartwick, Saxophone
Ralph Escudero, Bass   Sonny Greer, Drummer
Directions—Tim O'Donnell   Pat Casey Agency [8]

Sweatman opened at the Lafayette on Monday, March 5, 1923, for a standard seven-day run (ending Sunday, March 11). The Lafayette's ad in the *New York Age* made no mention of Sweatman but simply announced an "All-Star Vaudeville Show." The schedule called for nightly performances and daily matinees, a midnight show on Friday, and continuous entertainment from 2 P.M. to 11 P.M. on Sunday. Sweatman and his musicians shared the bill with several other acts, including comedians, singers, acrobats, and dancers.[9] The Lafayette's pit orchestra most likely accompanied these other performers.

Ellington gave a brief account of his stint with Sweatman: "We joined him in New York and played some split weeks in theatres. It was another world to us, and we'd sit on the stage and keep a straight face. I began to realize that all cities had different personalities, which were modified by the people you met in them. I also learned a lot about show business from Sweatman. He was a good musician, and he was in vaudeville because that was where the money was then."[10] Although Ellington had seen bands like Sweatman's at the Howard, this may have been his first onstage experience in a vaudeville show. Greer remembered that Sweatman had a "flash act" with a "beautiful stage setting" and "lots of drapes." The band was dressed immaculately. One unpleasant aspect, however, was Sweatman's insistence that his musicians use powder to lighten their complexions.[11]

Except for the new mode of stage presentation, Ellington may not have had difficulty adjusting to Sweatman's group. He was used to six-piece bands in Washington, and he may have taken jobs before with the tuba-player Ralph Escudero, who had been with Greer in the Howard Theater pit orchestra under Marie Lucas. Sweatman's repertory probably featured blues pieces with singer Flo Dade,

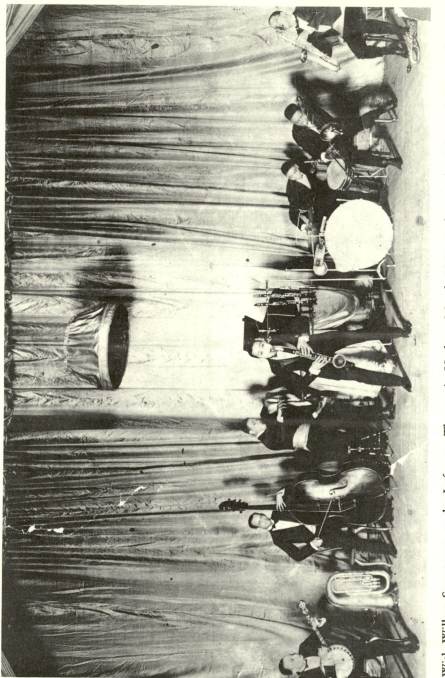

With Wilbur Sweatman at the Lafayette Theater in Harlem, March 1923. Left to right: Maceo Jefferson, banjo; Ralph Escudero, bass and brass bass; Ellington, piano; Wilbur Sweatman, clarinet/leader; Sonny Greer, drums; John Anderson, trombone; Otto Hardwick, saxophones (Frank Driggs Collection)

together with pop songs, jazz instrumentals, and novelty numbers. Perhaps Sweatman performed his famous three-clarinet version of Ethelbert Nevin's "The Rosary," a beloved piece from Ellington's childhood. It seems likely that the band did not play from music; for appearance' sake they either memorized arrangements or knew them well enough to fill in without resorting to the written page. (The *Clipper* photograph of Sweatman showed no music or stands, but this was customary for formal band portraits and need not have indicated performance style.)

Ellington, Greer, and Hardwick stayed with Sweatman for a few other jobs after his run at the Lafayette, including, in Greer's words, a "weekend of grief" on Staten Island. But when Sweatman followed the Keith Circuit to other cities, his three recruits from Washington chose to remain in New York. Accustomed to steady employment and a network of friends in Washington, the trio now found themselves out of work and on their own. Greer and Ellington stayed in Harlem with one of Sonny's aunts, while Hardwick roomed across the street with his own aunt.[12] Each day they started from scratch: "[We] hustled around playing pool. . . . The minute we got two dollars, we'd quit, go home, dress up, order two steak dinners, give the girl a quarter, and have a quarter left for tomorrow."[13] At night they visited clubs, sometimes lugging instruments with them, hoping to make enough in tips to keep them going.

Despite the difficulties, several factors eased Ellington's entry into New York. For one thing, Greer had a knack for making quick personal connections. As Ellington put it, "[He] had a lot of face. He would walk in any place, see someone he knew, and go over to him. 'Hey, So-and-so, remember me?' he'd say. 'Sonny Greer. Jersey kid. Remember?' And we'd be in."[14] Also, Greer and Ellington shared a buoyant optimism that kept them afloat. And Ellington's personal charm and smart style of dress—perhaps even more than his keyboard ability—helped him gain access to the now-legendary circle of pianists working the clubs and "parlor socials" of Harlem.

One of the first pianists Ellington met was Willie "the Lion" Smith. Apparently Greer took Ellington to see Smith at the Capitol Palace (575 Lenox Avenue at 139th Street) soon after arriving in New York. Greer used his New Jersey credentials to win the trust of the Newark-born pianist, who had a reputation for combative and crusty behavior. What struck Ellington about Smith was not his dashing style but the effect of his music on the environment: "Everything and everybody seemed to be doing whatever they were doing in the tempo The Lion's group was laying down. The walls and furniture seemed to lean understandingly—one of the strangest and greatest sensations I ever had. The waiters served in that tempo; everybody who had to walk in, out, or around the place walked with a beat."[15] Smith had a blustery self-confidence which, together with his formidable piano skills and feisty nature, put him in command of the downstairs club. Upon being introduced to the new arrival, he growled at Ellington: "Sit in there for me for a couple of numbers. D-flat. As one of those Western piano plonkers just fell in, I want him to take the stool so I can crush him later."[16]

Willie "the Lion" found Ellington a "good-looking, well-mannered fellow; one of those guys you see him, you like him right away; warm, good-natured."[17] Smith was no stranger to Washington musicians. In 1923 the band that preceded his own at the Capitol was Lionel Howard's Musical Aces, a group from Washington that included Cliff Jackson on piano, Prince Robinson on clarinet and tenor sax, and Dewey Beasley on drums.[18] He was also familiar with some of Ellington's Washington piano mentors—at least he recalled in his memoirs the names of Louis Brown, Louis Thomas, and Doc Perry. Although only a few years older than "Duke and his pals," Smith dispensed fatherly advice, encouraging them to stay in New York when they talked of returning to Washington. He offered them pocket money and free instruction: "We'd stand on street corners and I'd give them lectures each morning. I'd lecture them on the ladies. There was no way for them to miss."[19] At night, after the Lion had finished his regular job, Ellington and his friends roamed around with him and picked up other musical and drinking companions—James P. "The Brute" Johnson, Corky Williams, Alberta Simmons, Raymond "Lippy" Boyette, and Thomas "Fats" Waller. They would stop at Harry Pyle's speakeasy up on Fifth Avenue or make the rounds of apartments, often staying at sessions through the night into the middle of the next day. Occasionally James P. Johnson and Lippy passed on jobs to Ellington. According to Ellington, Lippy "had heard so much piano he couldn't play any more. He only thought piano."[20] For a newcomer to the city, Ellington was moving in good company.

Ellington's description of Harlem in 1923 makes it seem a playground in which he and his Washington friends romped each night. The clubs stayed open past dawn, the musicians floated from one joint to the next, and the free-flowing liquor—despite Prohibition —kept many of them well lubricated. Ellington heard bands led by Fess Williams, Jack Hatton, and Johnny Dunn. He was also introduced to players who would soon work with him: trumpeter James "Bubber" Miley was in Mamie Smith's band at the Garden of Joy (Seventh Avenue between 138th and 139th streets) and trombonist Joe Nanton was at the Bucket of Blood (West 129th Street). At the Capitol Palace he might have seen both Miley and trombonist Charlie Irvis sitting in with the band led by Willie "the Lion" Smith.

Yet after a while, as Ellington would recall, "things got kind of slim." [21] The strain of living without a regular income took away from the fun. Ellington and his friends—"more bored with our situation than desperate" [22]—decided to return home. After finding fifteen dollars on the street, the three hopped a train back to D.C., where they received a warm welcome, as Ellington would later recall: "We got to Washington on a Sunday morning. . . . I still remember the smell of hot biscuits when we walked in. There was butter and honey. My mother broiled six mackerel. There was lots of coffee. Uncle Ed [J.E.] got out the old decanter and we lay there drinking corn in the sunshine." [23] Ellington spent time with Edna and Mercer and resumed his band-booking and sign-painting business. Greer may have boarded with the Ellington family at 1212 T Street.[24] After the fast-paced nightlife and rigors of job-hunting in New York, Washington must have provided some peace and quiet.

But the return to Washington turned out to be only a brief interlude. Soon another New York opportunity arose, once again through the visit of a vaudeville act to Washington. The dancer Clarence Robinson had organized "Liza and Her Shuffling Sextet," which featured singer Katie Crippen and a five-piece band that included trombonist Lew Henry, clarinetist Garvin Bushell, trumpeter Seymour Irick, drummer Mert Perry, and Fats Waller on piano. The act had been traveling the Keith and Poli circuits; in Washington it appeared at the Gayety Theater. [25]

When the Shuffling Sextet got to Washington, a dispute threatened to break up the act. According to Garvin Bushell, Robinson decided to go his own way with a new band he had just discovered:

On a trip down to Washington, D.C., a few of us went to hear a band in a little backstreet place. This group was headed by Elmer Snowden, the banjo player. There was a youngster playing piano named Duke Ellington, Toby Hardwick was on saxophone, Schiefe [Arthur Whetsol] on trumpet, and Sonny Greer on drums. After we heard the band, Clarence and I got in a terrific argument, and we decided to split up. So Clarence went to Snowden and said, "I've got a job for you." I kept the original band, with Fats on piano.

In the meantime, we had six and a half more weeks booked with the act on the Poli time. Clarence figured that he could take this new band and do the gigs, but I decided to beat him to the punch. Early Monday morning I went up to the Palace Theater office in New York. I said, "Clarence and I split up, and he's bringing in a strange band. I have the original one. Now, I could get a new dancer, or what do you want to do?" They got leery and canceled the whole six and a half weeks. So when Clarence arrived in New York with Snowden, Duke, and that bunch, they didn't have any work—I'd canceled all their jobs. [26]

Other versions of this story follow the general lines of Bushell's narrative. Ellington claimed that he had a "chummy exchange" with Waller, whom he "had gotten to know . . . well when we were in New York with Sweatman." Waller notified Ellington that he planned to leave the act and invited him (as well as Greer and Hardwick) to come to New York the next week and join the band. [27] Elmer Snowden related the story a bit differently, with Clarence Robinson telling him he needed several musicians—but not a pianist, since Waller was staying—to work with him on the Keith Circuit. [28] Most sources agree that Snowden, Hardwick, Greer, and Whetsol took the train from Washington to New York without Ellington. A notice in the Baltimore *Afro-American* announced Elmer Snowden's Jazz Kings at Wonderland Park on June 8, 1923, so presumably his northern departure took place some time after. [29]

Snowden and his three fellow musicians arrived in New York to find no sign either of Waller or the promised job. After a week of living downtown and rehearsing, according to Snowden, they went to see Clarence Robinson in his Harlem home at 130th Street and Lenox Avenue. Robinson merely confirmed that Waller's location was unknown. Stuck in New York without a pianist, Snowden and the others wired Ellington to return, perhaps dangling before him the prospect of jobs. That same day Ellington took the train to New York, spending most of his money en route. Hardwick remembered meeting Ellington: "Artie [Whetsol] and I were the first there when he got in. . . . Duke was all smiles. 'Hi, fellows,' he said. 'Oh, we're so glad to see you,' we replied. 'Let's get on uptown. You've got cabfare, we hope!' "[30] Soon the Washington musicians were back on the street trying to scare up work. Sometimes the banjo-player Fred Guy, leading a band at the Orient (38 West 135th Street), let them sit in and divvy up the tips. They traveled downtown to the Strand building, where they auditioned for agents, with no results. Perhaps they answered ads like the following:

Dance Band Wanted
May to October
Broadway Engagement
Good dance band, 5 to 7 pieces; all summer
engagement. Must play GOOD DANCE MUSIC, sing and
entertain generally.
CHEAP JAZZ BANDS NEED NOT APPLY.[31]

Once they auditioned at the Everglades, a "beautiful downstairs club" on Broadway at 48th Street. According to Snowden, the manager liked the group but decided not to hire it after an argument broke out between Snowden and Clarence Robinson (who wanted to appear with the band as a dancer).[32] Finally, under Snowden's leadership the band found work late in June at the Music Box in Atlantic City, where they were advertised as the Washington Black Sox Orchestra. The name may have come from the Baltimore Black Sox, the Eastern Colored League baseball team from Snowden's hometown.

The first real break for the Washington musicians in New York did not occur until July or early August. Ada "Bricktop" Smith had met Ellington, Greer, and the others at Louis Thomas's Oriental Gardens in Washington. Now she was working at Barron Wilkins's club in Harlem. Apparently she and the club owner were on good terms, and Wilkins had come to rely on her musical judgment. After Bricktop had complained about the house band, Wilkins told her to let him know if she found another.[33] Soon she did.

When Bricktop learned that her friends from Washington needed work she suggested that Wilkins hire the band. Wilkins agreed, perhaps after hearing several of the musicians play with his house band. As Rex Stewart has recalled, this was a common way of finding employment: "The usual method of getting a job then was to descend upon a joint en masse and, one by one, get up on the bandstand and outblow the occupants until you got the crowd with you. The boss never failed to ask you if you wanted to work. When the originally employed musicians saw this happening, they knew that was their last night."[34] Wilkins let the house band go with two-weeks' pay, which meant that Snowden's group had to play for the first two weeks on tips alone. At Barron Wilkins's, however, this was no great hardship. Snowden claimed that each man made fifty dollars in tips the first night.[35] Ellington remembered the salary as thirty dollars (per man) weekly, with each musician taking in an extra twenty dollars a night in tips.[36] These wages, however, were hard earned. Regular hours were from 11 P.M. until 10 or 11 the next morning.

Barron Wilkins' Exclusive Club provided the Washington musicians with their first regular job at a prestigious Harlem location. Earlier Ellington had frequented Harlem clubs and made the rounds of parlor socials and all-night parties. But Barron Wilkins's was another kind of place, as Bricktop has recalled:

> Only light-skinned Negroes could get in, unless you happened to be someone special like Jack Johnson or the great Negro comic Bert Williams. Men had to wear jackets and ties, and women had to wear long dresses. It was *the* Harlem spot. Frank Fay, the actor . . . hung out there, and so did Al Jolson, and a chorus girl named Lucille LeSueur who would later be known as Joan Crawford. Every night the limousines pulled up to the corner of Seventh Avenue and 134th Street, and the rich whites would get out, all dolled up in their furs and jewels.[37]

Barron Wilkins had a history of advancing the careers of black musicians. In the early 1900s he had opened a club called the Little Savoy downtown on West 35th Street. According to Noble Sissle it was "the most important spot where Negro musicians got acquainted with the wealthy New York clientele, who became the first patrons of the music." The club's popularity and its array of fine black entertainers "sparked off the renaissance of the Negro musician in New York."[38] When Wilkins opened his cabaret uptown —where it was called the Astoria Café and Barron's Executive Club before becoming the Exclusive Club—it remained a place that attracted white patrons who came to hear black musicians. An observer in 1924 called Barron's "the rich man's black and white cabaret," where one went to soak up Prohibition liquor and African-American entertainment:

> Only members are admitted. It opens on week-days, at about eleven o'clock p.m., officially, but the place really never gets started before one o'clock at night. It is frequented by white men, with only a sprinkling of negroes, although it is known as a colored man's cabaret. *Bons viveurs* from all the strata of society, financiers, lawyers, and theatrical people, with their women or in search of them, are dancing to the negro jazz band, while expensive food and drinks are being served at the tables, and the thick smoke of cigars and perfumed cigarettes hovers low over the white-haired heads of the males and the wavy hair of the females.
>
> Between the dances a professional singer or dancer is doing his or her stunt, and as the entertainers are always negroes the art is generally a very special one, fit only for the sophisticates of Barron Wilkins' club. One must have his purse well garnished when visiting the place. A hundred-dollar bill will not go very far and is not intended to do much service in this luxuriously fitted-out cabaret. But what charm! What exoticism![39]

At times the "sophisticates" at Barron's yielded to another class. Snowden remembered gangsters occasionally stopping by, closing all the doors, and ordering the entire staff—band, chorus girls, and singing and dancing waiters—to put on a show.[40]

Snowden and his neatly dressed Washington musicians looked sharp and sounded good in Barron Wilkins' Exclusive Club. Arthur Whetsol, the minister's son, made sure certain standards were met. As Ellington put it: "We paid quite a lot of attention to our appearance, and if any one of us came in dressed improperly Whetsol would flick his cigarette ash in a certain way, or pull down the lower lid of his right eye with his forefinger and stare at the offending party."[41] Before coming to New York, Ellington went on to explain, two players had also developed musical styles that complemented the band's dignified image: "[Whetsol's] tonal character, fragile and genteel, was an important element in our music. As a result of playing all those society dances in Washington, we had learned to play softly, what is sometimes known as under-conversation music. Toby [Hardwick] also contributed much to this by playing sweet and straight on his C-melody saxophone."[42] Ellington was vague about the repertory at Barron's, simply calling it "conversation music, kind of soft and gutbucket."[43] The band's arrangements—probably many of pop songs—were either adapted from stocks or, more likely, worked out collectively by Ellington, Snowden, and the others.

While fine for Barron Wilkins's club, the style of Snowden's band may not have appealed to those who liked black music hotter and rougher. Snowden recalled that his group "played like most of the boys downtown" (i.e., the white bands in the Times Square district), avoiding the kind of low-down, growling brass effects produced by Bubber Miley and Charlie Irvis at the Bucket of Blood on 135th Street: "Whetsol wasn't doing any of that stuff. He used to use a cup under a hat, and his horn would sound like a saxophone."[44] Snowden has also suggested that prejudice against black musicians playing in a "sweet" style kept his band's first record from being released. That record was "Home," a song written by Ray Klages and Billy Fazioli and recorded by "Elmer Snowden's Novelty Band" for Victor on July 26, 1923. As Snowden told Stanley Dance, "Our music wasn't the kind of *Negro* music they wanted."[45]

During his first six months in New York Ellington took rooms in the apartments of various friends as he struggled to establish himself. Three early addresses listed in *Music Is My Mistress* are all in Harlem: with Leroy Jeffries's mother on 142nd Street, with Forny Brooks and his wife on 129th Street, and with Leonard Harper on Seventh Avenue between 123rd and 124th.[46] Through Harper, Ellington found another job opportunity.

Born the same year as Ellington in Birmingham, Alabama, Leonard Harper was a dancer on the vaudeville circuits and a producer of floor shows and revues. Earlier in 1923 he had staged the successful *Plantation Days,* starring Aida Ward and Florence Mills; it toured the States, then played at London's Empire Palace under the name *From Dover to Dixie.* While still in England, Harper was hired by Harlem businessman Joe Ward to work on more theater projects. The two planned to form a circuit of all-black revues which would perform in cabarets around New York and elsewhere in the country.[47]

Black floor shows were becoming increasingly popular in New York in 1923. The rise of theatrical stars like Gertrude Saunders and Florence Mills created a demand for cabaret entertainment featuring their talents. Another reason for the trend was supplied by James A. Jackson, editor of *Billboard*'s black music page: "Since prohibition has become more or less effective in the land it has been necessary for those restaurants that combined entertainment of sorts with their food and drink service to improve the character of their shows for the more sober and discerning patrons that the new conditions fostered. Colored performers have profited greatly by this change." As a result, Jackson noted, "Negroes have been the attraction in many of the most expensive places of the type."[48] According to Jackson, nineteen black floor shows were produced in New York in 1923—three of them by Leonard Harper.

In July 1923 Harper was hired to organize and stage a revue for Connie's Inn, a new Harlem cabaret that was opening next door to the Lafayette Theater. He and his wife, the dancer Osceola Blanks, starred in the revue, which had a cast of sixteen.

When Connie's Inn opened in the summer of 1923 it became an important club for Harlem. Like Barron Wilkins' Exclusive Club, Connie's was a sophisticated spot—"the swankiest of all the Harlem places," said Jimmy Durante.[49] But its policy toward customers was more liberal. Since Connie's admitted both blacks and whites, it was considered a "black and tan" cabaret. It was owned by the brothers Connie and George Immerman and staffed mainly by blacks. Harlem's *Amsterdam News* greeted Connie's arrival with enthusiasm: "Broadway at its jazziest and snappiest brought to Harlem! . . . The color scheme of this elegant new cafe is a vision of beauty. With its soft rose-tinted lights, its decorations in black and gold, tapestry, sunburst draperies over the raised dance floor, its spotless linen, its calcium lights and general artistic arrangements, it is the equal in beauty of any other similar place in New York City. It is, in short, something Harlem has never seen before."[50] The newspaper pointed out that black workers renovated the club and black artists decorated its interior. In all, Connie's employed seventy-one blacks (including members of the revue).

Ellington helped prepare Harper's revue for its premiere at Connie's. While playing nightly at Barron Wilkins's he served as Harper's rehearsal pianist during the day, accompanying performers who had been in the cast of *Plantation Days,* among them Trixie Smith, Billie Mitchell, the Silver-Tone Four, and also "seven of the peppiest and niftiest strutters you ever saw from the 'Liza' and 'Shuffle Along' chorus."[51] At Connie's, while working with seasoned professional entertainers, Ellington began learning first-hand about the musical structure of revues.

During Ellington's initial period in New York, Harlem served as his base of operations. He lived there, as did most of the musicians he met and played with. By 1923 Harlem was the center of New York's black population, and its theaters, clubs, and dance halls provided most of the jobs for the city's black musicians. At the time, the part of Harlem with the greatest concentration of black residents stretched roughly from 125th Street on the south to 145th Street on the north, and from Lexington Avenue on the east to Eighth and St. Nicholas avenues on the west.[52]

Harlem had much potential for inspiring a musician newly arrived from Washington. On any night Ellington could step outside Connie's or Barron's and see the crowd milling around the Lafayette Theater. There, under the Tree of Hope, he might spot such celebrities as Ethel Waters, Sissle and Blake, Miller and Lyles, and Fletcher Henderson. After-hours he could step downstairs to the Rhythm Club—located in the basement of a building next to the Lafayette Theater—where some of Harlem's best musicians gathered for jam sessions that lasted far into the night. On Sundays he might have strolled down Seventh Avenue, the "joy spot of America" for blacks, as one *Billboard* reporter put it, a street that had "more style, life, variety and novelty than can be observed in any similar length of thorofare in the country."[53]

But Ellington's ambitions also took him to another area located well south of the city's Black Belt. By the early twenties most of the city's important music publishers had offices in the vicinity of Times Square, especially between Broadway and 8th Avenue. "Tin Pan Alley," as the publishing district had long been called, now stretched from the upper 30s to the lower 50s and was concentrated in the mid-40s. Garvin Bushell has described the sound of the place:

"On 46th Street and 47th Street and 48th Street between 7th and 8th, Broadway and 8th, were all the song publishers. . . . You could go through those streets, and the windows were open, especially in the summertime, and you'd hear pianos. Everything was pianos . . . just one big ring of pianos." [54] Though the principal publishing companies were owned and staffed by whites, some black firms were located in the midtown area. In 1918 W. C. Handy and Harry Pace had brought their publishing business to New York from Memphis; in 1921 Pace broke away and started the Pace Phonograph Corporation. More recently established companies specializing in blues were headed by Perry Bradford, Spencer Williams, and Clarence Williams. Some black publishers had their own offices but were subsidized by whites: Jack Mills sponsored Down South (where Fletcher Henderson worked), Irving Berlin backed Rainbow (where Porter Grainger and Bob Ricketts were in charge), and Shapiro-Bernstein ran Skidmore. [55] Other white publishers had blacks on their staff: in September of 1923 the songwriter and publisher Fred Fisher employed Jo Trent as supervisor of its blues and recording division. James A. Jackson, *Billboard*'s black music editor, praised Fisher for his "broadminded courage and confidence in the business capacity of our group." [56]

In the summer of 1923 Ellington was one of a number of black songwriters who headed for Times Square, intent on selling songs. There he met Jo Trent, who introduced him to the "routines of the publishing world." [57] Trent, primarily a lyricist, liked Ellington and his songwriting ideas. Soon they were collaborating and auditioning their songs for publishers daily, though with little success. Finally Trent's boss, Fred Fisher, took interest in one of their creations. When Trent wanted a fifty-dollar advance for the song, Fisher asked for the lead sheet. Trent turned to Ellington, who remembered: "I had never made a lead sheet before, nor tried to write music of any kind, but it was 4:30 P.M. and I knew the checkbook would be closed at five. So, in spite of ten pianos banging away in ten different booths, I sat down and made a lead sheet. It was satisfactory. . . . I had broken the ice and at the same time gotten hooked on writing music." [58] This breakthrough in composing may have been with "Blind Man's Buff," Ellington's first copyrighted song. The only piece that Ellington alluded to from his first days in New York, however, was "Come Back to Me," a "jazz waltz" (never copyrighted or recorded).[59]

As a young songwriter hoping to sell his wares, Ellington had to produce pieces that met current criteria for popularity. In mid-1923 New York was still in the throes of a "blues fever" that had struck as early as 1920 with Mamie Smith's recordings for OKeh.[60] The popularity of blues songs accounted in part for the interest white companies were showing in black songwriters and recording artists. In September 1923 *Billboard* reported on the Jack Mills Company's decision to exploit blues songs. A month later the paper claimed Mills's catalog in this area was "so powerful that it is now believed to be second to none."[61] During the summer the company had concentrated on building up its blues listings. Ellington visited the Mills offices, joining other writers who would show up with lead sheets of "rather ordinary blues." There Ellington first met Irving Mills, Jack's younger brother, who was known as "the last resort for getting some money by those who had been peddling songs all day without success."[62] For tired, frustrated songwriters, a visit to Mills meant easy cash—twenty to thirty dollars outright if Mills accepted a song. Ellington did not mention the titles of any blues he sold to Mills. But he did acknowledge making this early connection with the man who later would play an important role in his career.

In August 1923 a band under Ellington's nominal leadership took part in a blues program broadcast by radio station WDT. It shared the bill with singers Trixie Smith and Rosa Henderson, the latter accompanied by Fletcher Henderson (no relation). An advertisement for the program listed the group as "Bruce Ellington and his Serenaders Orchestra."[63] Most likely this was Ellington with a few of his cronies—Hardwick, Greer, Whetsol, perhaps Snowden—using the old Serenaders name from their Washington days.

Ellington's first six months in New York were typical for a freelance musician seeking success in a new city. The period was marked by sporadic work, failed auditions, a temporary retreat and regrouping, and a few lucky breaks. By the end of the summer of 1923 he had made some inroads in New York's musical life. He had played at three important Harlem establishments: the Lafayette Theater, Connie's Inn, and Barron Wilkins' Exclusive Club. He had taken part in a record date for Victor and had performed at least once over the radio. He had become friendly with Willie "the Lion" Smith, James P. Johnson, Fats Waller, and other musicians whom he had met at clubs and jam sessions. And he had started writing songs and trying to sell them on Broadway. For the twenty-four-year-old pianist with Snowden's Black Sox Orchestra, New York held much promise.

7

Washingtonians on the Great White Way

SEPTEMBER 1923–1925

Broadway is a great place of health. It is a free electric-ray treatment. It is a tonic light-bath. Almost every one in the world feels better in health when he leaves the cross-streets and the inferior avenues to bask in the great open space in front of that New York temple, the Times building. Here voices are clearer, eyes brighter, and the whole body more vivid than anywhere else in New York.

Stephen Graham, *New York Nights*, p. 13

While Harlem provided black musicians with many playing opportunities, other parts of town offered attractive prospects for work. A number of Greenwich Village clubs featured jazz and a few East Side dance halls hired black bands. But in the early 1920s the center of commercial music activity was the Times Square area bordering Broadway in the 40s and lower 50s. The streets of New York's entertainment district were lined with theaters, restaurants, ballrooms, cabarets, and nightclubs. Most of the music publishers were located there, and radio and recording studios were close by. Music and musicians were in constant demand.

Yet Broadway was dominated by white enterprise, and blacks were not always welcome. Earlier, the Clef Club of James Reese Europe had helped combat discrimination in New York. But by the early 1920s its influence had waned and no comparable organization had emerged. The saxophonist and bandleader Benny Carter (b. 1907) has described the problems of a young black musician growing up in New York: "The 'downtown' white world was largely unavailable to us. It not only offered better pay for our sort of work but provided more opportunities in shows. . . . Of course many white musicians, making more than we did, came to listen to us and play with us. We welcomed them and enjoyed the jamming. But we couldn't go downtown to join them. We learned from each other and we didn't much blame the white musicians—we did envy them, though."[1] Cornetist Rex Stewart also recalled the frustration of having white musicians sit in with blacks in Harlem, but not enjoying the reciprocal freedom: "We couldn't find the records, and we couldn't get into any of the spots where [Paul] Whiteman was appearing. In those days there was a definite Jim Crow attitude. Downtown night clubs had a strict 'white only' policy."[2] Garvin Bushell has said that black musicians could see white bands in some downtown theaters, but only if they stayed in the balcony.

Despite the hegemony of white musicians, blacks were gradually breaking through color barriers downtown. In the autumn of 1921 Leroy Smith's band played at Reisenweber's restaurant on Eighth Avenue (where the Original Dixeland Jazz Band had appeared in 1917). Sometime in 1922 or 1923 a dance orchestra led by Fletcher Henderson worked opposite a white group at the Terrace Gardens (145 East 58th Street near Lexington Avenue). The *Chicago Defender* noted that Henderson's band was "so popular with the patrons that whenever the other orchestra played the dancers all rested, waiting for Henderson's crowd to begin."[3] In 1924, after six months at the Club Alabam (West 44th between Seventh and Eighth avenues), Henderson took his band into the famous Roseland Ballroom (Broadway and 51st Street). Earlier that May, Armand J. Piron and his New Orleans Orchestra had been the first black group featured there.

The history of black musicals on Broadway went back even further. The first had appeared in the 1890s, notably Bob Cole's *A Trip to Coontown* (1898) and Ernest Hogan and Will Marion Cook's *Clorindy; or, the Origin of the Cakewalk* (1898).[4] After a slow period in the 1910s, several black shows became successful in the early twenties, beginning with Noble Sissle and Eubie Blake's *Shuffle Along* (1921) and continuing with Maceo Pinkard's *Liza* (1922) and James P. Johnson's *Runnin' Wild* (1923). This theatrical activity often spawned black revues and floor shows in Times Square clubs and restaurants. In 1921 Gertrude Saunders, a star of *Shuffle Along,* sang at Reisenweber's for eleven weeks (black entertainment columnist James A. Jackson called her the first black woman to appear in a Broadway cabaret).[5] In February 1922 a revue with Florence Mills, Edith Wilson, trumpeter Johnny Dunn, and Tim Brymn's orchestra opened at the Plantation Café, a cabaret in the Winter Garden building (Broadway and 50th). Will Vodery became musical director for the revue in June.

Ellington joined this roster of black entertainers during the summer of 1923, when he and the other members of Elmer Snowden's band were invited to play some Sundays at the Plantation Café. Their appearances went unnoticed by the New York press.[6] But by the end of August they found their first steady downtown job right around the corner.

In the basement of a building on West 49th Street, on the short block between Broadway and Seventh Avenue, stood a club called the Palais de Dance. According to a *Billboard* announcement it was due to re-open September 1, 1923, as the Hollywood.[7] Leonard Harper had been hired to produce a revue for the cabaret; he and his wife, Osceola Blanks, were to be principals in a company of seventeen dancers and singers. The revue would be "elaborately staged with several new effects brought from Europe" and accompanied by Everard Dabney's Ginger Band, a six-piece outfit.[8]

For some reason Dabney's Ginger Band never opened at the Hollywood. Instead, Snowden and his Washington Black Sox Orchestra managed to land a six-month contract there.[9] Perhaps their auditions at the Strand building and appearances at the Plantation Café had brought them to the attention of the right people. Or Leonard Harper might have put in a good word for the group that included Duke Ellington, his young boarder and rehearsal pianist from Connie's Inn.[10]

The Hollywood did not make Snowden and his musicians an overnight sensation. But during the next four years it served as their home base. It saw the band through changes of leadership, personnel, and musical style. And it gave Ellington the opportunity to develop a range of skills. He entered the club a pianist playing with a little-known group from out of town. He emerged a successful bandleader, an experienced recording artist, and a promising composer.

Back in Washington, Daisy and J.E. Ellington may have been impressed when they heard that their son was now playing at a place called the Hollywood on Broadway. But the only glamorous aspects of the club were its name and location. A cramped cellar that Ulanov described as "turgid with alcoholic vapor and cigarette smoke," it held only slightly more than one hundred people. The ceiling was low and the bandstand was close to sewer pipes. One observer even reported that Sonny Greer had to play loudly to cover up the squeals of rats.[11] After the refined elegance of Barron Wilkins's, the Hollywood must have seemed like a dive.

Still, a band could get noticed there. A few months after the Hollywood's September opening, a review by Abel Green appeared in the *New York Clipper*. Green—later editor of *Variety*—was the trade paper's main popular music critic, and his piece was the first full-length article about the band in a major publication. It revealed important changes in Snowden's group, beginning with a new name:

The Washingtonians (7)
Hollywood, New York
   This colored band is plenty torrid and includes a trumpet player who never need doff his chapeau to any cornetist in the business. He exacts the eeriest sort of modulations and "singing" notes heard.
   The Hollywood, a comparatively new Times Square basement cabaret (it opened Sept. 1 last), is on West 49th Street. The band is the sole feature up to midnight, when Harper's Dixie Revue goes on, repeating again at 2 A.M.
   The boys can seemingly satisfy without exerting themselves, but for the benefit of the Clipper reviewer they brought out a variety of instruments upon which each demonstrated his versatility. And how!
   Elmer Snowden is the leader and banjoist, also doubling with soprano sax. "Bub" Miley is the "hot" cornetist, doubling with the melophone [*sic*]. John Anderson doubles trombone and trumpet; Sonny Greer specializes in the vocal interludes when not at

the traps; Otto Hardwick, sax and violin; Roland Smith, sax and bassoon; and Duke Ellington, piano-arranger.

The boys look neat in dress suits and labor hard but not in vain at their music. They disclose painstaking rehearsal, playing without music. They are well known in several southern places and were at the Music Box, Atlantic City, the past summer. They also broadcast every Wednesday at 3:45 from WHN (Loew State building) radio station. [12]

Such a positive review might have held special value for one of the few black bands playing in Times Square. Indeed, Snowden and company quickly capitalized on Green's critical endorsement for an advertisement in the *Clipper* (February 22, 1924). There they cribbed from the text of Green's November review under the lead: "Here's What ABEL Says About Us."

The Washingtonians, as they were now called, had grown larger and changed members since the summer. Both processes were to continue in the next several years. Unlike the stable membership of the Ellington orchestra in the 1930s, the personnel of the Washingtonians turned over quickly. After all, the band was not yet well established and could not hire and keep every musician its leader wanted. Such comings and goings were typical of mid-1920s jazz ensembles, as Rex Stewart has acknowledged: "Band personnels were not very stable in those days, and fellows were constantly jumping from band to band. . . . most bandleaders were also constantly on the lookout to find better sidemen to strengthen their groups." [13] Green's November 1923 review pointed out changes that had made the band stronger but also different.

At Barron Wilkins's the Washingtonians consisted of the quintet that had arrived in June 1923 hoping to work with Clarence Robinson. By November the group had grown to seven pieces and replaced one of its original members.

John Anderson joined as the Washingtonians' first trombonist. Ellington, Hardwick, and Greer had met him earlier in the year playing with Wilbur Sweatman. Like the other two new band members, Anderson became part of the group sometime between September 1 and mid-October.

Saxophonist Roland Smith (his first name appears also as Rollin or Rollen) appears to have had a brief tenure and little influence with the Washingtonians. He had played in the *From Dover to Dixie* revue during the summer of 1923 and was probably recommended to Snowden's band by Leonard Harper. Smith had recorded with Johnny Dunn and Lucille Hegamin and, according to Walter C. Allen in *Hendersonia,* may have been a member of the Black Swan house orchestra. As the first-known additional reed player for the Washingtonians, Smith was not mentioned by Ellington or other members as part of their group.

By contrast, a new cornetist made all the difference in the world. James "Bubber" Miley (1903–32) had joined after Arthur Whetsol decided to return to Washington, possibly intending to resume his schooling.[14] Born in South Carolina, Miley had moved with his parents to New York in 1909. In the winter of 1921, while on tour with singer Mamie Smith, he heard King Oliver in Chicago at the Dreamland. According to Garvin Bushell, also with Smith's Jazz Hounds at the time, Miley was captivated by Oliver's playing and soon began experimenting with a rubber plunger mute, finding ways to coax strange crying notes from his horn.[15] Later, back in Harlem, Ellington may have seen Miley in the house band at J. W. Connor's Café (135th Street off Lenox Avenue) or at the Garden of Joy, "an unusual open-air, canvas-enclosed dance pavilion located on top of a shelf of rock."[16]

Otto Hardwick remembered Miley as "a character . . . a happy-go-lucky, moon-faced, slim, brown boy with laughing eyes and a mouth full of gold teeth."[17] He also told how the Washingtonians had managed to recruit Miley: "One night after we finished work, we went up to Harlem, got Bubber stiff, and when he came to he was in a tuxedo growling at the Hollywood, on Broadway!" The new member had a dramatic impact on the sound of the Washingtonians, as is evident from Abel Green's allusion to Miley's "eeriest sort of modulations and 'singing' notes."

Apparently Snowden was not enthusiastic about Miley's "growling stuff" after Whetsol's sweeter style.[18] But Ellington disagreed: "Our band changed its character when Bubber came in. He used to growl all night long, playing gutbucket on his horn. That was when we decided to forget all about the sweet music."[19]

Ellington's statement pointed out a stylistic division between "sweet" white bands downtown (smooth, score-reading ensembles) and "hot" black groups uptown (rougher, improvising ones). Even if the sides were not so clearly drawn, people used these terms to describe differences in repertory and individual style—as when Green termed Miley a "hot" cornetist.

From their contrasting responses to Miley's arrival in the band—recollected, of course, many years later—it seems as though Snowden preferred his music sweet and Ellington liked it hot. Perhaps Miley brought the matter to a head. The opening of Green's review certainly suggests that the cornetist had become the dominant voice in the band. And Mercer Ellington has written that while in Washington his father had favored the lyrical approach of players like Whetsol and Hardwick, which suited the society dances they played, in New York "he got into a more gutty style . . . the 'growl' sounds of trumpets and trombones with plunger mutes."[20]

Miley's "hot" cornet was not the only reason for change in the Washingtonians' sound. Green's review showed Miley doubling on mellophone, an instrument he may have learned during a Navy stint in 1918 and 1919. Trombonist Anderson doubled on trumpet, saxophonist Roland Smith on bassoon. With Snowden already doubling on saxophone and Hardwick on C-melody and baritone, the addition of Miley, Anderson, and Smith increased the band's timbral variety.[21] Different textural effects were possible, such as two cornets (Miley and Anderson), or trombone, bassoon, and mellophone (Miley, Anderson, Smith). The group's versatility obviously impressed Green. It might also have inspired Sonny Greer's comment that the Washingtonians could sound "like a big band, but soft and beautiful."[22]

Playing nightly at the Hollywood brought Ellington closer to the power center of New York's music industry. In his efforts to get established as a songwriter and pianist, he made contact with several black musicians who helped him find publishing and recording opportunities.

Still living in Leonard Harper's Harlem apartment, Ellington visited downtown publishing offices in the afternoons, often spending time with Jo Trent (1892–1954). In a September 1923 *Billboard* article, James A. Jackson took note of Trent's position on Fred Fisher's staff, calling him "another of the many Negroes who have made places for themselves in the big amusement world that is fast learning to disregard anything but ability."[23] Trent had recently collaborated with Fletcher Henderson and pianist-songwriter

Roland C. Irving on "Oh Baby, How Long," which was published by Irving Berlin in August; in September Fred Fisher came out with Trent and Irving's "Sweet Pain" and "Oh, Oh, Please Don't." Trent then found a new collaborator in Ellington, and the two started writing songs together.

The first tangible evidence of Ellington's work with Jo Trent is "Blind Man's Buff." Never published, the song was copyrighted October 24, 1923 (E 576379), by the Fred Fisher Company. The copyright register states that the tune was "arranged" by "Geo[rge] R. Holman," who probably supplied an accompaniment for Ellington's melody. This version has not been found, but a lead sheet (probably made in the 1950s) and separate lyrics are in the Smithsonian's Duke Ellington Collection.[24] The verse of "Blind Man's Buff" is unusually chromatic for a song seeking popularity in 1923:

Example 14. "Blind Man's Buff," verse, mm. 1–4.

The chorus has a certain awkward quality, not just because the lyrics do not easily fit the melody but because the rhythmic patterns and chromatic inflections (especially in mm. 6–7) seem more instrumental than vocal in character:

Example 15. "Blind Man's Buff," chorus, mm. 1–7.

Ellington must have been proud to sell his first song to Fred Fisher, hailed by *Billboard* as "one of the most consistent producers of hits in the business" and renowned as author of the popular song of 1919, "Chicago."[25] And he must have been pleased when, at the end of December, he joined the Fisher staff, replacing Trent's former writing partner: "Duke Ellington, the pianist, at Hollywood Inn, has succeeded Roland Irving in the professional department of the Fred Fisher publishing house."[26]

Another black songwriter who befriended Ellington and helped the Washingtonians was Maceo Pinkard (1897–1962). By 1923 he was known as the composer of songs like "Mammy O' Mine," "Don't Cry Little Gal," and "Wonderful Pal," also of the hit revue *Liza*. Two years later he would have his biggest success with "Sweet Georgia Brown." (In his memoirs, Ellington remembered how Pinkard had played the song for him in his Broadway office before anyone else had heard it.) Like Trent, Pinkard was experienced not just in writing and publishing songs but in finding acceptance with white companies. He worked for a time with the Shapiro-Bernstein firm before launching out on his own with Attucks Songs, Inc. (presumably unrelated to the earlier Attucks Music Publishing Company), located in the Gayety Building. And like Perry Bradford, Clarence Williams, Spencer Williams, and other black music publishers, Pinkard had direct links to the recording industry. He became manager for Gertrude Saunders and accompanied her on his own "Potomac River Blues" in August 1923 for a Victor date. He also managed singer Rosa Motley.

Pinkard began helping the Washingtonians during their first month at the Hollywood. In September 1923 *Billboard* reported that he had placed the band with the Victor record company; in October he was described as "directing" the Washingtonians, the "recently arrived orchestra which is playing at a Broadway cabaret."[27] Snowden was an aggressive businessman, but he needed someone like Pinkard—an established songwriter and publisher—to get his band into the recording studio. As Ellington later wrote (putting his leadership of the band earlier than it actually took place), "Maceo Pinkard was the first to take me to a studio for the purpose of recording our group. When I think of how wonderful those men of that period in New York were, and of the way in which they received me, I always feel a glow of gladness and gratitude."[28]

By mid-October Pinkard's influence seems to have been working. After their disappointing session in July, the Washingtonians went back to the Victor studio—again under the name "Snowden's Novelty Orchestra"—and recorded two sides.[29] One was "Home," which had not been successful for the band on its previous visit. The other was "M.T. [or Empty] Pocket Blues," a piece the Fred Fisher Company was trying to promote. Written by Lewis Michelson and Eli Dawson and featured by Jim Barton in the play *Dew Drop Inn* (which ran from May 17 to June 30, 1923), "M.T. Pocket Blues" was making a bid "to be the outstanding hit of the firm's catalog."[30] Yet once again the performance by Snowden and his musicians may have been unacceptable; in any case, Victor did not issue either side.

Another figure in the music business who formed a friendship with Ellington was Will Marion Cook. A confident, imposing man, Cook moved easily from the performing arenas of concert hall and theater to the bustling corridors of music publishers. Ellington often saw "Dad" Cook on Broadway, followed him as he made the rounds, then shared a cab with him back to Harlem: "I can see him now with that beautiful mane of white hair flowing in the breeze as he and I rode uptown through Central Park in the summertime in a taxi with an open top."[31] Ellington learned wherever he went. He saw the respect Cook commanded when he walked into a publishing office, and he was impressed when a publisher gave Cook an advance just "to be on the right side with Dad." He also turned to Cook for composing advice. When Cook recommended that Ellington pursue formal training at a conservatory, Ellington answered, "Dad, I don't want to go to the conservatory because they're not teaching what I want to learn."[32] Then Cook would change his tactic, telling Ellington to trust his instincts in writing music: "First you find the logical way, and when you find it, avoid it, and let your inner self break through and guide you. Don't try to be anybody else but yourself."[33] For Ellington, anxious to gain a foothold in the conformist, highly competitive world of Tin Pan Alley, such words from a master musician made a deep and lasting impression.

Not all the activity of black songwriters was concentrated in

Times Square. In October 1923 Jo Trent and Clarence Williams sponsored a "Song Writers' Concert and Dance" at Harlem's New Star Casino (East 107th Street and 3rd Avenue). A number of prominent black musicians, composers, and publishers were slated to perform, among them Perry Bradford, Porter Grainger, Spencer Williams, and Lemuel Fowler. At least three orchestras were announced in the ads, together with a "blues contest between recorded artists."[34] Such occasions gave black songwriters a forum for presenting their recent songs, and white publishers and agents probably showed up to scout material and performers.

There were other ways to get known around town. Work at the Hollywood helped introduce the Washingtonians to a wider New York audience. Late in 1923 the *Clipper* noted that owners of some of the small Broadway cabarets were sending their revues to dance halls (before 11:00 P.M.) in order to "drum up business before the dance crowd."[35] A similar article appeared the following spring, stating that revues from the "less exclusive Broadway cabarets" had started visiting dance halls and theaters. Performers from both the Hollywood and the Club Alabam traveled to the Cinderella Ballroom (Broadway and 48th), where "these added attractions have been successful . . . and have been the means of drawing an element a bit above the usual dance hall following."[36] Such appearances may have brought bands additional jobs, thus benefiting the musicians as much as their club sponsors. When the Washingtonians made their Haverhill, Massachusetts, debut early in 1925, they were identified as coming not from the Hollywood but "direct from the Cinderella ballroom on Broadway."[37]

In 1923 club owners were just beginning to exploit radio as an advertising medium. Bands started broadcasting over station WHN in August. A month later the *Clipper* mentioned several Broadway cabarets that sent bands to the WHN studio, where they could plug their nightly entertainment. Orchestras from the Strand Roof and the Clover Gardens made the trip, as did the California Ramblers and "the Washingtonians, a colored band from Hollywood café, Harlem [*sic*]."[38] Regular broadcasts were good for the Hollywood's business and sent the sounds of the Washingtonians out beyond Times Square.

Early in 1924, before their first six months at the Hollywood were up, the Washingtonians chose a new trombonist, a new banjo player, and most important, a new leader.

The January 4 issue of the *Clipper* noted the first of these developments: "Charles Irvis is the new trombonist with the Washingtonians at the Hollywood, New York." He probably joined because of his friendship—both social and musical—with Bubber Miley. Rex Stewart has described how in the 1920s "a pair of brass men (trumpets and trombones) usually hung out as a team, eating and drinking and especially playing together."[39] Like Miley, Irvis (1899–1939) had gained experience accompanying blues singers (Lucille Hegamin and Eva Taylor) and playing in Harlem, especially with Willie "the Lion" Smith's group at the Capitol Palace. While John Anderson may have shone in vaudeville and novelty numbers (from his previous tenure with Sweatman), Irvis excelled at playing the blues. His nickname was "Plug" and he specialized in muting techniques. As Ellington later explained,

> Nobody ever really picked up on Charlie Irvis. He used an object that was very effective, and he played in a different register of the horn. There was a kind of mute they built at that time to go into the trombone and make it sound like a saxophone, but he dropped his one night and the darn thing broke into a million parts. So he picked up the biggest part that was left and started using it. This was *his* device and it was greater than the original thing. He got a great, big, fat sound at the bottom of the trombone—melodic, masculine, full of tremendous authority.[40]

Hardwick called Irvis "strictly a gutbucket trombonist"; this quality, as Ellington noted, helped add "new colors and characteristics" to the Washingtonians.[41]

Not long after Irvis joined the band, Snowden departed. He had been the band's nominal leader since the previous summer. Presumably he took care of business matters and provided musical direction by giving cues, setting tempos, and calling tunes (although Ellington may have introduced arranging ideas and some of his own pieces). Throughout the fall the group had been listed in the *Clipper* under Snowden's name, first as the Washington Black Sox Orchestra, then after December 14 as the Washingtonians (followed by Snowden's name in parentheses). But by mid-February of 1924 Snowden had been deposed. A special "Popular Music" issue of

The Washingtonians, early 1924. Left to right: Sonny Greer, Charlie Irvis, Bubber Miley (seated), Elmer Snowden, Otto Hardwick, Ellington (author's collection)

the *Clipper* noted the change in leadership. There, the Washingtonians (or Leo Bernstein, manager of the Hollywood) placed a large ad with a photograph and description of the band. Snowden was in the photo, but the text indicated that now George Francis played banjo and Ellington was in charge, leading from the piano and arranging the selections. The same issue announced that the Washingtonians had renewed their contract at the Hollywood for six months or more.[42]

Why did Snowden leave? He later described himself as a victim of mutiny: "One night, I went in there and heard the band talking about me in the girls' dressing room, talking about getting rid of me."[43] But several other sources point to a single reason for the band's rebellion: Snowden was discovered taking more than his share of the band's salary.[44] With his customary discretion, Ellington offered this explanation: "Snowden was the businessman of the group, and eventually he got so good at business that he went his way."[45] A bandleader was entitled to a larger share than his sidemen. But apparently Snowden went too far.

At first Ellington may have been reluctant to take over the band. Mercer Ellington has written that, after Snowden left "under a cloud," Greer briefly assumed leadership before handing it over to Duke.[46] And Snowden has claimed that Ellington "didn't really want the job as leader, because all he wanted to do was write songs and get them published."[47] Ellington, of course, knew what the job entailed. He had run bands in Washington for over a half-dozen years before moving to New York. He was experienced, self-assured, and ambitious. Perhaps, as Snowden suggested, Ellington viewed leadership more as a time-consuming chore than a privilege. On the other hand, as leader, Ellington could exert greater control over musical matters. Not only could he continue to write songs: he now had a band of his own to play them.

Under Ellington's leadership the Washingtonians remained at the Hollywood another six months, then six more, staying until January 1925. In November 1924, over a year after its last visit to Victor, the band recorded for Blu-Disc, a small company that was releasing sides by black artists. This time it had more success. On two sides, "Choo Choo" and "Rainy Nights," the full six-piece group appeared; on "Deacon Jazz" and "Oh How I Love My Darling," Hardwick and the rhythm section (Ellington, Francis, Greer) backed vocals by Jo Trent and Greer, respectively; and on "It's Gonna Be a Cold, Cold Winter" and "Parlor Social De Luxe," Greer and Ellington accompanied singer Alberta Prime. Also in November, Up-to-Date, a subsidiary of Blu-Disc, released a version of "How Come You Do Me Like You Do?" by singer Florence Bristol with assistance from Ellington and Hardwick. These records probably did not circulate widely. Judging from their rarity today, perhaps only a small number were pressed and released. The only known advertisement for Blu-Disc suggests that distribution was limited to lobbies of certain New York theaters.[48] But for a group that had no records on the market, it was at least a beginning. And for Ellington the records represented a personal breakthrough, since he received composer credit on three of the seven sides: "Choo Choo," "Deacon Jazz," and "Parlor Social De Luxe."[49]

Early in 1925 the Hollywood closed down for a while because of a fire; apparently those of the "mysterious-origin" variety were fairly common. As Sonny Greer said, "When business got slack, they'd torch the joint."[50] Luckily these blazes posed no physical threat to the Washingtonians. Whenever Leo Bernstein suggested that the musicians take their instruments home, they knew what to expect.

With the club closed for repairs, the Washingtonians went out on the road. In February 1925 they traveled north to Haverhill, Massachusetts, near the New Hampshire border, where they substituted for Mal Hallett, a popular white New England bandleader who had spent several successful seasons at Roseland. They returned to Haverhill later in the spring and then played other New England towns.

When the club re-opened, sometime in early spring of 1925, it looked the same and the menu had not changed. But its name was new: Club Kentucky. The owners had decided to turn from the glamorous allure of Hollywood to nostalgia for the Old South. This trend was already apparent in other clubs featuring black performers. Harlem had the Cotton Club, and Times Square had the Plantation Café, Club Alabam, Club Bamville, and Everglades. The Club Kentucky—more often referred to as the Kentucky Club—may have attracted customers with its suggestion of black entertainment.[51]

While playing nightly at the Kentucky Club, the Washingtonians also took part in vaudeville shows at Harlem theaters. Early in March 1925 they shared a bill at the Lincoln with five other acts: singer Gertrude Saunders; the Brown and McGraw Fast Steppers; the Three Danubes; Riggo and Dorothy; and Gilson, Wiles, and Their Midget. At the Lafayette the next month Gertrude Saunders "and her Washingtonians" entertained at a midnight show. In May the band was back at the Lincoln as Duke Ellington's Washington Orchestra, and a few months later Ellington returned with an augmented band to face off against the Will Tyler Orchestra.[52] Such work placed Ellington and his men in fast-stepping company, performing before audiences different from those downtown.

The band's appearances in larger halls may have led to more personnel changes. In May 1925 an ad for the Washingtonians in *Variety* indicated a "Jas. R. Robinson" playing saxophone.[53] This man—commonly known as Prince Robinson (1902–60)—brought the group's membership to seven. Ellington had lured the reed player away from a group led by Elmer Snowden. Doubling on clarinet, Robinson added to the Washingtonians' instrumental color and increased Ellington's options for arrangements.

About the same time that Robinson joined, Fred Guy replaced George Francis on banjo.[54] (Presumably Francis had been with Ellington since February 1924.) Guy, Ellington later wrote, was one of the "great, hospitable people" in Harlem who had welcomed the Washingtonians to the big city. Ellington and the others had known him since their first summer in New York, when they filled in for his group at the Orient. Yet by hiring Guy, Ellington was not simply repaying a favor but adding a solid musician: "He was rather a serious type fellow, and was always giving us advice, but his guitar was a metronome and the beat was always where it was supposed to be."[55]

The seven-piece version of the Washingtonians made no recordings in the spring of 1925. There has been speculation, however, about a summer recording session in which Prince Robinson was replaced by soprano saxophonist Sidney Bechet. Supposedly the band cut two sides for Brunswick, "Twelfth Street Rag" and "Tiger Rag."[56] In the 1950s Leonard Bechet, Sidney's nephew, said that Ellington had hired Bechet to help the band with New Orleans standards like "High Society."[57]

With banjo-player and guitarist Fred Guy, New York, ca. 1925 (Frank Driggs Collection)

In his memoirs Bechet described working with the Washingtonians in the mid-1920s and mentioned making records with the band, regretting that they were never released. He remembered Ellington fondly: "He had his feelings inside the music where they belonged, and none of any kind of meanness outside the music. . . . he wasn't as good a piano player as he is now, but he had right feelings, and he let the music come first."[58] Apparently, though, not everyone in the band restricted their "feelings" to the music. At first Miley was "in jail over some trouble concerning a girl" until the other musicians bailed him out. Then, Bechet recalled, Miley and Irvis started to squabble: "I could see Bubber and Charlie still had this trouble going. . . . There was a competition for the wrong things at the wrong time: all this tugging when they should be carrying, and sulking when they should be following, and this refusing to be with the music when they should be leading."[59] Such a glimpse inside the Washingtonians is rare, since Ellington almost never discussed personnel problems in the band. Perhaps the friction between Miley and Irvis influenced Bechet's decision to move on.

Another important change in the Washingtonians occurred in the summer of 1925 when a tuba joined the ensemble. The Kentucky Club was too small to permit many new players, and so far a double-bass had been expendable. But somehow they made room for Henry "Bass" Edwards (1898–1965).[60] Besides being a powerful player Edwards illuminated the ensemble: according to Sonny Greer he put "blinker lights" in the bell of his tuba and would often take several hot solo choruses "with the red and green lights twinkling over his head."[61]

In the fall of 1925, two years after he reported on the Washingtonians' first season at the Hollywood, *Variety* columnist Abel Green went back to the subterranean space and emerged with accounts of two visits there. "The Kentucky is a great drop-in place for a few laughs and a few times around on the floor," Green observed. It had "somewhat of an international aspect" with its "Dixie atmosphere, Chinese menu, cosmopolitan New York patronage and Oriental dances." In spite of the club's no-frills interior, Green noted that its "air is not so stuffy and the floor as microscopic as in most of the Broadway night clubs." Even so, it had its limitations. Julia Gerrity's voice, Green thought, was "a bit loud for a room with such a low ceiling," and some of the dancers' "terp stuff" was only "of fair order." [62]

A revue was still the centerpiece of the club's nightly entertainment. Each act was introduced by the master of ceremonies, who also filled in with patter and jokes. On his first visit Green saw Bobby Burns Berman (or B.B.B.), the "Human Broadcasting Station." Besides delivering gags in "a flip style," Berman sang "a 'hot' number convincingly" and danced a "nimble and strenuous Charleston." When Green went back in October Bert Lewis had taken over as m.c., "reeling off fast numbers in okay fashion." [63] Lewis soon became a fixture at the place, with later ads announcing the attraction of "Bert Lewis and His Hospitality Gang."

Each show at the Kentucky Club featured female singers and dancers. Some black vocalists in Times Square cabarets, like Florence Mills, Gertrude Saunders, and Ethel Waters, were well-known figures from theater and vaudeville. Although the Kentucky Club usually did not engage stars of this magnitude, it made an exception with the popular recording artist Alberta Hunter. She had appeared at the Hollywood in late 1923, billed as the "Paramount blues singer" who was "making white patrons like syncopated harmony." [64] But the singers heard by Abel Green in 1925 included Julia Gerrity (who earlier had appeared at the Little Club on West 44th Street, before it was renamed the Club Alabam), Jean Gaynor, and Ina Hayward. These performers were closely identified with the band; in fact, a *Variety* reporter (probably Green again) noted that "Duke Ellington's Band and Entertainers" was "one of the few Negro orchestras carrying singers as well as musicians." [65]

Also on the bill were dancers with names like Olive, Vernal, and Nadja, and the "shapely oriental dancer" Hazel Godrew (from *I'll Say She Is*), who provided "the real optical feast of the show." Chorus girls, Green wrote elsewhere, were the main attraction of black revues in Times Square cabarets, not just part of the scenery: "There are but few cabarets in New York where the artists are not requested to mix with the guests, with the girls paying special attention to male guests." [66] A hostess provided customers with female company, both at the club and perhaps later. As Sonny Greer put it: "Of course, they'd gig afterwards." [67]

Although Green devoted most of his September 1925 review in *Variety* to a description of the Kentucky Club revue and its personalities, he had only praise for the Washingtonians: "Duke Ellington's Orchestra of six pieces is still the musical attraction and in addition to the specialties it offers in the entertainment line ranks as one of the best 'hot' colored combinations in town." [68] In October he waxed even more ecstatic, calling the band "a wow" and "trojans for hard work." [69]

Another reviewer who visited the Kentucky Club, *Billboard*'s George D. Lottman, reacted to Ellington with similar gusto: "And now for the band! If anybody can tell us where a hotter aggregation than Duke Ellington and His Club Kentucky Serenaders can be found we'll buy for the mob. Possessing a sense of rhythm that is almost uncanny, the boys in this dusky organization dispense a type of melody that stamps the outfit as the most torrid in town." With unusual thoroughness Lottman listed each musician in the band, including a well-known intermission pianist:

> Duke Ellington, director, pounds the baby grand, and while he chow-meins in an adjacent eatery Thomas "Fats" Waller understudies. Both lads are deserving of all the available superlatives in the English language, while it is necessary to borrow a few from the Latin to adequately extol the performance of the latter. Sunny [*sic*] Greer is the third best drum showman in the country, with Vic Berton, of the Roger Wolfe Kahn Orchestra, and Willie Creeger [Creager], now a phonograph arranger, entitled, respectively, to first and second honors. Henry Edwards' tuba is all bent from the heat its owner gives it and "Bub" Miley "kills" 'em with his trumpet. Fred Guy plays banjo, Charley Irvis trombones, and Otto Hardwick supervises the sax. section. [70]

By bringing Greer in league with Vic Berton and Willie Creager, Lottman evaluated the Washingtonians not just as another " 'hot' colored combination" but as a professional ensemble that ranked with the best he knew.

Fats Waller played solo piano at the Kentucky Club and also accompanied Bert Lewis during Ellington's breaks. Wearing a jeweled turban, Waller would entertain the audience by posing as "Ali Baba, the Egyptian Wonder." [71] A more important aspect of Waller's work may have been his function as a kind of tutor to Ellington, giving instruction on matters of orchestration and arranging. According to Rex Stewart, Ellington eventually "absorbed Fats' teachings and proceeded to utilize them until he brought his own inventive mind to jazz."[72]

Kentucky Club nights were long: "If you must stay up until sunrise, we can't think of a better place to while away the small hours than at the Club Kentucky."[73] The Washingtonians began around nine or ten, then performed for two shows, usually at midnight and 2 A.M. During this time they accompanied songs, dance numbers, and comedy sketches and also provided the club's patrons with instrumentals for dancing. After-hours could stretch on and on. According to Fred Guy: "Once you put your horn in your mouth, you didn't take it out until." Until when? "Until you quit. Until period. You started at nine and played until."[74] The evening was not over after the second show, as Ellington remembered:

> I would send [the band] home and Sonny [Greer] and I would work the floor. I had one of those little studio upright pianos on wheels that you could push around from table to table, and Sonny would carry his sticks and sing. Answering requests, we sang anything and everything—pop songs, jazz songs, dirty songs, torch songs, Jewish songs. Sometimes, the customer would respond by throwing twenty-dollar bills away from him as though they were on fire. When business was slow, we'd sing "My Buddy." That was the favorite song of the boss, Leo Bernstein, and when we laid that on him he was expected to throw down some bills too.[75]

Tips formed a sizable part of the night's wages. Like many Times Square venues, the Kentucky Club attracted big spenders and celebrities who came to eat, drink, dance, meet friends, ogle the chorus girls, and hear hot jazz. "It was the era of the Big Shot," as Robert Sylvester wrote, and the nightclub was "the playground of the 'big names' from top society, the stage, Hollywood, early radio, and the various strata of the racketeering fraternity."[76] One evening, film star Tom Mix, outfitted in a ten-gallon hat, attempted to "carve" (or outplay) Sonny Greer on drums.[77] Entertainers who worked nearby, like Al Jolson, Harry Richman, and Jimmy Durante, often dropped in. Then there were the gangsters; according to Sonny Greer, owner Leo Bernstein had mob connections.[78]

The gregarious, jiving Greer was, as Ellington later wrote, "in his element" at the Kentucky Club. Besides drumming and singing, he mingled with the patrons, buttered them up, and often got a "sawbuck" for his efforts. He also kept an eye out for police and Federal agents who might try and close the club for selling liquor. Greer's eye may have been sharp, but not enough to keep Bernstein's establishment from being raided. The club was padlocked during the summer of 1926, probably because of liquor violations.

Many other musicians formed part of the Kentucky Club's regular clientele. As early as February 1924 the Hollywood had advertised itself as the place "where the Professional Musician Makes His Rendezvous."[79] Paul Whiteman stopped by to listen to the band after finishing at the Palais Royal around the corner. (He often left a fifty-dollar tip.) Vincent Lopez, Tommy Dorsey, and Miff Mole were also frequent visitors. They came to hear Miley's hot solos and Greer's entertaining vocals, and they may have been interested in Ellington's arrangements. Abel Green had remarked in his first review that the Washingtonians showed signs of "painstaking rehearsal, playing without music."[80] Sonny Greer expanded on this observation: "There were no small bands so well rehearsed as ours then. Most of them played stocks, which we never did. Duke wasn't writing so much, but he would take the popular tunes and twist them."[81] These "twisted" tunes included "Whispering," "Avalon," "St. Louis Blues," "Mighty Lak a Rose" (a feature for Otto Hardwick) and "I'll Follow the Swallow Back Home" (a feature for Sidney Bechet when he was in the band).[82] Greer remembered how Ellington could turn common tunes into something special, making the band sound "big, full, close, very close."[83]

Such arrangements were not Ellington's work alone but often the result of group effort. Sidney Bechet recalled a typical procedure: "At that time Otto, Duke and myself used to go over to Duke's place evenings to fool around on the piano, talk how we were going to build this thing with all the band. Duke, he'd be making arrangements for the band—not this kind of hit-parade arrangements I been saying about, but a kind of dividing of the piece, placing its parts. What we were after, it was to get the *feeling* for the band, playing it together. That way the music is working for itself."[84] This close collaboration—both in arranging and performing tunes—suggests that the communal spirit typical of the later Ellington was already present. For bandleaders like Whiteman and Lopez, such collaboration may have been one of the traits that made the Washingtonians so appealing. Many bands in the mid-twenties either used published stock arrangements (often "doctoring" them up) or played pop songs and blues more casually, filling in with ad lib phrases and harmonizations. The Washingtonians aimed for a balance between improvisation and composition, between the individual and the group. As Bechet said: "From hearing Otto play to me, me playing to Otto—playing *for* each other—we were making up what the band was to be, how it was to feel itself." [85]

From time to time, though, group discipline relaxed and gave way to a freer style of playing. Bechet, for example, apparently was invited to join the band after he showed up one night at the Kentucky Club, took out his soprano sax, and began trading choruses with Miley and Irvis. And once, at "some kind of charity affair" held at the Palais Royal, the Washingtonians won over the audience not with tight ensemble work but with improvised solos. Greer has described the occasion: "About the third tune we got into was one of those jam numbers we had then, and Bechet, Bubber, and Charlie came down front. Bechet had taken a table napkin and he held it in his mouth so that it hung down, and you couldn't see his fingers as he played his soprano. He cut everybody, Ross Gorman's band, everybody. When he had finished, the manager of the place came up to Gorman and said, 'Play waltzes. Don't play any more jazz.' That was our seven pieces." [86] Inside the Kentucky Club and without, the Washingtonians were building a reputation.

8

The Songwriter:
From "Jim Dandy" to "Yam Brown"

MARCH 1925–JUNE 1926

During his early years at the Kentucky Club, Ellington made slow progress writing music. Although he may have been concocting instrumental arrangements for the Washingtonians, he seems to have been more interested in writing and selling songs. By 1925 his output was still small: four songs are known, although he may have sold others outright, forfeiting copyright protection and royalties in exchange for a flat cash payment. Apparently this was a common practice of Fats Waller and other songwriters. In a 1962 interview Ellington mentioned "Come Back to Me" as one such tune he sold outright; it has not been located.[1]

Three songs by Ellington appeared on the Blu-Disc records of November 1924: "Deacon Jazz" and "Parlor Social De Luxe" written with Jo Trent, and "Choo Choo (I Gotta Hurry Home)" with Dave Ringle and Bob Schafer. Another Ellington-Trent tune from the same year was "Pretty Soft for You"; the Clarence Williams Music Publishing Company claimed copyright for it (November 1, 1924; E 602776). A photostat lead sheet of the chorus alone, in Ellington's hand, together with lyrics for both verse and chorus, is in bound volume T of the Smithsonian's Duke Ellington Collection. While "Choo Choo" was recorded by several other groups (see chapter 9), the songs Ellington wrote with Trent drew little interest. No recordings are known of "Blind Man's Buff" and "Pretty Soft for You," and no one besides Ellington seems to have recorded "Deacon Jazz." After working together for over a year, the pair had been unable to produce a song of any popularity. Their failure could not simply be attributed to discrimination; after all, Noble Sissle and Eubie Blake had been successful with "I'm Just Wild about Harry" (1921), Henry Creamer and Turner Layton, Jr., with "Way Down Yonder in New Orleans" (1922), and Cecil Mack and James P. Johnson with "Charleston" (1923). Rather, the strange alchemy behind a hit song—a matter of luck and timing, as well as appealing music and lyrics—eluded Ellington and Trent.

But in the spring of 1925 Ellington's luck turned. He and his songwriting partner got a chance to contribute songs to an all-black revue called *Chocolate Kiddies*. Although the show never reached Broadway it toured abroad for nearly two years, and it played a vital role in introducing Europeans to black-American performers and musical styles. As Ellington told the story:

> One day Joe Trent came running up to me on Broadway. He had a big proposition and there was urgency in his voice. "Tonight we've got to write a show," he said. *"Tonight!"*
>
> Being dumb and not knowing any better, I sat down that evening and wrote a show. . . . The next day we played and demonstrated our show for Jack Robbins, who liked it and said he would take it. [2]

The origins of *Chocolate Kiddies* went back to 1923, when *From Dover to Dixie,* the Plantation Café revue produced by Arthur S. Lyons and staged by Leonard Harper, traveled to England for several months. Later, when the Berlin-based impresario Leonidow made plans for a similar revue to tour the Continent, he turned to Lyons, who may have consulted both Harper and publisher Jack Robbins about possible cast members and songwriters.[3] What the producers needed was not an entire show—both book and music, as Ellington implied—but several new numbers around which the revue might be built. To these they would add comedy sketches, jazz instrumentals, and songs already popular. They needed, then, writers familiar with the conventions and requirements of black musical theater. Although Trent and Ellington lacked the experience of people like Luckey Roberts, Maceo Pinkard, and James P. Johnson, somehow they got the job.

The date of Ellington's night of labor on *Chocolate Kiddies* is not known. "Deacon Jazz," one of the songs used in *Chocolate Kiddies,* was recorded in 1924. But it probably was not written for the show. The "urgency" Ellington remembered in Trent's voice suggests that the commission dated closer to the time of the troupe's departure from New York. Since rehearsals began sometime in late April 1925, this would place the genesis of the four other Ellington-Trent tunes—"With You," "Love Is a Wish for You," "Jim Dandy," and "Jig Walk"—during that month or late in March.[4]

Beyond the $500 that Ellington claimed to have received for his work, he had little direct involvement with *Chocolate Kiddies* after writing the songs; he simply attended one or two rehearsals.[5] Rather than hiring the Washingtonians, the producers turned to another black musician, Sam Wooding, whose orchestra had had more stage experience and was known for its "symphonic jazz." Wooding and his band had toured with *Plantation Days* in 1923 and recently had been appearing at the Club Alabam, a spot famous for its floor shows and revues. The group Wooding took to Europe in May 1925 numbered eleven men: three trumpets, three reeds, one trombone, and four in the rhythm section. A photograph taken in Copenhagen showed the reed players sitting behind a battery of instruments—clarinets, saxophones, oboes, and rothophones. The Washingtonians could not match the Wooding orchestra in size or versatility. Act 2 of *Chocolate Kiddies,* for example, was titled, "Symphonic jazz concert by the Sam Wooding Orchestra at the Club Alabam in New York." The audience heard such numbers as Rudolf Friml's "Indian Love Call," W. C. Handy's "St. Louis Blues," and a "Medley of American Hits." Other examples of the band's symphonic jazz repertory are on recordings made by Wooding in 1925 for German Vox: Thurlow Lieurance's "By the Waters of Minnetonka," the pop song "O Katharina," and two "hot" dance tunes, "Shanghai Shuffle" and "Alabamy Bound."[6] But if Ellington was not to accompany *Chocolate Kiddies* to Europe, his music was heard and enjoyed in Hamburg, Berlin, Copenhagen, Stockholm—eventually even Leningrad and Moscow. While other jazz orchestras (Will Marion Cook, Paul Whiteman) and revues (*From Dover to Dixie*) had gone overseas, none had the sustained impact of Wooding's band with the *Chocolate Kiddies* troupe.

Chocolate Kiddies was a potpourri of African-American music, dance, and comedy. Although the revue's structure changed slightly over time, the program for the August 1925 performances in Stockholm indicates how the songs by Trent and Ellington were used.[7]

Following the overture, Act 1 opened with "Night Life in a Negro Cafe in Harlem in New York." The first song the audience heard was "Deacon Jazz," which described the irresistible force of this music. It was performed by Adelaide Hall, who later would record "Creole Love Call" with Ellington in 1927, and the *Chocolate Kiddies* chorus. After Wooding's symphonic jazz concert in Act 2, three more Ellington songs turned up in Act 3. The first part of the act was set in the South, "where the black people sing their songs and dance their dances and joke in the sunset" (Björn Englund's translation). It began with spirituals and two songs by Stephen Foster, "Old Black Joe" and "Old Folks at Home." Then, after Adelaide Hall's "Jungle Nights in Dixie" and a comedy routine by the "Three Eddies" (Tiny Ray, Chick Horsey, and Shaky Beasley), Jessie Crawford sang "Jim Dandy (A Strut Dance)," backed by chorus.

"Jim Dandy" (copyright December 3, 1925; E 627251) depicts a stereotyped character with origins in nineteenth-century minstrel songs like Dan Emmett's "Dandy Jim from Caroline" (1844). Rather vain and a fancy dresser, Jim Dandy represents a blend of different qualities—part pride, part self-parody, all dramatic flair. In Trent's lyrics he is a "stunning chappy," a "dashing, dusky fashion plate" who wins over the girls with his up-to-date style and good looks. As a "clever little sinner" he may have ulterior motives, but they matter less than the striking figure he cuts.

Ellington casts his song in a standard mold: introduction (8 bars), vamp (2), verse (16), and chorus (32). The verse begins with a chromatic melody unusual for its time and not so easy to sing:

Example 16. "Jim Dandy" (1925), verse, mm. 1–8.

The last eight bars are more common in their harmonies, melodic sequence, and diatonic profile, becoming chromatic only in the final lead-in to the chorus.

Ellington gives the chorus of his "Strut Dance" an old-fashioned flavor, using mild syncopation and a jaunty accompaniment to evoke an earlier era of cakewalk and ragtime songs:

Example 17. "Jim Dandy," chorus, mm. 1–8.

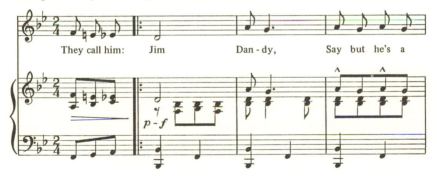

In keeping with the southern setting and nineteenth-century ambience, a quote from Dan Emmett's "Dixie" turns up in the first ending. One modern touch, however, results from the emphasis on both minor- and major-seventh chords. And the harmonic scheme of "Jim Dandy," with its plagal turn in the last eight bars, is similar to that found in other songs from the twenties such as "Somebody Stole My Gal" (1922) and "Baby Face" (1926).

Later in Act 3 the scene shifted back to Harlem. The cast performed a sketch based on the song "With You" (copyright December 3, 1925; E 627252), in which "members of the ensemble played the parts of a mother, children, a postman, a boy and, of course, a lover."[8] Trent's lyric for "With You" abounds in romantic clichés: if united, two lovers might lose themselves "in a dream world," a "cottage made of love dreams" where "life would be like summer sunshine." Yet such a straightforward expression of love sung by blacks was not so standard in 1925. A few years earlier Sissle and Blake had drawn criticism for putting "Love Will Find a Way" in *Shuffle Along* (although audiences received it warmly). Popular songs produced by blacks in the early twenties tended to be either blues numbers or jazz-related (e.g., "Way Down Yonder in New Orleans"). "With You," by contrast, is a sweet Tin Pan Alley ballad that avoids identification with stylized black-American speech or music.

Again, Ellington turns to the conventional verse-chorus form, although now the refrain is twenty-two bars instead of the more usual thirty-two or sixteen. And again, as in "Jim Dandy," the verse

Example 18. "With You" (1925), verse, mm. 1–4.

in their heart a trea - sure, fill - ing life with plea - sure.

is hard to sing—yet the difficulty seems less intentional than awk-ward on Ellington's part. Besides being a wayward, skipping tune, it drops nearly one-and-a-half octaves in the first four bars (see Example 18). After the descending lines and chromaticism of the verse, the smooth, arching, nearly pentatonic chorus provides welcome contrast:

Example 19. "With You," chorus, mm. 1–9.

With you all my joys will be com - plet - ed, with
you ev'-ry wish is just re - peat - ed, we two in a

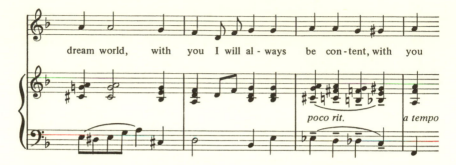

dream world, with you I will al - ways be con - tent, with you

With the line, "we two in a dream world," the chromatic flavor of the verse returns, especially in the snaky bass line of mm. 4–7. The gentle melody builds to a sudden climax and slowly winds down again, dropping in range and volume. At the words "you're mine" (chorus, m. 16) the move to V^7/ii signals a standard ii-V-I cadential pattern, but Ellington resists the temptation. By interpolating a dark $iv^{7(b3)}$ chord under "love dreams" he extends the phrase another four bars in an unexpected tag. Here, as elsewhere in the song, Ellington brings to his assignment fresh ideas instead of falling back on Tin Pan Alley formulas.

Near the end of Act 3 the *Chocolate Kiddies* ensemble came out and danced the Charleston—"New York's sensation"—to "Jig Walk" (copyright December 3, 1925; E 627250), the fourth song by Ellington and Trent used in the production (Example 20). Given the popularity of Cecil Mack and James P. Johnson's "Charleston," written for *Runnin' Wild* in 1923, it is not surprising to find the dance in this exported black revue. The hesitating Charleston rhythm—♩ ♪ ♪♩—and its accompanying dance movements helped make "Jig Walk" the hit of the show.

In Trent's lyrics, the phrase "Jig Walk" is synonymous with the Charleston dance: "There's a funny twisting step makes others seem a joke . . . Jig Walk, Come on and do the Jig Walk." But according to W. C. Handy, black minstrels had coined the phrase "jigwawk" to refer to a Negro.[9] Thus, in Trent's and Ellington's song, the dance step fuses with the identity of black Americans. Although Horst Bergmeier has speculated that "Jig Walk" was written earlier and not specifically for the *Chocolate Kiddies* revue, a lyric like "Show these kind folk New York's dancing craze / It has got that big Broadway ablaze" seems made to order for a troupe of black

Example 20

Jig Walk - Charleston

Words by
"JO" TRENT

Music by
DUKE ELLINGTON

PIANO

There's a fun - ny twisting step makes o - thers seem a joke

All you step - pers gather round and make your foot-sies smoke   You don't need no big brass band

Don't need no song   Ev'-ry - bo-dy pat your hands   get go-ing strong._____

Example 20

Example 20

cultural ambassadors.[10] Today the text may seem embarrassingly derogatory. But in 1925 "Jig Walk" made a proud statement about the power and influence of African-American music and dance.

Ellington seems more at home with the crisp dance rhythms of "Jig Walk" than with either the lyrical ballad or the older, ragtime "strutting" song. Indeed, the piece is just as successful played as it is sung and perhaps even started life as one of Ellington's piano solos. In the opening of the verse (mm. 9–16), the melody takes a backseat to rhythmically charged accompaniment. The vamp-like piano part carries echoes of James P. Johnson's stride and Spencer Williams's "I've Found a New Baby" (written the same year). The chorus owes something to Will Tyers's "Panama" (1911), a favorite instrumental number for jazz bands:

Example 21. "Panama," published stock, piano part, second strain, mm. 1–12.

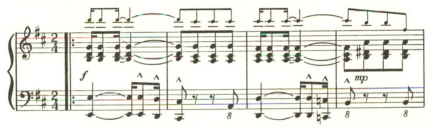

Other subsequent songs—Creamer and Layton's "Look What You've Done" (1918) and Con Conrad and J. Russel Robinson's "Singin' the Blues" (1920)—may have influenced Ellington's harmonic structure.

But "Jig Walk" is not all derivative. At the end of the verse (Example 20, mm. 21–25) Ellington leads up to a $\flat VI^{\flat 7}$-V^7 cadence with a descending, chromatic-tinged progression; similar patterns appear both in "With You" (chorus, mm. 7–9) and "Jim Dandy" (introduction, mm. 7–8). Such voice-leading and a preference for flatted VI and III chords turn up again and again in Ellington's later music.

The chorus of "Jig Walk" (AABA) features the Charleston rhythm in both A and B sections. Ellington does not write a new bridge but borrows from the verse, taking what before were straight quarters and adding Charleston syncopations (mm. 42–45). The appeal of the chorus comes not just from its rhythmic zest but from the harmonic coloring of the opening measures, once more highlighting the seventh scale-degree (see mm. 26–28). Although it has antecedents in "Panama" and "Singin' the Blues," this ii^7-V^7-I^7 chord pattern is more characteristic of the 1930s than the mid-1920s. Fats Waller's "I'm Crazy 'bout My Baby" (1931), for example, uses the same progression and stresses the same pitches in the same key. Another modern feature of "Jig Walk" is the unresolved I-IV^9 cadence that closes the song.

"Jim Dandy," "With You," and "Jig Walk" were copyrighted early in December 1925, more than six months after *Chocolate Kiddies* opened in Germany. Reflecting the transatlantic background of the show, the sheet music bears the imprint of its American publisher (Robbins-Engel, 1658 Broadway) and its Berlin representative (Victor Alberti). The three pieces cite not just the lyricist and composer but also Arthur S. Lyons, who presented the "colored revue." On the cover of all three is a caricature of the Three Eddies, who wear tuxedos, bowler hats, gloves and spats, and white rimless spectacles. Shoulder to shoulder, their arms akimbo and legs flung sideways at impossible angles, they seem to be in the midst of a wild Charleston (see p. 127).

The back page of "Jim Dandy" tells something about two additional Ellington-Trent songs. Incipits appear for "Love Is a Wish for You" and "Skeedely-Um-Bum." The former is a waltz starting, like

"Jig Walk," on ii[7]. The first four bars of "Skeedely-Um-Bum" have a blues flavor, while the last two suggest Ellington's later "jungle style," with the minor key, insistent accompaniment, and blue-note inflections:

Example 22. "Love Is a Wish for You" and "Skeedely-Um-Bum," incipits from back page of "Jim Dandy."

Despite the advertisement, these songs seem not to have been published by Robbins. Neither appears in the Library of Congress copyright records nor survives in sheet-music form. However, soon after the *Chocolate Kiddies* revue left for Europe, Jo Trent copyrighted "Love Is Just a Dream of You" (June 22, 1925), with no specific indication of composer. This may have become "Love Is a Wish for You" in its European incarnation.

In June 1925 *Variety* announced a recording of songs from *Chocolate Kiddies* by cast members:

All the principal numbers in the "Chocolate Kiddies" colored
show at the Admiral Palast, Berlin, have been recorded on the
"mechanicals" by the German branch of the Victor Company.
Jo Trent and Duke Ellington wrote all special numbers, which
have been acquired by Jack Robbins. . . . Among the leaders is
a fox trot-ballad, "With You," which Lottie Gee sings in German. A waltz number, "Love Is Just a Wish," also in German,
is rendered by Thaddeus Drayton (Greenlee and Drayton) and
Margaret Sims. A fast number, a Charleston, "The Jig Walk," is
introduced by Greenlee and Drayton and chorus. [11]

This notice confirms that "Love Is a Wish for You" was included in
the show. However, copies of the German Victor recordings have
not surfaced and may not have been issued.

Several of the Ellington-Trent tunes from *Chocolate Kiddies* were
recorded in the 1920s, but Ellington was involved directly with
only one, "Deacon Jazz." Ellington has sometimes been linked with
a piano nickelodeon roll of "Jig Walk" that was made in the late
1940s by the Wurlitzer company.[12] It gives a straightforward version of the tune with no improvisation, and the pianist, as Brooks
Kerr and others have agreed, does not sound like Ellington. Moreover, on two different occasions Ellington told ragtime historian
Mike Montgomery that he had never made piano rolls.[13]

The success of *Chocolate Kiddies* overseas inspired recordings
of numbers from the show by several European artists. In August
1925 Bernard Etté's dance orchestra recorded "Love Is a Wish for
You" in Berlin for Vox, which labeled the piece a "Valse Boston";
the next month pianist Mischa Spoliansky performed the same tune
for Odeon. In October, Odeon released a version of "Jim Dandy"
by Dajos Bela, a Hungarian bandleader.[14] But the story gets more
exotic. In 1976 Macs Elfstrom was browsing in a Scandinavian
record catalog from the 1920s when he came across a listing of
"Love Is a Wish for You" by Andreozzi's South-American Orchestra. The song was credited to Ellington and recorded by the
South Americans in Berlin in late 1925 or early 1926. Originally
released by the German Schallplatte Gramophon company, it had
been picked up by the Scandinavian Nordisk Polyphon Aktieselsk-
kab label and issued later in the twenties.[15] Back on 49th and
Broadway, Ellington might have been surprised that his song

enjoyed such international interest when it had no currency state-side.

"Jig Walk" has been recorded more than any other song from *Chocolate Kiddies*. Björn Englund has listed a dozen versions by both European and American orchestras, most from 1925 and 1926. In August 1925 Bernard Etté recorded it in Berlin for Vox; sounding quite Prussian and proper, Etté's band turns the snap of the Charleston into a hesitation fox trot. One of the first American recordings of "Jig Walk" was made December 10, 1925, by the Ipana Troubadors, a Sam Lanin band that included Red Nichols and Miff Mole (who may have heard "Jig Walk" played at the Kentucky Club). In some ways the Troubadors' arrangement followed the Arthur Lange orchestration published by Robbins-Engel in 1926. (The title page of Lange's arrangement read: "The International Success 'Jig Walk,' As Introduced in America by Paul Ash and His Gang [Chicago]." Similarly, an Okeh Syncopators recording from February 1926 appears to be a doctored version of Lange's stock.

"Jig Walk" outlasted the decade of the Charleston. The Ramblers, a Dutch band, recorded it in 1933, and Pee Wee Russell, Joe Sullivan, and Zutty Singleton improvised on the tune in 1941. In 1944 a stock arrangement by Will Hudson appeared, published by Robbins as part of "The New Duke Ellington Modern Rhythm Series." In the late thirties Ellington himself returned to "Jig Walk," possibly revising it for use in a downtown Cotton Club production. Two performances recorded from radio broadcasts in 1938 (May 22) and 1940 (September 26) show him completely overhauling the tune. And in the fluttering, trilled statement of the theme by the reeds, Ellington provides tongue-in-cheek commentary on old-fashioned performance practice.[16]

In the fall of 1925, while the *Chocolate Kiddies* troupe drew accolades on the Continent, Ellington and his band were beginning their third year in the basement club on 49th and Broadway. With Bass Edwards now a member, the regular Kentucky Club band used eight men; but on different occasions—record dates, engagements at other clubs—Ellington added extra players to bring the total to nine and sometimes ten. A bigger band called for different arranging techniques, and Ellington was clearly learning on the job, with varying results.

Between the fall of 1925 and late spring of 1926 the Washingtonians had three record dates: two for the Pathé label (September 7, 1925, and March 1926) and one for Gennett (April 1926). Bubber Miley is missing from all three. In September Pike Davis took his place; in both March and April Ellington expanded to two trumpets, using Harry Cooper and Leroy Rutledge.

Where was Bubber? Given the band's rare recording opportunities during this period, it seems unlikely that Ellington would have chosen to omit the outstanding hot soloist whose singular style had become part of the Washingtonians' identity. Was Miley out of the band periodically, or did he simply fail to appear sometimes? Miley could be unpredictable. Once, at a club where the manager wanted the band to play show tunes sweet and straight, Miley could not restrain himself any more and erupted on his horn like a volcano. Next night the Washingtonians arrived at the "swank spot" to find another band in its place on the stand. [17]

With or without Miley, in the spring of 1926 Ellington apparently enlarged his group to play at other clubs, including a revue at Ciro's, a restaurant and cabaret on West 56th Street that had opened the year before. Various saxophonists—Harvey Boone, Edgar Sampson, Benny Carter, and Don Redman—had brief stints with the band around this time, joining Hardwick and Robinson to form a three-piece reed team. Carter has recalled his experience with the group: "I was sort of a little insignificant musician around Harlem at the time . . . the Ellington band was at a club on 57th Street called Harry Richman's Club, and I sat in for Harvey Boone for a week or two . . . it may have been a number of days, and it just felt like a week or two." [18] Redman, the talented reed-man and arranger for Fletcher Henderson, took part in the Washingtonians' March and April record dates. He was needed, Ellington later explained, because "we were at the Kentucky Club with six pieces and the date called for ten." [19] (While Ellington and other musicians invariably referred to the Kentucky Club band as consisting of six pieces, contemporary newspaper evidence often indicated seven or eight.)

As new players came and went, the Washingtonians floated in and out of the Kentucky Club. In November 1925 they were out for a spell. The Baltimore *Afro-American* reported November 21 that the Washingtonians had just finished an engagement at the Lido

Club; yet no New York announcements had heralded an opening there. Later in the month they appeared at the Cameo Club and were fired the same night. After a brief vaudeville appearance with Ethel Waters and Earl Dancer (Fred Guy's former employer at the Orient) they were back at the Kentucky Club late in December. [20]

The band may not have chosen to switch jobs so frequently, but circumstances forced them to do so. Besides the fires that periodically closed down the club, the Kentucky Club management sometimes hired other bands. Also, late in 1925 the place was having trouble keeping its license—although it managed to beat a padlock injunction in early 1926. [21]

During their third year playing downtown, Ellington and his Washingtonians may have reached a professional plateau. Although now they could be billed as the "Famous Kentucky Club Band," [22] their brief appearances at downtown clubs suggest the exaggerated nature of the claim. They were still in the minor leagues compared to the orchestras of Paul Whiteman, Vincent Lopez, and Fletcher Henderson—all of which recorded more, performed in more elegant settings, and received more publicity. *Orchestra World,* one of the important trade publications for dance bands, mentioned Ellington and his band infrequently and then only in connection with their function at the Kentucky Club. By contrast, in the fall of 1925 the publication devoted a full-page article to the career of Fletcher Henderson, calling him "king of colored orchestra leaders." [23] The popular music monthly *Metronome* did not acknowledge the Washingtonians' existence. As late as 1927, when Ellington was cited as one of the co-writers of the song "Gold Digger," the *Metronome* editors let his last name slip by as "Yellington." [24]

After the cluster of songs in 1924 and the ones for *Chocolate Kiddies,* Ellington's composing activity in late 1925 and early 1926 seems to have dropped off sharply. Only two pieces survive: "Parlor Social Stomp" and "Yam Brown." Recorded by the Washingtonians in March 1926, "Parlor Social Stomp" was Ellington's first instrumentally conceived composition to appear on disc (see chapter 9 for discussion). It was neither copyrighted nor published.

"Yam Brown" (copyright May 4, 1926; E 640611) is another Ellington song with words by Jo Trent. Unlike "With You," it is an earthy love song that draws upon both musical and linguistic

African-American conventions. Yet "Yam Brown" lacks the charm or tunefulness of the songs from *Chocolate Kiddies*. The verse borrows from one of the most common vamp formulas around. The chorus is more inspired, especially in the first sixteen bars, where Ellington keeps up harmonic tension throughout a single, long melodic phrase:

Example 23. "Yam Brown" (1926), chorus, mm. 1–16.

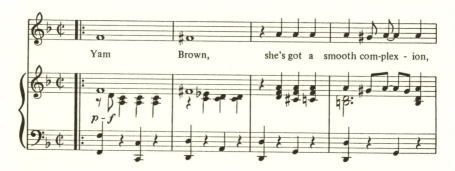

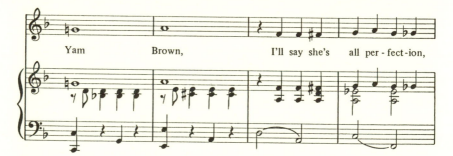

Spoon - ing,   she'll make you change your re-lig-ion,

But in the second half, rhythmic monotony, a big melodic leap, and a poor harmonic choice (an E appoggiatura over a B-natural diminished chord) make the tune fall flat.

In June 1926 the Washingtonians were out of the Kentucky Club again. They found a job at the more prestigious Plantation Café, but it ended quickly. On June 21 they returned to the Gennett studios. This time Miley made the date; the ensemble was better organized and played with verve. Although in some ways not as distinctive as "Choo Choo" and "Rainy Nights," these two sides— "(I'm Just Wild about) Animal Crackers" and "Li'l Farina"—were an improvement over the Washingtonians' earlier discs for Pathé and Gennett. "Li'l Farina," in particular, gave signs of promise for both Ellington and his band.

9

The First Recordings

NOVEMBER 1924–OCTOBER 1926

In the early 1920s jazz was supposed to be entertaining. Dancers thrilled to the music that gave them the shimmy, the toddle, the camel walk, and the Chicago flop. And listeners sitting in cabarets expected jazz bands to provide a few laughs, either from comical instrumental effects, bandstand antics, or the vaudevillian patter of a leader like Ted Lewis, forever asking, "Is Ev'rybody Hap-py?" Vincent Lopez recalled how his early band was made up of "whining and whistling clarinets, trombones that guffawed, trumpets that buzzed and fluttered, pianists that gyrated, and acrobatic drummers."[1] Ellington, too, acknowledged the music's origins in novelty: "When I began my work jazz was a stunt, something different. Not everybody cared for jazz and those who did felt that it wasn't the real thing unless they were given a shock sensation of loudness or unpredictability along with the music."[2]

By the mid-1920s bandleaders like Paul Whiteman and Jean Goldkette were stepping up their campaign to rid jazz of its "vulgar" aspects. In his Aeolian Hall concert of February 12, 1924, Whiteman demonstrated the old style of jazz with a raucous version of "Livery Stable Blues," then followed with the new, improved product, a stylish arrangement of "Mamma Loves Pappa." Yet despite the efforts of such reformers, many bands continued their imitation animal noises, solos on slide whistle and goofus, and good old-fashioned hokum.

In the fall of 1924, six months before *Chocolate Kiddies* took to the road, Ellington made his publishing and recording debut with a novelty song, "Choo Choo (I Gotta Hurry Home)" (copyright September 5, 1924; E 595558). A common theme in American music and poetry since the 1840s, trains had figured prominently in popular songs over the past several years. Between 1920 and 1924, both jazz bands and singers had recorded pieces like "Choo Choo Blues," "Choo Choo Charlie," "Freight Train Blues," "Railroad Blues," and "Railroad Man." Recently the singer Monette Moore had started making records with a group called the Choo Choo Jazzers featuring Bubber Miley on cornet. And train mania lay behind the choice of a subject by Ellington and his two collaborators, Dave Ringle (1893–1965) and Bob Schafer (1897–1943).

Ellington's partners were well acquainted with the business of selling songs. Ringle wrote contracts for publishing houses. Schafer served on the professional staff of various companies. Songwriter Sam Coslow called Schafer an "energetic hustler" who presented himself as a "songwriter's agent."[3] Perhaps Schafer served in this capacity for Ellington, thus winning a place on the title page of "Choo Choo." Although the song's credits do not indicate who did what, it seems likely that Ellington came up with the tune and Ringle (possibly with Schafer) supplied the words. In addition to publishing the sheet-music version, the Broadway Music Corporation issued a dance-band arrangement of "Choo Choo" by Louis Katzman. Ellington was in a good position to do business with the company: located on 7th Avenue at 48th Street, it was just one block away from the Kentucky Club.

By November 1924, when the Washingtonians recorded "Choo Choo," the tune had already become popular. In October it had been featured on discs by the Ambassadors (directed by Willie Creager), the Original Memphis Five, Earl Randolph's Orchestra, and the Goofus Five (with Adrian Rollini); the latter group released another version of the song November 12 under the name "Bailey's Dixie Dudes." Downtown white jazz bands were not the only ones interested in "Choo Choo"; a lively duet version appeared on Victor by comedians Billy Murray and Ed Smalle backed by an orchestra.

In some ways, the Washingtonians' performance of "Choo Choo" follows the tradition of jazz-as-novelty. Ellington's arrangement leaves no doubt that the subject is train travel: in the introductory vamp Charlie Irvis's trombone revs up the engines; midway through, George Francis rings the bell with tremolo banjo chords; and at the end, Irvis, Bubber Miley, and Otto Hardwick sound a D-minor wail that is echoed by five toots on a train whistle (probably blown by Sonny Greer). No one takes a vocal chorus, but Hardwick's frenetic alto sax captures the nervous quality of the text that appears in the sheet music:

> Choo Choo,
> I gotta hurry home.
> Choo Choo,
> This ain't no time to roam.
> I gotta travel
> I gotta travel
> You're slower than a cow,
> You're movin' now but how!
> Engine
> Come on and pull your freight,
> Shake it up and don't be late.
> Hurry up let's go,
> How come you're slow?
> Choo Choo,
> I gotta hurry home.

Yet Ellington and his band avoid the temptation to play "Choo Choo" for laughs. While Louis Katzman's stock arrangement of the piece takes off with a cliché—a diminished-seventh-chord whistle effect—Ellington begins with a fanfare in D major that slips down to the dominant C^7 at m. 7 (see Example 24). Throughout the record Ellington departs from both the structure of Katzman's arrangement and its details of part-writing.

The form of the Washingtonians' "Choo Choo" is straightforward:

Introduction	Hardwick, Miley, Irvis	8 bars
Vamp	Irvis + ensemble	8
Chorus 1	Ensemble, Miley lead	32
Verse	Ensemble, Hardwick lead	16
Chorus 2	Miley solo	32
"Patter" section	Irvis solo/Francis solo	8/8
Chorus 3	Ensemble	32
Coda	Ensemble + whistle	6

Example 24. "Choo Choo" (November 1924), introduction, mm. 1–8.

The three lead instruments' ensemble style is mostly homophonic. They show most independence in the first chorus, as Miley embellishes the melody, Hardwick alternates between sustained chord-tones and hyperactive triplets, and Irvis fills out the bottom with connecting phrases:

Example 25. "Choo Choo," first chorus, mm. 1–8.

The three horns return in the third chorus with a simple rhythmic variation of the theme:

Example 26. "Choo Choo," third chorus, mm. 5–8.

Except for occasional raggedness (e.g., Hardwick's late entrance at the beginning of the third chorus), the Washingtonians do sound, as Greer claimed, "well-rehearsed." In part this is because Ellington's arrangement leaves little room for improvising. Besides Miley's full chorus and Irvis's eight-bar solo, the only other place where a player can stretch out is during the four bars of stop-time (taken by Hardwick) toward the end of the third chorus. Just before this section Ellington gives the horns a break that combines both whole-tone and chromatic features:

Example 27. "Choo Choo," third chorus, mm. 21–24.

Such a passage shows young Ellington being fashionably modern in 1924.

A more original harmonic touch occurs at the opening of the chorus, in which an A^{b7} chord slides down to V^7/V before cadencing on the tonic F at m. 4. While the ^{b}III chord was common

in popular songs at the time, its function as secondary dominant
preparation was not. Ellington's novel idea gives the song a distinctive harmonic identity.

Two factors in the Washingtonians' performance of "Choo
Choo" help explain how they turn a novelty song into an effective
jazz instrumental. One is the strong playing of the rhythm section.
Ellington, Francis, and especially Greer provide a steady undercurrent that drives the train ahead yet holds back Hardwick's and
Miley's impatience to reach their destination. A good example of
their teamwork comes near the end of the first chorus (mm. 25–28),
when Greer's choked cymbal accents punctuate Ellington's walking bass line and make the rhythm rock. The other factor is Bubber
Miley's hot cornet solo. As Gunther Schuller has pointed out, it is
a paraphrase of the melody:[4]

Example 28. "Choo Choo," Bubber Miley solo.

* The plunger mute's tonal variation is not indicated.

Although simpler and more restrained than the solos Louis Armstrong was taking with the Fletcher Henderson band around the time, this was still "hot" in 1924.[5] Here Miley demonstrates the muting, growl, and bent-note techniques that were to figure so prominently later in Ellington's music.

"Rainy Nights" is the other instrumental on the November 1924 Blu-Disc session. Ellington may have had a hand in writing it, but the label credits [Jo] Trent, [Will] Donaldson, and [Vincent] Lopez.[6] Like "Choo Choo," "Rainy Nights" follows the standard pop song form with its sixteen-bar verse and thirty-two-bar (AABA) chorus. The chord progression, too, is rather ordinary; perhaps its most interesting (though not unusual) feature is the move to a $^{b}VI^{b7}$ chord in the second bar of the A section.

While Ellington's arrangement is more functional than creative, at least one inspired touch appears in the verse, a brief, dramatic crescendo carried by Irvis (with Ellington doubling the line):

Example 29. "Rainy Nights" (November 1924), verse, mm. 7–9.

The same passage turns up a few years later in the F-minor section of his piano solo "Swampy River" (1928), an early example of Ellington recycling his own materials.

"Rainy Nights" is dominated by Hardwick (first chorus and

verse following), Irvis (second chorus), and Miley (third chorus). All three hew close to the tune, approaching their solos more as opportunities to play the melody rather than to improvise around it. Hardwick turns in the "straightest" performance. He has a sweet, singing tone and favors a wide vibrato on held notes. Except for fluffing a note in the sixth bar of the verse, Hardwick takes a smooth and assured solo. Irvis, in his solo, does not growl or use a mute but instead plays lyrically on open horn.

But it is Miley who makes "Rainy Nights" memorable. As on "Choo Choo," he mutes his trumpet solo (either with a cup mute or his hand), breaking into the last two bars of Irvis's chorus with a hot growl. Miley's power comes not from volume or speed but from his subtle coloring of individual notes and his ability to create and sustain a mood—in this case, a wistful melancholy. Miley was a different kind of hot trumpeter from the brilliant and rhythmically daring Armstrong. The contrast is clear from a comparison of Miley's solo on "Rainy Nights" with Armstrong's on "Naughty Man"—both pieces were recorded the same month, and both use the same harmonies:[7]

Example 30. "Rainy Nights," Bubber Miley solo, beginning; "Naughty Man," Fletcher Henderson and his Orchestra (November 14, 1924), Louis Armstrong solo, beginning.

*No chord for Armstrong

Two years younger, Miley almost sounds like an old-timer when placed next to Armstrong, with the latter's rhythmic vitality and athletic leaps. Yet Miley's horn sings out with sincerity and feeling.

Nearly a year passed before the Washingtonians made another recording. (For vocal accompaniments from November 1924, see the discussion later in this chapter.) The time lapse reflected their status as one of many small dance bands in New York which had not yet made it big. By contrast, in 1925 the Original Memphis Five produced eighteen sides, Fletcher Henderson's orchestra over thirty, and the California Ramblers nearly seventy. Also, however, the assistance rendered earlier by Jo Trent and Maceo Pinkard may have faded in 1925. The Kentucky Club had been closed for part of the year and the band had been playing various places in and out of town. It was not until early September of 1925—between the seventh and the twelfth—that the Washingtonians returned to the studio for a session with Pathé.[8]

Unlike the shadowy and short-lived Blu-Disc label, Pathé was a solid company with European origins dating back to the 1890s. In 1925 its catalog advertised separate series for dance music, vocal music, opera, and race records. The California Ramblers (and one of its spin-off groups, Five Birmingham Babies) recorded for Pathé in 1925, as did the Original Memphis Five and Boyd Senter. Since Spencer Williams wrote both songs that the Washingtonians recorded for the company, he may have had something to do with arranging the date.

The A-side of the Washingtonians' first Pathé release featured "I'm Gonna Hang around My Sugar (Till I Gather All the Sugar That She's Got)" (copyright May 22, 1925; E 616174), a slightly racy song by Williams and Jack Palmer. The same team had scored a hit the year before with "Everybody Loves My Baby," also with another minor-key "baby" song earlier in 1925, "I've Found a New Baby." The lyrics (not sung on the Washingtonians' version) contain lines like, "I've got a lucky break and everything is cake," "Each honey bee just envies me/They buzz around her tryin' to make connection with my sweet confection," and "I'll give her all my attention / What we'll do is too numerous to mention." "I'm Gonna Hang around My Sugar" was never a great success for Williams and Palmer, but at least five other bands followed the Washingtonians in bringing it to the studio: the Original Indiana Five, Lanin's Red Heads, Fred Hall's Orchestra, the Varsity Eight (a Ramblers group with Adrian Rollini), and Perry's Hot Dogs (with Miff Mole and Arthur Schutt).

The Washingtonians seem to be playing a loosely sketched arrangement, not a published stock, with a few worked-out details. In the first chorus Pike Davis, substituting for Miley, dances around the melody with muted cornet for the first sixteen bars. In the second sixteen Charlie Irvis takes a solo that steers clear of direct references to the tune:

Example 31. "I'm Gonna Hang around My Sugar" (September 1925), Charlie Irvis solo.

Davis has the lead for the twenty-bar verse, then Hardwick follows with an alto solo interrupted toward the end by two blustery breaks from Prince Robinson's tenor sax. The next section is an interesting composed variation that may well be Ellington's own (Example 32). The key moves from B-flat up to E-flat and soon modern features appear, like the Charleston rhythm (m. 3), the tumbling sax break (m. 4), the sudden fanfare in triplets (m. 5), and the soaring ascent to the top of a ninth chord by Hardwick (m. 7). Toward the end of this chorus (mm. 13–17) the saxophones and trumpet momentarily evoke the sweet sound-world of Paul Whiteman:

Example 32. "I'm Gonna Hang around My Sugar," third chorus, mm. 1–18.

The last chorus brings back the full ensemble playing in a modified New Orleans style—cornet lead, saxes filling in the middle,
and tailgate trombone. The New Orleans connection becomes more
explicit when Robinson switches to clarinet. But the ensemble does
not mesh well enough to produce a true polyphonic chorus in the
New Orleans tradition; the players—especially Robinson—sound
stiff rather than fluid, more agitated than hot. (Fred Guy's per-
fectly executed glissando break is easily the high point.) And the
four-bar tag comes straight from the theater with its dramatic,
act-closing ritard, its "advanced" cadence (IV-^{b}VI^{b7}-I over a tonic
pedal), and its ultimate ninth chord.[9]

The other side of the Washingtonians' first Pathé release contains "Trombone Blues" (copyright January 14, 1925; E 606470),
another song by Spencer Williams, this time with words by Ted
Nixon. Ted (or Teddy) Nixon played trombone with Fletcher Henderson in 1923 and 1924. By late February 1925 the Henderson
band was associated with the tune: "The Melody Music Company
has just released a new song from the pen of Spencer Williams
. . . entitled 'Trombone Blues.' The number was recently tried in
vaudeville . . . by Wilbur C. Sweatman's orchestra and is now
being featured nightly at the Roseland . . . by Fletcher Henderson
and his Orchestra."[10] Later that year Henderson was praised in a
Billboard article for featuring numbers published by black firms
(e.g., Spencer Williams, Clarence Williams). The writer (probably
James A. Jackson) complained that too often black bandleaders
turned to material issued by white publishers.[11] But Henderson only
performed "Trombone Blues"; according to Brian Rust, the sole
recorded version is by the Washingtonians.

"Trombone Blues" has a twenty-four-bar chorus made up of two
twelve-bar sections (the first 4 + 4 + 4, the second 4 + 8). The ^{b}VI^{b7}
chord figures prominently in the song, appearing both in relation to
the tonic F (D^{b7}) and the subdominant B-flat (G^{b7}). Not surprisingly,
trombonist Charlie Irvis takes the lead in the first chorus; later during the reeds' chorus he punches out a two-bar break that inspires
a gutsy clarinet solo from Robinson. Pike Davis is the other main
soloist, taking a full chorus after Irvis's opening one and riding over
the final ensemble chorus.

But "Trombone Blues" shows the Washingtonians running into

problems. One is the constant interruption of forward motion by solo and duo breaks. Frequent breaks were characteristic of dance tunes of the time, but the best players—say, a Louis Armstrong or a Sidney Bechet—could seize the moment of rhythmic suspension, spin out a phrase or two, then set up the band's entrance in such a way as to make the interruption dramatic rather than disturbing. The breaks on "Trombone Blues" do not serve this function. Instead they make an already fragmented structure even choppier. Out of 139 measures of music (verse, four choruses, and trio), 25 are breaks; this works out to an average of a break every 5½ measures. A couple by Irvis are fiery (third and fourth choruses), one by the saxophones is comic (halfway through the second chorus), and a few are awkward (during the verse). There is a chromatic break after the trio for reeds and trumpet:

Example 33. "Trombone Blues" (September 1925), break.

Such a device shows Ellington—presumably the arranger—keeping up with contemporary novelty features yet not knowing how to use them effectively. Nor can his players lightly toss them off. The music sounds labored.

Indeed, the sound of both "Trombone Blues" and "I'm Gonna Hang around My Sugar" is another problem. The recording engineers must be held partly responsible. The balance of instruments is terrible, and if Greer is on the date at all, his drums cannot be heard. Moreover, the band simply does not perform well. The ensemble cohesion of "Choo Choo" and "Rainy Nights" has given way to a shaky rhythmic feeling, despite the presence of Bass Edwards. Also, Ellington's arrangements—especially on "Trombone Blues"

—revert to novelty: apparently he (or Pathé) wanted the band to sound up-to-date, even if this was not its strongest style. The results, as Schuller has noted, are two "typical numbers for dancing, with little 'Charleston' touches and many of the syncopated clichés of the time."[12]

When the Washingtonians next returned to Pathé's East 53rd Street studios around March 19, 1926, they recorded another Spencer Williams tune, "Georgia Grind" (copyright August 19, 1926; E 643753), this time paired with an Ellington original, "Parlor Social Stomp" (not copyrighted). The addition of Don Redman to the date gave Ellington his first three-piece reed section on record; with trumpeters Leroy Rutledge and Harry Cooper, the band numbered ten players. By 1925 this was a fairly standard instrumental line-up, but for Ellington it was not yet common.

In arranging for Fletcher Henderson's orchestra, Redman often pitted three brass and three reeds against each other in call-and-response fashion. This same device can be heard on the Washingtonians' "Georgia Grind." Yet a comparison of Ellington's "Georgia Grind" and Henderson's performance of "Tampeekoe"—recorded a few days later with Redman and the same ten-piece instrumentation—indicates striking differences. The Henderson group sounds like a well-oiled dance machine smoothly turning out a product that gleams with polish. The reed and brass sections play with excellent intonation and limber phrasing. The Washingtonians, on the other hand, seem to be struggling. They appear uncomfortable with the material and their rhythmic feeling is heavy. Perhaps it was the expanded ensemble's first encounter not just with the arrangement but with each other.

Earlier in 1926 "Georgia Grind" had received a slower, more comfortable performance by another studio-formed group in Chicago—Louis Armstrong's Hot Five. Yet Armstrong's musicians shared various experiences playing together and stood on common stylistic ground. The Hot Five version featured several instrumental choruses and vocals by Armstrong and Lil Hardin, the latter sounding the song's basic theme in her second stanza:

> I can shake it east, I can shake it west,
> But way down South I can shake it best

Doin' the Georgia Grind,
Oh that dirty Georgia Grind.

The versions of "Georgia Grind" recorded in August 1926 by the Georgia Strutters (a Perry Bradford group with Bubber Miley) and by Thomas Morris and his Seven Hot Babies (with Rex Stewart on cornet) resemble the Hot Five's performance, with their comic vocal choruses, spontaneous-sounding arrangements, and relaxed, bluesy, "southern" approach to the tune.

The Washingtonians' rendition is altogether different. The tempo is a quick $\downarrow$ = ca. 224. By using double-time, the arranger—either Ellington or Redman—turns Williams's twelve-bar blues into a twenty-four-bar structure. While the title refers to Georgia and the performance features a few stylistic hallmarks of New Orleans (e.g., the lead trumpet in the first chorus with tailgate trombone, and the freer polyphonic interplay of the final chorus), the band's approach to the piece is that of a "dicty" New York outfit.

The introduction sets the general tone, preparing the first theme with a flourish of triplets in the brass and an ascending wind-up phrase for the reeds. This curtain-raising gesture comes back after the piano solo, again with triplets and extended dominant preparation. Other showy features include a modulation before Redman's clarinet solo (to get from E-flat to B-flat) and, as in "I'm Gonna Hang around My Sugar," a slow, "conducted" coda ending with a ninth chord.

As an urban dance-band transformation of Williams's down-home tune, the Washingtonians' arrangement almost succeeds, despite the bad recording balance and the lack of tight ensemble playing. Two solos are notable: Ellington's rousing chorus of Harlem stride (see later in this chapter for discussion) and Hardwick's baritone sax solo, which shows technical facility and some sense of architectural shape. Ultimately, though, "Georgia Grind" resists Ellington's (or Redman's) fancy framework. The performance is too fast to be sensual, the players too nervous-sounding to be convincing. The grittier sounds of the Hot Five or the Georgia Strutters made for a better grind.

Despite the New York (or Washington) overtones in its title, "Parlor Social Stomp"—on the other side of "Georgia Grind"—*is* inspired by the South, specifically the multi-strain, ragtime-derived compositions played by Jelly Roll Morton and King Oliver's Creole Jazz Band. With each main section taking up sixteen bars, the form of Ellington's piece is:

Introduction
A
B
B
A^1
Transition
C   (Trio)
C^1 (trumpet solo)
D   (alto sax)
D^1 (trumpet)
D^2 (clarinet)
C^2 (ensemble)
Coda

In general the band sounds better on the second half of the tune —more relaxed and less at odds with the written arrangement. Some awkwardly executed breaks mar the B section, and Ellington's tricky introduction eludes the group entirely, even though this may have been their sixth attempt to get it right. (Timner lists six takes of the tune, the last of which was issued.)

In "Parlor Social Stomp" the performance problems stem mainly from an uneasy rhythmic relationship between the soloists and the rest of the ensemble. This tension, together with some poor note choices, makes the solo breaks more disruptive than exciting. The rhythm section fares better. Although Ellington can hardly be heard, Greer, Guy, and Edwards—by this time an established unit—work well together. Edwards lends especially strong support with his clipped quarter notes in the last chorus. Guy, too, effectively alternates two and four strums per bar and adds several fluent tremolos.

Less than two weeks after this last Pathé date, on March 30, 1926, Ellington took the same band into a different studio and chose a slightly different musical approach. The setting was the New York office of Gennett at 9-11 East 37th Street, and Ellington's material this time consisted of two pop songs with vocal choruses. Back home in its Richmond, Indiana, headquarters, the Gennett company had issued a number of important jazz recordings, many intended for the "race" market—among them King Oliver's first sides and Jelly Roll Morton's first piano solos, recorded in 1923.

"(You've Got Those) 'Wanna Go Back Again' Blues" (copyright February 16, 1926; E 634547)—the first of the Washingtonians' Gennett sides—is a Tin Pan Alley essay on nostalgia:

> When just a field of grain, shady lane,
> Makes you long for home once again
> You've got those "wanna go back again" blues.
> When swallows in the sky, flying by
> Make you brush a tear from your eye
> You've got those "wanna go back again" blues.

Wistful agrarian fantasies have a long tradition in American popular song, dating back at least to the influence of Thomas Moore's *Irish Melodies* in the early 1800s. Roy Turk and Lou Handman, the composers of " 'Wanna Go Back Again' Blues," do not quote Moore, but they do allude to Stephen Foster's "My Old Kentucky Home" in the bridge: "Altho' the sun shines bright it don't seem to shine for you." While " 'Wanna Go Back Again' Blues" has a cliché-ridden text and a slight tune, the Washingtonians bring to the piece a tongue-in-cheek attitude that saves the performance.

An arrangement of " 'Wanna Go Back Again' Blues" by Bob Haring ("Arranger of 1,000 Song Successes") was published in 1926 by Frank Clark, located at 1587 Broadway (on the corner of West 48th Street, just a block from the Kentucky Club). The title page advertises the tune as a "Novelty Fox-Trot Classic." The Washingtonians seem to be following Haring's version in the fourth chorus: the duo-trumpet break comes directly from the stock, as does the distribution of the tune for brass and reeds. The tag ending is exactly the same. Here, then, they play a heavily edited stock arrangement of a rather ordinary song more likely to appeal to the Broadway dance and theater crowd than to enthusiasts of African-American blues.

The Washingtonians skip the verse and play just four choruses: the first has Hardwick stating the melody on baritone with reed and brass commentary; the second is a paraphrase solo by Irvis on muted trombone (one of the few extended examples where he uses this technique); the third is a vocal by Greer, who sings the wrong

first two lines and then plays unmercifully with the rhythms to create a jarring effect with the accompaniment;[13] the fourth is a reprise
for full band. Only the first and final choruses offer much of the
full ensemble.

In doctoring the stock, Ellington (or whoever else is responsible)
goes for laughs. First the inevitable train whistle sounds in the introduction. Then, after Hardwick's sober first four bars, little tweets
appear in the reeds which develop into a crazy break and a Bronx
cheer from the brass:

Example 34. " 'Wanna Go Back Again' Blues" (April 1, 1926), first chorus,
mm. 5–8.

The humor gets broader when the reeds play a harmonized bugle
reveille against the tune. Despite the corny touches (right down to
the final "wheeee!" of the slide whistle), the band shows more unity
here than in the chaotic, ragged ensembles of the Pathé sides.

"If You Can't Hold the Man You Love (Don't Cry When He's

Gone)" (copyright March 31, 1926; E 635986) is a near-blues, or at least nearer to the real item than " 'Wanna Go Back Again' Blues." The white tunesmiths behind the song were Irving Kahal and Sammy Fain, better known for their later collaboration on "Let a Smile Be Your Umbrella," "Wedding Bells Are Breaking Up That Old Gang of Mine," and "I'll Be Seeing You." In late January 1926 *Phonograph and Talking Machine Weekly* announced that "If You Can't Hold the Man You Love" was "rapidly coming into its own in the popular music world." Next month Ethel Waters released her version of the tune accompanied by composer Fain at the piano.[14] Since Jack Mills published the song, Irving Mills may have pressed it upon Ellington.

Although lighthearted in tone, "If You Can't Hold the Man You Love" gets treated more seriously by Ellington's band than " 'Wanna Go Back Again' Blues." Jimmy Harrison at least acts his part on the vocal chorus, if not sounding fully convinced by the words. There are no humorous effects on the record, but the muted two-trumpet duet in the middle (based on the "patter" section of the published music) would have had some novelty appeal in 1926. As Schuller has pointed out, the duet emulates "the manner of Oliver and Armstrong [on the Creole Jazz Band sides], although it lacks their stylistic grace and precision."[15] Better muted playing can be heard in Irvis's half-chorus solo, especially in the last four bars where he "talks" and growls. And Fred Guy enters the spotlight briefly for eight bars of chordal shakes, slides, and raggy syncopation.

As in " 'Wanna Go Back Again' Blues," the Washingtonians appear to be following a stock in the verse (directly before the vocal) and, more loosely, in the final chorus. (Mills did issue a stock version arranged by Harold Potter in 1926.) The introduction and first chorus, however, were probably arranged for the date by either Ellington or Redman. In the first chorus the brass have a call-and-response with the reeds, using the kind of separation heard on Redman's arrangements for Henderson. Overall this is a fairly straightforward rendition of the tune—gone are the silly effects of " 'Wanna Go Back Again' Blues" and the nervous agitation of "I'm Gonna Hang around My Sugar." The band has settled down, almost to the point of complacency.

The Washingtonians showed more verve when they went back to the Gennett studios on June 21, 1926. Their first song that day was "(I'm Just Wild about) Animal Crackers!" (copyright June 3, 1926; E 641401), a novelty number by the songwriters Harry Link and Sam Coslow and bandleader Freddie Rich. Link worked for the publisher Waterson, Berlin, and Snyder; Sam Coslow described him as the "most successful promotion executive of the radio era," who was responsible for getting leading singers and bands to perform his company's compositions.[16] "Animal Crackers" had already been recorded by the California Ramblers and a Harry Reser group; Gennett probably wanted the Washingtonians to give their own "hot" version of a song already popular.

The Washingtonians' performance of "Animal Crackers" sticks fairly closely to the stock version arranged by Paul Van Loan and published by Waterson, Berlin and Snyder:

Stock (Key of B-flat)	Washingtonians (B-flat)
Introduction	Introduction
Chorus 1 Ensemble	Chorus 1 Ensemble
Chorus 2 Ensemble	Chorus 2 Piano solo/clarinet solo
Verse Ensemble	Verse Ensemble
Chorus 3 Ensemble	Chorus 3 Saxophone solos
(repeat ad lib)	Chorus 4 Trumpet solo
	Chorus 5 Ensemble
Tag	Tag

In the first chorus Ellington assigns the melody not to a saxophone trio, as in the stock, but to the trumpets of Miley and Charlie Johnson. The verse, final chorus, and tag, however, are nearly literal readings of Van Loan's arrangement. In the second, third, and fourth choruses Ellington simply makes room for individual soloists, providing reed backgrounds (drawn from the stock) only in the third chorus. The insertion of two hot solo choruses before the full ensemble reprise brings the arrangement up to the required recording length.

On these early recordings Ellington reveals a fondness for ear-catching introductions that often use surprising harmonic shifts (e.g., the move from D to F at the beginning of "Choo Choo" or the opening chromatic ascent of "If You Can't Hold the Man You

Love"). For "Animal Crackers," Ellington supplies a dramatic series of rising chromatic seventh chords for brass then alters both the harmonies and rhythms of the stock's fourth bar:

Example 35. "Animal Crackers" (June 21, 1926), introduction, mm. 1–5.

But "Animal Crackers" displays few other individual touches. The Washingtonians sound like an average mid-twenties dance band reading a stock. Their performance suffers from unsteady tempos: at the end of Ellington's piano solo, where he gets flustered and throws off Guy and Greer; during the last eight bars of the third chorus (Guy seems the culprit here); and in the last half of Miley's solo, where his rushing pulls along the rhythm section. (Schuller has termed this Miley's "headlong, devil-may-care feeling".[17])

Yet it is hard to complain about Miley. For once again his solo, as on the Blu-Disc records, is the high point of the performance. With his rough tone, blues phrasing, and rhythmic zest, Miley transforms the character of a banal tune. As Ellington has written of the trumpeter: "He was raised on soul and saturated and marinated in soul. Every note he played was soul filled with the pulse of compulsion." [18] The Washingtonians were fortunate to have a trumpet player who could pour such intensity even into a song like "Animal Crackers."

"Animal Crackers" shows Ellington spiking a published stock arrangement with solos and getting his band to sound passably hot. The other side of the record is a different story. In some ways the Washingtonians' performance of "Li'l Farina" resembles "Animal Crackers" because of its similar tempo (again, ♩ = ca. 232), key of B-flat, and structure (choruses for soloists and ensemble, verse inserted in the middle). However, "Li'l Farina" is more than a carbon-copy dance-band arrangement: it is a catalogue of Ellington's various musical influences, showing what he had absorbed as an arranger and bandleader, and hinting at future directions he might take.

"Li'l Farina" (copyright August 3, 1925; E 620240) was named after the urchin character in the *Our Gang* comedies, a series of two-reel silent films begun in 1922. Mercer Ellington has recalled that the films were quite popular in 1926: "We always went to see them; and when I realized [my father] had written a number with that title, it made quite an impression on me."[19] In fact, music publisher and songwriter Harrison Smith claimed authorship of the tune. Smith was the personal manager in 1926 for Allen Hoskins, the black child actor who played the part of "Li'l Farina." Whether or not Smith actually wrote "Li'l Farina"—he may have bought it outright from Ellington—his publishing office was reported as "cleaning up" with copies of the song in November 1926.[20] Smith later reported that the Gennett company considered Ellington's "Li'l Farina" the "hottest" of all their records up to that time, adding that people were amazed at Miley's "wah wah" work and could not understand why he did not "break a blood vessel" producing such sounds.[21] The connection with Li'l Farina had an additional benefit for Ellington, as Smith, in his expansive way, remembered: "Thru co-operation of Pathé Pictures Exploitation Department and 10,000 Gennett dealers—Duke's name became a household one and thru the recording I became Personal Representative of the Band and booked it in leading theatres."[22]

"Li'l Farina" is a bubbly, good-natured tune—although the tune seems less important than the simple chord progression which allows for comfortable soloing. Both the melody statements and solos are filled with variations on the ♩♩♩♪ rhythm. As Schuller has noted, this was a rhythmic pattern favored by Louis Armstrong in his recordings of 1924 and 1925 with Fletcher Henderson, the Clarence Williams Blue Five, and other groups. By 1926 the Armstrong influence could be heard in many trumpeters and bands. Miley's solo on "Li'l Farina" provides evidence of a stylistic connection, as does that of Joe Nanton, the new trombonist (see chapter 10). This becomes apparent in comparing them with a representative Armstrong solo from a few years earlier:

Example 36. "Go 'long Mule," Fletcher Henderson and his Orchestra (October 7, 1924), Louis Armstrong solo, mm. 1–8; "Li'l Farina" (June 21, 1926), beginning of solos by Joe Nanton and Bubber Miley.

Another Armstrong characteristic—the upward rip to a note—can be heard in a break for three saxophones (third chorus, m. 19). The Charleston rhythm present in previous Ellington arrangements is absent from "Li'l Farina." The band still has problems with rushing during Miley's solo and Robinson's tenor sax break, but overall, the more relaxed, rolling gait is an improvement over the stiffness of "Animal Crackers."

A second prominent influence in "Li'l Farina" is Don Redman, particularly his arrangements for the Fletcher Henderson band in the mid-twenties. Although Redman did not play on this date, as he had on the Washingtonians' two previous sessions for Pathé and Gennett, echoes of his style are heard in the riffs behind the clarinet solo in the first chorus, in the reed and brass separation of the fourth chorus, and in some of the ensemble breaks, like the whole-tone flourish for saxophones (third chorus, mm. 15–16). These features, like the ones mentioned above for Armstrong, were by no means Redman's alone. Many arrangers picked up such devices and many bands played them. Yet Redman was a natural figure for Ellington to emulate. A year younger than Ellington, he had developed both faster and further. His arrangements had helped make Fletcher Henderson's ensemble the most successful black band in New York. Ellington later wrote warmly of Redman, calling him "a forerunner, a wonderful writer and arranger," and admitting that when he first formed a big band in New York he wanted it to sound like Henderson's. [23]

Ellington had been interested in dramatic presentation since childhood. In New York he used to go with Sonny Greer to the Capitol Theater and study what the pit musicians were playing. Like other early sides by the Washingtonians', "Li'l Farina" begins with a flashy introduction. The band quotes the chorus of "Bon-Bon Buddy" (1907), written by Will Marion Cook and Alex Rogers and featured by George Walker in the 1908 Williams and Walker show, *Bandanna Land*. [24] The line of the song quoted—"Bon Bon Buddy the chocolate drop"—refers here to Li'l Farina. It is punctuated by military drum rolls from Greer. Then a chromatic waterfall of seventh chords brings the reeds smoothly down to F^7, preparing Nanton's solo entrance (see Example 37). A different kind of theatrical touch comes in the transition to the verse, after two thirty-two-bar solo choruses. Here the scene abruptly changes from Miley's torrid half-chorus solo to a sweet interlude for reeds beginning on $^\flat VI$ which quotes another song about a small boy—Ethelbert Nevin's "Mighty Lak a Rose" (1901)—and which suggests a modulation to D major before returning to B-flat (see Example 38). In this section one detects a trace of the symphonic jazz style which was favored by arrangers like Ferde Grofé and Bill Challis, and which

Ellington might have heard played by Whiteman or one of his followers, such as Sam Wooding. It is interesting to hear Ellington's
three reeds and single trombone bring off the effect and manage to
sound like a larger band.

Example 37. "Li'l Farina," introduction.

*Either Ellington does not play here, or his part is inaudible.

At least two other stylistic ingredients go into the "Li'l Farina" concoction. The last chorus features the reeds improvising in a quasi–New Orleans fashion behind the harmonized tune for brass, pushing through to the two-bar tag. Here are no tricky New York rhythms or effects, just a joyful Crescent City parade to the finish line. Also, Nanton and Miley growl during their solos, producing

Example 38. "Li'l Farina," transition to verse.

snarling effects with their mutes and throaty vocalizing. Ellington later acknowledged that these two brass players "founded a tradition we have maintained ever since."[25] In "Li'l Farina" one hears the roots of that tradition, before Ellington's imagination had fully grasped its meaning for orchestration.

"Li'l Farina," then, forms a map of influences: Louis Armstrong, Don Redman, Fletcher Henderson, Paul Whiteman, black musical theater, popular song, New Orleans, "jungle" brass. Where, in all of this, is Ellington?

He stands behind the scenes, plotting the sequence of events and directing the abrupt changes of mood from dramatic to hot, from sweet to stomping. The Ellington sound is taking shape in the chromatic tinge of the introduction, the ♭VI modulation in the middle, and in the fine blend of brass with their "wah" punctuations in the third chorus. In "Li'l Farina" Ellington emerges as someone who has absorbed much of the music around him, who can integrate diverse elements, and who demonstrates a strong hand both in ordering the arrangement and getting results from his musicians. In subsequent record sessions his strength would increase, and the influences would fuse more and more into something uniquely his own.

Critics have not always looked kindly on the Washingtonians' early recordings. In light of what Ellington achieved in 1927 and after, his first efforts in the studio have seemed slight. Peter Gammond, for one, has complained that the Washingtonians sound like a white band, that their arrangements show no signs of Ellington's "bold orchestration," and that the records from 1924 to 1926 are of "shady historical interest," giving "a tantalizing display of negative qualitites, of a magic that was not there." [26] Others have been less severe than puzzled, as when Gary Giddins admitted, "[It's] impossible to explain how Ellington progressed from these inauspicious beginnings to his first milestones, recorded in November of 1926 and 1927." [27] And in concluding his analysis of these recordings in *Early Jazz,* Gunther Schuller wrote: "We find rather ordinary material, a modicum of organization, one lovely tune ["Choo Choo"], and two fine Miley solos ["Choo Choo" and "Animal Crackers"]. . . . They certainly do not stand up in comparison to such contemporary masterpieces of both orchestration and formal structure as Jelly Roll Morton's *Black Bottom Stomp* [September 1926] or King Oliver's recording of *Froggie Moore* [April 1923]." [28]

But several factors must be considered when measuring the Washingtonians against their contemporaries or comparing Ellington's early efforts in the studio to his later achievements. First, as Schuller acknowledged, Ellington was considerably younger than either Morton or Oliver, thus his professional experience was more limited. Morton, for example, had over a dozen recording sessions behind him when he made "Black Bottom Stomp" with his Red Hot Peppers in 1926. And by April 6, 1923, the date of the first Creole Jazz Band session, Oliver (born in 1885) had been a performing musician for nearly as many years as Ellington had been alive. Second, as a working band the Washingtonians were only scantily represented on disc between November 1924 and June 1926. Out of five sessions for three different companies, at least two (March and April 1926) featured an expanded group. The lack of ensemble unity on these sides may have stemmed in part from the addition of extra players, from inadequate rehearsal, and from the absence of Bubber Miley (also missing from the September 1925 date). By contrast, Oliver, Morton, and Henderson often recorded with bands that performed together regularly.

The key factor, however, was the music recorded by Ellington. Nine of the ten early sides were pop songs in which the band mostly followed written parts or a set routine. The remaining instrumental by Ellington, "Parlor Social Stomp," was a pre-planned arrangement that offered individual players little freedom—or at least they chose not to exercise that freedom. Pieces like "I'm Gonna Hang around My Sugar," " 'Wanna Go Back Again' Blues," and "Animal Crackers" provided Ellington with few opportunities to show off his band. Besides, that may not have been the object: the record dates may have been set up by publishers (e.g., Mills, or Waterson, Berlin, and Snyder) as a way of promoting recent songs in their catalogs. If the Washingtonians had been better readers, like Fletcher Henderson's musicians, the results might have been more impressive. But Ellington did not have this kind of ensemble. His was a group accustomed to regular rehearsals, during which arrangements were worked out collectively and, for the most part, orally. Given a choice, Ellington probably would have recorded pieces his group played more often and cared more about.

To be sure, the first ten sides by the Washingtonians display rhythmic problems, poorly executed breaks and introductions, also cluttered and muddy textures. But Ellington had his hands full. Unlike Fletcher Henderson, he had no Don Redman on staff to arrange for him. He was just learning how to balance composing with leading the band, playing piano, and dealing with record companies. Under the circumstances, perhaps we should concentrate on what these records *do* reveal: a moderately accomplished dance band with one outstanding voice (Miley), three talented soloists (Hardwick, Irvis, Ellington), a good rhythm section, and a leader-arranger who was gaining in confidence and ability. Ellington was, as Martin Williams has suggested, "on the right track." [29]

Ellington as Accompanist

In the mid-twenties, when Ellington made his first recordings with the Washingtonians, it was common for blues and cabaret singers to go into the studio and record sides intended for what was called the "race" market. These events were informal and had little or no advance preparation. Sometimes the record companies used a back-up band of five or six pieces; otherwise they simply hired a pianist and perhaps a horn player. The material tended to be either twelve-bar blues or syncopated pop songs that were made to sound like blues. Such sessions were aimed at selling not just records but sheet music. In this way, black songwriters like Perry Bradford, Clarence Williams, Spencer Williams, Porter Grainger, Maceo Pinkard, and Jo Trent had an outlet for their wares, as did their white imitators (e.g., Irving Kahal and Sammy Fain in "If You Can't Hold the Man You Love").

Between November 1924 and October 1926 Ellington appeared on eight sides as an accompanist. This was a low number compared to a bandleader like Fletcher Henderson. But Henderson's earlier experience accompanying singers and plugging songs for Harry Pace and W. C. Handy made him better known. Ellington was not entirely lacking in such experience. At the Kentucky Club he and his band accompanied singers with some frequency, just as they had done at Barron's and before that at Louis Thomas's Oriental Gardens in Washington. And at the offices of Fred Fisher and other publishers, Ellington must have spent hours trying out new songs with singers. Even so, in his first three years in New York he was not in great demand as an accompanist.

Two of Ellington's horn players, however, Bubber Miley and Charlie Irvis, were in demand. They appeared on many blues dates in the early and mid-twenties, backing singers Eva Taylor, Sara Martin, Monette Moore, and others.[30] Yet Ellington did not use either of them on the vocal sides he accompanied. Instead he turned to his old friend from Washington, Otto Hardwick. Having a saxophone serve as a foil for a singer was not unheard of, but it was less common than trumpet or trombone. Hardwick seemed comfortable in the role. His slurred phrasing and fluid style worked well for the blues and blues-derived repertory.

Ellington never recorded with the big blues stars. His singers were lesser lights in their time; today they are obscure. He accompanied two Albertas—Prime and Jones—but not Alberta Hunter (at least not in the studio). He and Hardwick helped Florence Bristol make her first record; it was also her last. In 1926 the same team may have backed cabaret singer Zaidee Jackson on two sides that Gennett never released. But Ellington did accompany one singer, Irving Mills, who would soon prove a valuable contact.

The Washingtonians' first successful record date in November 1924 yielded five vocal sides. Four came out on the Blu-Disc label and one was issued by its subsidiary, Up-to-Date. Ellington scholar Jerry Valburn, among others, believes that all the November 1924 sides—both vocals and instrumentals—come from one session, possibly two. Until more information surfaces about Blu-Disc (i.e., studio logs, business records), this assumption will stand.

Alberta Prime filled two sides of a Blu-Disc record with "It's Gonna Be a Cold, Cold Winter" and "Parlor Social De Luxe." (This is her only known recording.) Like the better-known "Bricktop," Prime was a cabaret singer who ran her own clubs and performed in them. In 1925 *Variety* announced that she was opening "a new colored club at 60th Street and Broadway" with "four principals in the floor show and a chorus of six girls."[31] Judging from these two sides, she did not have much of a voice. Garvin Bushell has remembered her more as a great beauty than a great singer.[32] Such extramusical appeal may have led to her Blu-Disc date with Ellington.

"It's Gonna Be a Cold, Cold Winter" (copyright October 17, 1924; E 600653) was written by Porter Grainger and Jo Trent. After Ellington's introduction and vamp, Prime sings the verse (16 bars), chorus (24 bars), patter section (16 bars), and repeats the chorus. Ellington provides the sole support on piano and clucks "Poor thing!" during the patter section in mock sympathy with the singer's tale of hardship. Ellington gives Prime a full-bodied accompaniment with rolled tenths in the left hand and octaves and melody doublings in the right. He ends the record with a sudden outburst of energetic Harlem stride.

Sonny Greer joins Prime and Ellington on "Parlor Social De Luxe," which is credited to Trent and Ellington. The record label, in fact, simply lists the performers as "Alberta Prime and Sonny Greer." The smooth-talking drummer banters with Prime and goes through a studio reenactment of a Saturday night rent party, accompanied by Ellington's hard-driving piano and by police whistles and gun shots. It sounds like an impromptu performance. After the middle section, for example, where all hell breaks loose ("Help! Help! Murder!"), Greer is supposed to enter at the chorus but, unsure of the key, comes in too low and has to scoop upwards to reach the right pitch. Although of slight musical value, the performance has an air of authenticity about it. And Ellington can be heard playing various styles to good advantage: down-in-the-alley blues, pop song accompaniment, and galloping stride. Years later he would look back on the record as one of the first "happenings"—an early example of "theater of the absurd."[33]

Jo Trent had a hand in writing both Alberta Prime's songs and the Washingtonians' "Rainy Nights." He also attended the 1924 Blu-Disc date, singing "Deacon Jazz," one of his own pieces, backed by Greer, George Francis on banjo, and co-composer Ellington. Trent's vocal performance shows more enthusiasm than technique. He sounds like a composer belting out his own tune, and indeed, the record primarily served to plug the song. Trent talks through the verse and sings the chorus only once. The rest of the record is given over to instrumental solos based on the chorus.

If Greer is playing drums on "Deacon Jazz," he is buried by the poor sound quality. On the other side of the record, however, he steps front and center for a vocal feature on Harry Woods and Edgar Leslie's "Oh How I Love My Darling" (copyright November 10, 1924; E 601195). This Tin Pan Alley comedy number was published in 1924 by Clarke and Leslie (1591 Broadway) and recorded by several white bands that November, among them the Ambassadors (with Phil Napoleon and Miff Mole) and the Goofus Five (with Adrian Rollini). The Blu-Disc version by "Sunny and the D C'ns" was probably trying to cash in on a song of the moment. Such material circulated rapidly in the cabarets and restaurants of Times Square. The sheet music offered text for fifteen extra choruses, but supposedly Eddie Cantor sang ninety-six![34] Greer includes only one extra chorus (the fifth in the published version):

> I kiss her once, I kiss her twice
> Oh! How I love my darling.
> When I run short, and need a quart
> I get it from my darling.
> She's very lovely every time that we meet
> But she's so cross-eyed when she comes down the street
> She looks at you, then kisses me
> Oh! How I love my darling.

Greer's vocal delivery gives a good idea of how the "Sweet Singing Drummer" entertained Kentucky Club patrons after-hours. His style here has none of the black speech inflections of "Parlor Social De Luxe" but owes more to white entertainers like Jolson and Durante in its broad vowels ("Dahh-ling"), clipped consonants, and nasal tone. The band seems more confident with "Oh How I Love My Darling" than with "Deacon Jazz." Perhaps the song was more familiar.

Ellington's final vocal accompaniment from November 1924 was "How Come You Do Me Like You Do?" (copyright March 31, 1924; E 587204), a song by Gene Austin and Roy Bergere. It was released on Up-to-Date (one of the few records by this Blu-Disc subsidiary ever found). Ellington and Hardwick back Florence Bristol singing the tune. Bristol is not known to have recorded any other sides; she was probably a cabaret singer and perhaps appeared at the Kentucky Club. "How Come You Do Me Like You Do?" was popular in 1924. That spring the blues singers Viola McCoy and Rosa Henderson had recorded the song, and many bands followed later, among them the Original Memphis Five (September), Fletcher Henderson (November), and the Tennessee Tooters, a Red Nichols group (January 1925).

"How Come You Do Me Like You Do?" has a fairly typical structure: instrumental introduction and vamp; verse (in twelve-bar blues form); first vocal chorus; patter section; saxophone chorus; second vocal chorus; four-bar instrumental tag. The main interest is provided not by Bristol—who, on this record at least, proves to be a minor talent—but by Ellington and Hardwick. In the verse Ellington knocks out a rhythm— ♩ ⁊♪♩ ⁊♪|♩ ⁊♪♩ —that underlines the text ("Early this morning I come rappin' at your door"), then falls easily into a rolling accompaniment for the chorus, connecting phrases with eighth-note triplet sixths in the right hand. Hardwick, meanwhile, doubles and embellishes the melody an octave higher. But the high point comes in the saxophone solo after the patter section. Ellington varies the right-hand accompaniment figures every few bars while Hardwick paraphrases the melody using a rich tone and expressive slurs. In the bridge Ellington traverses the keyboard with fourths and single-notes before making a fast arpeggio that starts on a B^{o7} but higher up adds an A^{bmi6}:

Example 39. "How Come You Do Me Like You Do?" (November 1924), saxophone solo, mm. 11–12.

*Should be D♮?

Although somewhat out of place in the tune, Ellington's arpeggio shows that he commanded a certain degree of pianistic technique and that his harmonic thinking was not limited to the simple chord structures of the song.

"How Come You Do Me Like You Do?" is a pop song by two white writers trying to imitate black speech and musical conventions. On the other side of this Up-to-Date release is twenty-six-year-old Paul Robeson, accompanied by William Jones, performing "Since You Went Away," a gentle ballad by J. Rosamond Johnson. The striking contrast between the two songs and their singers—the raucous Bristol and the dignified Robeson—points up the broad musical territory covered by the "race record" category. [35]

After the November 1924 sides, two years passed before Hardwick and Ellington again accompanied a singer in the studio. However, in the summer of 1925 Ellington did participate in a session for Gennett with song-plugger and publishing representative Irving Mills; only a test pressing was made. Mills and Jimmy McHugh were responsible for "Eveything Is Hotsy Totsy Now," a light novelty number which was, by early May, "taking first place as the plug song of Jack Mills—mechanical releases by end of month will be 100 per cent—both instrumental and vocal versions will be released." [36] In fact, the California Ramblers had recorded the tune in April, and both the Original Indiana Five and Herb Wiedoft put out versions the next month. By August Jack Mills was running a big ad for the song in *Billboard* and by September *Variety* was referring to it as a "current dance favorite."[37]

It is not hard to see why "Eveything Is Hotsy Totsy Now" caught on. Full of word-play and repetition, the song is as contagious as a child's nursery rhyme:

> 'Cause I got myself a brand new hotsy,
> I'm her totsy and she's my hotsy,
> Everything is hotsy totsy now.
> And when we spoon she don't say stop-sy,
> Don't call Mom-sy or her Pop-sy
> Everything is Hotsy Totsy now.

On the Gennett performance, Mills is ever the exuberant song-plugger selling his wares; he steers wide of nuances or dynamics and cuts loose with his kazoo both in the introduction and half-way through Ellington's piano chorus. Ellington seems reasonably familiar with the song, although when Mills puts down his kazoo and starts singing again the pianist momentarily loses his way.

After making four sides for Gennett in April and June 1926, Ellington returned with Hardwick to the studio October 14 to accompany blues singer Alberta Jones. The session produced two songs by Jones and "the Ellington Twins": "Lucky Number Blues" (copyright September 29, 1926; E 648692) by Morris Eisenberg and Robert W. Phipps; and "I'm Gonna Put You Right in Jail" (copyright November 12, 1926; E 651633) by Lucky Johnson. Unlike Alberta Prime and Florence Bristol, Jones already had some reputation as a blues singer, having recorded two sides for Gennett in 1925 and three earlier in 1926. Of the early singers Ellington accompanied, Jones was the best. Her voice was expressive and her delivery sincere.

Both songs recorded by Jones are medium-slow in tempo, in B-flat, and simple enough to put the two instrumentalists at ease. Hardwick gets a half-chorus on "Lucky Number Blues" and a full one on "I'm Gonna Put You Right in Jail." Ellington's accompaniment is subdued on both sides, yet sympathetic with both singer and saxophonist. In the last chorus of "I'm Gonna Put You Right in Jail" he decorates the melody high in the treble (mm. 1–4) before filling out the phrase with a well-played trill and accented release.

On "Lucky Number Blues" he develops a tenor-range counter-melody (mm. 4–8) during Hardwick's solo which—like his imitation trombone break on the last chorus of "Everything Is Hotsy Totsy Now"—shows him using the piano orchestrally.

Throughout these sides Ellington displays little enthusiasm as a blues accompanist. Despite some high points, his performances are uneven and do not show the same growth as in his band's early recordings. Perhaps his mother's long-standing disapproval of the blues kept him at a distance from the idiom. Or perhaps he was simply more intrigued with the technical challenges and opportunities for display offered by ragtime than with the subtler art of vocal accompaniment. Whatever the reason, Ellington makes a stronger impression when the spotlight falls on him and him alone.

Ellington as Soloist

In later years with his orchestra, one of Ellington's favorite devices was to open a concert by introducing "our new, young apprentice piano player." After waiting a moment for this fellow to make his entrance, Ellington himself would walk to the piano and begin playing.[38] Ellington's stage manner was filled with such wry pokes at himself, and he frequently made mildly disparaging comments about his keyboard ability. When playing "Soda Fountain Rag," for example, he always broke off after a chorus or two, claiming that his first composition was "too hard." On the 1937 solo "Swing Session" he told the radio announcer, "I'll do [it first] so I won't forget the mistakes." Ellington's attitude served as a reversible coat: on one side modesty, on the other, defensiveness. For as the years passed and Ellington increasingly devoted more time and energy to writing music, he realized that certain aspects of his solo keyboard technique had slipped. Or, as he admitted to a 1972 Whitney Museum audience after a rough version of "Soda Fountain Rag," "Things ain't what they used to be." Ellington's early keyboard heroes were Luckey Roberts, James P. Johnson, and Willie "the Lion" Smith. Whenever he played Harlem stride, he remembered their prowess and remained in his mind's eye an apprentice.

Ellington always featured the piano in his band. He did not begin to give solo recitals until 1961, and even then they were infrequent. However, he made his first solo-piano recordings in 1928 for OKeh:

"Black Beauty" and "Swampy River." The former is a beautiful, blues-tinged tribute to Florence Mills, the latter another original composition that shares some traits (especially chromaticism and ninth chords) with "In a Mist," Bix Beiderbecke's piano piece of the same year. Before these two solo outings, however, it is possible to gain perspective on Ellington's pianistic ability from the records he made between 1924 and 1926. By this time Ellington had been a serious student of the instrument for nearly ten years, from his initial inspiration after hearing Harvey Brooks through his days as a Washington "piano plunker" and his New York experiences with various lions of the keyboard. His earliest recordings show him to be a pianist with a firm foundation in the stride style most closely associated with James P. Johnson and his student Thomas "Fats" Waller.

Of the eighteen sides Ellington recorded with various singers and the Washingtonians between November 1924 and October 1926, seven have piano solos: "Deacon Jazz," "Oh How I Love My Darling," "Parlor Social De Luxe," "I'm Gonna Hang around My Sugar," "Everything Is Hotsy Totsy Now," "Georgia Grind," and "Animal Crackers." In all of them Ellington draws upon the techniques of stride. He often builds his solos around the melody, embellishing it as he goes ("Animal Crackers," last half of "Deacon Jazz") or returning to it at the end of phrases ("Everything Is Hotsy Totsy Now"). At the beginning of the "Deacon Jazz" solo he touches on the tune in m. 1 then leaves it for the next sixteen bars. He gets off to a strong start, but at m. 13 his left hand begins to work against him (hence it is not included in the transcription below):

Example 40. "Deacon Jazz" (November 1924), piano solo, beginning.

*Should be:

His left hand remains shaky through the bridge and full recovery occurs only in the last eight bars. Of course, one could attribute the mistakes to nervousness; but other recordings show a similar weakness in Ellington's left hand, whereas his right hand always performs with greater assurance.

For overall conception and execution, Ellington's solo on "Georgia Grind" stands out from the rest. Instead of just stringing together standard stride devices Ellington achieves a sense of development over the course of twenty bars. He begins by decorating the melody, keeping its 2 + 2 phrase structure. Toward the end of the first eight bars he plays a figure that he uses as a beginning for the next section. Then he adds variety with a swift upward run which, like the preceding phrase, is played twice. To end he sweeps up and down with a wide-spanning arpeggio to prepare the band's entrance (humming as he goes):

Example 41. "Georgia Grind" (March 1926), piano solo.

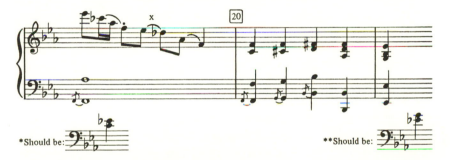

*Should be: **Should be:

Throughout this solo Ellington's rhythm is secure and his technique accurate (except for the final descending arpeggio). This is not, as Schuller has termed it, "very sloppy, helter-skelter sort of piano," but the work of a musician in control.[39]

The "Deacon Jazz" solo excerpt that appears above shows a rhythmic device of three-in-four (mm. 9–12) often used by Ellington and other stride pianists and later known as "secondary ragtime."[40] It also appears in Ellington's "Everything Is Hotsy Totsy Now" solo (although here it might come directly from the song's bridge, which features the same effect). Other recurring characteristics in his playing are left-hand tenths ("I'm Gonna Hang around My Sugar") and alternating right-hand thirds ("Deacon Jazz," "I'm Gonna Hang around My Sugar," "Animal Crackers"). The middle section of "Parlor Social De Luxe" is filled with Harlem piano

effects: broken tenths and walking octaves in the left hand, chromatic sequences, repeated treble riffs, and a type of right-hand
voicing found in the playing of James P. Johnson and Waller but also
prominent in the later work of another pianist who was absorbing
the same influences, William "Count" Basie:

Example 42. "Parlor Social De Luxe" (November 1924), middle section.

Johnson and Waller were only two of many pianists Ellington
heard and learned from. If their names dominate discussions of
1920s stride, it reflects not just superior ability but a lack of recordings by other players. Willie "the Lion" Smith, for example, cannot
be heard on recordings as a solo pianist until 1944; other legendary New York figures, like "Abba Labba" (Richard McLean) and
"The Beetle" (Stephen Henderson), did not record at all. However,
on the basis of the Lion's later recordings, few of his characteristics turn up in Ellington's early solos. (By contrast, the opening of
"Swampy River" in 1928 *does* sound Lion-esque.) Ellington occasionally employs devices not associated with the Johnson-Waller
axis. On the bridge of "Oh How I Love My Darling" he takes a
chime-like parallel-hand run down the keyboard and sticks with
the idea for eight bars. And on "Everything Is Hotsy Totsy Now"
he inserts two "trombone" breaks in the spirit (if not style) of Jelly
Roll Morton.

In his mid-twenties, Ellington was a capable pianist. Borrowing
much of his idiom from others, he had not yet developed a distinctive keyboard persona. But his talent was authentic, and his
intentions—as his solos demonstrate—were serious.

10

On Tour in New England

JULY–AUGUST 1926

In early July of 1926 Ellington and his Washingtonians left the hot streets of Manhattan and headed for New England. When the mercury climbed, the city slowed down. Throngs of New Yorkers fled to their favorite beaches and shore resorts, and the dance bands followed. Asbury Park and Atlantic City, both nearby in New Jersey, offered many musicians stable jobs from June through August. But in New England a band could travel from one ballroom to the next and find audiences everywhere it went, along the coast from Connecticut to Maine and inland from Massachusetts mill towns to New Hampshire lakeside hotels.

The man responsible for bringing Ellington to New England was Charles Shribman, an entrepreneur who owned the Charleshurst Ballroom in his hometown of Salem, Massachusetts. Shribman also managed the Mal Hallett Orchestra, a white group popular locally, and carried on an active band-booking business with his brother Sy. The Shribmans began bringing New York bands into New England ballrooms in the early twenties. In 1924 they joined with other ballroom managers in Massachusetts, Rhode Island, Connecticut, and Maine to form a circuit that featured "traveling crack orchestras in their dance halls through the warmer months as a business booster."[1] On this circuit, a band might set up headquarters in one town, travel to play one-nighters in other dance halls within driving distance, and repeat the sequence for a period of weeks. Summer was the main season for the ballroom circuits—"from Decoration

Day to Labor Day," as Sonny Greer remembered.[2] But bands visited at other times as well. Before his 1926 summer tour Ellington had already made several trips to New England.

The Washingtonians' first visit to the region had been in April 1924, when Charles Shribman needed a band in Salem. He learned that Ellington and his group were available and offered them the job.[3] On Easter Monday the Washingtonians were playing not for Broadway booze-hounds but for members of Salem's Young Men's Christian Temperance Society. Even though the band had yet to make a single record, it was billed as "Duke Ellington's Broadway Recording Orchestra."[4] The Washingtonians also appeared in Boston and in Lynn, Massachusetts, on a vaudeville bill at the Waldorf Theater. An article about the Waldorf engagement explained why the musicians were not at their usual job in New York:

> Real jazz music, the lively, tuneful, up-to-the-minute kind that is now at the height of its popularity in the restaurants along Broadway, will be the principal attraction at the Waldorf, Sunday afternoon and evening, presented by Duke Ellington's Hollywood Cafe Jazz Orchestra which has been filling a week's engagement in Boston since its own cafe was destroyed by fire. There are eight musicians in the act, each an expert soloist, and Sundays last summer played at the New York Winter Garden shows. Three other high class vaudeville acts, music by the Waldorf's own orchestra and "Storm Swept" for a feature picture will also be on the Sunday program.[5]

The next day—perhaps trying to attract an audience for Ellington's upcoming appearance—the *Salem Evening News* reported that the Washingtonians' visit to the Waldorf had been "the biggest sensation in the history of the theatre."[6] On Friday, April 25, Ellington held forth at Salem's College Inn, sharing the bandstand with Frank Ward, who was said to lead the "best orchestra in Boston."[7] The group went back to New York on Saturday.

Another fire at 49th and Broadway in the winter of 1925 freed the Washingtonians for a return engagement in New England. This time Shribman hired Ellington to take the place of Mal Hallett in Haverhill, Massachusetts, a town not far from Salem, near the New Hampshire border:

Mal Hallett to Introduce Orchestra New to City

Mal Hallett announced today that on Wednesday night at City Hall, he will introduce Duke Ellington and his Washingtonians, who will appear here for a few engagements while Mr. Hallett is fulfilling his contract in New York City.

The Washingtonians, who come direct from the Cinderella ball room on Broadway, have gained a nation-wide reputation during the past year that they have been featured by the Triangle and Blue Disc Record Company. They are one of the few colored orchestras that have made themselves popular on Broadway and this is no doubt due to the fact that they play the real southern style of jazz music. [8]

Once again Shribman inflated the reputation of Ellington's band, billing it as the "Cinderella Orchestra," those "Famous Recording Artists" who were "playing nightly with Paul Whiteman and Vincent Lopez on Broadway." [9] The Washingtonians seem to have been a success in Haverhill. They stayed on into early February and were "acclaimed by the audience at City Hall . . . as the equal of Mal Hallett." [10] Later the band returned to Haverhill a half-dozen times from March through July. [11]

When the Washingtonians traveled to Haverhill in 1925, they may have played other ballrooms in the area, even though newspapers did not record their appearances. A 1927 article in the *New York Tribune* mentioned a four-week New England tour in 1925 that came to "an abrupt end" when the band had to return to New York and fulfill a contract at the "Hollywood Inn" (although the place had re-opened that year as the Kentucky Club). According to the *Tribune* reporter, Ellington's group had roused New England dancers in a way that other orchestras—Paul Whiteman, Vincent Lopez, Ross Gorman, Coon-Sanders—had not: "[Their] entertainment was marvelous. They pounded out number after number that left the dancers standing firm on the floor, applauding, refusing to move, stamping their feet, screaming, practically demanding an encore, then another—and then—just one more. It required but one booking for the manager to ascertain that the dancers craved their music." [12]

By the summer of 1926, when the Washingtonians returned to New England for another tour, they had already made a name for themselves on local bandstands. They began the season with a July 12 appearance at Nuttings-on-the-Charles, a Shribman-owned ballroom in Waltham, Massachusetts. Advance publicity in the *Boston Post* hailed the band as "The Paul Whiteman of Colored Orchestras" and even singled out the star soloist: "This is positively the original band with that hot trumpet player (Bub) Miley . . . [known] all over America as the hottest Band on Broadway."[13]

Shribman arranged for the musicians to stay in Salem, which became their headquarters for the next five weeks. There the Washingtonians must have been something of an oddity. Unlike nearby Boston, Salem had few black residents. Quiet and proper, the town hardly seemed like a place that would appeal to fast-moving jazzmen from New York. But apparently Ellington and his band fit right in. They lived at the New Brunswick Hotel and got along well with the townspeople. Ellington became friendly with a police lieutenant who later became Salem's mayor.[14] When not in transit to the next job, the musicians enjoyed the fresh salt air, boat rides on the harbor, delicious fish dinners, and good-natured fun. Harry Carney, a sixteen-year-old saxophonist from Boston who occasionally played with the Washingtonians that summer, would later remember a prank pulled on him in Salem. After his fellow musicians had directed him to a house where he might have a romantic encounter, Carney found no willing woman but an angry man waving a pistol and accusing Carney of fooling with his wife. Carney ran for his life, hurried along by gunshots fired by the Salem police (who were cooperating with the practical jokers). For a black musician newly arrived in a nearly all-white town, such an episode must have been frightening.[15]

Most Tuesday nights the Washingtonians played in Salem's Charleshurst Ballroom. The Charleshurst was at Salem Willows, the town's summer recreation area located at the end of Salem Neck, a point of land that juts into the harbor; Beverly lies to the north, Marblehead to the south. In the twenties, Salem Willows was a thriving resort. People came for swimming, sailing, and picnics. The amusement center had a bowling alley, a pool hall (owned by the Shribmans), a shooting gallery, and a ride called the Whip. At night there were dances at the Charleshurst and the Willows Casino, and on Sundays local bands gave concerts in the pavilion.

Today most of the old buildings have vanished. The circular structure that once housed Brown's Electric Flying Horses (an elaborate carousel) is now used by a popcorn merchant. The Charleshurst Ballroom is gone, although the Willows Casino (with a new brick facade) still sits on the corner of Fort Avenue and Bayview Street. A few things have not changed. Now, as then, a cool breeze blows off the water and provides relief from the summer heat. And the stately old willows stand undisturbed, their branches gently rustling in the wind.

With Salem as their home base, the Washingtonians traveled to other New England dance halls (see itinerary, figure l). The Shribman publicity machine churned out enthusiastic press-releases for the newspapers, calling Ellington's group "The Hottest Band Boston Has Ever Heard" and "The Biggest Dance Sensation in Years."[16] Ads appeared for Duke Ellington and "his Washingtonians," or "his Serenaders," or "his Famous Orchestra." In Maine a paper announced the imminent arrival of "Luke Ellington and his Plantation Orchestra."[17]

Figure 1. Itinerary for the Washingtonians' 1926
Summer Tour of New England

DATE		PLACE	SOURCE
July	12 M	Nuttings-on-the-Charles, Waltham, Mass.	BP
	13 T	Charleshurst Ballroom, Salem, Mass.	SEN
	14 W	Arcadia, Gardner, Mass.	FS
	15 Th	Highland Park, Brockton, Mass.	BrPH
	16 F	Lincoln Park, Fall River, Mass.	FRHN
	17 Sa	Mohegan, Worcester, Mass.	WEG
	19 M	Nuttings-on-the-Charles, Waltham, Mass.	BP
	20 T	Charleshurst Ballroom, Salem, Mass.	SEN
	21 W	Crescent Gardens, Revere Beach, Mass.	SEN
	23 F	Roseland, Lawrence, Mass.	LS
	24 Sa	Arcadia, Gardner, Mass.	FS
	27 T	Commodore Ballroom, Lowell, Mass.	LS
	29 Th	Oakland Beach, Cranston, R.I.	PJ
	31 Sa	Charleshurst Ballroom, Salem, Mass.	BP
August	2 M	Nuttings-on-the-Charles, Waltham, Mass.	BP
	3 T	Charleshurst Ballroom, Salem, Mass.	SEN
	4 W	Fieldston, Marshfield, Mass.	BrPH
	5 Th	Miami Ballroom, Woonsocket, R.I.	PJ

6 F	Wilbur's, Somerset, Mass.	PJ
7 Sa	Mohegan, Worcester, Mass.	WEG
10 T	Charleshurst Ballroom, Salem, Mass.	SEN
12 Th	Old Orchard Pier, Old Orchard, Me.	PPH
13 F	Moseley's-on-the-Charles, Dedham, Mass.	BP
?	Orchard Beach, N.Y.	MM

Key to Sources:

BP	*Boston Post*		MM	*Music Is My Mistress*
BrPH	*Brockton Post Herald*		PJ	*Providence Journal*
FRHN	*Fall River Herald News*		PPH	*Portland Press Herald*
FS	*Fitchburg Sentinel*		SEN	*Salem Evening News*
LS	*Lowell Sun*		WEG	*Worcester Evening Gazette*

NOTE: The above list represents all known dates advertised in nine regional newspapers. Further research might yield information about other dates, although not every appearance by the Washingtonians may have been announced in the local press. The band was probably playing six or seven nights a week.

Other newspapers were searched that yielded no dates for the summer of 1926. They include: *Haverhill Gazette, Lawrence Evening Tribune, Lynn Daily Evening Item, Taunton Daily Gazette,* and the *Manchester Union.*

Whatever name it went by, Ellington's ensemble in the summer of 1926 was different from the seven-piece Kentucky Club band of the previous spring. Now it usually had ten players: two trumpets, trombone, three reeds, and four in the rhythm section.[18] The most important new member was trombonist Joseph Nanton (1904–46), who had replaced his friend Charlie Irvis during the Washingtonians' two-week stint at the Plantation Café in late June 1926. Nanton did not want to take the job away from Irvis, but Ellington apparently insisted. Things got off to a slow start, as Nanton recalled: "The first week I had to wait two days for my pay and the second week there wasn't any pay. So the place closed and we went to New England."[19] But there was more waiting ahead for Nanton. After playing Irvis's parts for several weeks, he was given no chance to solo—or, as it was called then, to "take a 'Boston.'" Most of the arrangements were built around Miley and Hardwick, and at first Ellington did not change them to feature his new trombonist. Finally Hardwick confronted Ellington: "For Christ's sake, Dumpy, how long are you gonna let this man sit here without taking a Boston?"[20] From then on Nanton was in.

Nanton was a New Yorker of West Indian descent. Like his predecessor Irvis, he had played extensively in Harlem night spots. Before joining Ellington he had performed with pianist Earl Frazier at Edmond's Cellar and with Cliff Jackson at the Nest Club. Rex Stewart has left a vivid portrait of him:

> Nanton was a gingerbread-colored man, kind of on the squatty side. His facial contours reminded me of a benevolent basset hound, with those big brown eyes that regarded the world so dolefully, framed in a long face with just a hint of dewlaps. . . . He had an indefinable quality about him even then that made him ageless. Perhaps it was his high, squeaky voice, which sometimes would fade away to a mere whisper. Or maybe it was his general air of insouciance. . . . [He] was sometimes called the Professor, because he knew something about almost everything. . . . He was well acquainted with such erudite and diverse subjects as astronomy, how to make home brew, and how to use a slide rule. He could recite poetry by ancient poets that most of us never knew existed, and he knew Shakespeare.[21]

Nanton, who was twenty-two when he joined Ellington in 1926, was to be a fixture in the band until his death in 1946.

Mack Shaw was the Washingtonians' new tuba player, having replaced Bass Edwards in April of 1926.[22] He was as tough as Nanton was learned—or so Ellington described him: "The police, gangsters, or somebody had caught Mack out in Chicago, beaten his face in and broken up all the bones. This cat would be blowing his tuba and blow out a loose bone. He had a whole lot of loose bones in his face, and he'd just put them together again and continue blowing! We had a terrific band then."[23] Supposedly Shaw could make ceiling beams shake from the force of his playing. As one of Ellington's men remarked, "He scared us."[24]

Ellington's second-trumpet player for the New England tour was probably Leroy Rutledge, who had appeared on the Washingtonians' record dates the previous March and April.

Various musicians joined Otto Hardwick in Ellington's reed section during the New England tour. Harry Carney (1910–74) substituted on occasion, a year before he became a full-time member. Carney usually gave 1927 as the year he joined Ellington. Yet a photograph from 1926 shows him with Bubber Miley pointing to a poster that announces the band's appearance Thursday, August

12, at the Ocean Pier in Old Orchard, Maine. Like Miley, Carney is dressed to play.[25] Moreover, Carney's appearance on a December 29, 1926, record date in New York suggests that Ellington may have used him earlier that year. Other saxophonists who appeared with the band were Harvey Boone, Percy Glascoe, and Freddie Skerritt.[26] Skerritt recalled going with Ellington on a short tour of Connecticut (organized by Harlem club-owner Happy Rhone) in the summer of 1926, just after the band finished at the Kentucky Club (i.e., June). He listed the other personnel as Hardwick, Miley, another trumpeter, Irvis, Harvey Boone, Guy, and Greer. In 1975 Greer confirmed this information, supplying the name of Leroy Rutledge as second trumpet.[27]

Although New England provided a welcome contrast to the Kentucky Club, it was hardly a vacation for the Washingtonians. Shribman often booked two bands for the same evening, advertising the event as a "Battle of Bands." This was partly a publicity device, partly a way of keeping the music and the dancers going nonstop, since one band could spell the other during breaks. (Roseland used the same policy.) On their first night at Nuttings-on-the-Charles the Washingtonians shared the bill with Mal Hallett. Later in the summer they were paired with Felix Ferdinando and his Havana Orchestra at the Charleshurst.[28] One night at Revere Beach Shribman had four bands rotating: Ellington, Mal Hallett, Speed Young, and the Crescent Gardens Broadcasting Orchestra.[29] According to Boston-born saxophonist Toots Mondello, who began playing with Mal Hallett in 1926, there was little competition at these "battles" —the bands just alternated sets. Mondello has recalled Ellington's group as being "more or less novelty," with Miley doing "all the tricky stuff."[30]

Ellington, however, recalled the New England dances as formidable occasions, with Hallett a stiff competitor. By 1926 Hallett, in addition to his experience playing for New England dancers, was a veteran of New York's Arcadia and Roseland ballrooms. *Variety* noted that he cared little for "flossiness" or "symphonic arrangements." Like any good dance-band leader, Hallett kept his eye on the audience and reacted with just the right tempos: "He gives them 'dirty' music when he senses they are primed for the 'low-down' indigo wails and switches as promiscuously to melody fox-trots, playing the latter, however, with a zest that is above average."[31]

Ellington remembered Hallett's band as playing "big, fat arrangements of dance music." When faced with the challenge of going up
against Hallett, Ellington chose an approach he had learned years
before when playing opposite the big brass bands at Virginia horse
shows: "We had a six-piece band and we used to play [Hallett]
contrast-wise. He'd know we were coming on and he'd blow up a
storm and lift the roof off. Then we'd crawl up there with our six
pieces and begin softly, and develop it, so that when we did play
loud it would seem as though we were playing louder than we actually were."[32] Ellington's "Whispering Tiger" (a version of "Tiger
Rag" he performed in the 1930s but never recorded) might have
evolved under such circumstances.

Most of the New York orchestras booked by Shribman—including those of Vincent Lopez, Ross Gorman, and Paul Specht—specialized in smooth performances of written arrangements. Fletcher
Henderson's band, one of the few black ensembles to play the New
England circuit, had men who were good readers and adept at a
wide variety of styles. To New England audiences, the Washingtonians were different. Instead of flashy orchestrations they offered, in
Ellington's words, "swing soul."[33] Many of their arrangements were
"conceived orally" and had the character of a "preserved jam session."[34] And while Hallett's and Lopez's players reproduced novel
orchestral or harmonic effects from the page, Ellington's men in-
vented their own devices on the spot. Nanton based his "tricks"
on an eerie, moaning "wah-wah" style. His ability soon won him
the nickname "Tricky Sam." Teamed up with Miley, "Tricky Sam"
Nanton worked out special choruses and dual plunger passages that
few other bands of the time could rival.[35]

The Washingtonians did well in New England. Although no
lengthy feature articles were written about them, a few newspaper
notices attested to their success. "Another crowd of enthusiastic
dancers was present at the second appearance of Duke Ellington,"
went an article in the July 21 *Salem Evening News*. And a few
weeks later the paper reported, "Duke Ellington and his Plantation Orchestra held forth at the Charleshurst last evening and in
spite of the intense heat a good house was present."[36] Looking
back at the 1926 tour from the vantage point of 1927, a writer
for the *New York Tribune* noted "one triumphant appearance after
another. They packed the ballrooms nightly."[37] Less impressed,

however, was the *Boston Post* reporter who wrote in August 1926 that visiting bands led by Ellington and Barney Rapp were "just good drawing cards" yet demanded "a higher price than the average local orchestra." The writer listed fees for various bands: $2,000 a night for Whiteman; $1,000 for Vincent Lopez; "less than $500" for the California Ramblers and Mal Hallett; $200 for the Memphis Five.[38] On the basis of these sums for well-known groups, Ellington's fee for a one-night stand was probably between $200 and $500.

The Washingtonians were able to command "a higher price than the average local orchestra" through the good offices of Charles Shribman. Shribman's strong managerial support came at a crucial time. In June 1926 Ellington and his band were in danger of drifting around New York from one short engagement to the next, but in July and August Shribman's circuit gave them structure and a stable financial base. It also improved their level of play: when sharing a bandstand with Mal Hallett or appearing in a ballroom the night after Vincent Lopez had been there, the Washingtonians were under more pressure to deliver their best. Shribman saw potential in Ellington's band and worked hard to develop it over time. Yet his motives were not strictly monetary, as Ellington noted when he paid tribute to the man: "[He] never owned a piece of any band or anybody. . . . I cannot imagine what would have happened to the big bands if it had not been for Charlie Shribman."[39]

On August 13, 1926, the Washingtonians gave their "farewell" New England performance at Moseley's-on-the-Charles. From there they headed back to New York, perhaps stopping to play at Orchard Beach. At this point song publisher Harrison Smith—co-composer of "Li'l Farina"—stepped in with an offer of more touring. Smith belonged to the Arthur Spizzi Syndicate, a booking organization that handled the bands of Vincent Lopez, Paul Specht, Isham Jones, Duke Yellman, and others.[40] Smith later claimed that, because of the Washingtonians' June appearance at the Plantation Café and the sales of their Gennett disc with "Animal Crackers" and "Li'l Farina," he was able to arrange a Stanley Circuit presentation tour for the band in Pennsylvania. The tour began in Pittsburgh (first week at the Liberty, second at the Schenley Theater), then moved on to North Kensington and Homestead, Pennsylvania, and the fourth week to Grafton and Wheeling, West Virginia. During the fourth week, however, as Smith told Marshall Stearns, Miley "got 'Lonesome for Harlem' and quit 'cold,' the Band got panicky and 'Duke' said 'No Dice' and the Boys headed for NYC leaving yours truly to wiggle out of said 'Play or Pay Contract' plus loss of commission on twenty [!] weeks."[41] In another account of this episode Smith remembered that when the Washingtonians played their first two weeks in Pittsburgh for theater manager Harry Davis, the latter wired New York with the comment, "Duke's is the Lousiest Band That I Ever Heard!"[42]

Smith also tried to get Ellington a job in Washington, D.C., at the Lincoln Theater. He suggested that theater-owner Harry Crandall hire Ellington and promote him as the "colored Paul Ash." But Crandall was not interested—perhaps he thought Smith's asking price of $1,000 per week too high for a native son.[43]

11

The Rise of Duke Ellington

SEPTEMBER 1926–DECEMBER 1927

Refreshed after a few months away from the city and seasoned by their experience on the road, the Washingtonians returned to New York. For a fourth consecutive fall they found themselves back at 49th and Broadway—this time with an eight-month contract.

The Kentucky Club had been padlocked for several months. "Entirely renovated" by owners Leo Bernstein and Frank Jerry, it re-opened September 25, 1926, with a new show featuring Bert Lewis as master-of-ceremonies, "rag singer" Julia Gerety [Gerrity?], soprano Eva Dowling, Bessie Kerwin, acrobatic dancer Olive Kendall, and the Washingtonians.[1] The following month *Orchestra World* reported the presence of other performers in the revue: the Hanley Sisters, who were "black bottomists," toe-dancer Ann Allison, entertainers Bigelow and Lee, and pianist Jack Carroll, who accompanied Bert Lewis. The place was serving "American and Oriental cuisine," the entertainment was "wonderful," and Ellington and his musicians were "burning 'em up with hot tunes. A wow of a band!"[2]

It looked as though the Washingtonians were in for a year much like the previous one. They had built up a reputation on the New England ballroom circuit and they could draw favorable notices from the New York press. Still, they were not getting many calls from record companies. In mid-October Ellington and Hardwick picked up one blues date, accompanying Alberta Jones for Gennett. The next month they may have recorded with Zaidee Jackson, although apparently no disc survives.[3]

But change was around the corner. One sign appeared late in October, when for the first time "Duke Ellington's Washingtonians" were listed in the "Leading Orchestras" section of *Variety*.[4] The Kentucky Club's owners might have been responsible for this publicity, or it may have been the work of Irving Mills.

Although it is difficult to know how close their association was in the mid-twenties, Ellington and Irving Mills probably had known each other for several years. During his first days in New York, Ellington had joined other songwriters who regularly visited the publishing executive's office hoping to sell a tune or two. He also spent time on the Mills company's "professional floor," where composers, lyricists, bandleaders, singers, and vaudevillians gathered.[5] Ellington's frequent trips to the publisher's building on West 46th Street may explain how he came to accompany Mills on the record of "Everything Is Hotsy Totsy Now," made in the summer of 1925. Mills also may have helped Ellington get recording dates for Gennett. "Everything Is Hotsy Totsy Now" was set for release by this label (but not issued), and on the Washingtonians' first Gennett session they played a tune from the Mills catalog, "If You Can't Hold the Man You Love."[6] During this period Mills devoted most of his energy to publishing and plugging songs. But at some point after hearing the Washingtonians at the Kentucky Club, Mills began to take an active interest in managing Ellington and his band.

Mills's discovery of the Washingtonians is one of those legendary events that defies precise dating and description. One version comes from songwriter Sam Coslow, who has suggested it happened early on. In the mid-twenties young Coslow was working for Mills Music as a "band-and-orchestra man." His job was "to visit the dance bands in the New York area and induce them to feature the firm's songs."[7] Coslow often went to the Kentucky Club, making it the last stop on his evening rounds because it "stayed open until dawn and became an early-morning rendezvous for show-business personalities after work." One evening Coslow approached Ellington about the possibility of recording:

The immediate gleam in Duke's eyes told me I had hit home.
"That's what I want to do more than anything in the world," he fairly shouted. "How do I get on records?"
"Well," I replied, "I was just thinking—my boss, Irving Mills,

has just started a new record company. Just a small label, sort of
a subsidiary of Mills Music. But I see no reason why he shouldn't
record you. I think your band has a great new sound for records.
Mills isn't getting any of the big name bands. Why not?" I'll never
forget Duke's hopeful look as I left him that morning. Sort of like
a prayer.[8]

As Coslow tells it, he persuaded Irving Mills to go down and hear
the band. After several trips Mills was impressed enough to set up
a record date for Ellington. More important, he wanted the Washingtonians to play Ellington's own compositions.

Coslow's account is intriguing, but it throws a stumbling block in
the path of the Ellington chronicler. If, as Coslow maintains, Mills
heard Ellington before he had made any recordings, the encounter
would have had to take place before the Blu-Disc session of 1924.
This, in turn, raises several possibilities: (1) Mills may have had
something to do with the Blu-Disc session; (2) Blu-Disc itself may
have been a recording venture undertaken by Mills Music (since
Coslow refers to "a small label, sort of a subsidiary of Mills"); (3)
Mills's use of Ellington as an accompanist the following year, and
his alleged role in getting Ellington on Gennett, had a precedent in
this early Blu-Disc episode.

What other evidence would support Coslow's story? As one of
the co-composers of "Animal Crackers," Coslow was surely aware
of Ellington's June 1926 recording of the tune—hence his conversation with Ellington must have occurred prior to June 1926. Two
other sources suggest a pre-1926 visit by Mills to the Kentucky
Club. One is a 1930 article in the New York Age, in which Mills
was reported to have discovered Ellington "when that personage
arrived from Washington, and with a five-piece colored orchestra
made his debut at the Kentucky Club."[9] The vague language and
lack of date make the information unreliable.

But the second source is more compelling. In 1981 Irving Mills
recalled that when he first visited the Kentucky Club, the manager told him he had "just hired a band from Washington." Mills
related his reaction: "I immediately thought of the quick change
that I could make between [Ellington] and Fletcher Henderson,
who had been working for me to do the background music for
my vocal artists that I had on my labels, black labels."[10] It is un-

clear what Mills might have meant by his "labels." But in 1923 and 1924 Fletcher Henderson was recording for many different companies, accompanying singers in vocal blues numbers (including Edna Hicks performing an Irving Mills song in January 1924, "Where Can That Somebody Be?").[11] Henderson was also working for the Down South Music Publishing Company, a subsidiary of Jack Mills, Inc. Perhaps, then, Blu-Disc was a Mills recording project, and the several vocal sides made for that company in 1924 by Alberta Prime and Florence Bristol represented Irving Mills's "quick change" between Henderson and Ellington.

Other sources, however, point to late 1926 as the starting-point for Mills's direct involvement with the Ellington band. A 1930 profile of Mills in *Metronome* reported that he had first heard the Washingtonians "some years ago" and that after he "expanded and developed the group" he "put them on a Victor record."[12] The band's first Victor date was January 10, 1927, backing Evelyn Preer. A Texas newspaper article from 1933 described a hot and humid summer night in 1926 when Mills visited the club and heard the Washingtonians playing many of Ellington's original compositions and arrangements.[13] (There is a problem with this account: the club was closed and the band out of town for most of that summer.) In 1952 Mills himself remembered dropping in late one night with *Variety* editor Sime Silverman and being impressed by "Black and Tan Fantasy."[14] Since the piece was not recorded until 1927, this, too, might argue for a date closer to 1926, and certainly after 1924. On the other hand, "Black and Tan Fantasy" may have been in the Ellington repertory before it was recorded, perhaps even before 1926. Also, Mills mentioned hearing a *five*-piece group in the Kentucky Club. The Washingtonians are not known to have played there with fewer than six pieces—unless Mills was not counting Ellington, in which case he might have heard the band with Miley, Irvis, Hardwick, Guy, and Greer, ca. 1924–25. By the fall of 1926, Ellington probably was using eight to ten musicians at the Kentucky Club.

Ellington suggested 1926 as the year of his discovery by Mills. In 1940 he recalled that the Washingtonians had been at the Kentucky Club "about three and a half years" (i.e., late fall of 1926) when Mills first heard them. Mills was impressed with their performance of "St. Louis Blues"; apparently Ellington's arrangement was so fancy that Mills failed to recognize Handy's tune and had to ask the bandleader what it was. Afterwards, Mills spoke with Ellington about making a record. Ellington was all for it: "Naturally, I agreed, and we got together four originals. They were for the Vocalion and Brunswick labels, and we made 'East St. Louis [Toodle-O]' and 'Birmingham Breakdown' for the first. On the second date . . . we waxed 'Emigration [*sic*] Blues.' "[15] While Ellington and Mills had done business before, they began a new phase of their relationship with the November 29, 1926, Vocalion date.

The first Vocalion session was a breakthrough for Ellington the composer. The band, identified on the label as the Kentucky Club Orchestra rather than the Washingtonians, recorded four pieces by Ellington: "A Night in Harlem," "East St. Louis Toodle-O," "Who Is She," and "Birmingham Breakdown." The company released only the second and fourth titles. (As of this writing, "A Night in Harlem" has not been located. "Who Is She" is a song Ellington wrote with Mills, Rousseau Simmons, and Bob Schafer.) Mills apparently believed that Ellington's compositions could compete commercially with popular songs. He also must have realized that the band was more distinctive when it performed Ellington's own music than when it played arrangements of Tin Pan Alley tunes.

Mills began to manage the Ellington band some time after the November Vocalion date, either in late 1926 or early 1927. The terms of Ellington's first agreement with Mills are unknown. Later, probably in the period 1928 through 1930, Ellington's contract gave himself 45 percent of his earnings, with 45 percent going to Mills and 10 percent to Mills's lawyer.[16] Using the same techniques applied to plugging songs, Mills sought to promote his client through recordings and press exposure. On December 29, 1926, exactly one month after its first visit to Vocalion, the Kentucky Club Orchestra returned to record two more Ellington originals, "Immigration Blues" and "The Creeper." Less than two weeks later Ellington and four sidemen went to the Victor studio to accompany Evelyn Preer singing "Make Me Love You" (never issued) and the Mills song "If You Can't Hold the Man You Love," previously recorded by the Washingtonians on Gennett. Both the frequency of record dates and the choice of material suggest the presence of Mills.

Late in 1926 an article in *Orchestra World* stressed the need for dance bands to have publicity that "keeps the leader and his orchestra in the limelight." [17] Because of Mills, perhaps, Ellington's publicity was improving. After first appearing October 27, 1926, on the list of "Leading Orchestras" in *Variety,* the Washingtonians stayed on the roster every week until January 26, 1927. The January 1927 issue of *Orchestra World* brought more attention with a big boxed ad:

Duke Ellington and his Washingtonians
Extend New Year Greetings to all their friends
Now in their Fifth Season at the Club Kentucky, New York City
Brunswick Artists [18]

The same issue contained the first article about Ellington to appear in the periodical. Under the heading, "Duke Ellington's Ripping Style," a short piece called the Washingtonians "a favorite Brunswick recording group," noting that the previous summer their New England tour had been extended from two weeks to six. Some of the language smacked of press-agent's propaganda: "So much of the charm of Duke Ellington lies in the grace of his musical translation that it is difficult to describe in cold, prosaic words. The lucently ripping style of his Washingtonians always scores heavily because it has a thrilling thread woven through it." [19] The article claimed that the band recorded only "Duke's own compositions, published by Jack Mills, Inc." However, it also mentioned "Rhapsody Jr." (copyright October 21, 1926, E 649276), "Mr. Ellington's latest composition" which was published by Robbins-Engel. Steven Lasker has located a reference to "Rhapsody Jr." in the Vocalion recording ledger under February 24, 1927, performed in Chicago by pianist Ford L. Buck. [20] Ellington's orchestra never recorded the piece, but Jimmie Lunceford's orchestra did in 1935. With its ninth and augmented chords, its whole-tone melodies and parallel triads, "Rhapsody Jr." shows Ellington displaying some of the hallmarks of mid-twenties jazz modernism.

Between November 1924 and June 1926 Ellington's band had visited record studios five times and produced only ten sides. By contrast, in the four months between January and April 1927, it made the same number of sides in seven sessions, and all but three of them featured compositions by Ellington himself. Ellington had left the small labels behind and was now affiliated with major recording companies. The Evelyn Preer date in January was for Victor, the session on March 22 for Columbia. Of the five other sessions, four were for Brunswick and one for its subsidiary, Vocalion. Brunswick brought Ellington better distribution and marketing than he had ever received before. As a result his name spread rapidly. According to an article by "W.E.B." in the August 7, 1927, *New York Tribune,* Ellington's first Brunswick record "was a huge success and those that followed proved to be leading sellers on the music market." This market stretched beyond the East Coast and Midwest. One Brunswick dealer in New York received an order from Australia for one hundred records by the Washingtonians.[21]

As Ellington's fame grew as a recording artist his stock rose as a composer. One direct result was the publication in 1927 of "Gold Digger," a jazz instrumental he had written some time earlier with Will Donaldson. An article in *Metronome* explained the reason for the delay:

> The "Gold Digger," a hot tune (fox trot) by Will Donaldson and Duke Yellington [*sic*], is starting to show up and is heard often on the air from the many broadcast stations in the East. There is a funny incident connected with this tune; it was written over five years ago and offered to all the publishers since then, but due to its radical departure from the usual conventional hot tune type it was rejected by them all. Recently Denton and Haskins heard it and inquired who wrote and who was publishing it. They thought, perhaps, the other publishers might have made a mistake and it was only a matter of a few minutes to get the writers to sign up. Today it is one of the outstanding numbers in their hot tune catalog.[22]

Most likely the piece was not five years old, since Ellington was still in Washington in 1922. But it may have dated from 1923 or 1924. By 1927 Ellington's hot jazz had become hot property. He no longer had to pound the pavement in search of publishers: they sought him out instead.

Chicago Defender columnist Dave Peyton had recognized Ellington's achievement in April that same year. Peyton was one of the major black music journalists of the day, also a well-known orchestra-leader based in Chicago. While his article seemed less obviously a "plug" than the January blurb in *Orchestra World,* its last section bore the stamp of Mills:

Duke Ellington's Success

From the Oriental cafe in Washington, D.C. to the Kentucky Club, one of the brightest spots in New York's gay night life, and one of the feature artists of the Brunswick Phonograph Co., is the record of Duke Ellington, conductor of what leading judges have called the foremost jazz orchestra in America.

Ellington, who is only twenty-eight years old, is a graduate of Armstrong Tech., of Washington, D.C. Attending in the course of his scholastic curriculum the Music School of Washington, Ellington was for some time a pupil of the famous Henry Grant, head of that school.

But in accounting for his success, Ellington insists that all his remarkable rhythms and harmonies would not be before so wide a public today were it not for Irving Mills of Jack Mills, Inc., New York music publishers. This firm, publishing such numbers of Duke Ellington's as "East St. Louis Todelo," "Birmingham Breakdown," "A Black and Tan Fantasy," "Down Home Stomp," and others, has enabled him to reach the broad-pinnacled heights of success. [23]

Ellington, of course, did not actually graduate from Armstrong, nor did he attend the Washington Conservatory. Either he inflated his credentials or he relayed the basic facts to Mills, who embellished them to make a stronger impression. It would be several years before Mills's publicity campaign for Ellington would go into high gear. But even here, in a 1927 article based on a press release, the general outlines of Mills's strategy can be gleaned. That strategy, as Mills explained years later, was "aimed at presenting the public a great musician who was making a lasting contribution to American music." [24] Instead of promoting Ellington merely as a popular bandleader and songwriter, Mills sought to make "his importance as an artist the primary consideration." When Peyton stressed Ellington's formal training and cited his talents as composer and as conductor of "the foremost jazz orchestra in America," he reinforced the sophisticated image that Mills wanted to highlight—an image which, to a great degree, Ellington had cultivated in Washington before coming to New York.

As the summer of 1927 approached and another season at the Kentucky Club wound down, Ellington and his men prepared for a return to New England. Once again the Shribman brothers arranged a ballroom circuit. A month before the band's first New England appearance, a notice in the *Salem Evening News* heralded the arrival of "Duke Ellington and his Washingtonians, Columbia and Brunswick Record Orchestra, Featuring Bub Miley, America's Hottest Trumpet Player."[25]

Ellington began to organize a group for the road tour ahead. Four years after coming to New York with Snowden, he had only a few of the original Washingtonians still with him: Hardwick, Greer, and, since the fall of 1923, Miley. Banjo-player Fred Guy and trombonist Joe Nanton were steady members, as was second trumpeter Louis Metcalf, who had joined early in the fall of 1926 out of Charlie Johnson's band.

The reed section, as usual, was in flux. Hardwick was there, but his section-mates between fall 1926 and spring 1927 are unknown. From time to time he may have been joined by Harvey Boone, Prince Robinson, and others.[26] But for the New England tour Ellington added two new reed players.

One was the Chicago-based clarinetist Rudy Jackson (1901– ca. 1968). Jackson had played in New York in 1925 at the Club Alabam, at the Club Petite on West 46th Street, and possibly at Roseland with Fletcher Henderson.[27] After touring with the *Lucky Sambo* company in 1926, he was back in Chicago with King Oliver at the Plantation Café by early 1927. Several months later he received a call from Ellington to join the Washingtonians in New England.[28]

The other reed player was not exactly new to Ellington. Harry Carney had played with the Washingtonians in New England during the summer of 1926 but had gone back to school that fall. However, when his schedule permitted he made trips to New York, where he sat in with Ellington's band or other groups in town. During his 1926 Christmas vacation he had gone to New York and participated in the Washingtonians' December 29 Vocalion date. He also appeared on all the Brunswick and Vocalion sessions of early 1927. On these recordings he played clarinet, alto, and baritone saxophone in the ensemble but did not solo. As a rule, Hardwick took the baritone solos, which later became Carney's specialty.[29]

On March 8, 1927, Carney left Boston with fellow saxophonist Charlie Holmes to live in New York.[30] Soon he found work with a "relief group" at the Savoy Ballroom, then with Henry Sapparo at the Bamboo Inn (although he had to get his mother's permission to join). For a Boston schoolboy, Harlem was a musician's paradise: "I couldn't believe it. I could see my favorite musicians every afternoon. Just to have the chance to talk with them meant so much to me. I used to eat at a restaurant at 131st Street. But this is how I ate: I'd order, and then run outside for a bit, then I'd come back in and eat a little, then I'd go outside again. I just didn't want to miss anything."[31] Ellington hired Carney for record dates and possibly for occasional Kentucky Club work; he also served as surrogate parent, looking out for the boy Sonny Greer called "Youth."[32] But Carney was not a typical teenager. He was "well-organized," according to Ellington, and already "owned a car and all his own instruments."[33] Realizing he could count on Carney for the upcoming tour, Ellington asked him along.

Ellington also took bassist Wellman Braud (1891–1966), a New Orleans native. Braud, who replaced Mack Shaw, was a powerful performer on string bass as well as tuba. When he joined the band, Ellington recalled, he was already a seasoned player and "a clean, neatly dressed coach who knew all the answers."[34]

The Washingtonians' 1927 summer tour resembled that of the previous year (see itinerary, figure 2). Once again the band was based in Salem and traveled around for one-nighters, playing in many of the same ballrooms. But now New England audiences were better acquainted with them. One ad called the Washingtonians a "Celebrated Orchestra," and a review claimed that "these noted players were at their best."[35]

Figure 2. Itinerary for the Washingtonians' 1927
Summer Tour of New England

DATE	PLACE	SOURCE
June 20 M	Nuttings-on-the-Charles, Waltham, Mass.	BP
22 W	Charleshurst Ballroom, Salem, Mass.	SEN
26 Su	Olympia Theater, Lynn, Mass.	LDEI
27 M	Nuttings-on-the-Charles, Mass.	BP
July 1 F	Crescent Park, near Providence, R.I.	PJ
2 Sa	Wilbur's, Somerset, Mass.	FRHN
3 Su	Charleshurst Ballroom, Salem, Mass.	BET
13 W*	Fieldston, Marshfield, Mass.	BrPH

	14 Th	Old Orchard Pier, Old Orchard, Me.	PPH
	16 Sa	Crescent Gardens, Revere Beach, Mass.	BP
	19 T	Charleshurst Ballroom, Salem, Mass.	BP
	22 F	American Legion Beauty Ball, Taunton, Mass.	TDG
	25 M	Old Orchard Pier, Old Orchard, Me.	PPH
	26 T	Charleshurst Ballroom, Salem, Mass.	SEN
	28 Th	New Joyland, Woonsocket, R.I.	TDG
	30 Sa	Blackbird Ballroom, Nashua, N.H.	MU
August	2 T	Charleshurst Ballroom, Salem, Mass.	SEN
	3 W	Arcadia, Gardner, Mass.	FS
	6 Sa	Highland Park, Brockton, Mass.	BrPH
	9 T	Charleshurst Ballroom, Salem, Mass.	SEN
	11 Th	Charleshurst Ballroom, Salem, Mass.	SEN
	12 F	Roseland, Lawrence, Mass.	LET
	16 T	Ocean Echo, Salisbury Beach, N.H.	LET
	18 Th	Whalom Park, Fitchburg, Mass.	FS
	19 F	Charleshurst Ballroom, Salem, Mass.	SEN
	20 Sa	Highland Park, Brockton, Mass.	BrPH
	23 T	Commodore Ballroom, Lowell, Mass.	LS
	30 T	Charleshurst Ballroom, Salem, Mass.	SEN
	31 W	Arcadia Ballroom, Manchester, N.H.	MU
September	1 Th	Whalom Park, Fitchburg, Mass.	FS
	3 Sa	Old Orchard Pier, Old Orchard, Me.	PPH
	4 Su	Arcadia, Gardner, Mass.	FS
	5 M	Whalom Park, Fitchburg, Mass.	FS

Key to Sources:

BP	*Boston Post*	LS	*Lowell Sun*
BET	*Boston Evening Transcript*	MU	*Manchester Union*
BrPH	*Brockton Post Herald*	PJ	*Providence Journal*
FRHN	*Fall River Herald News*	PPH	*Portland Press Herald*
FS	*Fitchburg Sentinel*	SEN	*Salem Evening News*
LDEI	*Lynn Daily Evening Item*	TDG	*Taunton Daily Gazette*
LET	*Lawrence Evening Tribune*	WEG	*Worcester Evening Gazette*

NOTE: The above list represents all known dates advertised in fourteen local newspapers. Also searched was the *Haverhill Gazette;* it yielded no dates for the summer of 1927.

*The *Fitchburg Sentinel* (July 8, 1927) announced that the Washingtonians would be appearing at the Arcadia in Gardner, Massachusetts, on the night of July 13.

Two other additions to the Ellington entourage were his wife Edna and eight-year-old son Mercer. While Edna had been with Duke in New York since 1923 or 1924, Mercer lived with J.E. and Daisy in Washington, usually visiting his parents during the summer months. Mercer has remembered the summer of 1927 in Salem as a pleasant period when he stayed in the New Brunswick Hotel, played in the firehouse nearby, and met certain Ellington band members for the first time. Miley and Hardwick took a friendly interest in the youngster. And Mercer was especially impressed by bassist Wellman Braud, "pulling the single strings up on one beat and slapping them against the board on the next."[36]

This tour, like the last one, had its share of "battles" with other bands. On Monday, June 20, their first night of the season, the Washingtonians faced off against Mal Hallett at Nuttings-on-the-Charles. Carney remembered that Hallett had "a helluva band" that included alto saxophonist Toots Mondello and drummer Gene Krupa.[37] Later the Washingtonians shared bills with McMullin's Orchestra (July 16), Phil Napoleon's "Victor Record Band" (July 19), Dick Voynow's Wolverines (July 26), a group from Argentina called the Gauchos (August 2), and Roane's Sensational Pennsylvanians (August 9 and 12). Reviews of these encounters reveal little. The day after Ellington battled Roane's Pennsylvanians, the *Salem Evening News* reported only that the two bands "put up a real good fight and some lively jazz was the result with continuous music throughout the evening."[38]

But not every night brought musical combat. A few days after their tour began, the Washingtonians provided music for a dancing party at the Charleshurst sponsored by the Young Men's Catholic Total Abstinence Society.[39] In mid-August they accompanied a "Miss America" dance in the same hall.[40] Most of these audiences must have been white. On Thursday, August 11, however, the band performed for a different event at the Charleshurst: "A colored dance night at the Willows is something new at the resort and undoubtedly will be one of the big nights of the season." The next day, the *Salem Evening News* reported that eight hundred people had turned out to hear Ellington.[41]

A preview article about Ellington in the *Fall River Herald News* gives an idea of the reception the band met on its travels. Parts of the piece were probably cribbed from Shribman's publicity ma-

terial, as when the group was called the "Famous Colored Recording Orchestra" and "The Paul Whiteman of Colored Orchestras."
But the writer also provided a glimpse of Ellington on the bandstand, mentioning that on the previous night in Providence "this
prince of melody and his band scored a tremendous hit, graciously
responding to repeated calls for encores." The hyperbolic language
exceeded anything written about Ellington the previous summer:
"Duke Ellington and his galaxy of Broadway stars are now engaged
in a whirlwind tour of the New England states. . . . Ellington,
pianist and director of this entertaining orchestra, is one of the
nation's foremost figures in the musical world. The inimitable presentation of the Southland's crooning melodies, masterfully blended
with modern-day jazz, will completely captivate everyone." The
writer concluded by predicting that the band's upcoming appearance at Wilbur's-on-the-Taunton—its only one of the summer—
would "attract one of the season's largest crowds." [42]

W.E.B's August 1927 piece in the *New York Tribune* also raved
about the band's New England tour. The Washingtonians were
"taking the territory by storm"; everywhere they drew "a capacity
gathering of dancers, young and old." W.E.B. was not sure how to
account for this success, but wrote that it may have stemmed from
the band's ability to create moods in slow pieces and to generate
excitement during fast ones: "Apparently there is nothing unusual
about this orchestra, yet, when you start dancing you don't want
to stop. When you waltz you sort of wander off into a dream, the
music is so soothing. Their slow fox trot, àla Southern style, brings
out that soft, weird, entrancing effect that sends you sort of creep-
ing over the floor, and when they play a fast one for contrast, they
simply sweep you off your feet." [43] Ellington's ensemble, W.E.B.
concluded, was "slowly and surely becoming New England's favorite dance orchestra." The proprietor of a ballroom in Maine received sixty-eight phone calls one week from people curious about
the group's next appearance. Enthusiastic patrons were filling up
the suggestion boxes of dance halls with slips of paper naming the
Washingtonians as their favorite group. And promoters were now
billing the Washingtonians as a "choice attraction" and mounting
heavy advertising campaigns for the band. [44]

W.E.B.'s article, which documented the Washingtonians' rising
fame, also described Ellington's working methods at the time. El-

lington's afternoons were given over to rehearsals, his evenings to performances, and afterwards he would often "sit up till the wee hours of the morning writing new arrangements or thinking of something different to please the dancer and promoter."[45] Already Ellington was forming work habits he would keep later, using the time directly after performances—when the sounds of his players still swirled in his head—to compose new music. W.E.B. also acknowledged the bandleader's ambition: "Duke is aiming for the top of the ladder, and that day is not far off."

Ten weeks after they opened at the Charleshurst, the Washingtonians made their farewell appearance at the Salem ballroom on August 30, once again battling a band led by Phil Napoleon, a founding member of the Memphis Five.[46] On Labor Day weekend they traveled to Old Orchard, Maine, for a dance that featured a personal appearance by "Miss Universe."[47] On their way back to New York they played one-nighters in Gardner and Fitchburg, Massachusetts. Then the season was over.

In September, for the first time since his move to New York in 1923, Ellington did not descend the steps of the Kentucky Club. Perhaps the club's management decided to get a different band, or else Irving Mills wanted to find other opportunities for Ellington and his musicians.

At first the Washingtonians landed a three-week job at Club Ciro's on West 56th Street. During the engagement the saxophonist and violinist Ellsworth Reynolds joined the band, and Mack Shaw temporarily replaced Wellman Braud on bass.[48] The Washingtonians then took to the stage. They had not played any theater dates since the fall of 1925—at least none were advertised. Now, on October 10, 1927, they were back in Harlem's Lafayette Theater for *Jazzmania*, a revue produced by Clarence Robinson. This time Ellington's group performed both on stage and in the pit. Starring in the revue were singers Edith Wilson and Lena Wilson (Edith's sister-in-law), the song-and-dance team of Buck and Bubbles, comedians Johnnie Vigal and Henry Jones, and the Royal Balalaika Orchestra from Europe. The latter ensemble accompanied the dance act of Rodrigo and Lila. Robinson's revue consisted of a typical mixture of songs, dances, and comedy routines. One member of the cast, Jack Blake, sang and danced to "Bugle Blues." The chorus also had some dance sequences, and Rodrigo and Lila did the tango and the "Apache" dance.[49]

Jazzmania was well received at the Lafayette and its run extended for another week. The *Age* claimed that no show had garnered such "unstinted praise" since Bill Robinson's last appearance. Best of all, the reviewer continued, "throughout its entire ninety minutes on the stage there was not one moment of smut." The *Age's* critic devoted a separate paragraph to Ellington, saving his highest compliment for the last sentence: "The music for *Jazzmania* was rendered by Duke Ellington's band, and what a band it is. Both in the orchestra pit and on the stage their performance was superb. With the possible exception of Fletcher Henderson's band, Duke Ellington seems to head the greatest existing aggregation of colored musicians."[50]

During October the Washingtonians performed for the revue *Messin' Around,* which was presented at the Plantation Café in the Winter Garden building. It was a gathering of old friends: Leonard Harper staged the show, and Maceo Pinkard wrote the music.[51]

Then in mid-November, less than a month after putting on *Jazzmania,* Clarence Robinson prepared another revue for the Lafayette. This one was called *Dance Mania,* and once more Robinson turned to Ellington's band for the music. Except for Lena Wilson and Johnnie Vigal, the cast of *Dance Mania* was different from that of *Jazzmania.* The show featured the comedy team of Joyner and Foster, Crawford Jackson, and "Go-Get-'Em" Rogers. But its star was Adelaide Hall, the young woman from Brooklyn who had been in the road cast of *Shuffle Along* (1922), in *Runnin' Wild* (1923), and in the first edition of *Chocolate Kiddies* (1925). Hall, the *Age* reviewer wrote, "can dance and sing and strum on a uke to one's unbounded delight." The writer also saluted Clarence Robinson as one of the "ablest young producers in the East" and described Ellington's band as "famous."[52]

Also in November songwriter Jimmy McHugh, former associate of Irving Mills at Mills Music, was busy planning a new revue for the Cotton Club, on Lenox Avenue at 142nd Street. Andy Preer's Missourians had been the house band at the Harlem nightclub since 1925. When Preer died in May of 1927, a new band was needed. Reportedly both King Oliver and Sam Wooding turned down job offers.[53] McHugh had been impressed by Ellington's band and per-

Ellington's orchestra at the Lafayette Theater, Harlem, fall 1927. Left to right: Ellington, Joe "Tricky Sam" Nanton, Sonny Greer, Bubber Miley, Harry Carney, Wellman Braud, Rudy Jackson, Fred Guy, Nelson Kincaid, Ellsworth Roy Reynolds (Frank Driggs Collection)

suaded Cotton Club manager Herman Stark and his partner Dan Healy to go hear it at the Lafayette in *Dance Mania*. Afterwards, according to Fred Guy, Ellington went with Stark and Healy to a tavern next to the theater. There he signed a contract to appear with his orchestra in the Cotton Club's upcoming revue.[54]

The next day, however, Ellington and his men left with the *Dance Mania* company for a tour on the Keith-Albee Circuit. (Ellington pared his group down to eight men for the road: trumpet, trombone, two saxes, piano, banjo, bass, and drums.[55]) Their first stop was Philadelphia, where the show was to play the Standard Theater for two weeks beginning November 21. A few days after opening in Philadelphia, Ellington's band—billed as "Duke Ellington's Great Jazzmania Orchestra"—appeared opposite Fletcher Henderson's orchestra at a Thanksgiving Day dance held at the Academy of Music.[56] But before *Dance Mania* had finished at the Standard its orchestra defected. Ellington and his musicians had been summoned back to New York.

It seems the owners of the Cotton Club had close connections with gangsters both in New York and Philadelphia. As the story goes, one of their thugs in the City of Brotherly Love approached the theater owner who had Ellington under contract for the week that the new Cotton Club show was scheduled to open. A few well-chosen words convinced the owner to let the musicians break their contract: "Be big or you'll be dead."[57] Ellington and his band were free to return to New York. They packed up their instruments and headed for Harlem.

12

A Composer and His Band

The recordings made by the Washingtonians between November 1924 and October 1926 had reflected Ellington's status as a relative newcomer to New York's competitive musical scene. Lacking a manager and a regular recording contract, Ellington ended up with a sporadic series of dates for Gennett, Pathé, and the obscure Blu-Disc company. Only four of the eighteen issued sides featured Ellington's regular working band: "Choo Choo" and "Rainy Nights" from November 1924 and "Animal Crackers" and "Li'l Farina" from June 1926. On the others Ellington either enlarged his group to accommodate record producers or pared it down to accompany singers. Moreover, Ellington probably had little control over the repertory he recorded. At the Kentucky Club he may have played popular songs like "Oh How I Love My Darling," "How Come You Do Me Like You Do?," and "Animal Crackers." But more likely these pieces appeared on his discs because recording and publishing executives wanted them there.

The Vocalion session of November 29, 1926, marked a turning point in Ellington's career. The recordings he was to make over the next year—and in the years ahead—differed in several fundamental ways from those that had come before.

On this session Ellington's band performed four pieces, all written by Ellington (alone or with collaborators). Previously, only four of Ellington's eighteen sides had featured his compositions; between November 29, 1926, and November 3, 1927, seventeen out of twenty-two would be by him.[1] This was the beginning of a pattern that was to hold the rest of his life: Duke Ellington's band would play Duke Ellington's music.

Various record companies helped introduce Ellington's compositions to the public. In 1927 his band appeared on two labels with race series aimed at black buyers—Vocalion and OKeh—but also recorded for three with a wider network of distribution: Brunswick (Vocalion's parent company), Columbia, and Victor. Affiliation with these labels spread the band's fame, and better recording equipment improved its sound.

Starting with the first Vocalion date, Ellington's records also took on a new function. Before, the Washingtonians had recorded pieces that were already published; their discs, then, were a form of song-plugging, helping to boost the sale of music already in circulation. Now the reverse process went into effect. As soon as Ellington's band had recorded a piece, Mills would publish it both in sheet-music and orchestral stock versions. People buying the sheet music for, say, "Black and Tan Fantasy" or "Birmingham Breakdown" got something fairly close to the text of Ellington's recorded performance. Indeed, solos improvised by Otto Hardwick and Bubber Miley were transcribed, often approximately, and included in the sheet music (see discussion of "The Creeper" and "Washington Wabble," following). Thus the published music preserved and promoted the identity of the band. And since Mills served as Ellington's manager as well as publisher, he made sure that most of the profits stayed in-house.

The twenty-two sides issued from November 1926 to November 1927 reveal how much Ellington's emerging compositional style depended on the musical personality of key figures in the band and, as a result, on the continuity of its membership. Just as Miley's presence on "Choo Choo" and "Rainy Nights" gave those pieces a quality missing from the early Pathé and Gennett sides, so his contributions during the next period—both as soloist and co-composer with Ellington—were indispensable. Miley became so closely identified with the Ellington repertory, in fact, that even when he missed a date—as on November 3, 1927—his replacement, Jabbo Smith, emulated his sound and approach. After Miley, Joe Nanton and Otto Hardwick were the other main soloists; each enhanced Ellington's sonic world: Nanton rough and guttural, Hardwick smooth and suave.

Above all, these recordings show Ellington coming into his own as a composer. Pieces like "Birmingham Breakdown" and "Washington Wabble" are successful examples of mid-twenties instrumental dance music. Even more impressive are the collaborative efforts like "Creole Love Call" and "Black and Tan Fantasy" in which Ellington weaves together motives and phrases contributed by his players to make unified musical compositions.

The pieces Ellington's band recorded between November 29, 1926, and November 3, 1927, fall into three general categories. A handful are popular songs or instrumentals by writers outside the band: "If You Can't Hold the Man You Love," "Song of the Cotton Field," "Soliloquy," "What Can a Poor Fellow Do?" and "Chicago Stomp Down." A second group is made up of fast, hot dance numbers written by Ellington and Hardwick, or by Ellington alone: "Birmingham Breakdown," "The Creeper," "Hop Head," "Down in Our Alley Blues," and "Washington Wabble." A third includes slower pieces that draw upon the blues for their form or melodic language and that feature Bubber Miley in a prominent role: "Immigration Blues," "New Orleans Low-Down," "Blues I Love to Sing," "Creole Love Call," "Black and Tan Fantasy," and "East St. Louis Toodle-O." The last two compositions, in particular, signaled the arrival of an ensemble with its own sound and style; they also represented the first major triumph of its ambitious young leader.

Songs and Stocks

During this period, the first time Ellington recorded someone else's music was January 10, 1927, when he took a reduced band into the Victor studio to accompany Evelyn Preer.[2] Besides Ellington, Greer, Hardwick, and Miley, the ensemble included both a clarinetist and a violinist who doubled on alto saxophone—the latter was probably Edgar Sampson, who had played with Ellington the previous year.[3] Preer was an actress who had appeared with the Lafayette Players and was well known for her roles in Oscar Micheaux's films made with all-black casts and intended for black audiences. A 1923 newspaper article called her "the dazzling and most beautiful Colored Actress of the screen," also "the first and only Colored girl to ever be starred in Broadway."[4] In 1926 she had recorded a few sides as a singer and on one date was backed by a group featuring Red Nichols and Miff Mole.

Ellington recorded two songs with Preer for this Victor date. "Make Me Love You" was rejected. The other side—a test pressing, according to Jerry Valburn—was a remake of "If You Can't Hold the Man You Love," first recorded by the Washingtonians in April 1926. This time, however, the vocal takes up most of the disc. But even in a secondary role Ellington shows imagination as an arranger and authority as a bandleader.

"If You Can't Hold the Man You Love" begins with Miley growling down a C-major scale as Ellington mirrors his line with parallel chords. After four bars the two altos enter with mock-classical arpeggios that are interrupted by a searing break from Miley:

Example 43. "If You Can't Hold the Man You Love" (January 10, 1927), introduction.

The tight arrangement relaxes on the first part of Preer's vocal, as clarinet and trumpet improvise loosely behind her on the verse and are joined by violin on the chorus. However, the patter section ("You can't hold a bird unless you feed him seed, / You can't hold a dog without the bones he needs," etc.) features a sweet, arranged accompaniment for altos and trumpet. When Preer goes back to the chorus, the saxes continue with arranged background figures and Miley ad libs. Preer's voice is just adequate for Sammy Fain's tune, but her acting ability helps bring the right kind of tongue-in-cheek approach to Irving Kahal's lyrics.

Ellington divides the final chorus into four sections, taking the first eight bars himself then following with Sampson's violin, Miley's trumpet, and Preer's vocal. He launches his own solo with a powerful rhythmic drive and never strays far from the melody. Both Sampson and Miley contribute solos that are strong and sure; Miley enhances his with expressive muted wah-wah tones. Greer's playing is notable throughout, from his dancing brush-strokes to his sharp cymbal punctuation. Altogether, "If You Can't Hold the Man You Love" is a considerable improvement over Ellington's earlier recordings with singers; the arrangement is well balanced and the performance flows.

In 1927 the only other singer to appear on disc with Ellington is Adelaide Hall, and on these few sides she functions as part of the band rather than as the headliner. (See pp. 236–42 for discussion.) A Vocalion date in November 1927, however, brought in Ellington and two others (violin and cello) to accompany Marguerite Lee in performances of "You Will Always Live on in Our Memory" and "She's Gone to Join the Songbirds in Heaven," and Walter Richardson in "Gone But Not Forgotten." The sides were announced in a Vocalion ad but never issued.[5]

On February 3, 1927, at his third session for Vocalion, Ellington recorded Porter Grainger's "Song of the Cotton Field" (copyrighted as "Song from a Cotton Field," July 6, 1927; E 670138). Grainger's composition may have been used for a theatrical production number depicting the plight of slaves in the South—or so the title implies. The voices of the singers in the "cotton field" are represented by the plaintive solos of Miley, Nanton, and a clarinetist (Rudy Jackson, according to Harry Carney[6]) growling in his low register. With its somber hues, minor key, and slightly ominous tone, "Song of the Cotton Field" bears a relationship to "East St. Louis Toodle-O," "Black and Tan Fantasy," and some of the "jungle" pieces from Ellington's Cotton Club period (e.g., "Jungle Nights in Harlem" and the middle section of "Echoes of the Jungle").

Unlike "If You Can't Hold the Man You Love," Ellington's version of "Song of the Cotton Field" shows scant evidence of his arranging skills. He may have written the gloomy baritone sax countermelody behind the solos of Miley, Nanton, and the clarinetist, also the brass figures in the third chorus. However, it sounds as though Ellington's brass- and reed-players may be reading the verse and the last part of the third chorus. The main interest in "Song of the Cotton Field" lies not in the arrangement but in the special tone-qualities Ellington coaxes from his musicians—the dark voicings and nearly human cries that lend the piece an atmosphere of mystery and sorrow.

Nearly three months later, on April 30, 1927, the Washingtonians recorded Rube Bloom's "Soliloquy" (copyright June 21, 1926; E 642522) for Brunswick. Gunther Schuller has written that Ellington tried to "hit the white market" with "Soliloquy" in an attempt to "cash in" on its popularity.[7] But since Mills Music published Bloom's piece, Irving Mills probably recruited Ellington to record it. The day after Ellington made his recording of the song, *Metronome* announced that "Soliloquy" was enjoying good sales, "catching well as a dance tune everywhere since the original dance arrangement was taken up by Paul Whiteman, who is featuring it at his cabaret."[8] Bloom himself recorded a solo piano version of his piece in April 1927 (as he had earlier in March 1926).

The same year that Ellington recorded "Soliloquy," Jack Mills published an arrangement of the piece by Phil Boutelje. Subtitled "A Musical Thought" and marked "Slow and sultry," the piece is filled with the stylistic hallmarks of mid-twenties modern jazz—rich ninth chords, mild dissonance (e.g., the unresolved augmented triad in the second bar of the theme), and syncopated phrases based on secondary ragtime.

The Washingtonians' version of "Soliloquy" is rhythmically square and somewhat lackluster. Miley's absence from the date may be partly responsible for the low level of intensity. But the main problem stems from the band's adherence to written notation; throughout, Ellington's players closely follow Boutelje's arrangement, perhaps under instructions from the Brunswick people to render it "straight." Miley's replacement, June Clark (from Long Branch, New Jersey, Greer's hometown), plays lead trumpet sweetly and accurately, occasionally adding melodic and rhythmic embellishments to make his part hotter. In his piano solo, Ellington shows that he could follow the printed page if he had to. But while this fidelity to the text leaves Boutelje's arrangement intact, it strips the Washingtonians of their identity. The performance is competent yet anonymous.

Miley is also missing from Ellington's first session for OKeh, on November 3, 1927. With Jabbo Smith taking his place, Ellington's group recorded two tunes, "Chicago Stomp Down" and "What Can a Poor Fellow Do?" Perhaps the OKeh producer or Irving Mills requested these pieces.

"Chicago Stomp Down" (copyright December 27, 1927; E 682360) was written by Henry Creamer and James P. Johnson and published by Jack Mills. The "stomp" of the title comes from the Charleston-like figure— ♩ ♪ —repeated five times during each twenty-bar chorus. The piece also has a novelty feature in the form of two descending chromatic passages inserted in the middle section.

The arrangement follows a standard form for pop songs, with two statements of the chorus leading to the verse, then three more choruses following. As in "Song of the Cotton Field" the band may be playing from a stock on the verse; the conventional harmonies and close scoring for full ensemble sound prepackaged. The rest of the arrangement is filled out with solos: Hardwick on alto, a wordless growl vocal for Adelaide Hall, Nanton on trombone, Rudy Jackson on clarinet, and finally an arranged chorus with Jackson soloing above the ensemble.

"What Can a Poor Fellow Do?" (copyright May 14, 1927; E 666878), by Billy Meyers and the prolific writer Elmer Schoebel, appears to be closely based on Schoebel's stock orchestration.[9] A short introduction leads to Jabbo Smith's muted horn stating the melody with interlocking accompaniment for trombone and clarinet:

Example 44. "What Can a Poor Fellow Do?" (November 3, 1927), first chorus, mm. 1–8.

This is a rhythmically altered version of the chorus that appears in the stock arrangement following the verse; perhaps Ellington did the doctoring. After the band plays the verse virtually as written in the stock, the chorus returns with Hardwick on lead and slightly different harmonies. The stock is the source for the surprising modulation from E-flat to D-flat, also for sections of the final chorus and coda.

Jabbo Smith, interviewed in 1987, remembered reading parts for "What Can a Poor Fellow Do?" and said the piece was not rehearsed in the studio. He credited Ellington with the arrangement. [10]

While several soloists bring interest to certain sections of "Song of the Cotton Field," "Soliloquy," "Chicago Stomp Down," and "What Can a Poor Fellow Do?" collectively the Washingtonians do not emerge on these sides as an outstanding ensemble. Often they sound like an average New York dance band playing somewhat generic arrangements. Fortunately for Ellington, he had other pieces in his repertory and the opportunity to record them.

Hot Jazz

In its ad for a July 1927 appearance in Maine by Ellington, the *Portland Press Herald* printed a reminder: "Bring Your Asbestos Ear Muffs to Hear the Hottest Blue Blowing Dance Band above the Earth!" [11] During their summer New England tours, the Washingtonians became known as a fiery jazz outfit that could send dancers spinning across the floor with brisk tempos, crackling rhythms, and sizzling solos. Earlier they had recorded a few hot numbers for Pathé ("Georgia Grind," "Trombone Blues," "Parlor Social Stomp") and Gennett ("Li'l Farina"). But after the summer of 1926 they showed greater skill with such fast, syncopated pieces for dancing.

Improvements in both Ellington's arranging and the band's performance are evident in the November 29, 1926, recording of "Birmingham Breakdown." Ellington casts the piece in strain form, the structure he preferred for all his hot tunes of this period:

c	Ab ────────►		c	Ab ──────────────►		Db ────────►		
Ensemble	Reeds	Brass	Ensemble	Alto Solo	Brass	Tpt. Duet	Bar. Solo	Ensemble
16	20	20	16	16	20	16	12	12
Introduction	A	A¹	Introduction	B	A¹	B¹	C	C¹

This old framework, familiar from nineteenth-century marches, ragtime, and earlier jazz, provides Ellington with built-in thematic and harmonic contrasts. To add variety, Ellington pits the loud introduction and B strain against the quieter A strain. He also varies the length of sections, giving the A strain a twenty-bar structure somewhat unusual for jazz and dance pieces of the day (although "not uncommon," Gunther Schuller has written, "in ragtime").[12] In place of the trio found in typical strain form, Ellington substitutes the twelve-bar blues. To some extent this undercuts the originality of the A strain, following its structural asymmetry with a predictable solution. Yet ending with the blues was a practical measure, too, allowing Ellington, in live performance, to stretch out his arrangement with solos. The time limits of recording permit only two choruses—the first a baritone sax solo for Hardwick, the second a relaxed New Orleans ride-out for ensemble, with Hardwick and the brass filling in with ad-lib phrases while two clarinets play arranged riffs.

Ellington's themes in "Birmingham Breakdown" are harmonic and rhythmic rather than melodic in character. In its first appearance, in fact, the A strain sounds like a chord progression, primarily because the recording levels cause the saxophones' backgrounds to cover up an Ellington piano solo. But when trumpets and trombone enter, the true theme emerges out of the reeds' opening chordal sketch:

Example 45. "Birmingham Breakdown" (November 29, 1926), A[1] strain, mm. 1–4.

Schuller has called this theme a "rhythmicized chromatic chord progression."[13] Ellington derives the rhythm from the introduction, thus relating two sections that otherwise differ in theme, key, and dynamic level:

Example 46. "Birmingham Breakdown" (November 29, 1926), introduction, mm. 1–4.

*Tpt. 2 plays c' at m. 8.

The theme of the B strain, too, is less a melody than a "rhythmicized" arpeggiated figure (see Example 47b).

On February 28, 1927, Ellington recorded "Birmingham Breakdown" again, this time for Brunswick. Except for adding reeds behind the brass's A¹ sections, Ellington retains his earlier arrangement. However, the band's performance is slightly faster, crisper, and cleaner (compare, for example, the execution of the trombone/trumpet/alto break, first B strain, mm. 7–8). In 1952 Ellington listed this performance as one of his eleven favorite records—the only one, in fact, to date from the 1920s.[14]

"Birmingham Breakdown" was copyrighted on February 10, 1927 (E 660361), shortly before the second version was recorded. Gotham Music Service, Inc.—a division of Mills Music—brought it out as "Birmingham Back-Down." Curiously, the published version put the introduction in A-flat major rather than Ellington's C minor. Otherwise the A and B strains are similar to those on both recorded versions, as is the three-instrument break mentioned above. The arrangement ends, however, not with Ellington's blues choruses but with a return to the syncopated theme of A¹.

"Birmingham Breakdown" was recorded by a few other bands in 1927 and 1928, among them the Arkansas Travelers, a Red Nichols-Miff Mole group, on September 14, 1927. Nichols, Mole, and Rube Bloom, the Travelers' pianist, may have heard Ellington play the piece at the Kentucky Club. Their "Birmingham Breakdown" has a slower tempo and a more rocking rhythm. They omit the B strain altogether and solo over the chord progression of A. (Mole takes one chorus of twelve-bar blues in the middle.) Also, they do not repeat the introduction until the end of the arrangement, using it to round off the piece. Two highlights of the Travelers' performance are the lyrical solo by Nichols and the solid stride chorus by Bloom. Here Ellington's multipart form is whittled down to serve as a vehicle for soloists.

Ellington's second Vocalion session, on December 29, 1926, produced "The Creeper" (copyright February 25, 1927; E 660468), another fast dance number that shares features with "Birmingham Breakdown." Again, Ellington builds the arrangement on three strains of different lengths, this time in three different keys: E-flat, B-flat, and A-flat. Whereas in "Birmingham Breakdown" he turned to the blues for the C strain (or trio), here he draws upon the thirty-two-bar chord progression of "Tiger Rag." "The Creeper" marks the first time on record that Ellington used this harmonic plan that would appear later in "Hot and Bothered" (1928), "Jubilee Stomp" (1928), "High Life" (1929), "Daybreak Express" (1933), "Braggin' in Brass" (1938), and other pieces.

Like "Birmingham Breakdown," "The Creeper" lacks striking tunes; its melodic material comes more from short, fragmented phrases. The sixteen-bar theme of the A strain—stated by Hardwick after Joe Nanton's opening solo chorus—is based on what jazz musicians might call a "lick." In its rhythmic profile and accented leaps it resembles the B theme of "Birmingham Breakdown" (also taken by Hardwick):

Example 47 a. "The Creeper" (December 29, 1926), A^1 strain, mm. 1–8.

47 b. "Birmingham Breakdown" (November 29, 1926), B strain, mm. 1–7.

Similarly, the reed section's variation on the B strain of "The Creeper" (following its first statement by the brass) strings together several ideas that could have come from an improvised saxophone solo. The close, three-part voicing resembles Don Redman's writing for Fletcher Henderson:

Example 48. "The Creeper," B¹ strain, mm. 1–7.

For his introduction to "The Creeper" Ellington simply borrows the third of these hot phrases.

The thirty-two-bar C strain based on "Tiger Rag" has no theme. It begins with a Hardwick alto solo and concludes with an ensemble chorus that leaves plenty of room for improvising. In the absence of a third-strain theme, the published version of "The Creeper" actually includes a transcription of Hardwick's solo, probably taken off the record by a member of Mills's staff (and transposed from A-flat to B-flat):

Example 49. "The Creeper," C strain, 1927 published version, mm. 1–16.

"The Creeper" has other hot features besides its themes. Trombonist Nanton takes two solos, the first on open horn, the second muted. In the second-to-last chorus, over a temporary minor-chord reharmonization of the "Tiger Rag" progression (mm. 17–20), Hardwick's growling alto and Fred Guy's throbbing banjo evoke the sound-world of Ellington's later "jungle" pieces. There are also many breaks for soloists, and in the last chorus the brass play an arranged break based on a secondary rag device:

Example 50. "The Creeper," C¹ strain, break.

This break, as Schuller has pointed out, appears on the 1923 record-ing of "Snake Rag" by King Oliver's Creole Jazz Band, and Elling-ton would use it again in his 1929 recording of "Tiger Rag." [15] Such borrowing gives a clue to Ellington's listening habits and suggests where he may have found formal models for his hot pieces.

Two takes of "The Creeper" were made. In each case the ar-rangement and individual solos vary only slightly. On the second take Hardwick is a bit shaky in his first solo, the rhythm section rushes in the A strain, and the clarinetist plays a few wrong notes in the minor-key section of the last chorus. Perhaps for these reasons the first take was released.

Otto Hardwick assumes a prominent role playing lead alto and soloing on both "Birmingham Breakdown" and "The Creeper." Some of Ellington's thematic variations (e.g., "The Creeper," sec-ond B strain) seem to be modeled on Hardwick's style, if not taken directly from his improvisations. Just a few months later, for the March 22, 1927, Columbia session, Hardwick would share com-poser credit with Ellington on two pieces: "Hop Head" and "Down in Our Alley Blues."

"Hop Head" (copyright July 12, 1927; E 672244) bears the stamp of different musical personalities in each of its strains, al-though it is impossible to verify individual contributors. The A strain theme is probably Hardwick's; it even turns up in one of his alto breaks on "The Creeper" from the year before: [16]

Example 51 a. "Hop Head" (March 22, 1927), A strain, mm. 1–2.

51 b. "The Creeper" (December 29, 1926), break.

The theme of the B strain (Example 52) may have also come from Hardwick; it is a syncopated sequence based on skips of a fourth that echoes the A theme of "The Creeper" (see Example 47a):

Example 52. "Hop Head," B strain, mm. 1–7.

In contrast to these two linear themes, that of the third strain is more harmonic in character, suggesting an idea worked out by Ellington at the keyboard. Moreover, it incorporates the same rhythmic figure (♪♩ ♪♩ ♩) Ellington uses in "Birmingham Breakdown."

"Down in Our Alley Blues" (copyright August 12, 1927; E 670901) has neither the harmony nor structure of the blues but is another fast dance piece in strain form. It is filled with the secondary rag rhythmic grouping of three-in-four. Ellington may have picked up this device during his ragtime apprenticeship or heard it in the playing of New York stride pianists and in Don Redman's arrangements for Fletcher Henderson. In "Down in Our Alley Blues" Ellington uses it to make a "trick" introduction, as the stuttering effect momentarily obscures the metric flow. The A theme, too, plays off this effect, with the tuba phrasing in 3 + 3 + 2 against a different pattern in the reeds (see Example 53). James P. Johnson often broke up his left-hand accompaniment into 3 + 3 + 2 units to heighten the rhythmic tension.[17] Ellington does the same in his capable piano solo on "Down in Our Alley Blues," providing a direct link between his keyboard style and arranging techniques.

Example 53. "Down in Our Alley Blues" (March 22, 1927), A strain, mm. 1–4.

As in "Li'l Farina" from the previous year, the rhythmic influence of Louis Armstrong can be heard in both "Hop Head" and "Down in Our Alley Blues," especially in the playing of trumpeter Louis Metcalf. In "Hop Head," Metcalf's B-strain solo and his break at the end of the C strain are steeped in Armstrong's style, as when he rips up to a high note and tumbles down with an arpeggio. The ♩♩♩ or ♩♩♩♪ pattern is common, too, just as it was both in "Li'l Farina" and in Nanton's opening solo on "The Creeper."

The harmonies of "Hop Head" and "Down in Our Alley Blues" resort frequently to ninth chords. The published version of "Hop Head"—issued under the title "Down in Our Alley Blues" (see below)—has a four-bar introduction not heard on Ellington's recording which ends with a series of chromatically ascending ninth chords:

Example 54. "Down in Our Alley Blues," 1927 published version (recorded as "Hop Head"), introduction.

Similarly, the main theme of "Down in Our Alley Blues" is based on a ii^9 chord (see Example 53) which is played eight times during each statement of the thirty-two-bar section. The chord itself becomes a kind of thematic device, since Ellington brings the A strain back both in the middle and at the end of the arrangement.

Piano arrangements of both "Hop Head" and "Down in Our Alley Blues" were published in the summer of 1927 with the titles reversed from the way they appeared on the recordings. Titles were treated very loosely. Many probably resulted in the recording studio as afterthoughts, making an error in labeling easily possible. Both titles are colorful and must have been intended to attract potential record-buyers. "Hop Head" refers to an opium addict, as in the line from Mamie Smith's "Crazy Blues" of 1920, "I'm gonna do like the Chinaman, / Get myself some hop." The music of "Down in Our Alley Blues" is neither blues-derived nor redolent of an alley, but the title makes the piece sound inviting.

The published versions of both pieces contain important thematic sections from the recordings as well as transcribed solos and breaks. One example of transcription can be seen in the B strain to "Down in Our Alley Blues" (i.e., "Hop Head" on the record), where the unpianistic right-hand voicings come directly from Ellington's reed section:

Example 55. "Down in Our Alley Blues," published version (recorded as "Hop Head"), B strain, mm. 1–11.

Elsewhere the piano reductions follow Ellington's scoring quite closely; if Ellington was not responsible for these arrangements, a staff arranger at Mills either produced them from Ellington's written parts (if any existed) or, more likely, took them off the recordings.

In 1927 Ellington's band recorded "Washington Wabble" for Victor on October 6 (three takes, two issued) and on October 26 (two takes, one issued). Like Ellington's other compositions in the hot jazz genre, "Washington Wabble" (copyright December 30, 1927; E 682389) is made up of contrasting strains, each distinguished more by a rhythmic figure or improvised solo than by an actual theme. The piece is filled with ninth chords and ternary phrase groupings, and occasionally features a Charleston-like rhythmic figure:

Example 56. "Washington Wabble" (October 26, 1927), C strain, mm. 9–15.

The last section provides a typically raucous finale: as the brass call out a phrase reminiscent of the final chorus of "Hop Head," Rudy Jackson solos over the ensemble, giving the illusion of a collectively improvised out-chorus.

In every take, "Washington Wabble" features a level of performance higher than that on the earlier hot pieces. From the opening salute the band builds momentum steadily, leading each section smoothly to the next and driving ahead to the final stomping bars. It sounds as though the musicians had played this arrangement many times. The ensemble passages are cohesive, and the solos of Metcalf, Jackson, Ellington, Hardwick, and Nanton are fairly set, as can be heard by comparing the three takes that were issued. One of the key players on "Washington Wabble" is bassist Wellman Braud. His sustained half-notes and pounding quarters help provide a solid rhythmic foundation. He takes a two-bar bass break—the earliest example on an Ellington record—in the repeat of the A strain. On the October 26 version Braud bows on the A strain behind Metcalf then switches to slapping pizzicato for Rudy Jackson's clarinet solo; this simple change creates an electric effect. Rudy Jackson is in fine form throughout. On the last chorus he brings a festive spirit to the proceedings, his high notes popping out like firecrackers. This is a band in command of its material, playing with verve and enthusiasm.

The published version of "Washington Wabble" keeps to Ellington's three-part form, although it gives the key areas as D, G, and C rather than the record's F, B-flat, and E-flat. The arrangement includes transcriptions of solos by Rudy Jackson and Otto Hardwick, also breaks played on the recording by Wellman Braud and Harry Carney.

These five pieces—"Birmingham Breakdown," "The Creeper," "Hop Head," "Down in Our Alley Blues," and "Washington Wabble"—show how Ellington could serve up hot dance music spiced with the favorite ingredients of the day: syncopated rhythmic figures, trick breaks, ninth chords, chromatic lines, and New Orleans–influenced final choruses. In concocting his arrangements, Ellington drew upon formal and stylistic conventions already established by Redman and other New York dance-band arrangers. And his rhythmic vocabulary blended the syncopated devices of ragtime and stride with the more recent swing of Armstrong.

The important soloists on these records are Hardwick, Nanton, Jackson, Metcalf, and Ellington. But what about Miley? Although advertised in the band's publicity as "America's hottest trumpeter," Miley does not play a major role in these hot pieces (although perhaps he did in live performances). Instead it is Metcalf, with his Armstrong-inspired phrasing and licks, who most often takes the lead.

Miley's hot trumpet filled a special function in Ellington's compositions. When the tempo slowed down and the lights dimmed, it was Miley's turn to step forward and play the blues. Inspired by the soul in Miley's horn, Ellington fashioned pieces that went beyond hot jazz and made his band sound like no one else's. In the process he discovered new paths as a composer.

A Composer and the Blues

Looking back at the twenties, Ellington recalled in his memoirs how musicians attempted to depict scenes or describe states of feeling in their solos: "Painting a picture, or having a story to go with what you were going to play, was of vital importance in those days. The audience didn't know anything about it, but the cats in the band did."[18] Among the "painters" singled out by Ellington were Sidney Bechet, Arthur Whetsol, Joe Nanton, and especially Bubber Miley, who "always had a story for his music."[19] The titles of Ellington's later compositions suggest that he, too, wanted to paint pictures with sounds. Some of his subjects were places ("Echoes of Harlem," "Isfahan"), people ("Portrait of the Lion," "Jack the Bear"), nature ("Dusk," "Sunset and the Mocking Bird"), trains ("Daybreak Express," "Happy-Go-Lucky-Local"), and emotions ("Mood Indigo," "Melancholia").

The origins of Ellington's tone pictures can be traced to pieces he first recorded in 1926 and 1927. They may have taken their pictorial quality from stage or dance acts they accompanied. Or they may have sprung directly from something Ellington or one of his musicians had felt or seen—as when Miley imagined "East St. Louis Toodle-O" to be about an old, tired man limping home after a day's work. Whatever their source, these mood or character pieces became Ellington's trademark. As Mercer Ellington has written, his father always tried to "make the listener *feel* experiences with the sound, almost as though he were creating apparitions within the music."[20]

By the mid-twenties, the term "blues" had taken on different meanings. It could refer to a melancholy emotional state or a musical and textual form which might (or might not) express sad feelings. It could also apply to pieces—for example, "Down in Our Alley Blues" or "Potato Head Blues"—which showed no trace of either the typical character or musical form of the blues. Singers like Bessie Smith, Ma Rainey, and Sippie Wallace, and instrumentalists like King Oliver, Louis Armstrong, and Sidney Bechet had demonstrated the artistic potential and emotional power of the blues on their recordings. At the same time, for many singers in the 1920s the blues represented more of a commercial phenomenon than a vehicle for conveying intense emotions.

The early blues pieces Ellington recorded between 1924 and 1926 come under the more commercial category. "It's Gonna Be a Cold, Cold Winter," "How Come You Do Me Like You Do?" and "If You Can't Hold the Man You Love" were considered blues songs in their time, even if they did not follow the twelve-bar form with its series of AAB stanzas and its basic chord progression built on tonic, sub-dominant, and dominant. " 'Wanna Go Back Again' Blues" is not a blues at all, simply a pop song that describes someone who is "blue" about being away from home. Both "Trombone Blues" and "Georgia Grind" feature the chord progression and formal outline of blues choruses, but their frenetic rhythms and tricky licks separate them from gutsier instrumental blues like the Creole Jazz Band's "Dippermouth Blues" (1923) or Jelly Roll Morton's "Dead Man Blues" (1926). Perhaps Ellington comes closest to the spirit of the blues on the recordings of "Lucky Number Blues" and "I'm Gonna Put You Right in Jail" with Alberta Jones, but here he is limited by mediocre material and a singer of modest ability.

Ellington's first important piece using the blues form is "Immigration Blues" (copyright February 25, 1927; E 660467), recorded at the second session for Vocalion on December 29, 1926. The piece does not strictly follow the formal structure of the blues. The first chorus is sixteen bars and based on an original chord progression.

It sounds reminiscent of a spiritual, in part because of what Schuller has termed the "organ-like" character of the opening, with its plagal cadences and hymn-like solemnity. Rudy Jackson states the theme on tenor saxophone, and Miley takes it up midway through on open horn. Nanton begins the next chorus, but after only eight bars there is an abrupt harmonic splice (from F to E-flat) and the twelve-bar blues progression begins.[21]

The rest of "Immigration Blues" features four solos: Hardwick on alto, Ellington at the piano, Miley with his plunger mute, and Hardwick again (with what sounds like a two-trumpet dialogue behind him). The band supports Hardwick both times and plays a little closing figure at the end of each chorus. Otherwise the sound of the full ensemble is withheld until the final chorus. This way Ellington keeps the focus on individual feeling, as the soloists present different facets of the same blue mood.

Perhaps Ellington supplied his players with a "picture" behind "Immigration Blues" to inspire such emotional consistency.[22] It might have depicted an uprooted black southerner living in the North (a number of popular songs on this theme had appeared since the Civil War). The opening section suggests the folk culture of the southerner, steeped in religion and expressed through the spiritual. The second section might have represented the southerner after relocation—now with a case of the blues. Such a meaning would not be farfetched in mid-1920s New York, a city with places like the Plantation Café and Cotton Club, where whites went to watch black entertainers re-enact scenes from southern life in songs, dances, and skits. Ellington and his musicians had played for such revues both downtown and in Harlem.

But Ellington does not just let the soloists have their say. To balance his composition he carefully arranges tone colors. He pairs Jackson's gruff tenor with Miley's open horn, then lets Nanton's muted trombone finish the A section before bringing in Hardwick's alto. After his own subdued piano chorus, Ellington closes with Miley growling and Hardwick playing it pretty (a coupling he would use in "Black and Tan Fantasy" to contrast the two main themes). In addition to ordering different timbres Ellington highlights the character of each soloist by giving him appropriate settings. During Miley's growl solo, for example, he emphasizes seventh chords in his piano voicings and calls for heavy back-beats in the accompaniment. When Hardwick returns for the final chorus, the sevenths recede and smooth quarter-note motion resumes in the rhythm section. By 1926 it was common for arrangers to adapt the textures and rhythms of accompaniments to fit individual soloists. But by using these techniques to enhance a poetic effect and achieve aesthetic unity, Ellington was breaking new ground.[23]

Although Ellington provides a folk-like melody for the first part of "Immigration Blues," he gives it a few sophisticated harmonic touches from the big city. Each eight-bar phrase of the A section ends with a movement by thirds, traveling from F (I) to C (V) by way of A major:

Example 57. "Immigration Blues" (December 29, 1926), first chorus, mm. 5–8.

This move to the sharp side of F is counterbalanced by the cadences on ${}^{b}VI^{b7}$ after the introduction and in Jackson's and Nanton's solos. Another advanced harmonic aspect comes in the middle of Miley's first solo, when a line descending by whole-steps prepares V. Here is the section as it appears in the published version:

Example 58. "Immigration Blues," 1927 published version, mm. 21–28.

In such a passage Ellington presents himself as a composer updating an older style.

"New Orleans Low-Down" (copyright June 23, 1928; E 694892) is another blues-based composition in which Ellington lets the individual character of soloists take precedence over thematic contrast. Less of a tone picture than "Immigration Blues," "New Orleans Low-Down" might make musical reference to the South in the arpeggiated tuba figure in the first and last choruses (a stylized Crescent City bass line?), also in Miley's muted solo, which clearly shows his respect for King Oliver. But the theatrical fanfare of the introduction (cf. "Georgia Grind"), the whole-tone passage for reeds in the fifth chorus, and the eight-bar modulatory section that follows make "New Orleans Low-Down" a piece that could only have come from a New York downtown band. As with "Birmingham Breakdown," the "New Orleans" of the title may have reflected Vocalion's marketing aims more than specific musical traits.

The opening ensemble chorus of "New Orleans Low-Down" does not have much of a theme, only the ♩ ♩ ♩ ♪ rhythmic figure placed against the ascending arpeggio on tuba (doubled by piano) that supports Louis Metcalf's lead trumpet. This chorus seems perfunctory, as though Ellington felt compelled to fill up twelve bars before introducing soloists. Miley is the first to enter, immediately bringing the piece back to basics with his raw emotion and gutbucket style. Once again Ellington varies the rhythm of the accompaniment behind soloists and alternates tone colors. He backs Hardwick's sweet alto with a quasi-martial rhythmic figure— ♪ ♫♩ ♩ ♩ —then follows with Nanton's plunger-mute chorus while Braud's tuba plays on beats two and four. Miley and Nanton sound remarkably close in timbre and even begin their solos the same way (on a sustained E-flat). As Ellington wrote of the pair, "They had such beautiful teamwork together. Everything they played represented a mood, a person, a picture." [24] On "New Orleans Low-Down," they seem to be describing the same thing—whatever it may be.

Lacking any distinctive themes, "New Orleans Low-Down" might have ended up a string of solos over a blues progression. But Ellington shapes the piece by having the ensemble round off each solo with the same cadential phrase and by modulating to B-flat for Nanton's second chorus. Also, the final chorus brings a twofold reprise of the opening section. First the ensemble repeats the theme based on the ♩ ♩ ♩ ♪ rhythm. Then Miley truncates the second statement into a four-bar coda that keeps the same figure and also echoes the phrase he used to begin his own solo.

The dark reed voicings behind Nanton's second solo foreshadow the unusual orchestrational effects that later became an Ellington specialty.[25] But for the most part, Ellington's soloists leave a stronger impression than does the composer-arranger. "New Orleans Low-Down" has many of the same components of "Immigration Blues"; as a composition, however, it holds together less well.

In "Creole Love Call" (copyright August 16, 1928; E 698167), recorded October 26, 1927, for Victor, Ellington transforms a series of blues choruses and the simplest of themes into a haunting southern landscape. The "Creole" in the title identifies the vicinity as somewhere near New Orleans. Adelaide Hall plays the part of a sultry southern siren, singing a wordless obbligato in the first and last choruses. At the outset her voice is high and clear, as though floating in from afar. By the end she has come closer, her tone more earthy than ethereal.

As Adelaide Hall tells it, she first heard Ellington's band play the piece that became "Creole Love Call" when she was traveling with it on the RKO theater circuit.[26] As Hall listened to the band from the wings, she started humming a countermelody in between phrases. Apparently Ellington liked what he heard: "[He] came right across the stage to the wing and said, 'Addie, that's what I wanted. . . . We're going to do it again.' I said, 'Do what?' . . . So he started from the beginning of the chorus with the orchestra, and I started this counter-melody."[27] After the show Ellington told Hall he wanted to record the piece with her "tomorrow or the next day." In the studio she repeated what she had done off-stage; Ellington gave her little or no advice about what to sing or how to sing it.[28]

Just as Ellington had earlier learned to pick up ragtime devices in Washington, so he "caught" Hall's part and immediately knew how to use it in his piece. But this was not the only music Ellington borrowed. The clarinet trio's main theme in "Creole Love Call" can be heard on the 1923 recording of "Camp Meeting Blues" by King Oliver's Jazz Band, specifically in Jimmie Noone's clarinet solo (which is related to the first strain of Oliver's piece):

Example 59 a. "Camp Meeting Blues," King Oliver's Jazz Band (October 16, 1923), clarinet solo.

59 b. "Creole Love Call" (October 26, 1927), first chorus. Only the pitches of Adelaide Hall's vocal have been transcribed.

All but the second and third of "Creole Love Call"'s six choruses are based on this theme. Rudy Jackson, who received joint composer credit with Miley and Ellington on "Creole Love Call," may have brought this theme into the band. On "Being Down Don't Worry Me," an OKeh record made about August 1925, Jackson had played the same tune behind singer Sippie Wallace.[29]

In the third chorus Rudy Jackson plays a melody on clarinet that also appeared on "Camp Meeting Blues," where it was stated by a trombonist (probably Ed Atkins) and embellished by Lil Hardin's accompanying piano:

Example 60 a. "Camp Meeting Blues," trombone solo.

60 b. "Creole Love Call," third chorus, clarinet solo.

Jackson could have learned the solo during his Chicago days with King Oliver, or even before. Judging from the way Atkins and Hardin perform the tune, it may have been an old blues familiar to New Orleans musicians or perhaps a solo that became well known and set over time (like Oliver's on "Dippermouth Blues").

This leaves the second chorus to account for—Bubber Miley's solo. Since Miley is listed as one of the composers, the theme may be his.

Example 61. "Creole Love Call," second chorus, Bubber Miley solo.

*In this solo, Miley plays ♩♩ as ♩³♪.

In the published version of "Creole Love Call," this twelve-bar theme (marked with repeats) makes up the second chorus; it is followed by two more statements of the "Camp Meeting Blues" chorus.

Adelaide Hall, Rudy Jackson, Bubber Miley, and King Oliver's Jazz Band were all important contributors to "Creole Love Call." As for Ellington, he probably decided upon an order for the various elements and varied the orchestration of the "Camp Meeting Blues" theme. The clarinet trio takes it down low in the first and sixth choruses, and two octaves higher in the fifth. The brass pick it up in the fourth chorus, answered by the reed players, who have switched to saxophones. Ellington also added low connecting phrases in the piano during Jackson's solo, the syncopated pattern in the brass that answers the high clarinet trio, and the *misterioso* ending based on a half-diminished seventh chord. These orchestrational touches helped Ellington integrate ideas he had borrowed from others. "Creole Love Call" shows a continuing development of the balanced timbres and ordered solos heard in "Immigration Blues" and "New Orleans Low-Down." Yet unlike these last two pieces, "Creole Love Call" had staying power. It was still in Ellington's active repertory in the 1970s.

The same October 26, 1927, Victor session yielded two takes of "Blues I Love to Sing" (copyright December 30, 1927; E 682387), another blues-derived composition featuring Adelaide Hall. Here, though, Ellington departs from the usual twelve-bar choruses, turning to an ABB¹A form with outer sections of twenty-four measures (8 + 4 + 8 + 4) and inner ones based on eight-bar lengths (B = 8 + 8, B¹ = 8). (In the final chorus, however, the last four bars of the A section serve as a standard tag using the I-V⁷/II-V⁷/V-V-I formula.) The theme of the A section may be Miley's invention, since he states it both times and receives co-composer credit with Ellington. Hall's wordless vocal in the reprise of the A section is based on this theme.

Although she uses her voice instrumentally, Hall is more of a human presence than on "Creole Love Call," interjecting spoken phrases like "Oh, you're killin' me," and "It won't be long now." She ends her gritty vocalise with half-swallowed reiterations of the refrain, "It's the blues I love to sing."

The A theme of "Blues I Love to Sing" has few blue notes (mm. 9–10), and while its chord progression shares some features with the standard twelve-bar form, it is different enough to sound original. Yet even without direct imitation the theme captures the melancholy essence of the blues. The B section, in the subdominant, also retains this character despite its quick harmonic rhythm and chromatically altered chords. The high point of the piece is Joe Nanton's solo:

Example 62. "Blues I Love to Sing," middle section, trombone solo.

This solo—like Miley's and Hardwick's—seems to have been set and not improvised. Both takes of "Blues I Love to Sing" contain only slight variations in solo and ensemble sections, indicating how well-rehearsed such a number was.

An interesting footnote: the B section theme of "Blues I Love to Sing," stated by Hardwick on alto, appears as the main theme of a 1927 Ellington composition called "Black Cat Blues" (copyright December 6; E 679305), which also quotes six bars of the Nanton solo mentioned above. Ellington did not record "Black Cat Blues."

"Blues I Love to Sing" reveals that Ellington was discovering how to depict a blue mood without falling back on old conventions. The piece has new themes, new chord patterns, and a rounded form. Yet it is imbued with the spirit of the blues—not the blues of Tin Pan Alley or theater revues but a blend of sad and joyful emotions distilled from black-American experience.

A Composer and His Muse

In the year before Ellington went into the Cotton Club, amidst the hot jazz, blues, and pop songs recorded by his band, two compositions stood out from the rest for their distinctive tonal and formal qualities: "Black and Tan Fantasy" and "East St. Louis Toodle-O."[30] Each was recorded on three separate occasions during this period, and "East St. Louis Toodle-O" appeared again on December 19, 1927—the first recording session after the band had entered the Cotton Club. More than anything Ellington had recorded until then, this music was unique. "East St. Louis Toodle-O" was Sonny Greer's favorite piece in the early days because it established the band's identity so strongly: "People heard it and said, 'Here they come!' "[31] Indeed, "East St. Louis Toodle-O" served as the band's theme song until about 1940 and stayed in the repertory for the rest of Ellington's life.

Bubber Miley played an important role in bringing both "Black and Tan Fantasy" and "East St. Louis Toodle-O" into being. Ever since joining the Washingtonians in 1923 Miley had been a key figure in defining the style of the band; now his sound permeated these two compositions, enriching them with drama and emotion.

Built on the twelve-bar blues form, "Black and Tan Fantasy" (copyright July 16, 1927; E 672246) belongs to the African-American tradition Ellington mined in pieces like "Immigration Blues" and "Creole Love Call." According to Miley, the main theme came from variations his mother used to sing on a spiritual she called "Hosanna." The "Hosanna" melody is related to the chorus of Stephen Adams's sacred song, "The Holy City":[32]

Example 63 a. Stephen Adams, "The Holy City" (1892), chorus, mm. 1–12.

63 b. Ellington, "Black and Tan Fantasy," 1927 published stock, trumpet part, mm. 1–12.

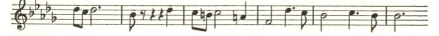

Although Miley states the opening in minor, later solos revert to Adams's original major mode.

The form of "Black and Tan Fantasy" was fairly well set by the time of its first recording for Brunswick on April 7, 1927. When Ellington returned to the piece in the fall, first for the October 26 Victor date, then on November 3 for OKeh (with Jabbo Smith taking Miley's place), the significant differences are in sound and tempo, not in the arrangement.[33] All three versions, however, have different qualities to recommend them. The opening chorus of the Brunswick session is almost fierce, while on Victor the slower tempo and relaxed pacing make it both more somber and more powerful. The eerie tone of Jabbo Smith gives the Columbia release a vague, dream-like quality. For overall conception and performance, however, the Victor disc has a slight edge over the others. It is the one described below.

"Black and Tan Fantasy" immediately plunges the listener into a dark, slightly forbidding tonal atmosphere. Miley states the tune with Nanton harmonizing underneath. There is no showy introduction or preliminary fanfare, just the plaintive melody and the stark accompaniment of piano, banjo, tuba, and drums:

Example 64. "Black and Tan Fantasy" (October 26, 1927), first chorus.

Suddenly Hardwick's silky alto enters with a new melody, this one as suggestive and alluring as the first was severe. It curls upward like a wisp of smoke, evoking the illicit pleasures and over-ripe atmosphere of a "black and tan" cabaret. Tailor-made for Hardwick's smooth style, the second theme is probably Ellington's own, beginning as it does on the $^{\flat}VI^{\flat 9}$ chord (in the new key of B-flat major) and having the syncopated phrase groupings of secondary ragtime:

Example 65. "Black and Tan Fantasy," second theme, mm. 1–8.

Schuller disparages this theme as "slick" and "trying-to-be-modern show music."[34] Yet it provides an effective contrast, both melodic and harmonic, to the opening chorus. And Hardwick plays it beautifully; his warm tone and sensuous phrasing—with the tossed-off downward lip slurs—make it hard to resist.

The next four choruses follow a straight twelve-bar blues pattern and feature soloists: Miley for two choruses, then Ellington, then Nanton. Beginning on a soft and high B-flat held for four bars, Miley constructs a solo that is impressive both in its careful control and spontaneous feeling. He bends notes and growls judiciously, using these techniques as embellishments rather than tricks.[35] By October 1927 his two choruses had become a fixed part of the composition. On later recordings of "Black and Tan Fantasy" other trumpeters played them virtually note-for-note.[36]

Ellington follows Miley with a chorus in which he brings back the ♭VI chord (m. 6). After Miley's concentrated statement, Ellington's solo is looser and more relaxed. Like Hardwick following Miley at the outset, Ellington provides relief to the tension, all part of the "fantasy" being spun out by the band. Then Nanton invokes the keening sound of a blues singer. Toward the end he gives out a comical whinny that must have made listeners smile, especially if they were beginning to get nervous from the intensity of expression. R. D. Darrell, in an early appreciation of Ellington's work from 1932, wrote of "Black and Tan Fantasy": "I laughed like everyone else over its instrumental wa-waing and gargling and gobbling. . . . But as I continued to play the record . . . I laughed less heartily and with less zest. In my ears the whinnies and wa-was began to re-solve into new tone colors, distorted and tortured, but agonizingly expressive. The piece took on a surprising individuality and entity as well as an intensity of feeling that was totally incongruous in popular dance music. Beneath all its oddity and perverseness there was a twisted beauty that grew on me more and more and could not be shaken off."[37]

In the final chorus Miley returns for a call-and-response sequence with the rhythm section. The rest of the brass and reeds enter at m. 8 to suggest the imminent end of the fantasy. For the coda, Ellington brings down the curtain with the famous Chopin "Funeral March" quotation (from Sonata No. 2, Opus 35, in B-flat minor).

The main compositional achievement of "Black and Tan Fantasy" lies in Ellington's discovery of an effective musical-dramatic frame-work within which to present his distinctive soloists. Although sharing qualities with "Immigration Blues," "Creole Love Call"—even with "New Orleans Low-Down"—"Black and Tan Fantasy" reveals a more skillful blending of older forms and greater emo-tional depth. Miley's thematic contributions and four pillar-like choruses—supporting beginning, middle, and end—have much to do with the piece's success. But it took Ellington to direct the action and make sure that individual contributions did not detract from the unity of the piece. The elements may derive from the blues, sacred song, King Oliver, Miley, and Chopin, but the final compound is pure Ellington.

Mills's Gotham Music Service published both a piano version of "Black and Tan Fantasy" and a stock arranged by Eddie Powell. The former contains four choruses drawn from the recorded arrangement: Miley's opening statement, Hardwick's secondary theme, Ellington's solo chorus, and the final call-and-response leading to the "Funeral March" tag. The first and last sections sound quite different because of the piano's inability both to bend notes and to suggest the brass timbres of Ellington's players. Unlike "Hop Head," "Washington Wabble," and other fast pieces by Ellington, "Black and Tan Fantasy" seems to have been conceived for the ensemble rather than at the keyboard. Powell's arrangement of the Ellington-Miley piece preserves many details from the record but assigns parts to different instruments. Thus, a band buying the Mills stock would have gotten only a skeleton of the piece: its heart lay in the performing style of individuals and could not be transmitted through notation.

Some of the pictorial qualities of "Black and Tan Fantasy" were realized in the 1929 film short *Black and Tan*, featuring Ellington and his orchestra and Cotton Club dancer Freddi Washington. At the beginning of the film Ellington is shown rehearsing his new piece with Arthur Whetsol. At the end, after Washington collapses at a "black and tan" while dancing (against doctor's orders), she asks Ellington to play "Black and Tan Fantasy." Ellington's musicians, joined by the moaning laments of the Hall Johnson Choir, perform the funereal piece as the dancer lies on her deathbed.

Another theatrical scenario for "Black and Tan Fantasy" was suggested in a description of the Ellington band by Frank M. Davis, a syndicated columnist for the Associated Negro Press. Writing to Marshall Stearns in 1949, Davis recounted a story—which he admits "may be pure fiction" but had been told to him as "the gospel truth"—in which Johnny Dunn and Bubber Miley scheduled a trumpet duel at the Lafayette Theater, sometime in the mid-twenties. First Dunn played. Handsome and confident, he stepped to center-stage in his white silk tuxedo and "ran his repertoire of hot stuff." The crowd responded enthusiastically. Then it was Miley's turn:

> The audience leaned forward. But instead of coming to the front of the stage to solo, the curtain lifted and it showed the interior of a backwoods church. Then Duke Ellington began playing in the background. After a few bars, there came a series of wails off-stage. They grew louder, and Bubber Miley appeared, dressed as a preacher. And while the Ellington band sent him with the sub-dued but pulsating background, Bubber took his rubber squeegee and provided wah-wah effects and wails which only Miley could do and which had never before been heard in Harlem. Bubber hadn't even reached the middle of his sermon before Johnny Dunn was observed to rise and walk quietly out of the auditorium.[38]

In such a setting, "Black and Tan Fantasy" may have been the piece Ellington chose to establish Miley's authority and to present his orchestra with dramatic flair.

Although "East St. Louis Toodle-O," unlike "Black and Tan Fantasy," is not based on blues form, it is suffused with the spirit of the idiom. It represents Ellington's highest compositional achievement from the early years.

Again, Miley provided the main melody. Apparently he conceived of the theme upon seeing a sign in the Boston area advertising Lewando's, a local dry cleaner's business (probably in the summer of 1926):

Example 66. "East St. Louis Toodle-O," first theme. [From Roger Pryor Dodge, "Bubber," *H.R.S. Rag* (October 15, 1940), p. 10.]

Miley may have known Fletcher Henderson's 1924 recording of W. C. Handy's "The Gouge of Armour Avenue." In the middle, trombonist Charlie Green plays a few phrases over a minor-mode vamp;[39] Miley's are remarkably similar:

Example 67. Top line: "East St. Louis Toodle-O"(November 29, 1926), first theme, Bubber Miley solo, mm. 1–15. Bottom line: "The Gouge of Armour Avenue," Fletcher Henderson and his Orchestra (July 31, 1924), Charlie Green trombone solo, mm. 17–23, mm. 8–15.

Both Louis Armstrong's "Yes! I'm in the Barrel!" (November 12, 1925) and "The King of the Zulus" (June 23, 1926) begin with a mournful solo over a static vamp. The melancholy character of these pieces, as well as the specific musical device they use, may have influenced Ellington's "East St. Louis Toodle-O."

"East St. Louis Toodle-O" must have been in the Washingtonians' repertory by October or November of 1926. When Ellington went into the Vocalion studio on November 29 for his first date using only original material, he chose it as one of four pieces to be recorded, and his band gave every sign of being familiar with the arrangement. The name of the piece, however, may have emerged during the record session. Apparently Vocalion wanted to increase sales in the largely black section of East St. Louis, Illinois, hence the place name in the title. [40]

The "Toodle-O" part of the title has an interesting history. In 1962 Ellington explained that this phrase—which he always pronounced "Toad'lo"—meant a kind of broken walk. Elsewhere he recalled the picture Miley imagined for the piece: "This is an old man, tired from working in the field since sunup, coming up the road in the sunset on his way home to dinner. He's tired but strong, and humming in time with his broken gait." [41] The term Ellington probably had in mind was "todalo," which referred to a specific dance style or step. [42] Through printing errors the title was spelled different ways as the piece was rerecorded. It started as "Toodle-O" (Vocalion, November 29, 1926, and Brunswick, March 14, 1927) and went on to "Toodle-Oo" (Columbia, March 22, 1927) and "Toddle-Oo" (Victor, December 19, 1927). Both the stock and piano versions published by Gotham in 1927 give it as "Toodle-O." The spellings seem less important than the correct pronunciation, which differs from the popular phrase for good-bye. Pronouncing the title Ellington's way links it to earlier pieces with "todalo" in the title—Eubie Blake's "Baltimore Todolo" (ca. 1907), Joe Jordan's "The Darkey Todalo" (1910), J. B. Brown and A. W. Walsh's "My Todalo Man" (1911)—and also lends support to Ellington's story relating the word to physical movement.

Since Ellington and his band recorded "East St. Louis Toodle-O" again in March 1927 for both Brunswick and Columbia, also later in December for Victor, it seems to have been an important part of their repertory. Gunther Schuller has acknowledged the piece's standing by discussing it in detail in his chapter on Ellington's style.[43] Schuller compares the four versions recorded between November 29, 1926, and December 19, 1927, showing how Ellington used the same arrangement for the three earliest versions then shifted two choruses and changed soloists for the "improved format" of the Victor date.

The form of "East St. Louis Toodle-O" is unusual not only for jazz compositions of the time, as Schuller notes, but for Ellington as well. His faster pieces from 1926 and 1927—like "Birmingham Breakdown," "Hop Head," and "Washington Wabble"—make use of the old strain-form principle, usually with several contrasting thematic and key areas. A slower, blues-inspired piece like "Immigration Blues" might have two contrasting themes (as does "East St. Louis Toodle-O"), but one simply follows the other, with no attempt at integration or balance. "Black and Tan Fantasy" also has two principal themes, but there Ellington builds the arrangement on a series of blues choruses, as in "Creole Love Call," rather than developing the material; except for harmonic allusions to it in Ellington's piano solo, Hardwick's secondary theme never returns after its first appearance. Perhaps the closest formal parallel to "East St. Louis Toodle-O" is found in "Down in Our Alley Blues," where the A strain makes a rondo-like return in the middle and at the end; similarly, in "East St. Louis Toodle-O" Ellington recalls the A section for the clarinet solo midway through the piece and for Miley's final reprise of the theme.

Another formal aspect that makes "East St. Louis Toodle-O" more an integrated structure than a string of solos is Ellington's withholding of the secondary theme until the piece is well underway. After Miley's thirty-two-bar, AABA opening strain in C minor, Nanton takes an eighteen-bar solo in the relative major of E-flat. But the theme that goes with this section is not heard until later, when stated by the brass:

Example 68. "East St. Louis Toodle-O" (December 19, 1927), secondary theme, mm. 1–8.

As Martin Williams has noted, this theme is closely related to the second strain of Scott Joplin and Louis Chauvin's "Heliotrope Bouquet" (1907).[44] And the basic outlines of its sixteen-bar chord progression can be found in many songs and ragtime pieces, among them Joplin's "Maple Leaf Rag," A. J. Piron's "I Wish I Could Shimmy Like My Sister Kate," and W. C. Handy's "Memphis Blues." On the three early recordings of "East St. Louis Toodle-O" this theme is repeated by both reeds and full ensemble before Miley's final reprise. But Ellington pares it down on the Victor date, partly because he has given Carney a solo on the same progression earlier and partly, perhaps, because of time limitations. Other Ellington arrangements from the same period, like "Birmingham Breakdown," show a similar delay in presenting themes, though not to the same extent as "East St. Louis Toodle-O." Later pieces such as "Old Man Blues" (1930) and "Diminuendo and Crescendo in Blue" (1937) follow the same procedure.

Beyond its formal features, "East St. Louis Toodle-O" is distinguished by a background accompanying figure for the reeds that serves as a countermelody to Miley's main theme. This returning, ominous undercurrent is as important to the piece as the theme itself, perhaps even more so. The bottom-heavy scoring of the original recording places three saxophones (two altos and baritone) in close harmony, with the tuba doubling one of the lines below. In the later Victor version Wellman Braud's bowed bass replaces Bass Edwards's tuba, and Ellington spreads out the voicings and supplies one of the lines on piano:

Example 69. "East St. Louis Toodle-O" (December 19, 1927), introduction, mm. 1–7.

The murky effect of this passage may result in part from poor balances in the recording studio. But Ellington may have wanted it to sound that way, too, as later recordings made with more advanced equipment suggest. The timbres of reeds, piano, and bass blend into a blurry wash behind Miley's growls and sharp articulation.

While the form of "East St. Louis Toodle-O" varies slightly in the December 19, 1927, Victor version, on the whole both solos and ensemble parts are quite close to those on the first recording. This, too, reflects the piece's composed quality: instead of being a vehicle for individual improvisation, it is more of a fixed statement for full ensemble, with each member taking preplanned roles.

Some of the compositional shaping processes in "East St. Louis Toodle-O" can be seen taking place over time. On the first recording, during the bridge of Miley's opening solo Ellington plays a single-note countermelody behind the trumpet. By March Nanton has taken up this line, which can be heard faintly on the Brunswick disc and with more clarity on the Columbia version made eight days later. By December, however, the counterpoint of the two brass parts is a primary feature of the section:

Example 70. "East St. Louis Toodle-O" (December 19, 1927), first chorus, mm. 17–22.

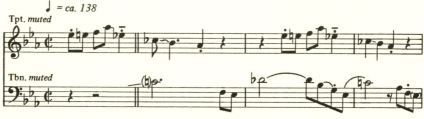

On the Victor version Ellington also provides a piano counterpoint to Harry Carney's solo, playing single-note lines in the range of a trombone:

Example 71. "East St. Louis Toodle-O" (December 19, 1927), Harry Carney baritone sax solo, mm. 1–7.

Ellington's linear use of the piano here—not just taking a solo or providing "oom-pah" accompaniment—represents a step toward integrating the instrument into the ensemble, a process he was to continue later.

Over a thirteen-month period, the tempo of "East St. Louis Toodle-O" went from quite fast (Vocalion) to moderate (Brunswick and Columbia) to rather slow (Victor). As Schuller has pointed out, the band "drags" on the Victor version, perhaps to a fault. Even so, a slower tempo for "East St. Louis Toodle-O," as for "Black and Tan Fantasy," enhances the mysterious mood of the piece. And when Ellington returned to both compositions in the late 1930s, he slowed the pace even more.

Beyond its distinctive form, orchestration, and mood, "East St. Louis Toodle-O" is notable for its structural balances. Framed by the eight-bar introduction and coda, the piece flows smoothly from one section to the next without interruptions. Gone are the awkward transitions or modulations, the solo breaks, and comic sound effects. Like "Black and Tan Fantasy," the piece displays both the forward momentum and overall architectural balance that mark many of Ellington's later masterpieces. For the first time, it seems, Ellington knew how to use the three-minute limit of a recording studio for maximum expressive effect, designing a shape that would contrast various elements while sustaining a line from beginning to end.

The published piano version of "East St. Louis Toodle-O" (copyright February 10, 1927; E 660364) preserves some, but not all, of the features from the recordings. The reeds' rising accompaniment beneath the opening melody is absent; in its place is an ineffectual (but pianistically more practical) bass line:

Example 72. "East St. Louis Toodle-O," 1927 published version, introduction and first chorus.

The form of the first chorus, too, has been altered. The arranger (presumably not Ellington) truncates both the second A section and the bridge, ending up with twenty-eight measures instead of Ellington's original thirty-two. The two main themes of "East St. Louis Toodle-O" are not equally successful in this piano adaptation; the second sounds fine on the keyboard, but Miley's melody makes little sense without his special tone-coloring and articulation.

The orchestral stock arrangement of "East St. Louis Toodle-O" is closer to the recorded versions of the piece. Of course, the composition is attributed to Ellington and "Bob Wiley," but there are no such glaring errors in the music. Ellington is credited with the arrangement, whether or not he was responsible. The piano part has the correct harmonies and seems close to what Ellington might play (although his single-note lines and sharp punctuating chords are lost). There are curious features to the orchestration, however, such as the role assigned the clarinet in the introduction:

Example 73. "East St. Louis Toodle-O," 1927 stock arrangement, introduction, mm. 1–7.

Still, the voicing of the saxophone chords is almost the same as that on the Vocalion version. If Ellington indeed was the arranger, perhaps he was simply keeping a larger ensemble occupied—one with four reeds instead of three.

As bandleader, arranger, and composer, Ellington achieved a breakthrough on recordings by late 1927. Using many of the same players who had been with him for years, he found a way to highlight their strong points—both alone and together—within the framework of

a well-constructed composition. Ellington now could devise textures for his ensemble—like the opening of "East St. Louis Toodle-
O" or the clarinet trio on "Creole Love Call"—that were just as
striking as the solo voices of Bubber Miley, Joe Nanton, or Otto
Hardwick. He could fashion whole pieces out of melodic threads
supplied by his players. Most important, perhaps, he had a band
which, through its distinctive sound and blend, could evoke new
states of feeling.

After long experience playing Tin Pan Alley pop songs, hot
jazz numbers, and the blues, Ellington had evolved a style that
drew upon all these genres, as well as African-American folk music,
both secular and sacred. He was still young, and the final important
phase of his musical education lay ahead. But in a way, even before
setting foot in the Cotton Club door, Duke Ellington had arrived.

APPENDIX

Compositions and Recordings of Duke Ellington

1914–NOVEMBER 1927

This is a chronological listing of Ellington's written and recorded works. Titles of Ellington's own compositions appear in boldface type. Titles of pieces written by others and recorded by Ellington, either with his band or vocalists, appear in italic type. This list does not include discographical data that can be found in Bakker, Timner, Rust, Volontè/Massagli/Pusateri, and other standard sources. Rather, it provides basic information about existing sources, publishers, first recordings, and copyright.

All recordings, unless otherwise noted, were made in New York City. Issue numbers are given here, not matrix numbers. For personnel on the recordings, see the discographies of Bakker, Timner, and the "Birth of a Band" series by Frank Dutton in *Storyville*.

Copyright information comes from the Library of Congress Copyright Division and *Music Is My Mistress* (compiled from ASCAP lists).

Abbreviations for Location of Sources

DEC   Duke Ellington Collection, Archives Center, Smithsonian National Museum of American History, Washington, D.C.
DLC   Library of Congress
NN   New York Public Library, New York

ca. 1914–15

Soda Fountain Rag [or *Poodle Dog Rag*]
Piano

SOURCE: No score has been located. Ellington mentioned the piece in *MM* and in interviews, calling it his first composition. It first appeared on disc as part of "Oklahoma Stomp," an ensemble arrangement recorded October 29, 1929 on Vocalion 1448 by the Six Jolly Jesters (pseudonym for an Ellington-led group). On May 8, 1937, Ellington performed a solo piano version on a radio broadcast of "The Saturday Night Swing Club," calling it "Swing Session." In the 1960s and 1970s Ellington played the piece on various occasions; an impromptu performance appears on a "Bell Telephone Hour" program shown October 13, 1967. Ellington made no commercial recordings of the piece.

COPYRIGHT: Not located at DLC. Listed as 1958 in *MM*.

Bitches' Ball
Piano

SOURCE: No score has been located. In 1971 Ellington told Brooks Kerr that his piano solo on "Beige" (third movement of *Black, Brown, and Beige,* first recorded January 23, 1943) was a piano piece with this title, composed in 1914. A note in Ellington's hand, within an envelope containing *Black, Brown, and Beige* materials, refers to "B. Ball" as part of the "Beige" movement (DEC).

COPYRIGHT: Not located at DLC.

ca. 1915–17

What You Gonna Do When the Bed Breaks Down?
Song

SOURCE: No score has been located. Mentioned by Ellington in *MM* as his second composition. In 1964, during an interview conducted by Byng Whitteker in Toronto, Ellington played a brief instrumental version of the song accompanied by a bassist and drummer. At a birthday party in New York in 1972, Ellington played and sang the piece, and Brooks Kerr memorized both music and text.

COPYRIGHT: Not located at DLC.

1923

Blind Man's Buff
Song

SOURCE: Unpublished song by Jo Trent (words) and Ellington (music), arranged by Geo[rge] R. Holman. A lead sheet with the melody (not in Ellington's hand and probably copied in the 1950s or 1960s) and a separate page with lyrics survive. Not recorded.

LOCATION: DEC, bound volume A

COPYRIGHT: Claimed by the publisher Fred Fisher, October 24, 1923, E 576379.

Home
(Ray Klages and Billy Fazioli)
Instrumental [?]

SOURCE: Unissued Victor test pressing (or trial recording) by Elmer Snowden's Novelty Orchestra, July 26, 1923.
COPYRIGHT: Not located at DLC.

Home
(Ray Klages and Billy Fazioli)
M. T. Pocket Blues
(Lewis Michelson, Eli Dawson, Victor Olivier)
Instrumentals [?]

SOURCE: Unissued Victor test pressing by Elmer Snowden's Novelty Orchestra, October 18, 1923. Ellington researcher Steven Lasker contends this session never happened, having found no evidence for it in Victor's files.
COPYRIGHT: Not located for "Home"; "M. T. Pocket Blues" claimed by Fred Fisher, September 18, 1923, E 571132.

ca. 1923

Come Back to Me
Song

SOURCE: Ellington mentioned writing this "jazz waltz" when he first came to New York, then selling it outright (WDE). No score or recording has been located.
COPYRIGHT: Not located at DLC.

1924

Choo Choo (I Gotta Hurry Home)
Song

SOURCE: Published by the Broadway Music Corporation (723 7th Avenue, corner of 48th Street) both in sheet music form and as a stock arrangement (by Louis Katzman) for dance band. Ellington shared composer credit with Dave Ringle and Bob Schafer. Its first recorded performance by the Washingtonians was in November 1924, Blu-Disc T-1002.

LOCATION: NN
COPYRIGHT: Claimed by Broadway Music Corp., September 5, 1924, E 595558. Title entered as "Choo-choo, I Gotta Hurry Home."

Pretty Soft for You
Song

SOURCE: Unpublished song, Jo Trent (words) and Ellington (music). A photostat of a lead sheet in Ellington's hand, from 1924, and a separate page with lyrics survive. Not recorded.
LOCATION: DEC, bound volume T
COPYRIGHT: Claimed by Clarence Williams Co., November 1, 1924, E 602776.

Parlor Social De Luxe
Song

SOURCE: Recorded by Alberta Prime with Ellington and Sonny Greer, November 1924, Blu-Disc T-1007. Listed on the record label as a "Vocal novelty," it is credited to Jo Trent and Ellington. A score for an instrumental version of the piece in Ellington's hand is in bound volume T, DEC, under the title "House Rent." This arrangement probably dates from the mid- or late 1930s.
COPYRIGHT: Not located at DLC.

Deacon Jazz
Song

SOURCE: Recorded by Jo Trent and the D C'ns, November 1924, Blu-Disc T-1003. Attributed to Trent and Ellington, it was performed in the *Chocolate Kiddies* revue, 1925. No score located.
COPYRIGHT: Not located at DLC.

It's Gonna Be a Cold, Cold Winter
(Jo Trent and Porter Grainger)
Vocal with instrumental accompaniment

SOURCE: Recorded by Alberta Prime with Ellington and Greer, November 1924, Blu-Disc T-1007.
COPYRIGHT: Unpublished song, claimed by Broadway Music Corp., October 17, 1924, E 600653.

Rainy Nights
(Jo Trent, [Will?] Donaldson, [Vincent?] Lopez)
Instrumental

SOURCE: Recorded by the Washingtonians, November 1924, Blu-Disc T-1002.

COPYRIGHT: Not located at DLC. *MM* gives a 1973 copyright date, attributing the piece to Ellington.

Oh How I Love My Darling
(Harry Woods and Edgar Leslie)
Vocal with instrumental accompaniment

SOURCE: Recorded by Sunny and the D C'ns, November 1924, Blu-Disc T-1003.

COPYRIGHT: Claimed by Clarke and Leslie songs, November 10, 1924, E 601195.

How Come You Do Me Like You Do?
(Gene Austin and Roy Bergere)
Vocal with instrumental accompaniment

SOURCE: Recorded by Florence Bristol with Ellington and Otto Hardwick, November 1924, Up-to-Date 2019.

COPYRIGHT: Claimed by Stark and Cowan, March 31, 1924, E 587204.

1925

Everything Is Hotsy Totsy Now
(Jimmy McHugh and Irving Mills)
Vocal with piano accompaniment

SOURCE: Test pressing recorded by the Hotsy Totsy Boys (Irving Mills, vocal, Ellington, piano), June 8, 1925, Gennett 9533-A (matrix number).

COPYRIGHT: Not located at DLC.

I'm Gonna Hang around My Sugar
(Jack Palmer and Spencer Williams)
Instrumental

SOURCE: Recorded by Duke Ellington's Washingtonians, September 1925, Pathé 36333.

COPYRIGHT: Unpublished song, claimed by Irving Berlin Inc., May 22, 1925, E 616174. Title entered as "I'm Gonna Hang around My Sugar, till I Gather All the Sugar That She's Got."

Trombone Blues
(Ted Nixon and Spencer Williams)
Instrumental

SOURCE: Recorded by the Washingtonians, September 1925, Pathé 36333.

COPYRIGHT: Unpublished song, words by Ted Nixon, music by Spencer Williams, claimed by Melody Music, January 14, 1925, E 606470.

Jig Walk—Charleston
Song

SOURCE: Sheet music published by Robbins-Engel (1658 Broadway). The music is by Ellington, the words by Jo Trent. The song was probably composed in late March or early April 1925. The European distributor of this and the other *Chocolate Kiddies* songs (see next two entries) was Victor Alberti, of the Musikalienhandlung Graphisches Kabinett, Berlin.

LOCATION: DLC

COPYRIGHT: Claimed by Robbins-Engel, December 3, 1925, E 627250.

Jim Dandy
Song

SOURCE: This Trent-Ellington song was written for *Chocolate Kiddies*. See entry for "Jig Walk."

LOCATION: DLC

COPYRIGHT: Claimed by Robbins-Engel, December 3, 1925, E 627251.

With You
Song

SOURCE: This Trent-Ellington song was written for *Chocolate Kiddies*. See entry for "Jig Walk."

LOCATION: DLC

COPYRIGHT: Claimed by Robbins-Engel, December 3, 1925, E 627252.

Love Is a Wish for You
Skeedely-Um-Bum
Songs

SOURCE: Incipits for both pieces appear on the back page of "Jim Dandy," but apparently the songs were not published. No complete versions or recordings have been located.

LOCATION: DLC

COPYRIGHT: Claimed by Robbins-Engel on the back page of "Jim Dandy," but entries for these songs have not been located at DLC.

1926

Parlor Social Stomp
Instrumental

SOURCE: Recorded by the Washingtonians, March 1926, Pathé 7504. No score located. Ellington receives label credit as composer.

COPYRIGHT: Not located at DLC.

Georgia Grind
(Spencer Williams)
Instrumental

SOURCE: Recorded by the Washingtonians, March 1926, Pathé 7504.

COPYRIGHT: Unpublished song, claimed by Bud Allen Music, August 19, 1926, E 643753.

(You've Got Those) "Wanna Go Back Again" Blues
(Roy Turk and Lou Handman)
Instrumental with vocal chorus

SOURCE: Recorded by Duke Ellington and his Orchestra, March 30, 1926, Gennett 3291.

COPYRIGHT: Claimed by Frank Clark, Inc., February 16, 1926, E 634547. Title entered as "You've Got Those Wanna Go Back Again Blues."

If You Can't Hold the Man You Love
(Irving Kahal and Sammy Fain)
Instrumental with vocal chorus

SOURCE: Recorded by Duke Ellington and his Washingtonians, April 1, 1926, Gennett 3291.

COPYRIGHT: Claimed by Jack Mills, March 31, 1926, E 635986. Title entered as "If You Can't Hold the Man You Love, Don't Cry."

Yam Brown [Fox Trot]
Song

SOURCE: The published sheet music attributes the piece to Jo Trent and Duke Ellington. Ukelele arrangement is by May Singhi Breen. No recordings located. A score for an instrumental version of the piece, possibly dating from the 1930s, is located in DEC, bound volume W, under the title "Yam."

LOCATION: DLC

COPYRIGHT: Claimed by Frazer-Kent Inc., Music Publishers (1650 Broadway), May 4, 1926, E 640611. Words by Trent, music by Ellington.

(I'm Just Wild about) Animal Crackers [Fox Trot]
(Fred Rich, Sam Coslow, Harry Link)
Instrumental

SOURCE: Recorded by Duke Ellington and his Washingtonians, June 21, 1926, Gennett 3342.

COPYRIGHT: Claimed by Henry Waterson, Inc., June 3, 1926, E 641401. Words by Rich and Coslow, music by Link. Title entered as "I'm Just Wild about Animal Crackers!"

Li'l Farina
(Harrison Smith and Alvano Mier)
Instrumental

SOURCE: Recorded by Duke Ellington and his Washingtonians, June 21, 1926, Gennett 3342.

COPYRIGHT: Claimed by Harrison Smith and A. Mier, August 3, 1925, E 620240. Title entered as "Lil' Farina, Everybody Loves You." Words by H. G. Smith, music by A. Mier.

Lucky Number Blues
(Morris Eisenberg and Robert W. Phipps)
Vocal with instrumental accompaniment

SOURCE: Recorded by Alberta Jones with Ellington and Hardwick ("The Ellington Twins"), October 14, 1926, Gennett 3403.

COPYRIGHT: Claimed by Morris Eisenberg, September 29, 1926, E 648692. Title entered as "(The) Lucky Number Blues."

I'm Gonna Put You Right in Jail [Slow Drag]
(Lucky Johnson)
Vocal with instrumental accompaniment

SOURCE: See above entry.

COPYRIGHT: Claimed by Anita J. Glander, November 12, 1926, E 651633.

Rhapsody Jr.
Piano/Instrumental

SOURCE: Mentioned by Ellington in *MM* as a piano solo written around the time of *Chocolate Kiddies*. No recording by Ellington. An undated lead sheet survives, probably from the 1920s. According to Steven Lasker, the Vocalion ledger indicates that pianist Ford L. Buck played the piece in Chicago, February 24, 1927; no recording, however, was issued. (Frank Dutton has speculated that the pianist may be Ford Lee "Buck" Washington, of the vaudeville team Buck and Bubbles.) A piano arrangement was published by Robbins in 1935, and Jimmie Lunceford and his Orchestra recorded the piece that year (Decca 639) in an arrangement by Eddie Durham and Edwin Wilcox.

LOCATION: Private collection

COPYRIGHT: Claimed by Robbins-Engel, October 21, 1926, E 649276.

East St. Louis Toodle-O
Instrumental

SOURCE: Recorded by Duke Ellington and his Kentucky Club Orchestra, November 29, 1926, Vocalion 1064. See next entry under the same title.

LOCATION: *Duke Ellington: Compilation Album "Hot"* (Paris: Editions Salabert)

Birmingham Breakdown
Instrumental

SOURCE: Recorded by Duke Ellington and his Kentucky Club Orchestra, November 29, 1926, Vocalion 1064. See next entry under the same title.

LOCATION: *Duke Ellington: Compilation Album "Hot"* (Paris: Editions Salabert)

Who Is She
Song/Instrumental

SOURCE: Unissued recording by Duke Ellington and his Kentucky Club Orchestra, November 29, 1926, Vocalion.

COPYRIGHT: Not located at DLC. Listed as 1962 in *MM* (probably a renewal), credited to Ellington, Irving Mills, Rousseau Simmons, and Bob Schafer.

A Night in Harlem
Instrumental [?]

SOURCE: Unissued recording by Duke Ellington and his Kentucky Club Orchestra, November 29, 1926, Vocalion. Ellington receives credit as composer.

COPYRIGHT: Not located at DLC.

They Say I Do It
(Booker-Ewingo)

Drifting from You Blues
(Booker-Ewingo)
Vocal with instrumental accompaniment

SOURCE: Rejected OKeh recording by Gussie Alexander "accompanied by Duke and Otto, piano and saxophone," December 1, 1926.

LOCATION: Steven Lasker claims there are no surviving master parts from this session, and tests are unknown. Lasker's research in the OKeh files indicated that another take of "Drifting from You Blues" was made by Alexander on December 1, accompanied only by piano (Ellington?).

Immigration Blues
Instrumental

SOURCE: Recorded by Duke Ellington and his Kentucky Club Orchestra, December 29, 1926, Vocalion 1077. A piano arrangement was pub-

lished in 1927 by Gotham Music Service, Inc., a division of Mills
Music (150 W. 46th Street).
LOCATION: *Duke Ellington: Compilation Album "Hot"* (Paris: Editions
Salabert)
COPYRIGHT: Claimed by Gotham Music Service, Inc., February 25, 1927,
E 660467.

The Creeper
Instrumental
SOURCE: Recorded by Duke Ellington and his Kentucky Club Orches-
tra, December 29, 1926, Vocalion 1077. A piano arrangement was
published in 1927 by Gotham Music Service, Inc.
LOCATION: Private collection
COPYRIGHT: Claimed by Gotham Music Service, Inc., February 25, 1927,
E 660468.

1927

If You Can't Hold the Man You Love
(Irving Kahal and Sammy Fain)
Vocal with instrumental accompaniment
SOURCE: Recorded by Evelyn Preer with a small group led by Ellington,
January 10, 1927, Victor test pressing, first issued on microgroove
ca. 1967 (Tax LP-9). ("Make Me Love You," by Porter Grainger and
Jo Trent, was recorded for the same date. It has not been issued, and
according to Steven Lasker the master parts have been destroyed.)
COPYRIGHT: See above entry under the same title.

New Orleans Low-Down
Instrumental
SOURCE: Recorded by Duke Ellington and his Kentucky Club Orchestra
February 3, 1927, Vocalion 1086.
LOCATION: *Duke Ellington: Compilation Album "Hot"* (Paris: Editions
Salabert)
COPYRIGHT: Claimed by Gotham Music Service, Inc., June 23, 1928,
E 694892. Title entered as "New Orleans Low Down."

Song of the Cotton Field
(Porter Grainger)
Instrumental
SOURCE: Recorded by Duke Ellington and his Kentucky Club Orchestra,
February 3, 1927, Vocalion 1086.

COPYRIGHT: Claimed by Gotham Music Service, Inc., July 6, 1927, E 670138. Title entered as "Song from a Cotton Field; Southern Classic."

East St. Louis Toodle-Oo
Birmingham Breakdown
Instrumentals

SOURCE: Recorded by Duke Ellington and his Kentucky Club Orchestra for Brunswick. Steven Lasker has established the date as February 28, 1927. "East St. Louis Toodle-Oo" was not issued; "Birmingham Breakdown" came out on Brunswick 3480. Piano arrangements of both pieces were published in 1927 by Gotham Music Service, Inc.

"East St. Louis Toodle-Oo" (or Toodle-O) is by Ellington and Bubber Miley. An orchestral stock arrangement credited to Ellington was published the same year.

LOCATION: "East St. Louis Toodle-Oo," private collection; "Birmingham Breakdown," in *The Great Music of Duke Ellington* (Melville, N.Y.: Belwin Mills, 1973).

COPYRIGHT: Claimed by Gotham Music Service, Inc., February 10, 1927: "East St. Louis Toodle-O," E 660364; "Birmingham Breakdown," E 660361.

East St. Louis Toodle-O
Instrumental

SOURCE: Recorded by Duke Ellington and his Orchestra, March 14, 1927, Brunswick 3480.

East St. Louis Toodle-Oo
Instrumental

SOURCE: Recorded by the Washingtonians, March 22, 1927, Columbia 953-D.

Hop Head
Down in Our Alley Blues
Instrumentals

SOURCE: Recorded by the Washingtonians, March 22, 1927. "Hop Head" was issued on Columbia 953-D, "Down in Our Alley Blues" on Columbia 1076-D.

Both pieces are credited to Ellington and Otto Hardwick. Piano arrangements were published in 1927 by Gotham Music Service, Inc., with titles reversed from the way they appear on the Columbia recordings.

Steven Lasker has seen the Columbia matrix cards that show "Hop Head" originally titled as "Surprise," "Down in Our Alley Blues" as "Indian Rubber." Lasker points out another probable mix-up in titles here, since "hop" and "Indian rubber" belong together as synonyms for opium.

LOCATION: "Hop Head," in *Duke Ellington: Compilation Album "Hot"* (Paris: Editions Salabert); "Down in Our Alley Blues," private collection

COPYRIGHT: Claimed by Gotham Music Service, Inc.: "Hop Head," July 12, 1927, E 672244; "Down in Our Alley Blues," August 12, 1927, E 670901.

Black and Tan Fantasy [Fox Trot]
Instrumental

SOURCE: Recorded by the Washingtonians, April 7, 1927, Brunswick 3526. The piece is credited to Ellington and Miley. Gotham Music Service published a piano version, also an orchestral stock arranged by Eddie Powell.

LOCATION: piano version, *Duke Ellington: Compilation Album "Hot"* (Paris: Editions Salabert); stock, private collection

COPYRIGHT: Claimed by Gotham Music Service, Inc., July 16, 1927, E 672246.

Soliloquy
(Rube Bloom)
Instrumental

SOURCE: Recorded by the Washingtonians, April 30, 1927, Brunswick 3526.

COPYRIGHT: Claimed by Triangle Music Publishing Co., June 21, 1926, E 642522.

Gold Digger
Instrumental

SOURCE: Published stock by Denton and Haskins, credited to Ellington and [Will] Donaldson, arranged by "Our Gang." Apparently the piece had been composed a few years earlier. It was not recorded by Ellington, but a version exists by Johnny Ringer and his Rosemont Ballroom Orchestra (Gennett 6280).

LOCATION: Private collection

COPYRIGHT: Claimed by Denton and Haskins, August 13, 1927, E 670985.

Washington Wabble
Instrumental

SOURCE: Recorded by Duke Ellington and his Orchestra, October 6, 1927; first issued on microgroove, take 2 in 1955 ("X" LVA 3037), take 1 in 1965 (Pirate MPC 510). Gotham Music Service published a piano arrangement.

LOCATION: *Duke Ellington: Compilation Album "Hot"* (Paris: Editions Salabert)

COPYRIGHT: Claimed by Gotham Music Service, Inc., December 30, 1927, E 682389.

Black and Tan Fantasy
Instrumental

SOURCE: Recorded by Duke Ellington and his Orchestra, Camden, N.J., October 26, 1927, Victor 21137.

Washington Wabble
Instrumental

SOURCE: Recorded by Duke Ellington and his Orchestra, Camden, N.J., October 26, 1927, Victor 21284.

Creole Love Call
Instrumental with vocal choruses

SOURCE: Recorded by Duke Ellington and his Orchestra, Camden, N.J., October 26, 1927, Victor 21137. The record credits the piece to Ellington, Bubber Miley, and Rudy Jackson. Piano arrangement published by Gotham Music Service, Inc.

LOCATION: *Duke Ellington: Compilation Album "Hot"* (Paris: Editions Salabert); *The Great Music of Duke Ellington* (Melville, N.Y.: Belwin Mills, 1973).

COPYRIGHT: Claimed by Gotham Music Service, Inc., August 16, 1928, E 698167. Composer listed as Ellington. Title entered as "The Creole Love Call."

Blues I Love to Sing
Instrumental with vocal chorus

SOURCE: Recorded by Duke Ellington and his Orchestra, Camden, N.J., October 26, 1927, Victor 21490. It is credited to Ellington and Miley.

LOCATION: *Duke Ellington: Compilation Album "Hot"* (Paris: Editions Salabert).

COPYRIGHT: Claimed by Gotham Music Service, Inc., December 30, 1927, E 682387.

What Can a Poor Fellow Do?
(Billy Meyers and Elmer Schoebel)
Instrumental

SOURCE: Recorded by Duke Ellington and his Orchestra, November 3, 1927, OKeh 8521.

LOCATION: The piano part to the 1927 stock arrangement by Elmer Schoebel is in the author's collection.

COPYRIGHT: Claimed by Elmer Schoebel, Inc., May 14, 1927, E 666878.

Chicago Stomp Down
(Henry Creamer and James P. Johnson)
Instrumental

SOURCE: Recorded by the Chicago Footwarmers, November 3, 1927, OKeh 8675.

COPYRIGHT: Claimed by Jack Mills, December 27, 1927, E 682360.

Black and Tan Fantasy
Instrumental

SOURCE: Recorded by Duke Ellington and his Orchestra, November 3, 1927, OKeh 8521.

You Will Always Live on in Our Memory
(Jo Trent)
Gone But Not Forgotten
(Mandy Lee and Bob King)
She's Gone to Join the Songbirds in Heaven
(Porter Grainger)
Vocals with instrumental accompaniment

SOURCE: Unissued recordings by Marguerite Lee with Duke Ellington Trio (first and third titles) and by Walter Richardson, accompanied by the Duke Ellington Trio ("Gone But Not Forgotten"), November 8, 1927. Steven Lasker has located this information in the Vocalion files.

Notes

List of Abbreviations
Used in Notes

Age	*New York Age*
Amsterdam News	*New York Amsterdam News*
Bakker	Dick M. Bakker. *Duke Ellington on Microgroove, Vol. 1, 1923–1936.* Alphen aan den Rijn, Holland: Micrography, 1977.
Bee	Washington *Bee*
Clipper	*New York Clipper*
DE	Barry Ulanov. *Duke Ellington.* 1946, 1947; rpt., New York: Da Capo, 1975.
DEC	Duke Ellington Collection, Archives Center, National Museum of American History, Smithsonian Institution, Washington, D.C.
Defender	*Chicago Defender*
DEP	Mercer Ellington with Stanley Dance. *Duke Ellington in Person: An Intimate Memoir.* 1978; rpt., New York: Da Capo, 1979.
EPY	Ellington Project, Oral History, American Music, Yale University
IJS	Institute of Jazz Studies, Rutgers University-Newark, Newark, New Jersey
JOHP	Jazz Oral History Project, Institute of Jazz Studies

MM   Duke Ellington. *Music Is My Mistress.* 1973; rpt., New York: Da Capo, 1976.

MSRC   Moorland-Spingarn Research Center, Howard University, Washington, D.C.

Timner   W. E. Timner. *Ellingtonia: The Recorded Music of Duke Ellington and His Sidemen,* 3rd ed. London and Metuchen, N.J.: Institute of Jazz Studies and Scarecrow Press, 1988.

WDE   Stanley Dance. *The World of Duke Ellington.* 1970; rpt., New York: Da Capo, [1981].

PREFACE

1. Floyd G. Snelson, "Story of Duke Ellington's Rise to Kingship Reads Like Fiction," *Pittsburgh Courier,* December 19, 1931.

2. Duke Ellington, "The Duke Steps Out," *Rhythm* (March 1931), p. 22.

CHAPTER ONE

1. *MM,* p. 17.

2. Constance McLaughlin Green, *The Secret City: A History of Race Relations in the Nation's Capital* (Princeton, N.J.: Princeton University Press, 1967), pp. 27–28.

3. Ibid., p. 89.

4. Booker T. Washington, *Up from Slavery* (1901; rpt., Booker Washington Birthplace, Va.: Booker T. Washington Centennial Commission, 1956), p. 62.

5. Constance McLaughlin Green, *Washington: Capital City, 1879–1950* (Princeton, N.J.: Princeton University Press, 1963), vii-viii.

6. Ronald M. Johnson, "Those Who Stayed: Washington Black Writers of the 1920's," *Records of the Columbia Historical Society* 50 (1980), p. 485.

7. *MM,* p. 15. These aunts were sisters of Ellington's father, James Edward Ellington.

8. Langston Hughes, *The Big Sea* (New York: Hill and Wang, 1940), p. 208.

9. Ibid., p. 206. Hughes also railed against Washington's black upper class in "Our Wonderful Society: Washington," *Opportunity* 5 (August 1927), pp. 226–27.

10. Sonny Greer, interviewed by Edith Exton and Brooks Kerr, New York, 1976. Tape copy in the collection of Brooks Kerr.

11. *MM,* p. 17.

12. Rayford W. Logan, "Growing Up in Washington: A Lucky Generation," *Records of the Columbia Historical Society* 50 (1980), p. 500.

13. For more on Dunbar High School see Mary Gibson Hundley, *The Dunbar Story, 1870–1955* (Washington, D.C.: Vantage Press, 1965); and Mary Church Terrell, "History of the High School for Negroes in Washington," *Journal of Negro History* 2 (July 1917), pp. 252–66.

14. *DEP,* p. 9.

15. Oscar Lucas, interview, Columbia, Maryland, September 12, 1983.

16. Dunbar High School *Liber Anni* (1923), [21–23]; Mercer Cook to Mark Tucker, July 27, 1984.

17. William H. Jones, *Recreation and Amusement among Negroes in Washington, D.C.* (1927; rpt., Westport, Conn.: Negro Universities Press, 1970), p. 79.

18. *The Star of Ethiopia,* in "Washington, D.C. Programs," Box 1, MSRC. For a text of the pageant see *Crisis* 7 (November 1913), pp. 339–41. A review of the Washington production is in the *Bee,* October 16, 1915.

19. W. Montague Cobb, telephone conversation, Washington, D.C., May 29, 1984.

20. Maud Cuney-Hare, *Negro Musicians and Their Music* (1936; rpt., New York: Da Capo, 1974), p. 208.

21. George Edmund Haynes and Sterling Brown, *The Negro in Detroit and Washington* (1936; rpt., New York: Arno Press/New York Times, 1969), p. 80.

22. See the *Bee,* December 4, 1920; March 5, 1921; October 22, 1921.

23. "An Operetta," *The Negro Musician* 1 (February 1921), p. 18.

24. W. E. B. Du Bois, ed., *Efforts for Social Betterment among Negro Americans* (Atlanta: Atlanta University Press, 1909), p. 106.

25. Duke Ellington, "The Most Essential Instrument," *Jazz Journal* 18 (December 1965), p. 15.

26. Maurice Banks, interview, Washington, D.C., September 29, 1983.

27. Doris McGinty, "The Washington Conservatory of Music and School of Expression," *The Black Perspective in Music* 7 (Spring 1979), p. 62.

28. Ibid., p. 63.

29. MSRC has the primary collection of Washington Conservatory materials. Recital programs show Claude Hopkins playing in 1909 and 1910 (folders 33, 35, 37), Gertrude Wells in 1910 (folders 37–38), and Louis Brown in 1915 (graduation program).

30. "Washington, D.C. Programs," Box 4, MSRC. The two concerts were held November 21, 1913, at the Metropolitan AME Church, and February 28, 1914, at the Howard Theater.

31. Bettye Gardner and Bettye Thomas, "The Cultural Impact of the Howard Theater on the Black Community," *Journal of Negro History* 55 (October 1970), p. 254.

32. *Bee*, November 3, 1917.

33. Hollie I. West, "Duke at 70: Honor from the President," *Washington Post*, April 27, 1969.

34. The *Bee* is the best source for Howard Theater programs. The performers and shows cited here come from the newspaper's listings, 1918–21.

35. The *Symphony in Black* soundtrack has been reissued on *Duke Ellington Band Shorts (1929–1935)*, Biograph BLP-M-2. Ellington's first performance of *Black, Brown, and Beige* is captured on *The Duke Ellington Carnegie Hall Concerts, January 1943*, Prestige P-34004.

36. MSRC has several issues of *The Music Master* (from 1919–20) and *The Negro Musician* (1920–21). The *Negro Music Journal* lasted only from 1902 to 1903; it has been reprinted by Negro Universities Press (Westport, Conn., 1970).

37. *Bee*, April 5, 1919.

38. *Bee*, October 1, 1921.

39. *Bee*, May 29, 1920.

40. *MM*, p. 26.

41. *Washington Tribune*, July 31, 1921. A cover story on Miller and his Community Civic Center Band appeared in *The Music Master* 2 (February 1920), pp. 6–7.

42. *Washington Tribune*, June 17, 1922.

43. For more on Ellington's relationship to these figures, see Mark Tucker, "The Renaissance Education of Duke Ellington," in *Black Music and the Negro Renaissance* (Westport, Conn.: Greenwood Press, 1990).

CHAPTER TWO

1. Ellington was aware that he had told only one part of the story. After *Music Is My Mistress* appeared, he said to his son Mercer, "We've written the Good Book and now we'll write the Bad Book!" (*DEP*, p. 172).

2. Lyrics from "My Mother, My Father," in *My People* script, DEC. In the original text all letters are capitalized.

3. No Ellingtons appear in the Washington city directories before 1891; however, Ruth Ellington Boatwright has stated that her father came to Washington at the age of seven (1886) (interview, New York, October 21, 1983).

4. Constance McLaughlin Green, *The Secret City: A History of Race Relations in the Nation's Capital* (Princeton, N.J.: Princeton University Press, 1967), p. 129.

5. *DE,* p. 2; Hollie I. West, "Duke at 70: Honor from the President," *Washington Post,* April 27, 1969.

6. *Boyd's Directory of the District of Columbia* (Washington, D.C.: William H. Boyd) was published annually and included blacks in its pages. Only in 1913 did a separate city directory for blacks appear: *Sherman's Directory and Ready Reference of the Colored Population in the District of Columbia* (Washington, D.C.: Sherman Directory Co.).

7. *MM,* p. 10.

8. *DE,* p. 2.

9. *MM,* p. 205.

10. Ruth Ellington Boatwright, interview, New York, October 21, 1983.

11. *DEP,* p. 8.

12. *MM,* p. 10.

13. J.E.'s obituary in the *Washington Tribune* (November 8, 1937) gave 1934 as the date of his retirement from the Navy Yard. However, both Mercer and Duke put the date around 1930, claiming that J.E. joined Ruth, Daisy, and Duke in New York the following year.

14. *MM,* p. 12.

15. Bernice Wiggins, interview, New York, September 6, 1983.

16. *WDE,* p. 287.

17. Florette Henri, *Black Migration: Movement North, 1900–1920* (Garden City, N.Y.: Anchor Press/Doubleday, 1975), p. 167.

18. Bernice Wiggins, telephone conversation, New York, February 16, 1985.

19. *MM,* p. 6.

20. *MM,* p. 15.

21. *DE,* p. 3.

22. Certificate of Marriage No. 3997, issued by the Marriage Bureau, Superior Court of the District of Columbia.

23. Ellington's Certificate of Birth, #100.207, issued by the District of Columbia Vital Records Office.

24. *Boyd's City Directory,* 1900.

25. Rayford W. Logan, "Growing Up in Washington: A Lucky Generation," *Records of the Columbia Historical Society* 50 (1980), p. 506.

26. Bernice Wiggins, interview, September 6, 1983; Ruth Ellington Boatwright, interview, October 21, 1983.

27. *MM,* p. 20; CBC interview #177 (April 1965), Ellington clipping file, IJS. Brooks Kerr once played Morrison's "Meditation" for Ellington, who confirmed that he knew the piece from childhood.

28. *DE,* p. 6; Ruth Ellington Boatwright, interview, October 21, 1983.

29. *DEP,* p. 10.

30. Stanley Dance, liner notes to *The Girls Suite,* Columbia EC38028 (1961).

31. *MM,* p. 15.

32. Nineteenth Street Baptist Church 68th Anniversary Program, 1907. A copy from the church's files was given to me in 1984 by Mrs. Etta Booker, then church clerk.

33. Ruth Ellington Boatwright, interview, October 21, 1983. Also see her EPY interview, November 11, 1977, p. 3. A fire in 1976 destroyed most of the John Wesley AME Zion records.

34. Essie Sorrel, telephone conversation, Washington, D.C., October 19, 1983.

35. Some years after Ellington studied with Mrs. Clinkscales, the *Bee* reported on at least two recitals of her pupils. The program for one, held June 26, 1915, at the Florida Avenue Baptist Church, suggests the kind of pieces Ellington might have learned if he had progressed far enough: "Dance of Moonbirds" (Stasney); "Shower of Roses" (Streabog); "Evening Schottische" (Elicker); "Fireside Memories" (Frailey); "Gleaming Waters" (Kimball).

36. *MM,* p. 9.

37. *DE,* p. 6; CBC interview #177, Ellington clipping file, IJS.

38. Bernice Wiggins, interview, New York, September 6, 1983. Also see her EPY interview, October 20, 1980, p. 6.

39. *MM,* p. 12.

40. *MM,* pp. 22–23. Pianist Brooks Kerr remembers how Ellington believed that shows should have a didactic purpose. This is evident in Ellington's larger productions (e.g., *Black, Brown, and Beige, Jump for Joy, My People*) and surfaces repeatedly in *Music Is My Mistress,* where Ellington finds something instructive or valuable in nearly every experience. In part it may derive from Ellington's early passion for Horatio Alger stories, which he once discussed with Kerr.

41. CBC interview #177, Ellington clipping file, IJS.

42. *MM,* p. 10; West, "Duke at 70."

43. Ruth Ellington Boatwright, interview, October 21, 1983.

44. Ibid. Also see Ruth Ellington Boatwright's EPY interview, November 11, 1977, p. 4.

45. Oscar Lucas, interview, Columbia, Maryland, September 12, 1983.

46. Catherine K. Clarke, "Conversation with William ('Billy') Taylor, the Jazz-Mobile Man," *The Black Perspective in Music* 10 (Fall 1982), p. 182.

47. *MM*, p. 457.

48. Information from Washington city directories (1910, 1913, 1915, 1916, 1918). Mercer Ellington reports that his grandmother worked "as a kind of receptionist and housecleaner" for Cuthbert. See *DEP*, p. 8.

49. According to Ulanov, Duke bought the house on 1212 T Street for his father; in *Music Is My Mistress* Ellington countered that J.E. bought it himself. The 1921–22 D.C. General Assessment lists both James E. Ellington and James W. Kennedy (Daisy's father) as owners of the property.

50. *MM*, p. 10.

51. Ruth Ellington Boatwright, interview, October 21, 1983.

52. West, "Duke at 70."

53. Green, *The Secret City*, p. 180.

54. *MM*, p. 17.

55. Ibid.

56. *MM*, pp. 23–24. Among the professional men who frequented the poolroom were Dr. Charles Drew and the lawyers Bub Boller and George Hayes.

57. Willie "the Lion" Smith with George Hoefer, *Music on My Mind: The Memoirs of an American Pianist* (1964; rpt., New York: Da Capo, 1978), pp. 38–44.

58. Ruby Berkley Goodwin, "Meet the Duke," *The Bronzeman* 9 (August 1932), p. 20. Ellington discussed his discovery of Harvey Brooks in *MM*, pp. 17–20. In the early 1920s Brooks performed with singer Mamie Smith and then led a group in California called the Harvey Brooks Quality Four, which later became Paul Howard's Quality Serenaders and recorded for Victor in 1929–30. On these sides Brooks plays in a conservative, stride-oriented style. Something of the "tremendous left hand" that impressed Ellington may be heard in his solo on *Quality Shout* (Victor V-38122, recorded April 29, 1929), especially in the last eight bars of his sixteen-bar chorus.

CHAPTER THREE

1. Hollie I. West, "Duke at 70: Honor from the President," *Washington Post*, April 27, 1969.

2. See Tom Davin, "Conversations with James P. Johnson, Part 2," *The Jazz Review* 2 (July 1959), p. 10; also Willie "the Lion" Smith with George Hoefer, *Music on My Mind: The Memoirs of an American Pianist* (1964; rpt., New York: Da Capo, 1978), pp. 52–53.

3. *DE*, p. 14.

4. Ibid.

5. *MM*, p. 20.

6. *DE*, pp. 10–11.

7. Ellington admitted he "didn't read very well way back there" in a CBC interview #193 (February 1966), Ellington clipping file, IJS; also see *MM*, p. 30.

8. Davin, "Conversations with James P. Johnson, Part 2," pp. 12–13.

9. Mercer Cook to Mark Tucker, June 24, 1984.

10. Smith, *Music on My Mind*, p. 23.

11. Herbert Saal, "The Duke at 70," *Newsweek* (May 12, 1969), p. 117. Throughout his later career listening was fundamental to Ellington's creative process. He referred to himself as "the world's greatest listener" (*MM*, p. 446) and claimed he kept his band together so he could hear his own music. Ellington's oft-repeated aesthetic credo was also based on the primacy of the ear: "If it sounds good, it's good music" (*MM*, p. 455). Tom Whaley, Ellington's copyist and "aide de camp," considered listening to have been Ellington's greatest asset (*WDE*, p. 47).

12. *MM*, pp. 24, 28; *DE*, p. 15; Duke Ellington, "Jazz As I Have Seen It," Part 3, *Swing* (May 1940), p. 10.

13. Much of the information in this paragraph comes from Rudi Blesh and Harriet Janis, *They All Played Ragtime*, 4th ed. (New York: Oak Publications, 1971), pp. 190–92.

14. Al Rose, *Eubie Blake* (New York: Schirmer Books, 1979), p. 46.

15. Edward Berlin, "Ragtime and Improvised Piano: Another View," *Journal of Jazz Studies* 4 (Spring/Summer 1977), pp. 7–8.

16. Rose, *Eubie Blake*, p. 42. In *Reminiscing with Sissle and Blake* (New York: Viking Press, 1973), Robert Kimball and William Bolcom define "trick," rather vaguely, as "a device intercalated within the musical texture of a given piece" (p. 48). As examples they cite Luckey Roberts's "blindingly fast chromatic scales in the right hand," James P. Johnson's "shimmering passagework in the extreme upper register," and Eubie Blake's tricks based on "the accent in all its forms."

17. Davin, "Conversations with James P. Johnson," *The Jazz Review* 2 (June 1959), p. 16.

18. Blesh and Janis, *They All Played Ragtime*, pp. 185–86.

19. Ibid., p. 193.

20. Davin, "Conversations with James P. Johnson," p. 17.

21. Nat Hentoff, "Garvin Bushell and New York Jazz in the 1920s," Part 1, *The Jazz Review* 2 (January 1959), p. 13.

22. Terry Waldo, *This Is Ragtime* (New York: Hawthorne Books, 1976), p. 102.

23. Piano rolls are not the most reliable basis for stylistic analysis. They can be played at different speeds, edited, and filled out with extra notes. Their rhythmic character usually does not capture that of the original performer.

24. "Charleston Rag" dates from 1899, according to Blake, but was not recorded on a roll until 1917. Its early origin might explain a few of its stylistic differences from Johnson's 1917 rolls. In 1921 Blake recorded the piece under the title "Sounds of Africa."

25. Davin, "Conversations with James P. Johnson, Part 2," p. 11.

26. Rose, *Eubie Blake*, p. 47.

27. Ellington more often referred to the piece as "Soda Fountain Rag." But in a 1940s interview he called the piece "Poodle Dog Rag" (Gretchen Weaver, "The Duke of Jazzdom," *Bandleaders* [n.d.], p. 42, Ellington clipping file, IJS). Elmer Snowden also referred to the "Poodle Dog Rag" in Stanley Dance, *The World of Swing* (1974; rpt., New York: Da Capo, 1979), p. 48.

28. Ruth Ellington Boatwright apparently has a lead sheet of "Soda Fountain Rag" in her files, but it is more likely the work of pianist Brooks Kerr (who recalls producing one for her) than of Ellington himself.

29. The Poodle Dog Café does not turn up in Boyd's city directories, nor in *Sherman's Directory and Ready Reference of the Colored Population in the District of Columbia* (1913).

30. *Bee,* October 3 and November 20, 1920.

31. George Hoefer, "Duke Ellington: Society Band Leader," *Washington Post Potomac* (May 20, 1962), p. 12.

32. The soundtrack for this program has not been issued on record. However, the documentary *On the Road with Duke Ellington,* released in 1974, incorporates all the footage from the "Bell Telephone Hour" program.

33. This 1937 broadcast has been issued on *Duke Ellington, Collector's Jackpot,* vol. 2, Jazz Archives JA-40.

34. I am indebted to Brooks Kerr, Jerry Valburn, and Jack Towers for their help with the history of "Soda Fountain Rag." Ellington also played the piece for a Chicago television show filmed in 1957 (issued on *One Night Stand with Duke Ellington,* Joyce LP-1023); during a reception held after his January 4, 1962, Museum of Modern Art solo piano concert; in Toronto in 1964 (issued on *Duke Ellington,* Rarities 29); in Paris in 1965 (issued privately by Sjef Hoefsmit on the cassette *10 Years Later*); at the Whitney Museum in 1972; and at the 1972 Newport in New York Jazz Festival.

35. Smith, *Music on My Mind,* p. 65.

36. This section of the A strain was selected for transcription because it contains the fewest mistakes (e.g., missed bass notes, blurred mid-register chords).

37. Brooks Kerr, interview, New York, November 12, 1983. "Bitches' Ball" could have been a piece Ellington heard other pianists play, and not necessarily his own invention. A note in Ellington's hand that gives a

structural breakdown of *Black, Brown, and Beige* also lists "B. Ball" at the head of the "Beige" section (DEC).

38. Cato Adams, interview, Washington, D.C., December 14, 1983.

39. Essie Sorrel, telephone conversation, Washington, D.C., October 19, 1983.

40. In *MM* Ellington claimed Edgar McEntree gave him his name (p. 20); in *DE* Ulanov attributed it to Ralph "Zeb" Green (p. 7).

41. *MM*, p. 20.

42. The performance is issued on *Duke Ellington,* Rarities 29.

43. Mercer Cook, interview, Silver Spring, Maryland, August 19, 1983.

44. *MM*, p. 26.

45. Oscar Lucas, interview, Columbia, Maryland, September 12, 1983; Mrs. Delia Perry, telephone conversation, Washington, D.C., November 17, 1983.

46. *MM*, p. 128.

47. *Bee,* February 10, 1917.

48. *MM*, p. 28.

49. Richard O. Boyer, "The Hot Bach," Part 3, *The New Yorker* (July 8, 1944), p. 28.

50. CBC interview #184 (1966), Ellington clipping file, IJS.

51. Mrs. Delia Perry, telephone conversation, November 17, 1983.

52. *MM*, p. 26.

53. Brown was born in Alexandria, Virginia. He attended Stevens Elementary School, Armstrong High School, and the Boston Conservatory. Later he worked in the Bureau of Engraving. (This biographical information was supplied by Cato Adams, Mrs. Essie Sorrel, and Lydia Magowan, Louis Brown's niece.) In 1950 Blesh and Janis described him as "the fine Washington ragtime pianist who now teaches the classics" (*They All Played Ragtime,* p. 191).

54. Mercer Cook, interview, Silver Spring, Maryland, August 19, 1983.

55. *MM*, p. 26.

56. Information drawn from Ellington's high-school transcript (1914–17), supplied by the D.C. public schools.

57. *MM*, p. 32.

58. The last grades on Ellington's Armstrong transcript are dated January 1917, so presumably he left shortly thereafter.

59. *MM*, p. 28.

60. West, "Duke at 70."

CHAPTER FOUR

1. Adam Clayton Powell, Sr., quoted in Jervis Anderson, *This Was Harlem: A Cultural Portrait, 1900–1950* (New York: Farrar Straus Giroux, 1981), p. 105.

2. Constance McLaughlin Green, *The Secret City: A History of Race Relations in the Nation's Capital* (Princeton, N.J.: Princeton University Press, 1967), pp. 184–85.

3. Ellington did register, when required by law, in 1918 (September 12). Registration card #A3156, obtained from General Services Administration, Federal Archives and Records Center, East Point, Georgia.

4. John Clagett Proctor, ed., *Washington Past and Present: A History,* 5 vols. (Washington, D.C.: Lewis Historical Publishing Co., 1930), 1:398.

5. *Bee,* June 16, 1917; July 28, 1917; August 25, 1917.

6. As might be expected with any "first" event in the life of someone interviewed extensively over many years, there are various versions of the Louis Thomas story. Both Charles E. Smith and Gretchen Weaver put the date at 1915, when Ellington was sixteen. See Smith, "The Duke Steps Out," *Jazz* 1 (January 1943), p. 12; Weaver, "The Duke of Jazzdom," *Bandleaders* [n.d.], p. 42, IJS clipping file. Ulanov gave the date as 1916 (*DE,* p. 17) but his anecdote involves Kern's "The Siren's Song," which was not written until 1917. My own view is that Ellington played for Thomas after he had left high school, probably in the fall of 1917.

7. Stanley Dance, *The World of Swing* (1974; rpt., New York: Da Capo, 1979), p. 31.

8. The first mention of Thomas's Capital City Clef Club in the *C and P Telephone Directory* appeared June 1, 1916, p. 71. A good photograph of the building—with the caption "Headquarters of Washington's Superior Colored Musicians"—is in *The Music Master* 2 (April 1920), p. 7, MSRC.

9. *Bee,* February 3, 1917.

10. *MM,* p. 30.

11. *DE,* pp. 17–18.

12. *MM,* p. 30.

13. Information from "Euterpeans" program, November 6, 1915, in "Programs," Box 4, MSRC.

14. Maurice Zolotow, "The Duke of Hot," *Saturday Evening Post* (August 7, 1943), p. 25. Charles E. Smith in "The Duke Steps Out" and Gretchen Weaver in "The Duke of Jazzdom" reported sixty players in Wooding's orchestra.

15. While Weaver and Smith stated that Ellington could not get a job with Wooding, Zolotow and Ulanov claimed he was fired after one per-

formance. Ellington did not mention the incident in *MM*, citing Wooding only as someone (like Louis Thomas) "who had the class work" (p. 30).

16. *DE*, p. 20.

17. *Bee*, January 27, 1917.

18. Washington Concert Orchestra program, December 28, 1913, in "D.C. Music" vertical file, MSRC.

19. *Bee*, November 25, 1916.

20. *Bee*, March 10, 1917.

21. George Hoefer gave an account of Ellington's "first job" in "Duke Ellington: Society Band Leader," *Washington Post Potomac* (May 20, 1962), p. 12; also see *DE*, p. 17. Supposedly Ellington played from 8:00 P.M. to 1:00 A.M. and made seventy-five cents.

22. Roy Ellis, telephone conversation, Washington, D.C., August 19, 1983.

23. In an interview on WMAL (Washington, D.C.) with Felix Grant, conducted April 29, 1964, Hardwick cited Lloyd Stewart as a member of one of Ellington's early groups, also Honey [?] White on banjo.

24. Dance, *World of Swing*, p. 66.

25. For an interview with Hardwick see *WDE*, pp. 55–62. Dunbar records, which are incomplete, do not show Hardwick as a student there; however, Oscar Lucas, a Dunbar graduate, recalled that Hardwick attended the school (interview, Columbia, Maryland, September 12, 1983).

26. *WDE*, p. 55.

27. *MM*, p. 50.

28. Jehu Hunter, interviewed by Mark Tucker and Spencer Crew, Washington, D.C., November 10, 1983. Mr. Hunter lived in Mrs. Schiefe's boardinghouse in the early 1920s. Apparently Whetsol had a sister who taught in a girls' school. Mr. Whetsol, Mrs. Schiefe's first husband, had died by this time.

29. Oscar Lucas, interview, September 12, 1983.

30. *MM*, p. 54.

31. *DE*, p. 13.

32. Rex Stewart, *Jazz Masters of the Thirties* (1972; rpt., New York: Da Capo, [1982]), pp. 81–82.

33. Address information drawn from the 1918 *C and P Telephone Directory* and the draft registration card Ellington filled out in September.

34. Bernice Wiggins, interview, New York, September 6, 1983.

35. Weaver, "The Duke of Jazzdom," p. 42.

36. *Bee*, August 31, 1918.

37. *Bee*, August 3, 1918.

38. An ad for Handy's performance at the Center Market Coliseum on May 5, 1919, appeared in the *Bee*, April 26, 1919.

39. *Washington Post,* June 27, 1918.

40. *C and P Telephone Directory,* June 16, 1919, p. 208.

41. *C and P Telephone Directory,* October 25, 1920, p. 126.

42. *MM,* p. 32.

43. Otto Hardwick, quoted in Hoefer, "Duke Ellington: Society Band-leader," p. 12.

44. Ibid.

45. *MM,* pp. 30–31. When small bands in Washington were averaging $5 a night, $100 for a solo job seems on the high side. But the place of employment (country club) and travel involved may have made such a fee plausible.

46. *MM,* p. 33.

47. Gwen Dobson, "Luncheon with . . . Duke Ellington," *Washington Evening Star,* April 23, 1971.

48. Eugene Scheel, *Culpepper: A Virginia County's History through 1920* (Culpepper, Va.: Culpepper Historical Society, 1974), p. 316.

49. *MM,* p. 32.

50. Ibid.

51. M. Louise Evans, *An Old Timer in Warrenton and Fauquier County, Virginia* (Warrenton, Va.: Virginia Publishing Inc., 1955), p. 135.

52. *DEP,* p. 14.

53. "The Crescendo Club of Singers and Players," *The Music Master* 2 (March 1920), p. 14; "Growth of the Crescendo Club," *The Music Master* 2 (April 1920), pp. 5–6.

54. *Bee,* February 19, 1916.

55. *Bee,* May 31, 1919.

56. *MM,* p. 33.

57. It is difficult to determine precisely when Ellington studied with Grant. Mrs. Alice Spraggins and Mrs. June Hackney, Grant's daughters, have said that Ellington was about seventeen when he came by their house for lessons, making it around 1916 or 1917. On the other hand, if Ellington sought out Grant after he had built up a reputation, these years are too early, and 1918 to 1919 seem more probable. Some of the following biographical information was provided by Mrs. Hackney and Mrs. Spraggins, in an interview conducted in Washington, D.C., October 11, 1983.

58. A number of Washington black public school teachers participated in important musical organizations and events at this time. In addition to Henry Grant and Mary Europe, the list includes Turner Layton, Sr., conductor of the Samuel Coleridge-Taylor Chorus; Ernest Amos, singer with the Afro-American Folksong Singers and teacher at the Washington Conservatory; and James Miller, community civic bandleader. Today, educator Dr. Billy Taylor—a product of Dunbar High School and a stu-

dent of Henry Grant—continues in this Washington tradition of teacher-performers.

59. The Music Division of the Library of Congress has a set of programs from the 1919 music festival at Dunbar.

60. *MM,* p. 28.

61. Ibid., p. 33.

62. *DE,* p. 9.

63. *Washington Tribune,* October 22, 1921.

64. *The Negro Musician* (February 1921), p. 9. I have been unable to locate issues with these proposed articles.

65. H. G. [Henry Grant], "*Shuffle Along* A Great Success," *The Negro Musician* (June 1921), p. 13.

CHAPTER FIVE

1. *MM,* p. 32.

2. Ellington's October 1919 ad in the *C and P Telephone Directory* gives the Sherman Avenue address.

3. CBC interview #193 (February 1966), Ellington clipping file, IJS.

4. *DEP,* pp. 14–15.

5. In his article "Jazz as I Have Seen It" (Part 3, *Swing* [May 1940]) Ellington claimed he was earning $150 to $200 a week during this period (p. 16). Mercer Cook remembered $5 as the fee for Ellington's group, which seemed high at the time: "In Harlem you could get Fats Waller for only $3!" (interview, Silver Spring, Maryland, August 19, 1983). Added support for the $5 figure comes from the *Bee* (January 8, 1921), which reported that Louis Brown broke an engagement at Odd Fellows Hall, for which his orchestra would have received $5.

6. Marc Crawford, "A Visit with Mrs. Duke Ellington," *Ebony* 14 (March 1959), p. 133.

7. *MM,* p. 10.

8. *Bee,* September 6, 1919.

9. *Bee,* September 27, 1919.

10. *MM,* p. 28.

11. Biographical sources on Snowden include John Hammond, "The Story of Duke's Boss," *Music and Rhythm* (June 1942), pp. 22–23; David Ives, "Elmer Snowdon [*sic*]," *Jazz Journal* (January 1963), pp. 26–27; Les Muscutt, "Discovering Elmer," *Storyville* (April/May 1968), pp. 3–7; a questionnaire that Snowden filled out for Leonard Feather's *Encyclopedia of Jazz,* Snowden clipping file, IJS.

12. Stanley Dance, *The World of Swing* (1974; rpt., New York: Da Capo, 1979), p. 47.

13. *Bee,* September 4, 1920.

14. *MM,* pp. 53–54.

15. *WDE,* p. 63. For more on Greer, see Orrin Keepnews, "Reminiscing in Tempo: Sonny Greer, Drums," *Record Changer* (July 1948), p. 14; Burt Korall, "The Roots of the Duchy," *Down Beat* (June 13, 1967), pp. 21–22; Lee Jeske, "Scrapple from the Apple," *Jazz Journal International* (November 1978), p. 22.

16. Sonny Greer, interviewed by Stanley Crouch, January 15, 1979, JOHP, p. 12.

17. Mercer Cook, interview, Silver Spring, Maryland, August 19, 1983.

18. Rhea, quoted in George Hoefer, "Discs in Orbit" [n.d.], p. 4, Ellington clipping file, IJS. Hardwick, too, recalled the playful competition at the supper shows, with Ellington's group "matching other bands' versions of the same popular tunes" (in Hoefer, "Duke Ellington: Society Band Leader," *Washington Post Potomac* [May 20, 1962], p. 12).

19. *Bee,* April 2, 1921; November 19, 1921.

20. Dance, *World of Swing,* p. 47.

21. Henry T. Sampson, *Blacks in Blackface: A Source Book on Early Black Musical Sources* (Metuchen, N.J.: Scarecrow Press, 1980), pp. 274–75, 287. For more on Marie Lucas, see D. Antoinette Handy, *Black Women in American Bands and Orchestras* (Metuchen, N.J.: Scarecrow Press, 1981), pp. 55–56.

22. Indianapolis *Freeman,* August 26, 1916.

23. *Bee,* February 3, 1917.

24. Both Snowden (in Dance, *World of Swing,* p. 47) and Tizol (interviewed by Patricia Willard, Los Angeles, November 15, 1978, JOHP, p. 39) mentioned Escudero as a member of the Howard pit band. In his JOHP interview, Tizol corrected the error in *Music Is My Mistress,* in which Ellington wrote that Lucas came to the Howard with the Puerto Ricans. She arrived before them.

25. Questionnaire sent to Juan Tizol by the author, filled out by Tizol August 26, 1983. Also see the Tizol JOHP interview, p. 29.

26. *Washington Tribune,* October 15, 1921.

27. Tizol, JOHP interview, p. 10.

28. William H. Jones, *Recreation and Amusement among Negroes in Washington, D.C.* (1927; rpt., Westport, Conn.: Negro Universities Press, 1970), p. 132.

29. Dance, *World of Swing,* p. 67.

30. *Bee,* February 5, 1921; October 1, 1921.

31. Jones, *Recreation and Amusement,* p. 126.

32. *Washington Tribune,* March 4, 1922; May 6, 1922.

33. *Defender,* January 6, 1923.

34. Quentin, "The New Cabaret," *Washington Tribune,* November 26, 1921.

35. Dance, *World of Swing,* p. 31.

36. *Washington Tribune,* April 15, 1922.

37. Jones, *Recreation and Amusement,* p. 133.

38. *Bee,* October 23, 1920.

39. Adding to the Poodle Dog mystery, at least two long-time Washingtonians have recalled no strong musical associations with the place. Mercer Cook described the Poodle Dog as a kind of social club intended to keep would-be troublemakers off the street (interview, Silver Spring, Maryland, August 19, 1983). And his friend Roy Ellis dismissed it as "honky-tonky . . . just another place" (telephone conversation, Washington, D.C., August 19, 1983).

40. *Washington Tribune,* October 7, 1922.

41. Jones, *Recreation and Amusement,* p. 133.

42. Duke Ellington, "Jazz As I Have Seen It," Part 3, p. 16.

43. *Washington Tribune,* August 6, 1921.

44. *Bee,* May 29, 1920.

45. *Bee,* September 11, 1920.

46. *Defender,* July 30, 1921.

47. *Washington Tribune,* June 17, 1922.

48. *Defender,* August 13, 1921.

49. *Defender,* September 10, 1921.

50. *Defender,* January 13, 1923.

51. *Washington Tribune,* February 4, 1922.

52. *Washington Tribune,* April 15, 1922.

53. Ellington, "Jazz As I Have Seen It," Part 3, p. 16.

54. Jay Bee, "Snowden-Diamond Jazzologists, Eccentric Musicians," *Washington Tribune,* January 21, 1922.

55. *MM,* p. 26.

56. *Defender,* September 24, 1921.

57. *Defender,* December 17, 1921. The New Liberty Hotel (New Jersey Avenue and D Street, N.W.) was a black-managed hotel that opened in December 1920. The *Defender* (August 20, 1921) called its garden "one of the city's most popular recreation centers."

58. *Defender,* December 3, 1921.

59. Duke Ellington, liner notes to *James P. Johnson, Father of the Stride Piano,* Columbia CL1780. These notes were reprinted in *MM,* pp. 93–95.

60. Ellington, "Jazz As I Have Seen It," Part 3, p. 23.

61. *Washington Tribune,* May 13, 1922.

62. *MM*, p. 49.

63. Mercer Cook, interview, Silver Spring, Maryland, August 19, 1983. When Bechet went abroad with Cook in June 1919, the ensemble was renamed the Southern Syncopated Orchestra. See John Chilton, *Sidney Bechet: The Wizard of Jazz* (London: Macmillan, 1987), pp. 33–34.

64. *MM*, p. 35. Elmer Snowden reported that by 1923 in New York all the members of his group were doubling. Snowden himself had received saxophone instruction from one of the "Cubans" (he probably meant Puerto Ricans) in the Howard Theater pit band. See Dance, *World of Swing*, p. 50.

65. *MM*, pp. 35–36.

66. See *MM*, p. 31.

CHAPTER SIX

1. *Washington Tribune*, April 29, 1922.

2. *WDE*, p. 63. Also see *DE*, pp. 22–23.

3. Tim Weiner, "Keeping Time with Sonny Greer," *Soho Weekly News*, June 15, 1979. This is the only reference I have seen to an appearance by Ellington in New York at such an early date. In other interviews Greer did not mention Busoni's Balconnade. Greer may have been referring to the Balconnades Ballroom, located near Broadway and 66th Street, which featured bands such as the Original Memphis Five and the New Orleans Five.

4. From a 1950 interview with Williams by Ed Kirkeby, cited in Tom Lord, *Clarence Williams* (Chigwell, England: Storyville Publications and Co., 1976), p. 21.

5. Harrison Smith, "Wilbur Sweatman: Original Jazz King," *Record Research* (July 1961), p. 9.

6. A notice in the *Washington Tribune* (May 27, 1922) stated that Sweatman was booked to play Baltimore, Philadelphia, and Washington. No documentation has been found for the exact date of his visit. At least two sources have claimed Sweatman came through Washington in the winter of 1922 but provide no evidence. See Samuel B. Charters and Leonard Kunstadt, *Jazz: A History of the New York Scene* (1962; rpt., New York: Da Capo, 1981), p. 210; also James Lincoln Collier, *Duke Ellington* (New York: Oxford University Press, 1987), p. 37.

7. See *WDE*, pp. 56–57.

8. *Clipper*, February 28, 1923, p. 24.

9. *Age*, March 3, 1923; *Age*, March 10, 1923; *Amsterdam News*, March 7, 1923.

10. *MM*, p. 36.

11. Greer, interviewed by Stanley Crouch, January 15, 1979, JOHP, p. 17. In 1976 Greer said that his experience with Sweatman had been "horrible" (interview with Greer by Edith Exton and Brooks Kerr, New York, 1976; tape copy in the collection of Brooks Kerr).

This was not the last time Ellington would face such onstage color codes. When his band appeared in the films *Black and Tan* (1929) and *Check and Double Check* (1930), trombonist Juan Tizol and clarinetist Barney Bigard were forced to "blacken up" so that audiences would not think them white.

12. Sonny Greer, interview with Exton and Kerr.

13. *MM*, p. 36.

14. Ibid.

15. Ibid., p. 90.

16. Ibid.

17. Willie "the Lion" Smith with George Hoefer, *Music on My Mind: The Memoirs of an American Pianist* (1964; rpt., New York: Da Capo, 1978), pp. 149–50.

18. George Hoefer, booklet notes, *The Sound of Harlem,* Jazz Odyssey, Columbia C3L 33, p. [26].

19. Smith, *Music on My Mind,* p. 150.

20. Ellington, "Jazz As I Have Seen It," Part 3, *Swing* (May 1940), p. 23.

21. Ellington, interviewed by Max Jones and Humphrey Lyttleton, May 13, 1964, EPY, Tape 500k.

22. *MM*, p. 37.

23. Richard O. Boyer, "The Hot Bach," Part 3, *New Yorker* (July 8, 1944), pp. 28–29.

24. *DE,* p. 29. The 1923 Washington City Directory (probably compiled the previous year) shows both Edward K. and James Edward Ellington at the 1212 T Street address. Either Ellington had moved his family out of the Sherman Avenue house or Edna was living there without him.

25. Stanley Dance, *The World of Swing* (1974; rpt., New York, Da Capo, 1979), p. 48. An itinerary for the group has not yet been found.

26. Garvin Bushell as told to Mark Tucker, *Jazz from the Beginning* (Ann Arbor: University of Michigan Press, 1988), p. 47.

27. *MM*, p. 69. Also see *DE,* pp. 30–31.

28. Dance, *World of Swing,* pp. 48–49. Snowden gave the same version in the questionnaire he filled out for Leonard Feather's *Encyclopedia of Jazz,* IJS, Snowden clipping file. Hardwick remembered Waller telling Snowden of the opportunity (*WDE,* p. 57).

29. Frank Dutton, "Birth of a Band," Part 3, *Storyville* 98 (December 1981-January 1982), p. 45. David Ives gave June 18 as the date Snow-

den left Washington for New York. He also reported that Bill Beasley —the drummer in Snowden's Murray's Casino house band—did not want to go to New York, hence Greer went instead. See David Ives, "Elmer Snowdon" [sic], *Jazz Journal* (January 1963), p. 26.

30. *WDE,* p. 57.

31. *Variety,* March 8, 1923, p. 35.

32. Dance, *World of Swing,* pp. 50–52.

33. Bricktop with James Haskins, *Bricktop* (New York: Atheneum, 1983), pp. 77–78.

34. Rex Stewart, *Jazz Masters of the Thirties* (1972; rpt., New York: Da Capo, [1982]), p. 55.

35. Les Muscutt, "Discovering Elmer," *Storyville* 16 (April-May 1968), p. 4.

36. Nat Shapiro and Nat Hentoff, eds., *Hear Me Talkin' to Ya* (New York: Rinehart and Co., 1955), p. 230. Sam Wooding, who played at Barron's around 1922, gave a comparable figure: forty dollars for the leader, twenty-five to thirty dollars for sidemen (Sam Wooding, interviewed by Chris Albertson, New York, April 22, 1975, JOHP, p. 109).

37. Bricktop, *Bricktop,* p. 75.

38. Noble Sissle, "Show Business," *Age,* October 23, 1948, cited in Jervis Anderson, *This Was Harlem: A Cultural Portrait, 1900–1950* (New York: Farrar Straus Giroux, 1981), p. 16.

39. Konrad Bercovici, "The Black Blocks of Harlem," *Harper's* (October 1924), cited in Anderson, *This Was Harlem,* p. 172.

40. Dance, *World of Swing,* p. 52.

41. *MM,* p. 70.

42. Ibid.

43. Shapiro and Hentoff, *Hear Me Talkin' to Ya,* p. 230.

44. Dance, *World of Swing,* p. 53.

45. Ibid. According to Steven Lasker, who has closely examined Victor's files, "Home" appears to have been a trial recording rather than an actual test pressing.

46. *MM,* xi. The New York City directories of 1924 and 1925 show both Ellington and Hardwick occupying rooms in Harper's home at 2067 Seventh Avenue.

47. *Billboard,* September 1, 1923, p. 19.

48. *Billboard,* December 15, 1923, p. 100.

49. Jimmy Durante and Jack Kofoed, *Night Clubs* (New York: Knopf, 1931), p. 115.

50. *Amsterdam News,* July 25, 1923.

51. Ibid.

52. A map showing these boundaries for "Negro Harlem, 1925," ap-

pears in James Weldon Johnson, *Black Manhattan* (1930; new ed., New York: Atheneum, 1968), opposite p. 146. For more on Harlem in the 1920s see Jervis Anderson, *This Was Harlem;* David Levering Lewis, *When Harlem Was in Vogue* (New York: Vintage, 1982); Gilbert Osofsky, *Harlem: The Making of a Ghetto* (New York: Harper's Torchbooks, 1968); Nathan Irvin Huggins, *Harlem Renaissance* (New York: Oxford, 1971). George Hoefer's splendid essay for the booklet accompanying *The Sound of Harlem* gives the most comprehensive history of Harlem nightspots and lists many of the musicians who played there.

53. *Billboard,* November 3, 1923, p. 82.

54. Patrick Gaffey, "Garvin Bushell: Jazz Roots from the Beginning," *Arts Alive* [Las Vegas, Nevada] (May/June 1983), p. 20.

55. *Billboard,* November 10, 1923, p. 14.

56. *Billboard,* September 15, 1923, p. 52. Fisher's was not the only company to hire blacks. Two weeks earlier *Billboard* announced that Andrew Sissle, brother of Noble, had joined the staff of Jack Mills.

57. *MM,* p. 70.

58. Ibid., pp. 70–71.

59. *WDE,* p. 13.

60. See James A. Jackson, "Blues Seem to Have Taken Over," *Amsterdam News,* July 11, 1923. Also, "Getting a Slant on Our Performers and Song Writers on the 'Big Time,'" *Amsterdam News,* August 6, 1923.

61. *Billboard,* September 1, 1923, p. 20; October 13, 1923, p. 22.

62. *MM,* p. 72.

63. From *Pittsburgh Courier,* August 18, 1923, cited in Walter C. Allen, *Hendersonia* (Highland Park, N.J.: published by the author, 1973), p. 63. Thomas Walker—or Waller, as Allen supposes—accompanied Trixie Smith.

CHAPTER SEVEN

1. Morroe Berger, Edward Berger, and James Patrick, *Benny Carter: A Life in American Music,* 2 vols. (Metuchen, N.J.: Scarecrow Press, 1982), 1:45.

2. Rex Stewart, *Jazz Masters of the Thirties* (1972; rpt., New York: Da Capo, [1982]), p. 74.

3. Cited in Walter C. Allen, *Hendersonia* (Highland Park, N.J.: published by the author, 1973), p. 41.

4. See Thomas L. Riis, *Just Before Jazz* (Washington, D.C.: Smithsonian Institution Press, 1989), pp. 75–80.

5. Baltimore *Afro-American,* May 26, 1922.

6. The only reference to this activity found so far appears in the *Lynn* [Massachusetts] *Daily Evening Item*, April 18, 1924.

7. The club was referred to as the Hollywood Café, Hollywood Cabaret, Hollywood Inn, or simply the Hollywood. From May 1924 through the summer of 1926 the Manhattan telephone directory listed it as the Hollywood Restaurant, 203 West 49th Street.

8. *Billboard*, September 1, 1923, p. 19.

9. Samuel B. Charters and Leonard Kunstadt, *Jazz: A History of the New York Scene*, (1962; rpt., New York: Da Capo, 1981), p. 212.

10. While Barry Ulanov, in *DE* (p. 34), cited Harper as the main contact for the Hollywood job, one aspect of his narrative is incorrect and another is questionable. First, he stated that banjo-player Fred Guy replaced Snowden directly after the stint at Barron Wilkins's. But a review of the band in the fall of 1923 identified Snowden as leader. Second, Ulanov claimed that it was up to Ellington to decide whether the band would take a job uptown at Connie's or downtown at the Hollywood. Since Snowden was in charge, it was probably he who seized a last-minute opportunity to substitute for Everard Dabney.

11. Harrison Smith to Marshall Stearns, [n.d.], IJS vertical file.

12. *Clipper*, November 23, 1923, p. 12.

13. Stewart, *Jazz Masters of the Thirties*, p. 132.

14. Most accounts state that Whetsol left to attend medical school at Howard University. But Dennette Harrod, president of the Washington chapter of the Duke Ellington Society, has searched Howard's records without turning up Whetsol's name. Moreover, trombonist Lawrence Brown, who roomed with Whetsol in the 1930s, told Harrod he had never heard anything to suggest that the trumpeter had received medical training. In his memoirs, Ellington wrote simply that Whetsol left "to continue his studies at Howard University," thus skirting the issue of whether Whetsol actually did so.

15. Garvin Bushell as told to Mark Tucker, *Jazz from the Beginning* (Ann Arbor: University of Michigan Press, 1988), p. 25.

16. George Hoefer, booklet notes, *The Sound of Harlem*, Jazz Odyssey, Columbia C3L 33, p. [29].

17. This and the following quote are taken from an interview with Hardwick by Inez M. Cavanaugh, "Reminiscing in Tempo," *Metronome* (November 1944), p. 17.

18. Stanley Dance, *The World of Swing* (1974; rpt., New York: Da Capo, 1979), p. 53.

19. Nat Shapiro and Nat Hentoff, eds., *Hear Me Talkin' to Ya* (New York: Rinehart and Co., 1955), p. 231.

20. *DEP,* p. 23.

21. Green's claim that Hardwick doubled on violin is supported by no other evidence.

22. *WDE,* p. 66.

23. *Billboard,* September 15, 1923, p. 52.

24. In Volume A of the bound notebooks.

25. *Billboard,* October 13, 1923, p. 22.

26. *Billboard,* December 22, 1923, p. 54.

27. *Billboard,* September 22, 1923, p. 55; October 27, 1923, p. 22.

28. *MM,* p. 102.

29. Since the Victor files tend to give just instrumentation, not names of players, the personnel for this date remains a mystery. All sources agree on the presence of Ellington, Hardwick, Snowden, and Greer. But Dutton puts the number at six, with Miley and Anderson in; Bakker adds Roland Smith to Dutton's list to make seven in all; and Timner also has seven but with Whetsol on trumpet instead of Miley. Rust lists Irvis on trombone, but as Dutton has pointed out, the *Clipper* did not announce Irvis's arrival in the band until January 1924. See Frank Dutton, "Birth of a Band," Part 2, *Storyville* 91 (October-November 1980), p. 8.

Steven Lasker believes that this October 18 session never took place, having found no evidence of it in the Victor files. If this is true, where did earlier discographers get their information, and how did they arrive at the titles of the two pieces?

30. *Talking Machine Journal,* October 1923, p. 49. The only other known recording of the song is by Emma Gover, accompanied by Horace Henderson (September 10, 1923, Pathé Actuelle and Perfect).

31. *MM,* p. 95.

32. Hollie I. West, "Duke at 70: Honor from the President," *Washington Post,* April 27, 1969.

33. *MM,* p. 97.

34. *Amsterdam News,* October 10, 1923.

35. *Clipper,* December 14, 1923, p. 24.

36. *Clipper,* March 13, 1924, p. 18.

37. *Haverhill Evening Gazette,* January 26, 1925.

38. No reviews have been found for the Washingtonians' radio performances. Late in 1923 the *Clipper*'s radio page began covering music broadcast Wednesday evenings—when the white bands tended to play—but not Wednesday afternoons, the Washingtonians' time slot. Green's November 23, 1923, review cited the Washingtonians' weekly WHN broadcasts, but by March 6, 1924, the band's name was not mentioned in a list of groups appearing on the station.

39. Stewart, *Jazz Masters of the Thirties,* pp. 105–6.

40. *WDE,* p. 7.

41. Hardwick in Cavanaugh, "Reminiscing in Tempo," p. 17; *MM,* p. 71.

42. *Clipper,* February 22, 1924, p. 35. In its schedule of "Bands and Orchestras," the *Clipper* went on listing Snowden as leader for several more issues. But like the mid-December 1923 acknowledgement of the band's new name, this probably reflected out-of-date information that no one bothered to correct.

According to Dutton, nothing is known about George Francis. See "Birth of a Band," Part 2, *Storyville* 91 (October-November 1980), p. 8.

43. Dance, *World of Swing,* p. 53.

44. *DE,* p. 33. Interviews with Tommy Benford (Mount Vernon, New York, January 8, 1985) and Garvin Bushell (Las Vegas, Nevada, April 9, 1985) have confirmed this version of the story.

45. *MM,* p. 70.

46. *DEP,* p. 22.

47. Dance, *World of Swing,* p. 53.

48. The ad was reprinted in *Record Research* (June 1973), p. 7.

49. For a discussion of these recordings, see chapter 9.

50. Sonny Greer, interviewed by Stanley Crouch, January 15, 1979, JOHP, p. 40.

51. The first ad for the Kentucky Club appeared in *Variety,* April 1, 1925, p. 44, in a review of a March 28 performance.

52. Ads for these theater dates are from the *Age,* March 7, 1925; *Amsterdam News,* April 8, 1925; *Age,* May 16, 1925; *Variety,* July 8, 1925, p. 47.

53. *Variety,* May 13, 1925, p. 26.

54. Ibid. Although Elmer Snowden said that he rejoined the Washingtonians for a time after his initial departure, no documentation supports his claim.

55. *MM,* p. 109.

56. Both Bakker and Timner give the date as mid-1925. Yet according to Jerry Valburn, no card for this session has ever turned up in the Brunswick files.

57. Berta Wood, "The Duke and Sidney Bechet," *Jazz Journal* (July 1958), p. 25.

58. Sidney Bechet, *Treat It Gentle* (1960; rpt., New York: Da Capo, 1978), p. 141. It is difficult to establish precisely when Bechet played with the Washingtonians. In *MM,* Ellington gave the date as the summer of 1926 (p. 47), but Bechet was in Europe then. In a 1936 interview for *Swing Music,* saxophonist Benny Carter recalled that he and Bechet went with James P. Johnson's band into the Kentucky Club (then the Hollywood) in

the spring of 1924, taking the place of Ellington, who went out touring (see John Chilton, *Sidney Bechet: The Wizard of Jazz* [New York: Oxford University Press, 1987], pp. 67–70). Then, upon Ellington's return, apparently manager Leo Bernstein requested that Ellington add Bechet to his group. This may have been in late April or early May, after the Washingtonians came back from engagements in Massachusetts (see p. 184).

I think it also possible that Bechet played with the Washingtonians in the spring of 1925 and occasional dates that summer in New England, perhaps after leaving the show *Seven-eleven* and before opening his Club Basha in New York.

59. Bechet, *Treat It Gentle,* p. 142.

60. Dutton has speculated that Edwards joined around June 1925 (in Dutton, "Birth of a Band," Part 1, *Storyville* 80 [December 1978-January 1979], p. 49).

61. *WDE,* p. 67.

62. *Variety,* September 16, 1925, p. 45, and October 14, 1925, p. 46. The first of these reviews is unsigned but seems to be Green's work. In other contemporary sources Gerrity's name is spelled as "Gerety" and "Gerity."

63. *Variety,* October 14, 1925, p. 46.

64. *Billboard,* February 2, 1924, p. 52.

65. *Variety,* September 16, 1925, p. 43.

66. *Clipper,* February 22, 1924, p. 15.

67. Greer, JOHP interview, p. 20.

68. *Variety,* September 16, 1925, p. 45.

69. *Variety,* October 14, 1925, p. 46.

70. *Billboard,* December 5, 1925, p. 22.

71. Apparently the Washingtonians, Waller, and Bert Lewis once performed together in a revue at the New Amsterdam Theater. No contemporary references have turned up for these appearances, perhaps because they took place when the house was dark. See Maurice Waller and Anthony Calabrese, *Fats Waller* (New York: Schirmer Books, 1977), pp. 56–57.

72. Stewart, *Jazz Masters of the Thirties,* p. 21.

73. *Billboard,* December 5, 1925, p. 22.

74. Richard O. Boyer, "The Hot Bach," Part 3, *New Yorker* (July 8, 1944), p. 29.

75. *MM,* p. 72.

76. Robert Sylvester, *No Cover Charge* (New York: Dial Press, 1956), pp. 128, 138.

77. Harrison Smith to Marshall Stearns, [n.d.], IJS vertical file.

78. Greer, JOHP interview, p. 19.

79. *Clipper,* February 22, 1924, p. 15.

80. *Clipper,* November 23, 1923, p. 12.

81. *WDE,* pp. 65–66.

82. These titles are drawn from Tim Weiner, "Keeping Time with Sonny Greer," *Soho Weekly News,* June 15, 1979; Shapiro and Hentoff, *Hear Me Talkin' to Ya,* p. 231; an interview with Russell Procope by Brooks Kerr.

83. Weiner, "Keeping Time with Sonny Greer."

84. Bechet, *Treat It Gentle,* pp. 142–43.

85. Ibid., p. 143.

86. *WDE,* p. 66.

CHAPTER EIGHT

1. *WDE,* p. 13.

2. *MM,* p. 71.

3. Horst J. P. Bergmeier, "Sam Wooding Recapitulated," *Storyville* 74 (December 1977-January 1978), p. 44.

4. In "Chocolate Kiddies Company Sails for Germany" (*Pittsburgh Courier,* May 16, 1925), Floyd G. Snelson wrote that the show had been in rehearsal several weeks at Bryant Hall.

5. Garvin Bushell, interview, Las Vegas, Nevada, April 9, 1985.

6. For more on the history of *Chocolate Kiddies* see Björn Englund, "Chocolate Kiddies: The Show that Brought Jazz to Europe and Russia in 1925," *Storyville* 62 (December 1975-January 1976), pp. 44–50; John and Hans Larsen, "The Chocolate Kiddies in Copenhagen," *Record Research* (April 1965), pp. 3–5; Bernhard H. Behncke, "Sam Wooding and the Chocolate Kiddies at the Thalia-Theater in Hamburg, 28 July 1925 to 24 August 1925," *Storyville* 60 (August-September 1975), pp. 214–19; Garvin Bushell as told to Mark Tucker, *Jazz from the Beginning* (Ann Arbor: University of Michigan Press, 1988), pp. 54–71.

7. See Englund, "Chocolate Kiddies," pp. 45–47.

8. Behncke, "Sam Wooding and the Chocolate Kiddies," p. 217.

9. W. C. Handy, *Father of the Blues: An Autobiography,* ed. Arna Bontemps (1941; rpt., New York: Collier, 1970), p. 122.

10. See Bergmeier, "Sam Wooding Recapitulated," p. 44.

11. *Variety,* June 17, 1925, p. 40.

12. John Steiner (the record producer who put "Jig Walk" out on microgroove) to Mark Tucker, February 23, 1985.

13. Brooks Kerr, interview, New York, December 11, 1983; Michael Montgomery to Mark Tucker, February 8, 1985.

14. Björn Englund, "Two Obscure Ellington Tunes," *Doctor Jazz* (February-March 1974), p. 4. In his discography for *Chocolate Kiddies,* printed in *Storyville* 62, p. 50, Englund gave the titles as "(Love Is Just a

Wish) With You," thus conflating two songs from the show: "Love Is a Wish for You" and "With You."

15. *Record Research* (February-March 1976), p. 11.

16. The 1938 performance can be heard on *Duke Ellington: Live Recording at the Cotton Club,* Vol. 1, Jazz Anthology, 30 JA 5168. The same arrangement played with more fire in 1940 appears on *Reflections in Ellington,* Everybodys 3005.

17. Hardwick in Inez M. Cavanaugh, "Reminiscing in Tempo," *Metronome* (November 1944), p. 26. Hardwick claimed this incident occurred at Ciro's, Ulanov at the Flamingo Club (*DE,* pp. 54–55).

18. Benny Carter, interviewed by Morroe Berger, Princeton, New Jersey, October 13–14, 1976, JOHP, cassettes 1–2, p. 36.

19. *MM,* p. 95.

20. *Variety,* November 25, 1925, p. 42; *Defender,* December 26, 1925.

21. *Variety,* January 6, 1926, p. 45.

22. *Age,* December 12, 1925.

23. *Orchestra World,* October 1925, p. 8.

24. *Metronome,* August 1, 1927, p. 20. In both *Metronome* and *Orchestra World* white orchestras received far more coverage than black.

CHAPTER NINE

1. *Down Beat* (March 1939), cited in Samuel B. Charters and Leonard Kunstadt, *Jazz: A History of the New York Scene* (1962; rpt., New York: Da Capo, 1981), p. 78.

2. Gunnar Askland, "Interpretations in Jazz: A Conference with Duke Ellington," *Etude* (March 1947), p. 134.

3. Sam Coslow, *Cocktails for Two* (New Rochelle, N.Y.: Arlington House, 1977), p. 36.

4. Gunther Schuller, *Early Jazz* (New York: Oxford University Press, 1968), p. 323.

5. Apparently the hot trumpet solo was a fixture in "Choo Choo." Katzman's stock arrangement calls for one, and in the Original Memphis Five version Phil Napoleon takes a muted chorus of his own.

6. "Rainy Nights" seems not to have been copyrighted in the 1920s. In 1973 Ellington copyrighted it under his own name, and some microgroove reissues of "Rainy Nights" also list Ellington as composer. The Broadway 78 r.p.m. issue gives the title "Rainy Nights (Rainy Days)." While both Bakker and Timner list two issued takes of "Rainy Nights" (T-2006-1 and T-2006-2), both are pressings made from the same master.

A song by Porter Grainger called "Rainy Days" was copyrighted July 11, 1924 (E 589831), but this may have been a different piece.

7. "Naughty Man," credited to Don Redman and Charlie Dixon, was recorded by Fletcher Henderson's orchestra on November 7, 1924, also a week later. The composers of "Rainy Nights" may have borrowed from "Naughty Man." But as Martin Williams has pointed out, the borrowing could have gone in the other direction since the exact date of the "Rainy Nights" session is unknown. See Williams, *The Jazz Tradition* (New York: Oxford University Press, 1970), p. 90.

8. Bakker gives September 7 as the date, while Dutton comes up with ca. September 12 from a matrix-comparison estimate. See Frank Dutton, "Birth of a Band," Part 2, *Storyville* 91 (October-November 1980), p. 9.

9. "Rainy Nights" ends with the same chord. As Schuller noted in *Early Jazz*, the device "had become 'hip' in the middle 1920s, after seventh-chord endings had begun to pale with much overuse" (p. 323).

10. *Defender*, February 21, 1925, cited in Walter C. Allen, *Hendersonia* (Highland Park, N.J.: published by the author, 1973), p. 131.

11. *Billboard*, April 25, 1925, p. 50.

12. Schuller, *Early Jazz*, p. 320.

13. Some discographies list George Thomas as the vocalist here. Brooks Kerr is sure it's Greer, and I concur.

14. Recorded February 20, 1926, for Columbia, 14134-D. When I played the Washingtonians' version for Fain, on April 12, 1985, he commented on the fast tempo, saying that the studio probably told Ellington they wanted something "hot." Fain's own performance with Waters is somewhat slower and more relaxed.

15. Schuller, *Early Jazz*, p. 321.

16. Coslow, *Cocktails for Two*, pp. 71–72.

17. Schuller, *Early Jazz*, pp. 322–23.

18. *MM*, p. 106.

19. *DEP*, p. 16.

20. *Billboard*, November 13, 1926, p. 25. Smith also laid claim to various compositions written by Jelly Roll Morton.

21. Harrison Smith, letters to George Hoefer, May 24, 1942, and Marshall Stearns, [n.d.], IJS vertical file.

22. Harrison Smith to George Hoefer, May 24, 1942, IJS vertical file.

23. *MM*, pp. 95, 419.

24. See Thomas L. Riis, *Just Before Jazz* (Smithsonian Institution Press, 1989), pp. 119, 271–74. Louis Armstrong uses the same quotation in his introduction to "Shine" (1931).

25. *MM*, p. 420.

26. Peter Gammond, *Duke Ellington: His Life and Music* (1958; rpt., New York: Da Capo, 1977), p. 71.

27. Gary Giddins, "Ellington, Music, and Poker," *Village Voice* Jazz Supplement (August 28, 1984), p. 68.

28. Schuller, *Early Jazz,* p. 324.

29. Williams, *The Jazz Tradition,* p. 89.

30. See Timner (pp. 485ff.) for a listing of these dates.

31. *Variety,* October 21, 1925, p. 40.

32. Garvin Bushell, interview, Las Vegas, Nevada, April 10, 1985.

33. Personal communication from Ellington to Brooks Kerr, ca. 1971.

34. *Phonograph and Talking Machine Weekly,* October 29, 1924, p. 38.

35. This must be one of Robeson's first recordings, if not the first. The Blu-Disc ad (reprinted in the June 1973 *Record Research,* p. 7) noted that Robeson was the star of "All Gods Chillen Got Wings."

36. *Billboard,* May 2, 1925, p. 25.

37. *Variety,* September 9, 1925, p. 39.

38. *MM,* p. 3.

39. Schuller, *Early Jazz,* p. 322.

40. See Edward A. Berlin, *Ragtime: A Musical and Cultural History* (Berkeley: University of California Press, 1980), pp. 130–34.

CHAPTER TEN

1. *Clipper,* March 13, 1924, p. 15.

2. *WDE,* p. 69.

3. In *MM* Ellington wrote that Shribman had hired the band to work around New England for six weeks right after New Year's, 1924. Yet notices for the band do not turn up until April and then only for two weeks of jobs.

4. *Salem Evening News,* April 18, 1924.

5. *Lynn Daily Evening Item,* April 18, 1924.

6. *Salem Evening News,* April 21, 1924.

7. *Salem Evening News,* April 24, 1924.

8. *Haverhill Evening Gazette,* January 26, 1925.

9. Ibid.

10. *Haverhill Evening Gazette,* February 5, 1925.

11. According to *Variety,* the band played in Haverhill March 4 and 11, April 8 and 29, May 27, and July 8. These scattered dates suggest that, after spending the latter part of January and early February 1925 in New England, the Washingtonians made occasional overnight trips to Haverhill.

12. Quoted in the *Chicago Defender*, August 27, 1927. The original *Tribune* source has not been found.

13. *Boston Post*, July 9, 1926. The Paul Whiteman tag was common for the time and did not necessarily reflect on Ellington's music. In Chicago Dave Peyton and his Symphonic Syncopators were advertised the same way, and in Denver George Morrison was called "the colored Paul Whiteman." Similarly, white bandleader Jean Goldkette was billed as "the Paul Whiteman of Detroit."

14. *DE*, p. 52.

15. Ibid., pp. 60–62. Apparently Carney was not the only hapless victim of this joke. See *DEP*, p. 19.

16. *Boston Post*, July 31, 1926; *Providence Journal*, July 25, 1926.

17. *Portland Press Herald*, August 9 and 12, 1926.

18. Ads in the *Boston Post* (July 10, 1926) and *Providence Journal* (July 25, 1926) referred to ten pieces in the band.

19. Inez M. Cavanaugh, "Reminiscing in Tempo," *Metronome* (February 1945), p. 17.

20. Rex Stewart, *Jazz Masters of the Thirties* (1972; rpt., New York: Da Capo, [1982]), p. 108.

21. Ibid., pp. 104–7.

22. Frank Dutton, "Birth of a Band," Part 2, *Storyville* 91 (October-November 1980), p. 9.

23. *WDE*, p. 10.

24. *DE*, p. 53.

25. See *DEP*, opposite p. 100.

26. A photo taken at Orchard Beach, New York, in August 1926 shows Percy Glascoe and, in the front row, an unknown musician who may have been the third reed player but who is not Edgar Sampson (as the caption on p. 74 of *MM* claims). See Dutton, "Birth of a Band," Part 1, *Storyville* 80 (December 1978-January 1979), p. 51. The same photo identifies a person who was probably bassist Mack Shaw as clarinetist Rudy Jackson.

27. "Freddie Skerritt Tells His Story" to David Griffiths and Albert Vollmer (with additional information from Peter Carr), *Storyville* 66 (August-September 1976), pp. 215–16.

28. *Boston Post*, August 10, 1926.

29. *Boston Post*, July 20, 1926.

30. Toots Mondello, interview, February 7, 1985.

31. *Variety*, January 21, 1925, p. 40.

32. *WDE*, pp. 10–11.

33. *MM*, p. 75.

34. *DEP*, p. 24.

35. Nanton described his partnership with Miley in Cavanaugh, "Reminiscing in Tempo," p. 17.

36. *Salem Evening News,* August 4, 1926.

37. Quoted in the *Defender,* August 27, 1927.

38. A.L.H., "Ballrooms This Week," *Boston Post,* August 2, 1926.

39. *MM,* p. 99.

40. *Record Research* (January 1962), p. 11.

41. Harrison Smith to Marshall Stearns, [n.d.], IJS vertical file. In *MM* Ellington alluded to early work in Pennsylvania, but according to Nanton the band refused to go on a tour to Huntington, West Virginia, because it "sounded like the South" (in Cavanaugh, "Reminiscing in Tempo" [February 1945], p. 17).

42. "Ellingtonia," 1944 American Jazz Institute, typescript, IJS vertical file.

43. Smith to Stearns, [n.d.], IJS vertical file. In the opinion of several people who knew him, Harrison Smith was not an entirely reliable source of information. Indeed, his accounts of contact with Ellington are full of garbled dates and facts. Yet it seems possible that he might try to to get $1,000 a week for Ellington in 1926, when a bandleader like Vincent Lopez was earning the same amount for a single night's work.

CHAPTER ELEVEN

1. *Billboard,* September 25, 1926, p. 22.

2. *Orchestra World* (November 1926), p. 13. *Orchestra World* spelled some surnames differently from *Billboard:* Julia Gerety appeared as "Gerity," Eva Dowling as "Downling," and Olive Kendall as "Vernall."

3. Both Bakker and Timner list the Jackson session; Jerry Valburn has been unable to find any evidence for it in the Gennett files.

4. *Variety,* October 27, 1926, p. 102.

5. Mitchell Parish, interview, New York, December 1, 1984.

6. Harrison Smith may have also played a role in getting the Washingtonians on Gennett. The band recorded his song "Li'l Farina" for Gennett in June of 1926, and Harrison once described himself as an "Advisor and Record Jobber" for the company. See Harrison Smith to George Hoefer, May 24, 1942, IJS vertical file.

7. Sam Coslow, *Cocktails for Two* (New Rochelle, N.Y.: Arlington House, 1977), p. 40.

8. Ibid., pp. 40–41.

9. *Age,* July 12, 1930, cited in Samuel B. Charters and Leonard Kunstadt, *Jazz: A History of the New York Scene* (1962: rpt., New York: Da Capo, 1981), p. 208.

10. Irving Mills, interviewed by Irene Kahn Atkins, April 23, 1981, EPY. At the time Mills was eighty-seven years old.

11. Walter C. Allen, *Hendersonia* (Highland Park, N.J.: published by the author, 1973), p. 96.

12. Stephen Kemp, "New Talent His Specialty," *Metronome* (April 1930), p. 31.

13. John Rosenfield, Jr., "From Dance Musician to Jazzist," clipping from *Dallas News* (1933) in a Mills press book, personal collection of Stanley Dance.

14. Irving Mills as told to Charles Emge, "I Split with Duke When Music Began Sidetracking," *Down Beat* (November 5, 1952), p. 6.

15. Duke Ellington, "Jazz As I Have Seen It," from *Swing* (1940), reprinted in Nat Shapiro and Nat Hentoff, eds., *Hear Me Talkin' to Ya* (New York: Rinehart, 1955), pp. 231–32. Like Ellington, both Stanley Dance in *WDE* and Peter Gammond in *Duke Ellington: The Man and His Music* have linked Mills to the first Vocalion date. Ulanov (p. 58) claimed that Mills offered to get Ellington on Columbia, but this did not occur until March 1927.

16. *DE,* p. 58.

17. *Orchestra World* (December 1926), p. 19.

18. *Orchestra World* (January 1927), p. 21. The identification with Brunswick came from the four Vocalion sides the band had made in November and December 1926; Vocalion had been taken over by Brunswick in 1925. The first records by Ellington that actually appeared on the Brunswick label were made February 28, 1927.

The "Fifth Season" description requires explanation. As Frank Dutton has written, "a season . . . in club parlance . . . appears to be an elastic period stretching from as little as two weeks or so to many months!" ("Birth of a Band," Part 1, *Storyville* 80 [December 1978-January 1979], p. 51). A possible tally of the Washingtonians' "seasons" at the Hollywood/Kentucky Club might run as follows:

First   September 1923-August 1924 (two six-month contracts)
Second September 1924-February 1925 (after six months, fire closes the club)
Third   March 1925-August 1925 (six months)
Fourth   September 1925-April 1926 (eight-month contract)
Fifth   September 1926-April 1927 (eight months)

19. *Orchestra World* (January 1927), p. 15.

20. Steven Lasker to Mark Tucker, January 6, 1990.

21. Quoted in the *Defender,* August 27, 1927.

22. *Metronome* (August 1, 1927), p. 20.

23. *Defender*, April 16, 1927. "Down Home Stomp" is a Jo Trent and Ellington collaboration, with a 1962 copyright (or renewal notice) given in *MM* (p. 514). Ellington did not record it, and no published copy of the piece has been located.

24. This quotation and the following one are from Mills as told to Emge, "I Split with Duke," p. 6.

25. *Salem Evening News*, May 21, 1927.

26. Bakker has speculated on the reed personnel from November 29, 1926, through April 30, 1927, without drawing any firm conclusions (*Ellington on Microgroove*, pp. 10–11). Dutton's "Birth of a Band" series in *Storyville* grew out of an investigation of this very problem, but at the end of Part 3, after much dogged detective work and assistance from researchers worldwide, Dutton was forced to admit: "And we haven't even begun to scratch the surface of the sax-team problem!" (*Storyville* 98 [December 1981-January 1982], p. 12).

27. Allen, *Hendersonia*, p. 166.

28. Rudy Jackson, "My Story," *Jazz Music* 13/6 (1947), pp. 3–4.

29. Carney identified soloists on these recordings for Stanley Dance, who included them in the liner notes for the LP *Duke Ellington: The Beginning, Volume 1, 1926–28,* MCA-1358. The baritone solos, according to Carney, are all by Hardwick.

Carney's appearance on record dates did not always coincide with weekends or school vacations. As Phil Schaap pointed out to me, Carney must have been truant when he joined Ellington's band in the studio on February 3, 1927 (Thursday), and February 28, 1927 (Monday).

30. Charlie Holmes, interviewed by Phil Schaap, April 1977.

31. "The Carney Chronicle," *Down Beat* (November 27, 1958), p. 19.

32. *MM*, p. 111.

33. Ibid., p. 109.

34. In *MM* Ellington claimed Braud joined in 1926, not 1927, but this seems unlikely.

35. *Salem Evening News*, June 20 and 23, 1927.

36. *DEP*, p. 26.

37. "The Carney Chronicle," p. 19.

38. *Salem Evening News*, August 10, 1927.

39. *Salem Evening News*, June 23, 1927.

40. *Salem Evening News*, August 19, 1927.

41. *Salem Evening News*, August 10 and 12, 1927.

42. *Fall River Herald News*, July 2, 1927.

43. Quoted in the *Defender*, August 27, 1927.

44. Ibid.

45. Ibid.

46. *Salem Evening News,* August 30, 1927.

47. *Portland Press Herald,* August 30, 1927.

48. Information from Ellsworth Reynolds included in Dutton, "Birth of a Band," Part 1, *Storyville* 80 (December 1978-January 1979), pp. 52–53; and Part 2, *Storyville* 91 (October-November 1980), p. 10. Apparently this was Reynolds's first job with the band, and he consulted his scrapbook for confirmation of the date.

49. *Age,* October 8, 1927.

50. *Age,* October 15, 1927.

51. The only source for this is Ellsworth Reynolds's scrapbook. See Dutton, "Birth of a Band," Part 1, pp. 52–53; Part 2, p. 10.

52. *Age,* November 18, 1927.

53. *DE,* p. 66; Garvin Bushell as told to Mark Tucker, *Jazz from the Beginning* (Ann Arbor: University of Michigan Press, 1988), p. 73.

54. John McDonough, "Reminiscing in Tempo: Guitarist Freddy Guy's Ellington Memories," *Down Beat* (April 17, 1969), p. 16.

55. Photograph in Baltimore *Afro-American,* November 19, 1927.

56. Allen, *Hendersonia,* p. 217.

57. *DE,* p. 67.

CHAPTER TWELVE

1. Only eleven different pieces by Ellington appear on these records, but several were recorded more than once, raising the total to seventeen.

2. In December 1926 Ellington and Otto Hardwick accompanied Gussie Alexander on two sides—"They Say I Do It" and "Drifting from You Blues"—but OKeh rejected them, and no master parts survive. See Appendix.

3. Timner lists Rudy Jackson as the other reed player, while Bakker makes no identification. Both discographers suggest Otto Hardwick as the violinist, which is unlikely. Garvin Bushell, who played with Hardwick in the early 1930s, has stated that the alto saxophonist never played violin (interview, Las Vegas, Nevada, April 10, 1985). And as Brooks Kerr has asked logically (interview, New York, November 5, 1984), if Hardwick played violin this well, why didn't Ellington feature him on the instrument more often? Abel Green's November 1923 *Clipper* review of the Washingtonians is the only source linking Hardwick with the violin.

Brooks Kerr has suggested Sampson's name for the unknown saxophonist/violinist. A comparison of some of the violin solos Sampson played with Fletcher Henderson (e.g., "House of David Blues," recorded July 17, 1931) to the one on "If You Can't Hold the Man You Love" reveals similarities, especially in the double stops and intonation.

4. Baltimore *Afro-American*, October 19, 1923.

5. Steven Lasker's research on the Vocalion files has established that the date for this session was November 8, 1927. The Lee sides were planned for release but unissued; the Richardson side was rejected. Lasker has noted that all three songs were tributes to Florence Mills, who had died seven days earlier.

6. Stanley Dance, liner notes, *Duke Ellington: The Beginning, Vol. 1, 1926–1928*, MCA-1358.

7. Gunther Schuller, *Early Jazz* (New York: Oxford University Press, 1968), pp. 340–41.

8. *Metronome* (May 1, 1927), p. 19.

9. The piano part of this orchestration was made available to me by James Dapogny, who received it from Lawrence Gushee.

10. Jabbo Smith, interview, New York, February 4, 1987.

11. *Portland Press Herald*, July 24, 1927.

12. Schuller, *Early Jazz*, p. 334. Occasionally pop songs had twenty-bar choruses, such as Shelton Brooks's "Darktown Strutters' Ball" (1917) and Henry Creamer and Turner Layton, Jr.'s "After You've Gone" (1918).

13. Ibid.

14. *Down Beat*, November 5, 1952, p. 3.

15. Schuller, *Early Jazz*, p. 335.

16. Similarly, the first theme of "Down in Our Alley Blues" is closely related to both "Hop Head" and "The Creeper." Hardwick may have had an unacknowledged role in the latter's composition. The main theme of "Hop Head" also appears in the coda to "Steppin' on the Gas," recorded in New Orleans by Sam Morgan's Jazz Band for Columbia on April 14, 1927.

17. Schuller, *Early Jazz*, pp. 218, 221.

18. *MM*, p. 47.

19. *MM*, p. 106.

20. *DEP*, p. 29.

21. The published version of "Immigration Blues" has three sixteen-bar sections before the final blues (marked with repeats). Its keys are C and B-flat, and the tempo is marked "Lively" in contrast to the slow, weary gait on the recording.

22. Various anecdotes about Ellington's rehearsals describe the way he used visual images to elicit musical responses from his players. For one, see Rex Stewart, *Jazz Masters of the Thirties* (1972; rpt., New York: Da Capo, [1982]), pp. 97–98.

23. In a performance like "Dead Man Blues" (September 21, 1926), Jelly Roll Morton shows a similar sensitivity to details of orchestration that provide variety without breaking the spell of a piece. Like Elling-

ton, Morton had players whose disciplined improvising helped him realize compositional goals.

24. *WDE,* p. 7.

25. Bakker believes someone played bass clarinet on the date, which may have contributed to this special sound (*Ellington on Microgroove,* p. 37). For a discussion of the "Ellington effect" in connection with the background figures for "East St. Louis Toodle-O," see Schuller, *Early Jazz,* p. 327.

26. Hall and Ellington appeared together in Clarence Robinson's *Dance Mania* in November 1927. But since "Creole Love Call" was recorded the previous month, perhaps Hall had been in *Jazzmania* in early October. Newspapers did not mention her in the New York cast, but she may have joined when *Jazzmania* took to the road.

27. Interview with Adelaide Hall on "Ellington Is Forever," broadcast February 14, 1985, on WNYC, New York.

28. Adelaide Hall, interviewed by Beverley Tucker, London, February 19, 1985.

29. Walter C. Allen and Brian Rust, *King Joe Oliver* (Highland Park, N.J.: published by the authors, 1955), p. 65.

30. For "East St. Louis Toodle-O" I am using the form of the title that appears on the first recorded version and on the copyrighted composition. See pp. 250–51.

31. Tim Weiner, "Keeping Time with Sonny Greer," *Soho Weekly News,* June 15, 1979.

32. Roger Pryor Dodge, "Harpsichords and Jazz Trumpets," *Hound and Horn* (July-September 1934), p. 603. Dodge was the first to document this source. He performed with Miley (as a dancer) and knew the trumpeter in his last years.

33. The one exception is in the first take from November 3, when Nanton has the first solo after the theme. By the second take, Ellington had given it back to the trumpet. Perhaps Nanton was showing newcomer Jabbo Smith how the solo should go, and the first take served the purpose of rehearsal.

34. Schuller, *Early Jazz,* p. 330.

35. A possible source for the triplets in Miley's first chorus (mm. 9–10) is the "Holy City" theme (mm. 5, 7). Schuller cites another: trumpeter Johnny Dunn, whose plunger-mute style may have influenced Miley. For a discussion and transcription of Miley's solo on October 26, 1927, see Schuller, *Early Jazz,* pp. 330–31.

36. Arthur Whetsol reproduced the choruses on the soundtrack of the 1929 film *Black and Tan,* reissued on *Duke Ellington's Band Shorts (1929–1935),* Biograph BLP-M-2. Cootie Williams embellished them on

the 1938 recording of "Prologue to Black and Tan Fantasy," included on *Duke Ellington 1938*, Smithsonian Collection P2 13367.

37. R. D. Darrell, "Black Beauty," *Disques* (June 1932), p. 153.

38. Frank M. Davis to Marshall Stearns, June 4, 1949, IJS vertical file.

39. Trombonist Dicky Wells played this solo on Lloyd Scott's 1927 recording of "Symphonic Scronch" (Allen, *Hendersonia*, p. 113). And Ellington may have borrowed the minor-vamp idea later for the background to Barney Bigard's solo in "Rockin' in Rhythm" (1931).

40. Harrison Smith recalled that Jack Kapp of Brunswick "asked Duke to knock out a tune for Vocalion's East St. Louis trade" (letter to Marshall Stearns, [n.d.], IJS vertical file). And Irving Mills supposedly told Pat Willard, one of Ellington's publicity people, the same thing (interview with Brooks Kerr, March 20, 1985).

41. *MM*, p. 106. Ellington related the same story during his 1962 interview with Jack Cullen, available on the LP *Duke*, Varèse International VS81007.

42. Chadwick Hansen has convincingly demonstrated the link between "todalo" and dancing in "Jenny's Toe Revisited: White Responses to Afro-American Shaking Dances," *American Music* 5/1 (Spring 1987), pp. 1–19. See also my response to Professor Hansen's article: "On Toodle-Oo, Todalo, and Jenny's Toe," *American Music* 6/1 (Spring 1988), pp. 88–91. More commentary on the term appears in the "Can't We Talk It Over?" sections of *Storyville* 132 (December 1, 1987), pp. 210–11, and *Storyville* 133 (March 1, 1988), p. 15.

43. Schuller, *Early Jazz*, pp. 326–29.

44. Martin Williams, *The Jazz Tradition*, new and rev. ed. (New York: Oxford University Press, 1983), p. 109.

Note on Sources

Beginning in the 1930s, when Duke Ellington had attained celebrity status both in the United States and abroad, a steady stream of articles about him appeared in the popular press and in music publications. Little bibliographic control of these writings exists. Some of them provide information relating to the early years; occasionally that information came from Ellington himself or, more likely, from press releases and publicity material supplied by his agents. The Institute of Jazz Studies, at Rutgers University-Newark, New Jersey, contains in its clipping files many such press releases as well as a few publicity kits. In addition, articles on Ellington in American and European music periodicals are located in the Institute's Harold Flakser Collection. The other major repository of Ellington periodical literature is the Duke Ellington Collection in the Archives Center of the Smithsonian's National Museum of American History. Most of the press clippings there date from around 1930 through the late 1960s. Smaller samplings of articles may be found in New York at the Music Division of the Lincoln Center Library of the Performing Arts (Duke Ellington vertical file) and at the Schomburg Center for Research in Black Culture (on microfiche).

The single most helpful article for this study was a four-part series by Frank Dutton entitled "Birth of a Band" that appeared in the British periodical *Storyville* from 1979 to 1983. Assisted by Ellington scholars world-wide and relying upon newspaper research by the late Walter C. Allen, Dutton was able to construct a preliminary chronicle of Ellington's career, focusing on the years in New York up until 1927 and speculating on the personnel of various record dates. In many cases, Dutton's "Birth of a Band" suggested research trails to follow, especially concerning

Ellington's itinerary. I was then able to confirm and discover additional performing dates through examining local newspapers in New England, New York, and Washington, D.C.

An essential source for the study of Ellington's life and music is his autobiography, *Music Is My Mistress,* published in 1973. The book is especially rich in information about the early years, beginning with the opening chapter in which Ellington discusses his family and his exposure to music and musicians in Washington's black community. Some of the material is out of chronological sequence, and Ellington's dates and facts are not always reliable. Yet *Music Is My Mistress* is invaluable for providing Ellington's own view on his career and development—often filtered through layers of protective coating, diplomatic tact, and historical self-consciousness. Large sections of the manuscript for *Music Is My Mistress* —written in longhand on hotel stationery from around the world—are now in the Smithsonian's Duke Ellington Collection.

The first extensive treatment of Ellington's early years appeared in the first full-length biography, Barry Ulanov's *Duke Ellington* (1946). Ulanov undertook his work when many of the figures from Ellington's childhood and most of the important musicians associated with him in New York were still alive. As a result, the first five chapters (taking Ellington to 1927) are filled with colorful anecdotes and personal recollections. Two years before, in July 1944, Richard O. Boyer contributed a lengthy three-part profile of Ellington to the *New Yorker* that ran under the title, "The Hot Bach." Besides providing a fascinating glimpse of Ellington behind the scenes, Boyer included a biographical section based, apparently, on interviews with Ellington.

Since the 1940s a number of biographical and critical studies have appeared. Peter Gammond's *Duke Ellington: His Life and Music* (1958) contains a slightly abridged version of Richard Boyer's *New Yorker* piece, as well as essays by Stanley Dance and others and decade-by-decade surveys of Ellington's recordings from the 1920s through the 1950s. Two full-length biographies that focus more on the man than the music are Derek Jewell's *Duke: A Portrait of Duke Ellington* (1977) and James Lincoln Collier's *Duke Ellington* (1987). A candid first-hand account of life with Ellington may be found in *Duke Ellington in Person: An Intimate Memoir* (1978), written by Mercer Ellington with Stanley Dance. Less valuable, and more lurid, are the recollections of songwriter Don George in *Sweet Man: The Real Duke Ellington* (1981). Perhaps the most insightful account of how the Ellington organization worked comes from the cornetist Rex Stewart, whose articles written for *Down Beat* in the 1960s were collected in *Jazz Masters of the Thirties* (1972).

There are three major collections of interviews relating to Ellington:

the Jazz Oral History Project at the Institute of Jazz Studies, Rutgers University, funded by the National Endowment for the Arts; the Ellington Project, part of Vivian Perlis's Oral History, American Music program at Yale University; and tapes of meetings of the New York Chapter of the Duke Ellington Society, housed at the Schomburg Center for Research in Black Culture, the New York Public Library. These interviews, many with musicians who played under Ellington, contain biographical and historical information, opinions, impressions, and anecdotes unavailable elsewhere. At present the Smithsonian is also embarking on an oral history project in conjunction with its Duke Ellington Collection.

Published interviews help fill in the picture of Ellington's early years. Stanley Dance is responsible for two of the most informative collections: *The World of Duke Ellington* (1970), which contains interviews with Ellington and many of his musicians; and *The World of Swing* (1974), featuring commentary on the Washington and New York musical scenes by Elmer Snowden, Claude Hopkins, and Sandy Williams. Another gathering of interviews and previously published pieces is *Hear Me Talkin' to Ya* (1955), edited by Nat Shapiro and Nat Hentoff. The chapter on Ellington reproduces excerpts from "Jazz As I Have Seen It," an article written by Ellington (with Helen Oakley Dance's assistance) in 1940 and published serially in the magazine *Swing*.

Discographical sources on Ellington abound. For his early years the most useful are: Dick M. Bakker, *Duke Ellington on Microgroove-Volume 1, 1923–1936* (1977); W. E. Timner, *The Recorded Music of Duke Ellington and His Sidemen,* 3rd edition (1988); and the standard reference work by Brian Rust, *Jazz Records 1897–1942,* 5th revised edition [1983]. The first Ellington discography was *The "Wax Works" of Duke Ellington,* compiled by Benny Aasland in 1954. The most thorough discographical undertaking has been that of Luciano Massagli, Liborio Pusateri, and Giovanni M. Volontè, appearing in separate volumes under the title *Duke Ellington's Story on Records.* The global interest in Ellington's music is reflected in the nationalities of the discographical scholars listed above, representing Holland, Canada, Great Britain, Sweden, and Italy, respectively.

Relatively few analyses of Ellington's early music and recordings have been published. Most significant is Gunther Schuller's chapter in *Early Jazz* (1968), "The Ellington Style, Its Origins and Early Development," most of which first appeared in the pages of *The Jazz Review.* Schuller's precise analytical skills and incisive commentary help illuminate Ellington's first efforts as a composer, pianist, and bandleader in the recording studio. Another valuable critical discussion of Ellington's recordings and his development as a composer appears in Martin Williams, *The Jazz Tra-*

dition (1970; new and revised edition, 1983). Curtis B. Taylor takes a close look at one early Ellington piece in an unpublished M.A. thesis, "The Transcription and Stylistic Comparative Analysis of Duke Ellington's *Black and Tan Fantasy*" (Cornell University, 1974).

Two other studies are useful for documenting aspects of New York's musical life in the 1920s: Walter C. Allen's massive *Hendersonia* (1973), and Samuel B. Charters and Leonard Kunstadt's *Jazz: A History of the New York Scene* (1962). Drawing heavily upon contemporary newspapers and periodicals, the authors incorporate important primary sources and provide a useful historical framework.

After years of inaccessibility, Ellington's personal library of music and memorabilia was acquired by the Smithsonian in 1988. This collection will form the cornerstone for much future Ellington research, containing as it does an extraordinary cache of Ellington original scores, orchestral parts, and sketches. However, after spending two months in the summer of 1988 surveying the collection, I found little relating directly to Ellington's life and music before 1930. The collection does have the only known copies of two early Ellington songs, "Blind Man's Buff" and "Pretty Soft for You"; otherwise, Ellington's career during the twenties seems, at this stage at least, scantily represented in its holdings. Nevertheless, as the collection is processed and eventually used by scholars, it might yield more information —both musical and biographical—about Ellington's early years.

The Music Division of the Library of Congress has a representative sampling of Ellington's works in sheet-music form, together with scores issued by Tempo, Ellington's publishing company. (Few of these, however, are actual arrangements played by Ellington's orchestra—for these, the Smithsonian has the primary collection.) The Copyright Division of the Library of Congress keeps records of copyright registration for most of Ellington's early compositions, although the actual music is not available for every title. At present, the musicologist Erik Wiedemann, of the University of Copenhagen, is in the process of compiling a complete catalogue of Ellington's works.

Yet another forthcoming work which will bear on Ellington's early years is *Duke Ellington's Music on Record, 1924–1974,* an annotated overview of all of Ellington's recordings by the late Eddie Lambert, a dedicated scholar of Ellingtonia; Dan Morgenstern, director of the Institute of Jazz Studies, is preparing it for publication.

Recordings of early Ellington can be difficult to locate. While the Brunswick and Victor sides from 1926–27 have been reissued at various times, the Blu-Disc, Gennett, and Pathé records from 1924–26 are considerably rarer. The following selected reissues—some already out of print —contain music from the 1924–27 period:

Duke Ellington, Archive of Jazz, Vol. 21, BYG 529.071

Duke Ellington and His Orchestra—Early Ellington (1927–1934), Bluebird 6852-2-RB

Duke Ellington: Brunswick-Vocalion Rarities, MCA-1374

Duke Ellington 1927–1934, BBC CD 643

Duke Ellington: The Beginning, Vol. 1, 1926–1928, MCA-1358

The Essential Duke Ellington, November 1924 to March 14, 1927, VJM, VLP.71

The Essential Duke Ellington, 22 March 1927 to 19 December 1927, VJM, VLP.72

Hot'n'Sweet: The Birth of a Band, EPM Musique (France) FDC-5104

The Indispensable Duke Ellington, Vol. 1/2, Double Black and White, RCA PM 43687

Further sources of study appear in the Bibliography.

Interviews

Unless otherwise specified, the following interviews were conducted by Mark Tucker and tape copies or notes are in his files.

Cato Adams, Washington, D.C., December 14, 1983
Maurice Banks, Washington, D.C., August 3, 1983, September 29, 1983
Tommy Benford, Mount Vernon, New York, January 8, 1985
Ruth Ellington Boatwright, New York, October 21, 1983
Lawrence Brown, Los Angeles, April 13, 1985
Garvin Bushell, Las Vegas, Nevada, April 9–10, 1985
W. Montague Cobb (telephone conversations), Washington, D.C., May 2, 1984, May 29, 1984
Mercer Cook, Silver Spring, Maryland, August 19, 1983
Stanley Dance, Vista, California, April 13, 1985
A. P. Davis, Washington, D.C., March 13, 1984
Bessie Dudley, New York, March 22, 1985
Roy Ellis (telephone conversation), Washington, D.C., August 19, 1983
Sammy Fain, Los Angeles, April 12, 1985
Sonny Greer, interviewed by Edith Exton and Brooks Kerr, New York, 1976 (tape copy in the collection of Brooks Kerr)
June Hackney and Alice Spraggins, Washington, D.C., October 11, 1983
Adelaide Hall, interviewed by Beverley Tucker, London, February 19, 1985
Otto Hardwick, interviewed by Felix Grant, Bethesda, Maryland, April 29, 1964
Revella Hughes, New York, December 12, 1984

Jehu and Alice Hunter, interviewed by Spencer Crew and Mark Tucker, Washington, D.C., November 10, 1983

Brooks Kerr (many interviews and telephone conversations), New York, 1983–88

Percy G. Lee, Beverly, Massachusetts, November 21, 1984

Oscar Lucas, Columbia, Maryland, September 12, 1983

Toots Mondello, New York, February 7, 1985

Mitchell Parish, New York, December 1, 1984

Delia Perry (telephone conversation), Washington, D.C., November 17, 1983

Phil Schaap, Newark, New Jersey, February 22, 1985

Jabbo Smith, New York, February 4, 1987

Essie Sorrel (telephone conversation), Washington, D.C., October 19, 1983

Juan Tizol (questionnaire), Los Angeles, August 26, 1983

Jerry Valburn, Plainfield, New York, February 19, 1985, March 15, 1985

Bernice Wiggins, New York, September 6, 1983, November 18, 1983, May 24, 1985, (telephone conversation) February 16, 1985

Bibliography

Books and Articles

Allen, Walter C. *Hendersonia: The Music of Fletcher Henderson and His Musicians: A Bio-Discography*. Highland Park, N.J.: published by the author, 1973.

————, and Brian Rust. *King Joe Oliver*. Highland Park, N.J.: published by the author, 1955.

Anderson, Jervis. *This Was Harlem: A Cultural Portrait, 1900–1950*. New York: Farrar Straus Giroux, 1981.

Askland, Gunnar. "Interpretations in Jazz: A Conference with Duke Ellington." *Etude* (March 1947), pp. 134, 172.

Bakker, Dick M. *Duke Ellington on Microgroove, Vol. 1, 1923–1936*. Alphen aan den Rijn, Holland: Micrography, 1977.

Bechet, Sidney. *Treat It Gentle*. 1960; rpt., New York: Da Capo, 1978.

Behncke, Bernhard H. "Sam Wooding and the Chocolate Kiddies at the Thalia-Theater in Hamburg 28 July 1925 to 24 August 1925." *Storyville* 60 (August-September 1975), pp. 214–21.

Berger, Morroe, Edward Berger, and James Patrick. *Benny Carter: A Life in American Music*. 2 vols. Metuchen, N.J.: Scarecrow Press, 1982.

Bergmeier, Horst P. "Sam Wooding Recapitulated." *Storyville* 74 (December 1977-January 1978), pp. 44–47.

Berlin, Edward. *Ragtime: A Musical and Cultural History*. Berkeley: University of California Press, 1980.

————. "Ragtime and Improvised Piano: Another View." *Journal of Jazz Studies* 4 (Spring/Summer 1977), pp. 4–10.

Blesh, Rudi, and Harriet Janis. *They All Played Ragtime*. 4th ed. New York: Oak Publications, 1971.

Boyer, Richard O. "The Hot Bach." *The New Yorker* Part 1 (June 24, 1944), pp. 30–34, 37–38, 40, 42, 44; Part 2 (July 1, 1944), pp. 26–32, 34; Part 3 (July 8, 1944), pp. 26–31.

Bricktop [Ada Smith], with James Haskins. *Bricktop*. New York: Atheneum, 1983.

Bushell, Garvin, as told to Mark Tucker. *Jazz from the Beginning*. Ann Arbor: University of Michigan Press, 1988.

"The Carney Chronicle." *Down Beat* (November 27, 1958), p. 19.

Cavanaugh, Inez M. "Reminiscing in Tempo: Toby Hardwicke thinks back through the years with Ellington: The Lion, Lippy, Bubber . . ." *Metronome* (November 1944), pp. 17, 26.

———. "Reminiscing in Tempo: Tricky Sam goes over the great times he had with Duke, with Bubber, Freddie Jenkins." *Metronome* (February 1945), pp. 17, 26.

———. "Reminiscing in Tempo: Vexatious Rexatious recalls the balls with and without Duke." *Metronome* (November 1945), pp. 19, 48.

Charters, Samuel B., and Leonard Kunstadt. *Jazz: A History of the New York Scene*. 1962; rpt., New York: Da Capo, 1981.

Chilton, John. *Sidney Bechet: The Wizard of Jazz*. London: Macmillan, 1987.

Clarke, Catherine K. "Conversation with William ('Billy') Taylor, the Jazz-Mobile Man." *The Black Perspective in Music* 10 (Fall 1982), pp. 178–88.

Collier, James Lincoln. *Duke Ellington*. New York: Oxford University Press, 1987.

Coslow, Sam. *Cocktails for Two*. New Rochelle, N.Y.: Arlington House, 1977.

Crawford, Marc. "A Visit with Mrs. Duke Ellington." *Ebony* 14 (March 1959), pp. 132–36.

Cuney-Hare, Maud. *Negro Musicians and Their Music*. 1936; rpt., New York: Da Capo, 1974.

Dance, Stanley. *The World of Duke Ellington*. 1970; rpt., New York: Da Capo, [1981].

———. *The World of Swing*. 1974; rpt., New York: Da Capo, 1979.

Darrell, R. D. "Black Beauty." *Disques* (June 1932), pp. 152–61.

Davin, Tom. "Conversations with James P. Johnson." *The Jazz Review* 2 (June 1959), pp. 14–17.

———. "Conversations with James P. Johnson, Part 2." *The Jazz Review* 2 (July 1959), pp. 10–13.

Dobson, Gwen. "Luncheon with . . . Duke Ellington." *Washington Evening Star*, April 23, 1971.

Dodge, Roger Pryor. "Bubber." *H.R.S. Rag* (October 15, 1940), pp. 10–14.

————. "Harpsichords and Jazz Trumpets." *Hound and Horn* (July-September 1934), pp. 588–608.

Du Bois, W. E. B., ed. *Efforts for Social Betterment among Negro Americans.* Atlanta: Atlanta University Press, 1909.

Durante, Jimmy, and Jack Kofoed. *Night Clubs.* New York: Knopf, 1931.

Dutton, Frank. "Birth of a Band." *Storyville* 80 (December 1978-January 1979), pp. 44–53; 91 (October-November 1980), pp. 7–12; 98 (December 1981-January 1982), pp. 45–47; 103 (October-November 1982), p. 32.

Ellington, Duke. "Jazz as I Have Seen It," Part 1. *Swing* (March 1940), pp. 9, 32.

————. "Jazz as I Have Seen It," Part 3. *Swing* (May 1940), pp. 10, 23.

————. Liner notes. *James P. Johnson, Father of the Stride Piano.* Columbia CL1780.

————. *Music Is My Mistress.* 1973; rpt. New York: Da Capo, 1976.

————. "The Most Essential Instrument." *Jazz Journal* 18 (December 1965), pp. 14–15.

Ellington, Mercer, with Stanley Dance. *Duke Ellington in Person: An Intimate Memoir.* 1978; rpt., New York: Da Capo, 1979.

Englund, Björn. "*Chocolate Kiddies:* The Show that Brought Jazz to Europe and Russia in 1925." *Storyville* 62 (December 1975-January 1976), pp. 44–50.

————. "Two Obscure Ellington Tunes." *Doctor Jazz* (February-March 1974), pp. 4–5.

Fletcher, Tom. *100 Years of the Negro in Show Business.* 1954; rpt., New York: Da Capo, 1984.

Gaffey, Patrick. "Garvin Bushell: Jazz Roots from the Beginning." *Arts Alive* [Las Vegas, Nevada] (May-June 1983), pp. 18–20, 33–34.

Gammond, Peter, ed. *Duke Ellington: His Life and Music.* London: Phoenix House, 1958.

Gardner, Bettye, and Bettye Thomas. "The Cultural Impact of the Howard Theater on the Black Community." *Journal of Negro History* 55 (October 1970), pp. 253–65.

Goodwin, Ruby Berkley. "Meet the Duke." *The Bronzeman* 9 (August 1932), p. 20.

Graham, Stephen. *New York Nights.* New York: George H. Doran Co., 1927.

Green, Constance McLaughlin. *The Secret City: A History of Race Relations in the Nation's Capital.* Princeton, N.J.: Princeton University Press, 1967.

————. *Washington: Capital City, 1879–1950.* Princeton, N.J.: Princeton University Press, 1963.

Groves, Paul A. "The Development of a Black Residential Community in Southwest Washington: 1860–1897." *Records of the Columbia Historical Society* 50 (1980), pp. 260–70.

Handy, D. Antoinette. *Black Women in American Bands and Orchestras.* Metuchen, N.J.: Scarecrow Press, 1981.

Handy, W. C. *Father of the Blues: An Autobiography.* Ed. Arna Bontemps. 1941; New York: Collier Edition, 1970.

Hasse, John Edward, ed. *Ragtime: Its History, Composers, and Music.* New York: Schirmer Books, 1985.

Haynes, George Edmund, and Sterling Brown. *The Negro in Detroit and Washington.* 1936; rpt., New York: Arno Press/New York Times, 1969.

Henri, Florette. *Black Migration: Movement North, 1900–1920.* Garden City, N.Y.: Anchor Press/Doubleday, 1975.

Hentoff, Nat. "Garvin Bushell and New York Jazz in the 1920s," Part 1. *The Jazz Review* 2 (January 1959), pp. 10–14.

Hoefer, George. "Duke Ellington: Society Band Leader." *Washington Post Potomac,* May 20, 1962, pp. 11–12.

———. Booklet notes, *The Sound of Harlem,* Jazz Odyssey, Columbia C3L 33.

Huggins, Nathan Irvin. *Harlem Renaissance.* New York: Oxford University Press, 1966.

Hughes, Langston. *The Big Sea.* New York: Hill and Wang, 1940.

———. "Our Wonderful Society: Washington." *Opportunity* 5 (August 1927), pp. 226–27.

Hundley, Mary Gibson. *The Dunbar Story, 1870–1955.* Washington, D.C.: Vantage Press, 1965.

Ingle, Edward. *The Negro in the District of Columbia.* 1893; rpt., Freeport, N.Y.: Books for Libraries Press, 1971.

Ives, David. "Elmer Snowdon [*sic*]." *Jazz Journal* (January 1963), p. 26.

Jackson, Rudy. "My Story." *Jazz Music* 13 (1947), pp. 3–4.

"James Reese Europe." *Record Research* 1 (December 1955), pp. 3–5.

Jasen, David A., and Trebor Jay Tichenor. *Rags and Ragtime: A Musical History.* New York: Seabury Press, 1978.

Jeske, Les. "Scrapple from the Apple." *Jazz Journal International* (November 1978), pp. 22–23.

Johnson, James Weldon. *Black Manhattan.* 1930; new edition, New York: Atheneum, 1968.

Jones, William H. *Recreation and Amusement among Negroes in Washington, D.C.* 1927; rpt., Westport, Conn.: Negro Universities Press, 1970.

Keepnews, Orrin. "Sonny Greer, Drums." *Record Changer* (July 1948), p. 14.

Kendziora, Carl. "Behind the Cobwebs" [on the Blu-Disc label], *Record Research* (June 1973), p. 7.

Kimball, Robert, and William Bolcom. *Reminiscing with Sissle and Blake.* New York: Viking Press, 1973.

Korall, Burt. "The Roots of the Duchy." *Down Beat* (June 13, 1967), pp. 21–22.

Larsen, John, and Hans Larsen. "The Chocolate Kiddies in Copenhagen." *Record Research* (April 1965), pp. 3–5.

Lewis, David Levering. *When Harlem Was in Vogue.* New York: Vintage, 1982.

Logan, Rayford W. "Growing Up in Washington: A Lucky Generation." *Records of the Columbia Historical Society* 50 (1980), pp. 500–507.

Lord, Tom. *Clarence Williams.* Chigwell, England: Storyville Publications, 1976.

McDonough, John. "Reminiscing in Tempo: Guitarist Freddy Guy's Ellington Memories." *Down Beat* (April 17, 1969), pp. 16–17.

McGinty, Doris. "The Washington Conservatory of Music and School of Expression." *The Black Perspective in Music* 7 (Spring 1979), pp. 59–74.

Mills, Irving, as told to Charles Emge. "I Split with Duke When Music Began Sidetracking." *Down Beat* (November 5, 1952), p. 6.

Muscutt, Les. "Discovering Elmer." *Storyville* 16 (April/May 1968), pp. 3–7.

"The New Dunbar High School, Washington, D.C." *Crisis* 13 (March 1917), pp. 220–22.

Osofsky, Gilbert. *Harlem: The Making of a Ghetto.* New York: Harper's Torchbooks, 1966.

Proctor, John Clagett, ed. *Washington Past and Present: A History.* 5 vols. Washington, D.C.: Lewis Historical Publishing Co., 1930.

Riis, Thomas L. *Just Before Jazz.* Washington, D.C.: Smithsonian Institution Press, 1989.

Rose, Al. *Eubie Blake.* New York: Schirmer Books, 1979.

Rust, Brian. *The American Record Label Book from the 19th Century through 1942.* New Rochelle, N.Y.: Arlington House, 1978.

————. *Jazz Records 1897–1942.* 5th ed. New Rochelle, N.Y.: Arlington House, [1983].

"Saluting Duke Ellington." *Record Research* (July 1974), pp. 3–8.

Schuller, Gunther. *Early Jazz.* New York: Oxford University Press, 1968.

Shapiro, Nat, and Nat Hentoff, eds. *Hear Me Talkin' to Ya.* New York: Rinehart and Co., 1955.

Smith, Charles E. "The Duke Steps Out." *Jazz* 1 (January 1943), pp. 11–12.

Smith, Harrison. "Wilbur Sweatman: Original Jazz King." *Record Research* (July 1961), p. 9.

Smith, Willie "the Lion," with George Hoefer. *Music on My Mind: The Memoirs of an American Pianist.* 1964; rpt., New York: Da Capo, 1978.

Southern, Eileen. *Biographical Dictionary of Afro-American and African Musicians.* Westport, Conn.: Greenwood Press, 1982.

———. *The Music of Black Americans: A History.* rev. ed. New York: W. W. Norton, 1984.

Stewart, Rex. *Jazz Masters of the Thirties.* 1972; rpt., New York: Da Capo, [1982].

Sylvester, Robert. *No Cover Charge.* New York: Dial Press, 1956.

Terrell, Mary Church. "History of the High School for Negroes in Washington, D.C." *Journal of Negro History* 2 (July 1917), pp. 252–66.

Timner, W. E. *Ellingtonia: The Recorded Music of Duke Ellington and His Sidemen.* 3rd ed. London and Metuchen, N.J.: Institute of Jazz Studies and Scarecrow Press, 1988.

Tucker, Mark. "The Early Years of Edward Kennedy 'Duke' Ellington, 1899–1927." Ph.D. diss., University of Michigan, 1986.

———. "The Renaissance Education of Duke Ellington." In *Black Music and the Negro Renaissance.* Edited by Samuel A. Floyd, Jr. Westport, Conn.: Greenwood Press, 1990.

Ulanov, Barry. *Duke Ellington.* 1946, 1947; rpt. New York: Da Capo, 1975.

U.S. Bureau of Statistics. "The Standard of Living in Washington." *Survey* 38 (October 20, 1917), pp. 68–69.

Waldo, Terry. *This Is Ragtime.* New York: Hawthorn Books, 1976.

Waller, Maurice, and Anthony Calabrese. *Fats Waller.* New York: Schirmer Books, 1977.

Washington, Booker T. *Up from Slavery.* 1901; rpt., Booker Washington Birthplace, Virginia: Booker T. Washington Centennial Commission, 1956.

Weaver, Gretchen. "The Duke of Jazzdom." *Bandleaders* [n.d.], p. 12 (IJS clipping file).

Weiner, Tim. "Keeping Time with Sonny Greer." *Soho Weekly News* 6/5 (1979).

West, Hollie I. "The Duke at 70: Honor from the President." *Washington Post,* April 27, 1969.

Williams, Martin. *The Jazz Tradition.* New York: Oxford University Press, 1970; new and revised ed., 1983.

Zolotow, Maurice. "The Duke of Hot." *Saturday Evening Post* (August 7, 1943), pp. 24–25, 57.

Newspapers and Periodicals

Baltimore *Afro-American*
Billboard
Boston Post
Chicago Defender
Crisis
Down Beat
Haverhill [Massachusetts] *Evening Gazette*
Indianapolis *Freeman*
Metronome
The Music Master
The Negro Musician
Negro Music Journal
New York Age
New York Amsterdam News
New York Clipper
Orchestra World
Phonograph and Talking Machine Weekly
Pittsburgh Courier
Record Research
Salem [Massachusetts] *Evening News*
Variety
Washington *Bee*
Washington Tribune

General Index

Note: Pages with illustrations and musical examples
are indicated in italics at the end of entries.

Aasland, Benny, 311
Abba Labba (Richard McLean),
    35, 182
Adams, Cato, 41
Adams, Stephen, 243
Adams, Wellington A., 13, 28, 44,
    54, 61
Admiral Palast (Berlin), 134
Aeolian Hall (New York), 140
Afro-American Folk-Song Singers, 11,
    59, 61, 285 n58
"After You've Gone," 9, 306 n12
Alberti, Victor, 132, 264
Alexander, Gussie, 267, 305 n2
Allen, Walter C., 101, 309, 312
Ambassadors, The, 141, 173
Amos, Ernest, 10, 11, 59, 285 n58
Amphion Glee Club, 8
Anderson, John, 80, 99, 100, 102,
    107, 294 n29, 82
Anderson, Marian, 7
Anderson Open Air Gardens, 71
Andreozzi's South-American Orches-
    tra, 134
Arcadia Ballroom (New York), 190

Arkansas Travelers, 221–22
Armstrong High School, 7, 10, 14, 28,
    41, 46, 51, 52, 53, 59, 201, 282 n53
Armstrong, Louis, 147, 148–49, 154,
    155, 156, 160, 163–64, 165, 168,
    227, 230, 231, 232, 250; Hot Five,
    155–56
Asbury Park, N.J., 26–27, 65, 183
Ash, Paul, 135, 193
Astoria Café (New York), 89. *See also*
    Barron Wilkins' Exclusive Club
Atkins, Ed, 239, 240
Atlantic City, N.J., 26, 36, 64, 73, 87,
    100, 183
Austin, Gene, 174, 263
Australia, 200

Bakker, Dick M., 259, 307 n25, 311
Baltimore, Maryland, 30, 31, 33, 58,
    64, 66, 74
Baltimore Black Sox, 87
Bamboo Inn (New York), 203
Bamboula, 67
Banjo, 64, 65
Banjorine, 49, 65

Banks, Maurice, 10
Barron Wilkins' Exclusive Club (New York), 87–90, 91, 92, 94, 99, 100, 171, 293 n10
Barron's. *See* Barron Wilkins' Exclusive Club
Barron's Executive Club (New York), 89. *See also* Barron Wilkins' Exclusive Club
Basie, Count, xi, 182
Beasley (or Beaseley), Bill, 58, 69, 70, 73, 74, 291 n29
Beasley, Dewey, 84
Bechet, Leonard, 111
Bechet, Sidney, 154, 231, 232, 289 n63; and the Washingtonians, 111, 113, 117–18, 295–96 n58; heard by DE in Washington, 75
Beetle, The (Stephen Henderson), 182
Beiderbecke, Bix, 178
Bela, Dajos, 134
Belasco Theater (Washington, D.C.), 75
Bergere, Roy, 174, 263
Bergmeier, Horst, 126
Berlin, Irving, 33, 93, 103; publishing company, 263
Berlin, Germany, 120, 132, 134, 135, 264
Berman, Bobby Burns, 114
Bernard, Mike, 29
Bernstein, Leo, 109, 110, 116, 194, 296 n58
Berton, Vic, 115
Bigard, Barney, 38, 290 n11, 308 n39
Black and Tan (film), 247, 290 n11, 307 n36
Black Diamond. *See* Diamond
Black Sox Orchestra. *See* Washington Black Sox Orchestra
Black Swan (record company), 101
Blake, Eubie, 26, 30–31, 32, 33, 35, 41, 64, 74, 250, 280 n16, 281 n24. *See also* Sissle and Blake
Blanks, Osceola, 91, 98
Bloom, Rube, 216, 217, 222, 270

Blu-Disc (record company), 109, 110, 119, 162, 185, 196–97, 211, 261, 262, 263, 312; recordings by the Washingtonians in 1924, 141–49, 171–74
Blues, 20, 94, 106, 158, 159–60, 170–72, 173, 174–75, 176–77, 194, 213, 220, 222, 228, 231–42, 243, 246, 248, 251, 258
Boatwright, Ruth Ellington. *See* Ellington, Ruth
Bond, Carrie Jacobs, 20
Boone, Harvey, 136, 190, 202
Boston Conservatory, 30, 282 n53
Boston, Mass., 184, 186, 190, 203, 248
Boston, Miss R. A., 25
Boutelje, Phil, 217
Bowser, Clarence, 30, 46
Boyd, Carroll, 69
Boyer, Richard O., 310
Boyette, Raymond "Lippy." *See* Lippy
Bradford, Perry, 93, 104, 106, 156, 171
Braud, Wellman, 205, 207, 230, 236, 253; joins Washingtonians, 203, 209
Brauner, "Shrimp," 44
Breen, May Singhi, 265
Bricktop (Ada Smith), 67, 87–88, 172
Bristol, Florence, 110, 171, 174–75, 176, 197, 263
Broadway Music Corporation (publishing company), 141, 261, 262
Broadway Rastus, 12, 54
Brooks, Forny, 90
Brooks, Harvey, 27, 28, 34, 178, 279 n58
Brooks, Shelton, 53, 306 n12
Brown, Chauncey, 57
Brown, J. B., 251
Brown, Lawrence, 293 n14
Brown, Louis N., 9, 10, 30, 47, 48, 49, 50, 52, 53, 58, 69, 72, 84, 275 n29, 282 n53, 286 n5; admired by DE, 45–46

Brown, Sterling, 7
Brunswick (record label), xi, 111, 198, 199, 200, 201, 202, 212, 216, 217, 221, 244, 250, 251, 255, 269, 270, 303 n18, 312
Brymn, Tim, 98
Buck, Ford L., 199, 266. *See also* Buck and Bubbles
Buck and Bubbles, 207, 266
Bucket of Blood (New York), 85, 90
Bud Allen Music (publishing company), 265
Burleigh, Alston, 6
Burleigh, Harry T., 6, 22, 61
Bushell, Garvin, 32, 85–86, 92–93, 97, 101, 172, 305 n3
Busoni's Balconnade (New York), 80, 289 n3

Cakewalk, 9, 123
California Ramblers, 106, 149, 150, 161, 175, 192
Cameo Club (New York), 137
"Camp Meeting Blues," 237–41, *237, 239*
Cantor, Eddie, 173
Capital City Clef Club, 48–49, 58, 64, 67, 283 n8
Capitol Palace (New York), 83, 84, 85, 107
Carnegie Hall, 39
Carney, Harry, xiii, 205, 216, 230, 252, 254, 304 n29; moves to New York in 1927, 202–3; plays with DE in 1926, 186, 189–90, *209*
"Carolina Shout," 31, 32, 34, 74
Carroll's Columbia Orchestra, 50, 51
Carter, Benny, 97, 136, 295–96 n58
Center Market Coliseum (Washington, D.C.), 59, 71, 284 n38
Challis, Bill, 165
Charleshurst Ballroom (Salem, Mass.), 183, 186–88, 191, 203–4, 205, 207
Charleston (dance), 114, 120, 126, 132, 134, 135, 151, 155, 164, 194, 217, 229, 264

"Charleston Rag," 32, 281 n24, *32*
Chauvin, Louis, 252
Check and Double Check (film), 290 n11
"Chevy Chase, The," 31, 35, 36, *35–36*
Chicago, Ill., 101, 155, 189, 199, 200, 202, 266
Chilton, John, 75
Chocolate Kiddies, 120–35, 137–38, 140, 208, 262, 264, 266
Choo Choo Jazzers, 141
Chopin, Frédéric, 246, 247
Cinderella Ballroom (New York), 106, 185
Ciro's (New York), 136, 207
Clarence Williams Music Publishing Company, 119, 153, 262
Clark, June, 217
Clarke, Blanche, 69
Clarke and Leslie (publishing company), 173, 263
Clef Club, 14, 48, 75, 96
Clinkscales, Marietta (Mrs. M. Harvey), 23, 28, 278 n35
Club Alabam (New York), 97, 106, 110, 114, 121, 202
Club Bamville (New York), 110
Club Ciro's. *See* Ciro's
Club Petite (New York), 202
Cobb, W. Montague, 8
Cole, Bob, 97. *See also* Cole and Johnson
Cole and Johnson, 62, 66
Coleridge-Taylor, Samuel, 9, 11
Collins, Alonzo "Shrimp," 58, 74
Collins, Cleota, 61
Collins's Alabama Minstrels, 12
Colored American Opera Company, 8
Columbia (record company), 32, 54, 79, 80, 200, 202, 212, 250, 251, 253, 255, 269, 303 n15
Columbia Conservatory, 13, 28
Columbian Orchestra, 48, 69
Conaway (or Conway), Ewell, 48, 63, 65

Conaway (or Conway), Sterling, 48, 65, 73, 68
Connie's Inn (New York), 91–92, 94, 98, 293 n10
Conrad, Con, 132
Convention Hall (Washington, D.C.), 9, 61, 71, 74
Cook, Mercer, 7, 30, 43, 45, 65, 75, 286 n5, 288 n39
Cook, Will Marion, 7, 11, 14, 30, 59, 75, 97, 121, 165, 289 n63; friendship with DE, 105
Coon-Sanders Orchestra, 185
Cooper, Harry, 136, 155
Coslow, Sam, 141, 161, 195–96, 265
Cotton Club (New York), xi, xii, xiii, 110, 135, 208, 210, 233, 242, 243, 247, 258
Crandall, Harry, 193
Crandall's Theatre Corporation, 69
Crawford, Jessie, 122
Crawford, Joan, 88
Creager, Willie, 115, 141
Creamer, Henry, 217, 272
Creamer and Layton, 120, 132
Creamer and Rogers, 66, 306 n12
Creole Jazz Band. See Oliver, King, Creole Jazz Band
Crescendo Club, 14, 58
Crescent Gardens Broadcasting Orchestra, 190
Crippen, Katie, 85
Crisis magazine, 6
Crowder, Henry, 58, 70
Cuthbert, Middleton F., 17–18, 25, 48

Dabney, Everard, 98, 293 n10
Dabney, Ford, 12, 14, 61, 64, 75
Dade, Flo, 81
Dance, Helen Oakley, 311
Dance, Stanley, 22, 90, 304 n29, 310, 311
Dance Mania, 208, 210, 307 n26
Dance music, 219–31
Dancer, Earl, 137
Dancers and dancing, 41, 42–43, 44, 50, 57, 58–59, 69, 71–72, 89, 90, 91, 97, 98, 102, 106, 114, 154, 183–92, 202–8, 210, 219, 250–51, 308 n42. See also Charleston
Darktown Frolics, 54
Darrell, R. D., 246
Davis, Frank M., 247
Davis, Harry, 193
Davis, Meyer, 48, 56
Davis, Pike, 136, 150, 151, 153
Dawson, Eli, 105, 261
Denton and Haskins (publishing company), 200, 270
Dett, Nathaniel, 61
Diamond ("Diamond" Elbert, "Black Diamond"), 64, 65, 72, 73, 74
Dishman, Lester, 30, 46
Diton, Carl, 61
Dixon, Charlie, 299 n7
Dodge, Roger Pryor, 307 n32
Donaldson, Will, 147, 200, 262, 270
Dorsey, Tommy, 117
Douglass, Frederick, 9
Douglass, Joseph, 9
Down South Music Publishing Company, 93, 197
Drayton, Thaddeus, 134. See also Greenlee and Drayton
Dreamland (Chicago), 101
Dreamland (Washington, D.C.), 65, 69–70
Drew, Charles H., 7, 279 n56
Drummers, 73, 115
Du Bois, W. E. B., 6, 7
Dudley, S. H., 54
Duke Ellington Collection at the Smithsonian Institution, 103, 119, 309, 310, 311, 312
Duke's Serenaders, The, 51–52, 54, 59, 63, 66, 94, 55, 60
Dunbar, Paul Laurence, 12
Dunbar High School, 6, 7, 10, 24, 43, 45, 50, 51, 52, 59, 61, 65, 69
Duncan, Mose, 74
Dunn, Johnny, 85, 98, 101, 247–48, 307 n35
Durante, Jimmy, 91, 116, 174

Durham, Eddie, 266
Dutton, Frank, 259, 266, 303 n18, 304 n26, 309
Dvořák, Antonin, 11

Ebbitt House, 45
Edmond's Cellar (New York), 189
Edwards, Henry "Bass," 115, 135, 154, 157, 189, 253; joins Washingtonians, 113
Eichberg, Julius, 8
Eisenberg, Morris, 176, 266
Elbert, "Diamond." See Diamond
Elfstrom, Macs, 134
Ellington, Daisy Kennedy (mother), 18–20, 22, 23, 24, 25, 51, 85, 99, 177, 205, 279 n48; musical talent, 20, 22; spirituality, 19–20
Ellington, Edna (wife), 53, 63, 64, 85, 205, 290 n24
Ellington, Edward Kennedy "Duke," 21, 68, 82, 108, 112, 209. See also Duke Ellington Collection at the Smithsonian Institution; Duke's Serenaders; Washington Black Sox Orchestra; Washingtonians.
—as bandleader: assumes leadership of Washingtonians, 107, 109; at Cotton Club, 208, 210; early band members, 14, 51–53, 284 n23; first professional job, 50, 284 n21; in New England, 183–93, 201–7; in New York, 109–18, 135–37, 194–95, 207–10; the Six Jolly Jesters (group), 34, 260; in Washington, D.C., 49–56, 58–59, 71–72
—biographies of: Duke Ellington (Ulanov), 310; Music Is My Mistress (Ellington), xi, 3, 16, 17, 18–19, 20, 23, 34, 44, 58, 276 n1, 278 n40, 310
—childhood, 20–27
—as composer: early compositions, 29, 33–43, 72, 93–94, 103–4; emerging compositional style, 168, 212–13; first important blues composition, 232–35; first instrumen-
tally conceived composition on record, 137, first published composition, 140–41; "jungle music," 133, 168, 216, 224; orchestrational effects, 236, 252–53, 307 n25; as songwriter, 41–43, 93–94, 102–4, 119, 137–39, 198; sources of inspiration, xii, 4, 6, 12, 22–23, 25, 72; tone pictures, 231–32, 233
—early employment: as commercial artist, 48, 63, 85; in New York, 79–87, 289 n3; in Washington, D.C., 8, 46, 48, 72
—education, 25–26, 41, 46; conservatory training, rejection of, 105; early musical instruction in Washington, 23, 45; Henry Grant, lessons with, 59, 61–62; music-reading skills, 29, 45, 49, 61, 280 n7
—fame, xi-xii, 201, 206–8
—family, 5, 16–17, 19, 25, 274 n7 (see also listings under Ellington and Kennedy); birth of son Mercer, 63; marriage, 53
—financial matters: 56, 63–64, 88, 93, 116, 121, 198, 284 n21, 285 n45, 286 n5, 291 n36, 302 n43
—image of, 3–4, 41, 45, 84, 201
—influences on, xii, 4, 6, 12; individuals, 16, 18–22, 24–25, 27, 29–30, 44–45, 59, 61–62, 71–72, 74–75, 94, 198; ragtime, 28–29, 30–34; sacred music, 22–23
—as pianist, 27, 28–29, 33–41, 73–74, 162, 177–82, 226, 254–55; as accompanist, 170–77; first professional jobs, 48–49, 283 n6; pianistic technique, 29, 41, 175, 178–82; plays with Elmer Snowden at Barron's, 87–90; as rehearsal pianist, 92, 98
—personality: ambition, 207; artistic talent, 46; didactic tendencies, 278 n40; dramatic introductions, fondness for, 156, 161, 165, 235; as listener, 280 n11; optimistic outlook, 83; refusal to be categorized,

Ellington, Edward Kennedy "Duke"
—personality (continued)
xii, 6; theatrical flair, 23–24, 248;
work habits, 206–7
Ellington, James Edward "J.E."
(father), 17–20, 24, 25, 51, 53,
64, 85, 99, 205, 276 n1, 277 n13,
290 n24; employment, 17–18, 25,
48; energy, 18; exaggerating tenden-
cies, 24, 64; musical talent, 20; way
of speaking, 18
Ellington, John (uncle), 17
Ellington, Mercer (son), 16, 18, 19,
58, 63, 85, 102, 109, 163, 205, 231,
276 n1, 279 n48, 310
Ellington, Ruth (sister), 16, 18, 19, 22,
24, 51, 276 n1, 281 n28
Ellington, William "Sonny" (cousin),
17
Ellington, William (uncle), 17
Ellis, Roy, 50–51, 64, 288 n39
Emmett, Dan, 122, 124
Englund, Björn, 122, 135
Escoffery, William, 51, 52
Escudero, Ralph, 66, 81, 287 n24, 82
Esputa, John, 8
Etté, Bernard, 134, 135
Europe, James Reese, 6, 7, 11, 14, 48,
58, 64, 96
Europe, Mary L., 6, 9–10, 12,
285 n58
Euterpeans, The, 11
Everglades Club (New York), 87, 110
Evolution of the Negro in Picture,
Song, and Story, The, 12
Ewell, Sammy, 30

Fain, Sammy, 160, 171, 215, 265,
268, 299 n14
Fauset, Jessie, 6
Fay, Frank, 88
Fazioli, Billy, 90, 261
Federated Choral Society, 9
Ferdinando, Felix, 190
15th Street Presbyterian Church
(Washington, D.C.), 59

Fisher, Fred, 93, 102, 103, 104, 105,
171, 261
Five Birmingham Babies, 149
Foster, Stephen, 122, 158
Fowler, Lemuel, 106
Francis, George, 109, 110, 111, 142,
146, 173
Frank Clark (publishing company),
158, 265
Frank Holliday's poolroom, 26
Frazer-Kent Inc. (publishing com-
pany), 265
Frazier, Earl, 189
Friml, Rudolf, 33, 121
From Dover to Dixie, 90, 101,
120, 121
Fuller, Earl, 54

Gammond, Peter, 168–69, 310
Gangsters, 89, 116, 189, 210
Garden of Joy (New York), 85,
101
Garnet Elementary School, 23, 52
Garrison Junior High School, 25
Gayety Theater (Washington, D.C.),
24, 80, 85
Gaynor, Jean, 114
Gee, Lottie, 134
Gennett (record label), 136, 139, 157,
161, 163, 165, 171, 175, 176, 192,
194, 195, 196, 198, 211, 212, 219,
263, 265, 266, 312
Gerrity (or Gerety, Gerity), Julia, 113,
114, 194
Gibbs, Harriet Marshall, 10
Giddins, Gary, 169
Glascoe, Percy, 69, 190, 301 n26
Godrew, Hazel, 114
Goldfield Hotel (Baltimore), 30, 33
Goldkette, Jean, 140, 301 n13
"Go 'long Mule," 164
Goofus Five, The, 141, 173
Gorman, Ross, 118, 185, 191
Gotham Music Service, Inc., 221,
247, 268, 269, 270, 271. See also
Mills Music

"Gouge of Armour Avenue, The," 248–49, *249*

Gould, Walter, 30

Grainger, Porter, 93, 106, 171, 172, 216, 268, 272

Grant, Henry Fleet (singer, teacher), 8, *59*

Grant, Henry Lee (pianist, DE's teacher), 6, 7, 8, 9, 10, 11, 12, 13, *52*, 59, 61–62, 72, 201, 285–86 n58

Green, Abel, 99–100, 101, 102, 113, 114–15, 117, 305 n3

Green, Charlie, 249

Green, Constance McLaughlin, *5*

Greenlee and Drayton, 134

Greenwich Village, 96

Greer, Sonny, xiii, 6, 39, 67, 70, 73, 79, 80–81, 83, 85, 86–87, 94, 99, 100, 102, 109, 113, 114, 115, 184, 190, 197, 202, 203, 217, 243; as singer, *73*, 110, 158–59, 172, 173–74, 299 n13; at the Kentucky Club, 116–17; featured on DE's recordings, 142, 145, 146, 154, 157–59, 162, 165, 172–74, 213, 215, 262, 294 n29; meets DE in Washington, *65, 68, 82, 108, 209. See also* Washingtonians

Grofé, Ferde, 165

Guy, Fred, 115, 116, 137, 153, 157, 160, 162, 190, 197, 202, 210, 224, 293 n10; befriends DE in New York in 1923, 87; joins Washingtonians, 111, *112, 209. See also* Washingtonians

Hackney, June, 61, 285 n58

Hall, Adelaide, 122, 208, 215, 218, 240, 241, 307 n26; and "Creole Love Call," 236–38

Hall, Fred, 150

Hall Johnson Choir, 247

Hallett, Mal, 110, 183, 184–85, 190–91, 192, 205

Hamilton, West, 7

Hammerstein's Victoria Theater (New York), 80

Handman, Lou, 158, 265

Handy, W. C., 54, 75, 80, 93, 121, 126, 171, 198, 248, 252. *See also* Pace and Handy

Hardin, Lil, 155, 239, 240

Hardwick, Otto "Toby," xiii, 56, 61, 64, 65, 69, 73, 81, 83, 86–87, 94, 100, 101, 102, 107, 115, 117, 118, 136, 188, 189, 190, 194, 197, 202, 205, 263, 266, 267, 304 n29, 305 n2; as co-composer with DE, 225–26, 269–70, 306 n16; featured on DE's recordings, 142–48, 151, 156, 158–59, 170, 171, 174, 176–77, 212, 213, 218, 219, 220, 222, 223, 224, *230*, 231, 233, 234, 236, 242, 247, 251, 258, 294 n29; meets DE in Washington, 51–53; saxophone style, 90, 148, 171, 245, *82, 108. See also* Washingtonians

Haring, Bob, 158

Harlem, 110, 111, 122, 124, 203, 233; appeal for DE, 75; as DE's base of operations, 92; "black and tan" cabarets, 91, 245; jam sessions, 92, 97; nightlife, 84–85, 87–92, 94–95; pianists, 83–84

Harlem stride. *See* Stride

Harper, Leonard, 90–92, 98, 99, 101, 102, 120, 208, 293 n10

Harrison, Jimmy, 160

Harry Richman's Club (New York), 136

Hastie, William H., 7

Hatton, Jack, 85

Haverhill, Mass., 106, 110, 184–85, 300 n11

Hawkins, Coleman, 74

Hayes, Roland, 7

Hayward, Ina, 114

Healy, Dan, 210

Hegamin, Lucille, 69, 74, 101, 107

Henderson, Fletcher, 14, 51, 72, 92, 93, 94, 97, 102, 136, 137, 147,

Henderson, Fletcher (continued)
149, 153, 160, 163, 165, 168, 169,
170, 171, 174, 196–97, 202, 210,
223, 226, 248, 305 n3; hears DE
in Washington, 74–75; orchestra
admired by DE, 165; orchestra com-
pared with the Washingtonians, 155,
208; orchestra in New England,
191
Henderson, Rosa, 94, 174
Henderson, Stephen ("The Beetle").
See The Beetle
Henry, Lew, 85
Henry Waterson, Inc. (publishing
company), 265
Herbert's Minstrels, 12
Herbert, Victor, 33
Hiawatha Theater (Washington,
D.C.), 70
Hicks, Edna, 197
Hoefer, George, 58
Hoefsmit, Sjef, 281 n34
Hoffman, Elzie, 8, 13, 14
Hogan, Ernest, 97
Hollywood, The (New York), xiii,
98–99, 101, 102, 104, 106, 109,
117, 185, 293 n7, 303 n18; changes
name to Kentucky Club, 110; fires,
110, 184; Washingtonians reviewed
at, 99–100. See also Kentucky Club
Holman, George R., 103, 260
Holmes, Charlie, 202
"Holy City, The," 243, 307 n35, 243
Hopkins, Claude, 10, 28, 34, 44,
48, 52, 65, 67, 69, 70, 73, 79,
275n29, 311
Hoskins, Allen, 163
Howard, Paul, 279 n58
Howard Theater (Washington, D.C.),
10, 11–13, 48, 61, 63, 69, 80; jazz
at, 51, 54, 64, 65–67, 72, 73, 81,
287 n18; pit orchestra, 64, 65–67,
72, 287 n24, 289 n64
Howard University, 4, 5, 7, 8, 10, 11,
13, 20, 22, 47, 293 n14; Choir, 10;
Girls Glee Club, 61; Glee Club, 10
Howard, Lionel, 84

Howells, William Dean, 12
Hudson, Will, 135
Hughes, Langston, 5, 6
Hunter, Alberta, 114, 171
Hyman, Earl, 44
Hymns, 20, 22

Improvisation, 31, 41, 101, 148, 223
Immerman, Connie, 91
Immerman, George, 91
Industrial Café (Washington, D.C.), 70
Institute of Jazz Studies (Rutgers
University), 309, 311
Ipana Troubadors, 135
Irick, Seymour, 85
Irving, Roland C., 103, 104
Irvis, Charlie, 90, 115, 118, 190,
197; featured on DE's recordings,
141–54, 170, 171, 294 n29; joins
Washingtonians, 107; leaves Wash-
ingtonians, 188–89; relationship
with Bubber Miley, 107, 113, 108.
See also Washingtonians

Jack the Bear, 33
Jack Mills, Inc. (publishing company),
93, 94, 160, 170, 175, 176, 197,
199, 201, 217, 265, 272. See also
Mills Music
Jackson, Cliff, 84, 189
Jackson, Crawford, 208
Jackson, James A., 91, 93, 98, 102,
153
Jackson, Rudy, 216, 218, 230, 231,
233, 235, 301 n26, 305 n3; con-
tribution to "Creole Love Call,"
238–40, 271; joins Washingtonians,
202, 209
Jackson, Zaidee, 171, 194
Jazz, 220, 258; in Washington, D.C.,
circa 1918, 53–54; in the early
1920s, 140. See also Howard The-
ater, jazz at
Jazzmania, 207–8, 307 n62
Jefferson, Maceo, 81, 82
Jeffries, Leroy, 90
Jerry, Frank, 194

Jeter, Leonard, 11, 59
John Wesley AME Zion Church
  (Washington, D.C.), 22, 59
Johnny, Blind, 30, 73
Johnson, Charlie, 161, 202
Johnson, J. Rosamond, 8, 61, 175
Johnson, Jack, 88
Johnson, James P., 26, 30, 31–32, 33,
  34, 35, 41, 84, 95, 98, 120, 126,
  131, 177, 217, 272, 295 n58; meets
  DE in Washington in 1921, 74;
  piano rolls heard by DE, 29; piano
  style compared to DE's, 36, 178,
  182, 226
Johnson, James Weldon, 8
Johnson, Lucky, 176, 266
Jolson, Al, 88, 116, 174
Jones, Alberta, 171, 176, 194, 232,
  266
Jones, Bill (drummer), 14, 58, 73
Jones, G. Frank, 58, 74
Jones, Henry, 207
Jones, Isham, 192
Jones, Sissieretta ("the Black Patti"),
  12
Jones, William (accompanist), 175
Jones, William H. (sociologist), 7, 67,
  69, 70
Joplin, Scott, 31, 33, 252
Jordan, Joe, 250–51
Joseph, "One-Leg" Willie, 30
Joyner and Foster, 208
"Junk Man Rag, The," 31, 36
J. W. Connor's Café, (New York), 101

Kahal, Irving, 160, 171, 215, 265, 268
Kahn, Roger Wolfe, 115
Katzman, Louis, 141, 142, 261,
  298 n5
Keith-Albee Circuit, 210
Keith Circuit, 65, 80, 83, 85, 86
Kennedy, Alice Williams (grand-
  mother), 19
Kennedy, Florence (aunt), 19, 20
Kennedy, Gertrude (aunt), 19, 20
Kennedy, James William (grand-
  father), 19

Kennedy, James William, Jr. (uncle),
  19
Kennedy, John (uncle), 19
Kennedy, Marie (aunt), 19
Kennedy, Maud (aunt), 19
Kentucky Club (New York), xiii, 110–
  11, 119, 139, 149, 158, 171, 174,
  185, 188, 190, 201, 203, 207, 211,
  222, 295 n58, 303 n18; fires, 137,
  184; Washingtonians' performances
  in 1925, 113–18, 135–37; Wash-
  ingtonians' performances in 1926,
  194–99. See also The Hollywood
Kern, Jerome, 49
Kerr, Brooks, 43, 134, 260, 277 n27,
  278 n40, 281 nn28,34, 305 n3
Kincaid, Nelson, 209
King, Bob, 272
Klages, Ray, 90, 261
Krupa, Gene, 205

L'Allegro Glee Club, 10, 12, 59
L'Enfant, Pierre, 5
Lafayette Players, 213
Lafayette Theater (New York), 80–81,
  83, 92, 94, 111, 207–8, 210, 247;
  pit orchestra, 81, 82, 209
Lamb, Joseph, 31
Lange, Arthur, 135
Lanin's Red Heads, 150
Lanin, Sam, 135
Lasker, Steven, 199, 261, 266, 267,
  268, 269, 270, 272, 306 n5
Lawson, Warner, 10
Layton, John Turner, Jr. (songwriter,
  pianist), 9, 61, 120, 132, 306 n12
Layton, John Turner, Sr. (teacher,
  conductor), 9, 285 n58
Lee, Mandy, 272
Lee, Marguerite, 216, 272
Lee, Roscoe, 44, 58
Leonidow, 120
Leslie, Edgar, 173, 263
Lewis, Bert, 114, 115, 194, 296 n71
Lewis, J. Henry, 8–9, 10
Lewis, Ted, 140
Library of Congress, 133, 259, 312

Lido Club (New York), 136–37
Lieurance, Thurlow, 121
Lincoln Colonnade (Washington, D.C.), 63, 69
Lincoln Theater (New York), 111
Lincoln Theater (Washington, D.C.), 5, 45, 69, 80, 193
Link, Harry, 161, 265
Lippy (Raymond Boyette), 84
Little Savoy (New York), 88
Liza and Her Shuffling Sextet, 85
Liza, 92, 97, 104
Locke, Alain, 4
Logan, Rayford W., 6, 7, 20
Lopez, Vincent, 117, 137, 140, 147, 185, 191, 192, 262, 302 n43
Lottman, George D., 115
Lucas, Marie, 64, 66, 81
Lucas, Oscar, 7, 44
Lucas, Sam, 24, 66
Lunceford, Jimmie, 199, 266
Lyons, Arthur S., 120, 132

M Street High School. *See* Dunbar High School
McCoy, Viola, 174
McHugh, Jimmy, 175, 208, 263
Mack, Cecil, 120, 126
Mack, Sticky, 30, 46
McLean, Richard "Abba Labba." *See* Abba Labba
McMullin's Orchestra, 205
Maine, 187, 190, 206, 207, 219
Martin, Sara, 79, 171
Maryland, 58
Massagli, Luciano, 259, 311
Matthews, J. H., 71, 74
Melody Music Company, 153, 263
Memphis Five. *See* Original Memphis Five
Mendelssohn, Felix, 11
Messin' Around, 208
Metcalf, Louis, 202, 227, 230, 231, 236
Meyers, Billy, 218, 272
Micheaux, Oscar, 213

Michelson, Lewis, 105, 261
Mier, Alvano, 266
Miley, James "Bubber," xiii, 85, 99, 107, 113, 115, 117, 118, 139, 150, 156, 171, 186, 188, 189–90, 193, 197, 202, 205, 217, 269, 270, 271, 307 nn32,35; encounter with Johnny Dunn, 247–48; featured on DE's recordings, 141–49, 161–70, 212–16, 231–58, 294 n29; and Joe Nanton, 191, 236; joins Washingtonians, 101–2; trumpet style, 90, 101–2, 147, 148–49, 162, 167–68, 246; unpredictability, 136, *108, 209*. *See also* Washingtonians
Miller and Lyles, 92
Miller, "Devil," 14, 51, 52
Miller, Bill, 14, 51, 52, 69
Miller, Felix, 14, 51, 52
Miller, James E., 14, 51, 285 n58
Mills, Florence, 90, 91, 98, 114, 178, 306 n5
Mills, Irving, 94, 160, 171, 175–76, 207, 208, 212, 216, 217, 224, 229, 247, 263, 267, 303 n15, 308 n40; begins managing DE's band, 198; discovery of DE's band, 195–98; publicity strategy for DE, 201. *See also* Gotham Music Service, Mills Music
Mills Music (publishing company), 195, 208, 216, 221, 247, 268
Minor, Bud, 30
Minstrelsy, 12, 122, 126
Mitchell, Abbie, 11
Mitchell, Billie, 92
Mix, Tom, 116
Mole, Miff, 117, 135, 150, 173, 213, 221
Mondello, Toots, 190, 205
Montgomery, Michael, 134
Moore, Monette, 141, 171
Moore, Old Man Sam, 30
Moore, Thomas, 158
Morgan, Sam, 306 n16
Morris, Thomas, 156

Morrison, C. S., 20, 277 n27
Morrison, George, 301 n13
Morton, Jelly Roll, 157, 158, 169, 182, 299 n20, 306–7 n23
Motley, Rosa, 104
Mu-So-Lit Club, 8
Murray's Casino (Washington, D.C.), 5, 63, 67, 69, 71
Murray's Palace Casino. *See* Murray's Casino
Murray, Billy, 141
Music Box (Atlantic City), 87, 100
Musical theater and revues, 90–92, 97–98, 106, 114, 120, 121, 165, 168, 172, 194, 207–8, 210, 233, 242
Music Master, The, 13

NAACP, 46
NANM. *See* National Association of Negro Musicians
Nanton, Joseph "Tricky Sam," xiii, 85, 202; and Bubber Miley, 191; featured on DE's recordings, 163, 165, 167, 212, 216, 218, 222, 224, 227, 230, 231, 233, 235, 236, 241, 242, 244, 251, 253, 258, 307 n33; joins DE's band, 188–89, 209
Napoleon, Phil, 173, 205, 207, 298 n5
National Association of Negro Musicians, 61
"Naughty Man," 299 n7, *148–49*
Negro Music Journal, 13
Negro Musician, The, 9, 13, 61
Nest Club (New York), 189
Nevin, Ethelbert, 20, 50, 83, 165
New Ebbitt Café (Washington, D.C.), 48
New England, 110, 219, 300 n11; "battles" of bands in, 190–91, 205; Washingtonians' first visit to, 184; Washingtonians' 1926 summer tour, 183–92, 199 (itinerary, 187–88); Washingtonians' 1927 summer tour, 201–7 (itinerary, 203–4)
New Fairmount Park, 71

New Orleans, La., 203, 235, 236, 306 n16
New Orleans Five, 289 n3
New Orleans style, 111, 153, 156, 167, 168, 220, 230, 235
New Star Casino (New York), 106
New York: black musicians in, 97–98, 105–6, 165, 203; discrimination in, 96–97; ragtime, 31; recording studios in, 96, 170–71. *See also* Harlem; Times Square; Tin Pan Alley
Nichols, Red, 135, 174, 213, 221
Nineteenth Street Baptist Church (Washington, D.C.), 10, 22
Nixon, Ted, 153, 263
Noone, Jimmie, 237
Nordisk Polyphon Aktieselskab (record label), 134
Nuttings-on-the-Charles (Waltham, Mass.), 186–87, 190, 203, 205

Oberlin College, 10
Odd Fellows Hall (Washington, D.C.), 59, 64, 72, 286 n5
Odeon (record company), 134
OKeh (record label), xi, 94, 177–78, 212, 217, 238, 267, 272, 305 n2
Okeh Syncopators, 135
Oliver, King, 101, 202, 208, 232, 235, 240, 247; Creole Jazz Band, 157, 158, 160, 169, 225, 232, 237, 240
Olivier, Victor, 261
Orient, The (New York), 87, 111, 137
Oriental Gardens (Washington, D.C.), 67, 87, 171, 201, *68*
Oriental Grill. *See* Oriental Gardens
Original Dixieland Jazz Band, 54, 80, 97
Original Indiana Five, 150, 175
Original Memphis Five, 141, 149, 174, 192, 207, 289 n3, 298 n5
Orpheum Circuit, 80

Pace, Harry, 93, 171. *See also* Pace and Handy Music Company

Pace and Handy Music Company, 54
Pace Phonograph Corporation, 93
Palace Theater (New York), 86
Palais Royal (New York), 117, 118
Palmer, Jack, 149–50, 263
"Panama," 131, *131*
Paradise Café (Washington, D.C.), 70
Paramount (record label), 114
Parham, Florence, 74
Pathé (record company), 136, 139, 149, 153, 155, 157, 159, 165, 211, 212, 219, 263, 264, 265, 312
Pennsylvania, 192
Perkins, Lutice "Cutie," 65
Perry, Delia, 44
Perry, Mert, 85
Perry, Oliver "Doc," 30, 47, 48, 49, 51, 52, 53, 54, 58, 59, 64, 65, 71, 72, 73, 74, 84; as role model and tutor for DE, 44–45, 46
Perry's Hot Dogs, 150
Peyton, Dave, 200–201, 301 n13
Philadelphia, Penn., 31, 210
Phipps, Robert W., 176, 266
Pianists. *See* Ellington, as pianist; Harlem, pianists; Ragtime; Stride; Washington, D.C., black community, pianists
Piano rolls, 29, 32, 134, 280 n32
Pinkard, Maceo, 97, 104–5, 120, 149, 171, 208
Piron, Armand J., 97, 252
Pittsburgh, Penn., 192–93
Plantation Café (Chicago), 202
Plantation Café (New York), 98, 110, 139, 188, 192, 208, 233
Plantation Days, 90, 92, 121
Poli Circuit, 85, 86
Poodle Dog Café/Poodle Dog (Washington, D.C.), 34, 70, 281 n29, 288 n39
Potter, Harold, 160
Powell, Adam Clayton, Sr., 47
Powell, Eddie, 247, 270
Pratt Institute, 46
Preer, Andy, 208

Preer, Evelyn, 197, 198, 199, 213, 215, 268
Prime, Alberta, 110, 171, 172–73, 176, 197, 262
Prohibition, 85, 89, 116–17
Publishers. *See* Times Square, music publishers
Puerto Rico, 66, 287 n24, 289 n64
Pusateri, Liborio, 259, 311
Pyle, Harry, 84

Quality Amusement Corporation, 66

Radio, 94, 96, 100, 106, 135, 161, 200, 294 n38
Ragtime, 20, 28–41, 62, 123, 131, 134, 156, 177, 220, 226, 230, 237, 252; repertory, 33; secondary ragtime, 181, 217, 224, 226, 245. *See also* Strain form
Rainbow Music Corporation (publishing company), 93
Rainey, Ma, 232
Ramblers, The, 135
Randolph, Earl, 141
Rapp, Barney, 192
Redman, Don, 72, 136, 155–56, 160, 168, 170, 223, 226, 230, 299 n7; influence on DE's arranging style, 165
Reisenweber's restaurant (New York), 97, 98
Reser, Harry, 161
Reynolds, Ellsworth, 207, *209*
Rhea, Jerry, 66
Rhone, Happy, 190
Rhythm Club (New York), 92
Rich, Freddie, 161, 265
Richardson, Walter, 216, 272
Richman, Harry, 116. *See also* Harry Richman's Club
Ricketts, Bob, 93
Ringer, Johnny, 270
Ringle, Dave, 119, 141, 261
RKO Circuit, 237

Roane's Sensational Pennsylvanians, 205
Robbins, Jack, 120, 134
Robbins-Engel (publishing company), 132, 133, 135, 199, 264, 266
Roberts, Luckey, 12, 31, 32, 36, 73, 74, 120, 177, 280 n16
Robeson, Paul, 64, 175, 300 n35
Robinson, Bill, 208
Robinson, Clarence, 85–87, 100, 207–8, 307 n26
Robinson, J. Russel, 132
Robinson, Prince, 84, 111, 136, 151, 153, 164, 202
Rochester, Joe, 47, 64, 65
Rogers, "Go-Get-'Em," 208
Rogers, Alex, 165
Rollini, Adrian, 141, 150, 173
"Rosary, The," 20, 50, 83
Roseland Ballroom (New York), 97, 110, 153, 190, 202
Runnin' Wild, 98, 126, 208
Russell, Pee Wee, 135
Rust, Brian, 153, 259
Ruth, Babe, 70
Rutledge, Leroy, 136, 155, 189

"St. Louis Blues," 117, 121, 197
St. Luke's Episcopal Church (Washington, D.C.), 59
Salaries. See Ellington, Duke, financial matters
Salem Willows, 186–87, 205
Salem, Mass., 183–84, 186–88, 190–91, 202, 203–5, 207
Sampson, Edgar, 136, 213, 215, 301 n26, 305 n3
Samuel Coleridge-Taylor Choral Society, 9, 285 n58
Samuel Coleridge-Taylor Trio, 11
Sapparo, Henry, 203
Saunders, Gertrude, 12, 67, 91, 98, 104, 111, 114
Savoy Ballroom (New York), 203
Schaap, Phil, 304 n29
Schafer, Bob, 119, 141, 198, 261, 267

Schalplatte Gramophon (record company), 134
Schoebel, Elmer, 218, 272
Schuller, Gunther, 146, 155, 160, 162, 163, 169, 181, 216, 220, 225, 233, 245, 251, 255, 311
Schutt, Arthur, 150
Scott, James, 31
Scott, Lloyd, 308 n39
Senter, Boyd, 149
Shapiro-Bernstein & Company (publishing company), 93, 104
Shaw, Mack, 189, 207, 301 n26
Shribman, Charles, 183–87, 190–91, 202, 203, 205; managerial support of Washingtonians, 192
Shribman, Sy, 183, 202
Shuffle Along, 12, 61–62, 67, 92, 97, 98, 124, 208
Silverman, Sime, 197
Simmons, Alberta, 84
Simmons, Rousseau, 198, 267
Sims, Margaret, 134
Singleton, Zutty, 135
"Siren's Song, The," 49
Sissle, Andrew, 292 n56
Sissle, Noble, 64, 88–89. See also Sissle and Blake
Sissle and Blake, 12, 61–62, 67, 92, 97, 120, 124
Skerritt, Freddie, 190
Skidmore Music Company, 93
Slade, Walter, 73
Smalle, Ed, 141
Smith, Ada "Bricktop." See Bricktop
Smith, Bessie, 232
Smith, Harrison, 163, 192–93, 266, 299 n20, 302 nn6,43, 308 n40
Smith, Jabbo, 212, 217, 218, 219, 244, 307 n33
Smith, Leroy, 75, 97
Smith, Mamie, 12, 74, 85, 94, 101, 228, 279 n58
Smith, Roland (or Rollin, Rollen), 100, 102, 294 n29
Smith, Trixie, 69, 92, 94, 292 n63

Smith, Willie "the Lion," 26, 29, 30, 35, 36, 41, 95, 107; meets DE in New York, 83–85

Snowden, Elmer, 52, 64–66, 69, 71, 72, 73, 74, 79, 86, 94, 95, 98, 99, 100–102, 104, 105, 111, 177, 182, 202, 261, 289 n64, 293 n10, 294 n29, 295 n42, 311; band plays at Barron's in 1923, 87–90; leaves Washingtonians, 107, 109, *108. See also* Washingtonians

Songwriting, 93–94, 102–6, 141, 149–50, 153, 171, 172–73, 195. *See also* Ellington, Duke, as composer

Sorrel, Essie, 22, 41

Spangler, Roy, 29

Specht, Paul, 191, 192

Spirituals, 22, 122, 233, 243

Spoliansky, Mischa, 134

Spraggins, Alice, 61, 285 n58

Standard Theater (Philadelphia), 210

Star of Ethiopia, The, 7, 8, 12

Stark and Cowan (publishing company), 263

Stark, Herman, 210

Stearns, Marshall, 193, 247

Stewart, Lloyd, 51

Stewart, Rex, 52–53, 88, 97, 100, 107, 115, 156, 189, 310

Stock arrangements, 51, 67, 90, 117, 135, 150, 158–59, 161–62, 217–19, 247, 256–57, 261, 269, 298 n5

Strain form, 156–57, 219–20, 222, 225–26, 229, 251

Strand building (New York), 87, 98

Strayhorn, Billy, 6

Stride, 32, 38, 131, 156, 172, 173, 177–82, 226

Strut Yo' Stuff, 12, 67

Suburban Gardens, 71

Sullivan, Joe, 135

Sweatman, Wilbur, 80–81, 83, 86, 100, 107, 153, 289 n6, *82*

Sylvester, Robert, 116

Symphonic jazz, 121, 122, 165–66

Talbert, Florence Cole, 61

Taylor, Billy, 24–25, 285 n58

Taylor, Eva, 107, 171

Tchaikovsky, Peter Ilyich, 11

Tempo (publishing company), 312

Tennessee Tooters, The, 174

Terrace Gardens (New York), 97

Theater orchestras, 66, 165. *See also* Howard Theater, pit orchestra; Lafayette Theater, pit orchestra

Thiers, Will. *See* Tyers, Will

Thomas, A. Jacob, 13

Thomas, Andrew, 11, 48

Thomas, George, 299 n13

Thomas, Harry, 29

Thomas, Louis, 30, 48, 52, 56, 58, 64, 65, 67, 73, 75, 84, 87, 171, 283 n6, 284 n15; hires DE in Washington in 1917, 49

Thomas, Sylvester, 10, 48, 69

Thompson, Edna. *See* Ellington, Edna

Thornton, Caroline, 74

Three Eddies, The, 122, 132

Tibbs, Roy W., 10, 22

"Tiger Rag," 111, 191, 222, 223, 224

Times Square, 98, 99, 106, 110, 114, 116, 173; black bands playing in, 96–97, 100; music publishers, 92–93, 96, 104, 105, 171

Timner, W. E., 157, 259, 311

Tin Pan Alley, 92–93, 105, 124, 158, 173, 198, 242, 258. *See also* Songwriting

Tizol, Juan, 287 n24, 290 n11; meets DE, 66–67

Toronto, Ont., 42, 43, 260

Towers, Jack, 281 n34

Trent, Jo, 93, 102–3, 106, 110, 137–39, 149, 171, 172, 260, 262, 265, 268, 272; collaboration with DE on songs for *Chocolate Kiddies,* 119–35, 264

Triangle (record label), 185

Triangle Music Publishing Company, 270

True Reformers' Hall (Washington, D.C.), 5, 10, 50, 51, 53, 59, 62, 69, 72
Tucker, George H., 71, 74
Turk, Roy, 158, 265
Turk, William, 30
Tyers (or Thiers), Will, 33, 131
Tyler, Will, 111

Ulanov, Barry, 17, 19, 20, 23, 52, 61, 99, 310
Up-to-Date (record label), 110, 172, 174–75, 263

Valburn, Jerry, 172, 214, 281 n34, 295 n56
Van Loan, Paul, 161
Varsity Eight, 150
Vaudeville, 80–83, 85–87, 107, 111, 114
Verdi, Giuseppe, 8
Victor (record company), xi, 54, 90, 104, 105, 109, 134, 141, 197, 198, 199, 205, 212, 213, 214, 229, 236, 241, 244, 251, 253, 254, 255, 261, 268, 271, 312
Vigal, Johnnie, 207, 208
"Viper's Drag," 38, 38
Virginia, 56–57, 72, 191
Vocalion (record label), 198, 199, 200, 202, 211, 212, 215, 216, 222, 232, 235, 250, 255, 257, 266, 267, 268, 272, 303 n15, 303 n18
Vodery, Will, 12, 61, 98
Volontè, Giovanni M., 259, 311
Vox (record company), 121, 134, 135
Voynow, Dick, 205

Waldo, Terry, 32
Waldorf Theater (Lynn, Mass.), 184
Walker, George, 165. See also Williams and Walker
Walker, Louise, 69
Wallace, Sippie, 232, 238
Waller, Thomas "Fats," 35, 38, 39, 65, 84, 85, 86, 95, 119, 132, 178, 182, 286 n5, 292 n63, 296 n71; at the Kentucky Club, 115; as tutor for DE, 115–16
Walsh, A. W., 251
Ward, Aida, 12, 90
Ward, Frank, 184
Ward, Joe, 90
Washington, Benjamin, 22
Washington, Booker T., 5
Washington, Freddi, 247
Washington, D.C., black community: antebellum period, 4; bands, 13–14; cabarets and dance halls, 5, 63, 67–71; class structure, 6; concert music, 8–13; discrimination faced by, 4, 20; expectations of achievement, 24–25; high school cadet corps, 6, 7; historical pageants, 7–8; musical life, 8–15, 22–23, 30, 44–46, 47–56, 58–75; newspapers and periodicals, 13; opera in, 8, 9; pianists, 29–30, 44; piano contests, 14, 73–74; pride in, 6, 25–26; public schools, 5, 6, 13, 25–26, 285–86 n58; singers, 69–70
Washington Black Sox Orchestra, 87, 95, 98, 107
Washington Concert Orchestra, 10
Washington Conservatory of Music, 10, 13, 28, 59, 201, 285 n58
Washingtonians: 99–118; collective arranging, 170, 191; contracts at Hollywood, 98, 109, 303 n18; contracts at Kentucky Club, 194, 303 n18; critical reaction to recordings, 168–70; DE's arrangements for, 117–18, 197–98; first major review, 99–100; first visit to New England, 184; muted brass, 101–2, 107, 147, 148, 167–68; name change, 99–100; personnel, 99–102, 111, 113, 135–36, 155, 169, 188–90, 202, 294 n29; publicity for, 99–100, 106, 187, 190, 195,

Washingtonians (continued)
199, 200–201, 205–6; reed section,
136, 155, 188–90, 202–3; repertory
at Kentucky Club, 117, 211; rhythm
section, 146, 157, 170; schedule at
Kentucky Club, 116; size of band,
100, 111, 115, 118, 191, 197, 210,
211; versatility, 99–100, 102, 108
Washingtonians, recordings: from
1924, 109–10, 140–49; from
September 1925–June 1926, 136,
139, 149–68; from November
1926–November 1927, 198, 199–
200, 211–58; reissues, 312–13
Waters, Ethel, 92, 114, 137, 160,
299 n14
Waterson, Berlin, and Snyder (publishing company), 161, 170
"Way Down Yonder in New Orleans,"
9, 120, 124
Webb, Chick, 51
Weir, Felix, 11, 59
Wells, Dicky, 308 n39
Wells, Gertrude (Gertie), 10, 44, 64–
65, 67, 69, 71, 74, 275 n29
Wheeling, W.Va., 192
Whetsol, Arthur, 51, 61, 65, 67, 69,
79, 86–87, 94, 231, 247, 284 n28,
294 n29, 307 n36; leaves Washing-
tonians, 101, 293 n14; personal and
musical style, 52, 89–90, 102
White, Clarence Cameron, 61
White, Eddie, 65
White, Mabel, 69, 70
Whiteman, Paul, 97, 117, 121, 137,
140, 151, 166, 168, 185, 186, 192,
206, 216, 301 n13
Whitney Museum (New York), 177

Whitteker, Byng, 42, 43, 260
Wiedemann, Erik, 312
Wiedoft, Herb, 175
Wiggins, Bernice, 16, 19, 22, 53
Wilcox, Edwin, 266
Williams, Bert, 88. See also Williams
and Walker
Williams, Clarence, 80, 93, 104,
106, 171; Blue Five, 163. See also
Clarence Williams Music Publishing
Company
Williams, Cootie, 307–8 n36
Williams, Corky, 84
Williams, Fess, 85
Williams, Martin, 170, 252, 299 n7,
311
Williams, Sandy, 14, 51, 67, 311
Williams, Spencer, 93, 104, 106,
131, 149–50, 153, 155–56, 171,
263, 265
Williams and Walker, 62, 165
Willis, J. H., 13
Wilson, Edith, 98, 207
Wilson, Lena, 207, 208
Winter Garden building (New York),
98, 184, 208
Wodehouse, P. G., 49
Wooding Jubilee Quintet, 9
Wooding, Russell, 9, 49, 58, 283–
84 n15
Wooding, Sam, 10, 121, 166, 208
Woods, Harry, 173, 263
Woodson, Carter G., 4
World War I, 47, 65

Yellman, Duke, 192
Young, Speed, 190

Index of Compositions, Recordings, and Arrangements of Duke Ellington

Note: Pages with musical examples are indicated in italics at the end of entries.

"Animal Crackers," 139, 161–62, 164, 169, 170, 178, 181, 192, 196, 211, 265, *162*
"Arabian Lover," 72

"Birmingham Breakdown," 198, 201, 212, 213, 219–22, 223, 225, 226, 230, 235, 251, 252, 267, 269, *220–21, 223*
"Bitches' Ball," 39, 41, 260, *40–41*
"Black and Tan Fantasy," 197, 201, 212, 213, 216, 233, 242–48, 251, 255, 270, 271, 272, 312, *243–45*
"Black Beauty," 178
Black, Brown, and Beige, 6, 12, 23, 39–41, 260, 278 n40, *40–41*
"Black Cat Blues," 242
"Blind Man's Buff," 93, 103–4, 119, 260–61, 312, *103*
"Blues I Love to Sing," 213, 241–42, 271, *242*
"Braggin' in Brass," 222

"Chicago Stomp Down," 213, 217–18, 219, 272
"Choo Choo (I Gotta Hurry Home)," 109–10, 119, 139, 141–47, 154, 161, 169, 211, 212, 261–62, 298 n5, *143–46*
"Come Back to Me," 94, 119, 261
"Come Sunday," 12, 23
"The Creeper," 198, 212, 213, 222–25, 226, 227, 230, 268, 306 n16, *222–25, 226*
"Creole Love Call," 122, 213, 236–41, 243, 246, 251, 258, 271, *238–40*
"Creole Rhapsody," xi

"Daybreak Express," 222, 231
"Deacon Jazz," 109–10, 119, 120, 122, 134, 173, 174, 178–79, 181, 262, *178–79*
"Diminuendo and Crescendo in Blue," 252

"Down Home Stomp," 201, 304 n23
"Down in Our Alley Blues," 213, 225, 226–29, 230, 232, 269–70, 306 n16, *227–29*
"Drifting from You Blues," 267, 305 n2
"Dusk," 231

"East St. Louis Toodle-O," 198, 201, 213, 216, 231, 242, 243, 248–57, 258, 266–67, 269, *248–50, 252–57*
"Echoes of Harlem," 231
"Echoes of the Jungle," 216
"Everything Is Hotsy Totsy Now," 175–76, 177, 178, 181, 182, 195, 263

"Georgia Grind," 155–56, 178, 179–81, 219, 232, 235, 265, *180–81*
The Girls Suite, 22
"Gold Digger," 137, 200, 270
"Gone But Not Forgotten," 216, 272

"Happy-Go-Lucky-Local," 231
"High Life," 222
"Home," 90, 105, 261
"Hop Head," 213, 225–26, 227, 228, 230, 247, 251, 269–70, 306 n16, *225–26*
"Hot and Bothered," 222
"How Come You Do Me Like You Do?" 110, 174–75, 211, 232, 263, *175*
"Hymn of Sorrow," 23

"I'm Gonna Hang around My Sugar (till I Gather All the Sugar That She's Got)," 149–53, 154, 156, 160, 170, 178, 181, 263, *150–52*
"I'm Gonna Put You Right in Jail," 176, 232, 266
"If You Can't Hold the Man You Love (Don't Cry When He's Gone)," 159–60, 161, 171, 195, 198, 213, 214–15, 216, 232, 265, 268, *214–15*

"(I'm Just Wild about) Animal Crackers." *See* "Animal Crackers"
"Immigration Blues," 198, 213, 232–35, 236, 241, 243, 246, 251, 267–68, 306 n21, *234–35*
"Isfahan," 231
"It's Gonna Be a Cold, Cold Winter," 110, 172, 232, 262

"Jack the Bear," 231
"Japanese Dream," 72
"Jig Walk," 121, 131–32, 133, 134, 135, 264, *127–30*
"Jim Dandy," 121, 122–24, 132, 134, 264, *122–23*
"Jubilee Stomp," 222
Jump for Joy, 278 n40
"Jungle Nights in Harlem," 216

"Li'l Farina," 139, 162–68, 192, 211, 219, 227, 266, *164, 166–68*
"Love Is a Wish for You," 121, 132–34, 264, *133*
"Lucky Number Blues," 176–77, 232, 266

"M. T. Pocket Blues," 105, 261
"Make Me Love You," 198, 214, 268
"Melancholia," 231
"Mood Indigo," xi, 231
"My Mother, My Father," 16
My People, 6, 16, 278 n40

"New Orleans Low-Down," 213, 235–36, 241, 246, 268
"Night in Harlem, A," 198, 267

"Oh How I Love My Darling," 109–10, 173–74, 178, 182, 211, 263
"Oklahoma Stomp," 34–35, 39, 259–60, *35*
"Old Man Blues," 252

"Parlor Social De Luxe," 110, 119, 172–73, 174, 178, 181–82, 262, *182*

"Parlor Social Stomp," 137, 155, 156–57, 169–70, 219, 264
"Poodle Dog Rag," 33, 70, 259, 281 n27. *See also* "Soda Fountain Rag"
"Portrait of the Lion," 231
"Pretty Soft for You," 119, 262, 312
"Prologue to Black and Tan Fantasy," 308 n36

"Rainy Nights," 109, 139, 147–49, 154, 173, 211, 212, 262–63, 298–99 n6, 299 n7, *147–49*
"Rhapsody Jr.," 199, 266
"Rockin' in Rhythm," 39, 308 n39

"She's Gone to Join the Songbirds in Heaven," 216, 272
"Skeedely-Um-Bum," 132–33, 264, *133*
"Soda Fountain Rag," 33–41, 45, 70, 177, 259–60, 281 nn27, 28, 34, *39*
"Soliloquy," 213, 216–17, 219, 270
"Solitude," xi
"Song of the Cotton Field," 213, 216, 217, 219, 268–69
"Sophisticated Lady," xi
"Sponge Cake and Spinach," 38
"Sunset and the Mockingbird," 231
"Swampy River," 147, 178, 182

"Swing Session," 34–38, 177, 260, *36–38*. *See also* "Soda Fountain Rag"
Symphony in Black, 12

"They Say I Do It," 267, 305 n2
"Tiger Rag," 225
"Trombone Blues," 153–55, 219, 232, 263, *154*

" 'Wanna Go Back Again' Blues," 158–59, 160, 170, 232, 265, *159*
"Washington Wabble," 212, 213, 229–30, 247, 251, 271, *229*
"What Can a Poor Fellow Do?" 213, 217, 218–19, 272, *218*
"What You Gonna Do When the Bed Breaks Down?" 41–43, 260, *42–43*
"Whispering Tiger," 191
"Who Is She," 198, 267
"With You," 121, 124–26, 132, 137, 264, *124–26*

"Yam Brown," 137–39, 265, *138–39*
"(You've Got Those) 'Wanna Go Back Again' Blues." *See* " 'Wanna Go Back Again' Blues"
"You Will Always Live on in Our Memory," 216, 272

Note on the Author

Mark Tucker is co-author, with Garvin Bushell, of *Jazz from the Beginning* and a member of the Music Department at Columbia University.

Books in the Series Music in American Life

Only a Miner: Studies in Recorded Coal-Mining Songs
Archie Green

Great Day Coming: Folk Music and the American Left
R. Serge Denisoff

John Philip Sousa: A Descriptive Catalog of His Works
Paul E. Bierley

The Hell-Bound Train: A Cowboy Songbook
Glenn Ohrlin

Oh, Didn't He Ramble: The Life Story of Lee Collins
as Told to Mary Collins
Frank J. Gillis and John W. Miner, Editors

American Labor Songs of the Nineteenth Century
Philip S. Foner

Stars of Country Music: Uncle Dave Macon to Johnny Rodriguez
Bill C. Malone and Judith McCulloh, Editors

Git Along, Little Dogies: Songs and Songmakers of the American West
John I. White

A Texas-Mexican *Cancionero*: Folksongs of the Lower Border
Americo Paredes

San Antonio Rose: The Life and Music of Bob Wills
Charles R. Townsend

Early Downhome Blues: A Musical and Cultural Analysis
Jeff Todd Titon

An Ives Celebration: Papers and Panels of the Charles Ives
Centennial Festival-Conference
H. Wiley Hitchcock and Vivian Perlis, Editors

Sinful Tunes and Spirituals: Black Folk Music to the Civil War
Dena J. Epstein

Joe Scott, the Woodsman-Songmaker
Edward D. Ives

Jimmie Rodgers: The Life and Times of America's Blue Yodeler
Nolan Porterfield

Early American Music Engraving and Printing: A History
of Music Publishing in America from 1787 to 1825
with Commentary on Earlier and Later Practices
Richard J. Wolfe

Sing a Sad Song: The Life of Hank Williams
Roger M. Williams

Long Steel Rail: The Railroad in American Folksong
Norm Cohen

Resources of American Music History: A Directory of Source Materials
from Colonial Times to World War II
D. W. Krummel, Jean Geil, Doris J. Dyen, and Deane L. Root

Tenement Songs: The Popular Music of the Jewish Immigrants
Mark Slobin

Ozark Folksongs
Vance Randolph; Edited and Abridged by Norm Cohen

Oscar Sonneck and American Music
William Lichtenwanger, Editor

Bluegrass Breakdown: The Making of the Old Southern Sound
Robert Cantwell

Bluegrass: A History
Neil V. Rosenberg

Music at the White House: A History of the American Spirit
Elise K. Kirk

Red River Blues: The Blues Tradition in the Southeast
Bruce Bastin

Good Friends and Bad Enemies: Robert Winslow Gordon
and the Study of American Folksong
Debora Kodish

Fiddlin' Georgia Crazy: Fiddlin' John Carson, His Real World,
and the World of His Songs
Gene Wiggins

America's Music: From the Pilgrims to the Present,
Revised Third Edition
Gilbert Chase

Secular Music in Colonial Annapolis: The Tuesday Club, 1745–56
John Barry Talley

Bibliographical Handbook of American Music
D. W. Krummel

Goin' to Kansas City
Nathan W. Pearson, Jr.

"Susanna," "Jeanie," and "The Old Folks at Home": The Songs of
Stephen C. Foster from His Time to Ours
Second Edition
William W. Austin

Songprints: The Musical Experience of Five Shoshone Women
Judith Vander

"Happy in the Service of the Lord": Afro-American Gospel
Quartets in Memphis
Kip Lornell

Paul Hindemith in the United States
Luther Noss

"My Song Is My Weapon": People's Songs, American Communism,
and the Politics of Culture
Robbie Lieberman

Chosen Voices: The Story of the American Cantorate
Mark Slobin

Theodore Thomas: America's Conductor and Builder of
Orchestras, 1835–1905
Ezra Schabas

"The Whorehouse Bells Were Ringing" and Other Songs Cowboys Sing
Guy Logsdon

Crazeology: The Autobiography of a Chicago Jazzman
Bud Freeman, as Told to Robert Wolf

Discoursing Sweet Music: Town Bands and Community Life in
Turn-of-the-Century Pennsylvania
Kenneth Kreitner

Mormonism and Music: A History
Michael Hicks

Voices of the Jazz Age: Profiles of Eight Vintage Jazzmen
Chip Deffaa

Pickin' on Peachtree: A History of Country Music in Atlanta, Georgia
Wayne W. Daniel

Bitter Music: Collected Journals, Essays, Introductions, and Librettos
Harry Partch; Edited by Thomas McGeary

Ethnic Music on Records: A Discography of Ethnic Recordings
Produced in the United States, 1894 to 1942
Richard K. Spottswood

Downhome Blues Lyrics: An Anthology
from the Post–World War II Era
Jeff Todd Titon

Ellington: The Early Years
Mark Tucker